ISBN 978-1-330-25819-4
PIBN 10003992

1 MONTH OF
FREE
READING

at

www.ForgottenBooks.com

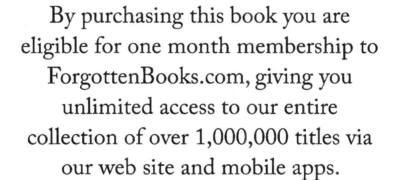

By purchasing this book you are eligible for one month membership to ForgottenBooks.com, giving you unlimited access to our entire collection of over 1,000,000 titles via our web site and mobile apps.

To claim your free month visit:

www.forgottenbooks.com/free3992

A STREAM IN ULU

THE EAST AFRICA PROTECTORATE

BY

SIR CHARLES ELIOT, K.C.M.G.

LATE H. M. COMMISSIONER FOR THE PROTECTORATE

AUTHOR OF "TURKEY IN EUROPE" (BY "ODYSSEUS")

WITH ILLUSTRATIONS AND MAPS

LONDON

EDWARD ARNOLD

Publisher to H. M. India Office

41 & 43 MADDOX STREET, BOND STREET, W.

1905

PREFACE

In the following pages I have endeavoured to give some account of the British East Africa Protectorate, that is, roughly speaking, our territories between Lake Victoria and the Indian Ocean, whose value is only now beginning to be understood. While omitting no aspect of the country which seemed likely to prove interesting, my special object has been to point out the opportunity which it offers for European colonisation and the interesting effect which such a colony may have on the future development of Africa.

After a brief historical retrospect, I have devoted three chapters to an account of the physical features of the country. Much of the territory is still imperfectly known, and even those who have claims to special knowledge are continually surprised by the discovery of new districts, healthy, fertile, and suitable as a residence for Europeans. In this year, though six weeks of it have not yet elapsed, I have received reports of two such districts in parts of the Protectorate which were supposed to be barren, one in the north of the Rift Valley, and one near the western extremity of the German boundary. After giving some account of the country, I have touched on the various tribes which compose the somewhat scanty native population, and then, assuming that the reader has acquired a sufficient acquaintance with the lie of the land and the character of its inhabitants, have proceeded to discuss the prospects which it holds out to intending colonists, and such questions as climate, health, and products. I have next examined some problems connected with our administration, and suggested some improvements in the present somewhat imperfect system. Chapters follow on the Uganda

Railway, trade, and missionary work, which has formed so large and bright a feature in the history of these possessions; and since no country can be isolated from its surroundings, I have added some account of the Italian and German possessions in East Africa, as well as of Uganda and its connection with Egypt through the Sudan.

My best thanks are due to many friends in East Africa for information or photographs, which I hope will add much to the value of this book, and particularly to Mr. Ainsworth, H.M. Sub-Commissioner at Nairobi; Mr. Bowring, Treasurer of the Protectorate; Mr. Hinde, Sub-Commissioner of the Kenya Province (to whom I am indebted for a map of the environs of Mount Kenya); Mr. Marsden, Chief of Customs; and Mr. Powter, of the Treasury Department. I must also specially thank Mr. Hollis, Secretary to the Administration, whose assistance materially lightened my labours when I was Commissioner of the Protectorate, and who has given me much valuable information respecting native tribes and historical questions.

I was H.M. Commissioner for the East Africa Protectorate from January 1901 till June 1904, and these were perhaps the happiest and most interesting years of my life, but to my deep regret I felt obliged to resign my post. I have thought it well to exclude personal matter from the present book, and not to give any account of the events connected with this step. I take this opportunity, however, of saying that the official papers published on the subject [1] give, in my opinion, a very erroneous impression both of the issues involved and of what actually occurred. No opportunity was given me of making any statement, and the two summaries prepared in the Foreign Office [2] can easily be shown to be full of inaccuracies in dates, geography, and facts. The selection of papers obscures the important aspects of the question at issue, and gives unnecessary prominence to subsidiary points.

[1] "Africa," No. 8, 1904.
[2] The prefatory minute in the Parliamentary paper, and Despatch No. 27.

I tendered my resignation because I was ordered to cancel grants made by me to private persons in conformity with my general instructions, and to cancel them in a way which seemed to me wholly unjust and liable to accusations of favouritism, for I was at the same time directed to give the East Africa Syndicate a grant of ten times the size of the others, and in the same district, on unusually favourable terms, which were in themselves disadvantageous to the general interests of the Protectorate. The reason assigned for these instructions was that the relatively small private grants were an infringement of native rights, because the district in which they were situated was to be made a native reserve. If no grants whatever had been made in this area, the decision would have been just, though its wisdom might be doubted ; but it appeared (and still appears) to me that the position of an officer who revokes a grant which he has made on the ground that it interferes with native rights, and at the same time gives in the same district a large concession to a Syndicate which must interfere far more with native rights, is untenable. I would gladly have reasoned with the Foreign Office, but it was not possible. I telegraphed home that the instructions sent me were based on incorrect information, but they were maintained and repeated in a more categorical form. I could not go to England and discuss matters, because the Deputy-Commissioner who should have replaced me was on leave, and as the Foreign Office were not disposed to pay any attention to the arguments which I submitted, I do not see what alternative I had but to resign.

CONTENTS

CHAPTER   PAGE

  I. Introductory 1

  II. General Geography and History 6

  III. The Coast Lands: Zanzibar, Jubaland, Tanaland . 31

  IV. The Coast Lands: Seyidie, Mombasa, Teita . . 51

  V. The Interior and Highlands 63

  VI. The Natives of East Africa: General . . . 91

  VII. The Natives of East Africa: Swahilis, Somalis,
    and Bantu-speaking Tribes 112

  VIII. The Natives of East Africa: The Masai, Suk,
    Nandi, &c.. 132

  IX. East Africa as a European Colony: Health,
    Climate, Food Supply, &c. 150

  X. East Africa as a European Colony: Minerals,
    Vegetable Products 158

  XI. East Africa as a European Colony: Pasturage,
    Land Questions, Zionists, Indians . . . 169

  XII. Administration: Present Arrangements, Ways and
    Means 180

  XIII. Administration: Suggestions for the Future . 193

  XIV. The Uganda Railway 208

  XV. Trade 223

  XVI. Slavery and Missions 231

  XVII. The Neighbours of British East Africa . . 248

  XVIII. Animals 262

ix   *b*

CHAPTER   PAGE

XIX. A Journey down the Nile 280

XX. Recapitulation and Conclusion 303

APPENDICES—

    A. Latest Information respecting the Protectorate . 313

    B. The Temporary British Protectorate over Mombasa in 1824 316

INDEX 319

LIST OF ILLUSTRATIONS

A Stream in Ulu		*Frontispiece*
Swahilis in Full Dress	*To face page*	14
Ivory Horn from Siu	,, ,,	14
Siu Fort	,, ,,	38
Ruins of Nabahan Palace and Graves at Pate	,, ,,	38
A Lady of Lamu Walking under a Tent Carried by Servants	,, ,,	44
Arabs	,, ,,	44
Mombasa Harbour	,, ,,	54
The Tsavo River	,, ,,	62
View of Lake Olbolosat from the Settima Hills	,, ,,	78
Anthills near Baringo	,, ,,	78
Lake Hannington and Flamingoes	,, ,,	78
Ruins of Ancient Stone Kraals on the Uasin Gishu	,, ,,	86
A Bamboo Forest in Kikuyu	,, ,,	86
A Native of Kavirondo	,, ,,	114
Machakos Fort	,, ,,	114
Masai Warriors	,, ,,	138
In the Settima Hills	,, ,,	138
A Path in the Woods near Kericho	,, ,,	170
Nyeri Hills	,, ,,	170
Naivasha	,, ,,	178
Masai Cattle	,, ,,	178
Uasin Gishu Plateau from the Sirgoit Rock	,, ,,	178

CROSSING THE ATHI .   .   .   .   .   .   *To face page* 190

THE ATHI RIVER .   .   .   .   ,,   ,,   206

MOUNT KENYA FROM THE FOOT OF THE SETTIMA HILLS   ,,   ,,   244

SIMBA : A HUNTER'S PARADISE .   .   .   .   ,,   ,,   244

KIMAA .   .   .   .   ,,   ,,   244

TAPPING A COCOANUT PALM FOR TODDY .   .   .   ,,   ,,   270

THE ZEBRA FARM NEAR NAIVASHA .   .   .   .   ,,   ,,   270

A SWAMPY RIVER .   .   .   .   ,,   ,,   294

MAP OF THE SOUTHERN PORTION OF THE KENYA PROVINCE   *at end*

  ,,   BRITISH EAST AFRICA.   .   .   .   .   .   ,,

THE EAST AFRICA PROTECTORATE

CHAPTER I

INTRODUCTORY

MY object in writing this book is to give some account of the British East Africa Protectorate, and especially of the attractions and advantages which it offers, both in climate and products, as a field for European colonisation. This Protectorate is often, but incorrectly, confounded with Uganda. The confusion is not unnatural, for it must be confessed that the name British East Africa is unfortunate, ·as it suggests a general geographical designation for our territories in this region rather than the name of a particular administrative section. That, however, is its proper official signification, and it is probably now too late to alter the expression, inconvenient though it is.

Our possessions, then, in East Equatorial Africa are organised under two fairly natural divisions. To the west and north of Lake Victoria is the Protectorate of Uganda, consisting of the native kingdom of the same name, and other territories, such as Unyoro, Usoga, Ankole, and Toru. It is at present a black man's country and hardly suited to European colonisation, being low, hot, thickly populated with native races, and largely covered with forests or tall grass. To the east of Uganda, between Lake Victoria and the Indian Ocean, lies the East Africa Protectorate, somewhat varied in scenery and character, but on the whole a white man's country,

A

inasmuch as it contains large open tracts over five thousand feet high, with a scanty native population, a healthy, temperate climate, and a soil excellent for both pasturage and agriculture. It may be added—for the nomenclature in common use is very confusing—that the British Central Africa Protectorate has nothing to do with Uganda (which well might bear the name), and is not central, but lies to the south and east of Lake Nyassa; that the Uganda Railway is not in Uganda, but wholly within the limits of the British East Africa Protectorate; and that the Somaliland Protectorate lies on the Gulf of Aden, and has nothing to do with the northern districts of the East Africa Protectorate, which are inhabited by Somalis, and are sometimes called Somaliland, but preferably Jubaland.

In my opinion, founded on a residence of about three and a half years as His Majesty's Commissioner, the East Africa Protectorate is, in virtue of its position and natural character, a possession of no small importance. It merits far more attention than it has received. It must always be to the interest of the Empire to see that its valuable assets are properly tended and utilised, but this case presents the special feature that we have made an outlay of about six millions on the Uganda Railway, and expended annually two or three hundred thousand pounds on grants in aid to the Protectorate without any appreciable return. I consider that the construction of the Uganda Railway can be justified, though I deplore the unnecessary expenditure which accompanied it; but it surprises me that the public, after having expended this enormous sum on building a railway, should take so little interest in the result of the expenditure and the administration of the countries through which the railway passes. Yet this administration must clearly be one of the chief factors in deciding whether these countries are to remain a burden to the taxpayer, or become self-supporting and perhaps wealthy.

It is not my intention to criticise the past administration

of the Protectorate more than may be incidentally necessary to show what should be done in the future. I resigned my post as His Majesty's Commissioner because I felt unable to execute the instructions which I received, and which appear to me incompatible with the welfare of the country. But the past is past: though the country has not made such progress as it might, it has not been spoiled, and we may reasonably hope that when it is transferred to the Colonial Office, and managed with more system and experience, it will rapidly advance in prosperity. We have in East Africa the rare experience of dealing with a *tabula rasa*, an almost untouched and sparsely inhabited country, where we can do as we will, regulate immigration, and open or close the door as seems best. This lessens the difficulty of administration, but it increases the responsibility and the need for reflection.

Whatever East Africa is in ten years' time will be the result not of circumstances or of things beyond our control, but simply of what we do now. If we administer the government with foresight and rectitude, if we avoid crazy projects and execute the dictates of common-sense without muddling, few who know the country can doubt that it will shortly be a flourishing European colony. And it will be more than this. As a European colony in Equatorial Africa it will have in virtue of its position a more than national importance: its development will mean the opening of a new world, and its destinies will influence the whole continent. On the west it borders on Uganda and the sources of the Nile, whence it is now proposed to regulate the water-supply of Egypt. There is already fairly regular communication with Khartum in the north, and through Tanganyika and Nyassa with the south. Both travellers and goods are beginning to use the Uganda Railway as a route to the Congo. On the eastern side the accessible information is ampler for the British possessions than for others, but it would seem that the high healthy plateau is continued, at least intermittently, through German and Portuguese territory to Rhodesia and the Transvaal. To the north, in Abyssinia and Somaliland, there are at any rate healthy patches. There is, therefore, a considerable area in which Europeans can live, and from which they can direct the exploration and development of the territories less suited to their residence.

The past of Africa has been, except in the north, uneventful and gloomy. This is mainly due to the physical configuration, which has on nearly all sides interposed some obstacle— deserts, marshes, or jungles—between the coast and the interior. The timid and backward natives have not broken through these barriers from the inside; from the outside they have been penetrated by few beneficent influences, and chiefly by the evil emissaries of the slave trade. But there is no reason to suppose that Africa differs essentially from the remaining divisions of the earth. The other continents were once covered with forests and marshes, which have disappeared under the hand of man. Nature and mankind interact on one another. Nations and races derive their characteristics largely from their surroundings, but, on the other hand, man reclaims, disciplines, and trains Nature. The surface of Europe, Asia, and North America has submitted to this influence and discipline, but it has still to be applied to large parts of South America and Africa. Marshes must be drained, forests skilfully thinned, rivers be taught to run in ordered courses, and not to afflict the land with drought or flood at their caprice; a way must be made across deserts and jungles, war must be waged against fevers and other diseases whose physical causes are now mostly known. A good beginning has been made, and the future is full of hope. No doubt a large part of Africa is low-lying and tropical, and such countries are at the best not well suited to the higher races, but is there any reason why in time it should not be as civilised and humanised as Southern India?

I doubt not that before Africa can be thus changed hecatombs of lives will be offered in every important locality, but to me this contest with the powers of Nature seems a nobler and more profitable struggle than the international quarrels which waste the brain and blood of Europe and Asia. A time must come when militarism will be felt to be intolerable, and it will be recognised that the fighting and self-sacrificing instincts find a better expression in feats of endurance and exploration than in obeying the dictates of national animosities.

CHAPTER II

GENERAL GEOGRAPHY AND HISTORY

THE East Coast of Africa has played but a small part in history, and has hitherto attracted less attention than the western side of the continent. This is mainly due to the fact that the most remarkable and important territories are situated at some distance in the interior, whereas the coast is either barren and inhospitable, or else a narrow fertile strip succeeded after a few miles by a useless and almost impenetrable jungle. Hence there was no room for the establishment of any large kingdom, and the history of the coast is practically a chronicle of petty conflicts between Arab adventurers from the north and the Portuguese who came into collision with them in journeying round the Cape to India. For neither party, however, were the East African settlements a matter of primary importance. The Portuguese appear to have valued them chiefly as stages on the road to India, and at the end of the fitful struggle· the Arabs remained in possession until the establishment of British and German influence in the last century.

For the history of the interior we have really no materials whatever except native tradition going back a few generations, and such speculations as to the movements of races as are suggested by anthropology and linguistic science. The region about Lake Victoria is indeed one of the most inaccessible in the world. On the east the character of the coast has acted as a barrier; on the west lie the vast forests of the Congo, which have only been traversed in recent years; on the north are the stony deserts of Somaliland and the regions round Lake Rudolf; and farther west the marshes of the southern Sudan, which largely deprive the higher waters of the Nile of their value as a means of communication. On the south indeed there is no natural obstacle to communication, but also no civilisation or any known element likely to influence the character of neighbouring nations. On the whole, whatever traces of superior civilisation can be discovered seem to have entered these regions from the north, either by way of the Nile or from the Gallas and Somalis, who had relations with Abyssinia, and perhaps with Arabia. The inhabitants of Equatorial Africa clearly prefer the low and somewhat swampy country round the great lakes, for the high plateaus to the east of them are scantily or not at all inhabited, and have produced no political organisation which can be compared to the kingdoms of Uganda and Unyoro. Yet the most important physical character of East Africa is precisely this ridge of high country, rising to as much as 10,000 feet above the level of the sea, without counting peaks, which seems suited to be the residence of a European race.

Professor Gregory in his interesting work on the foundation of British East Africa says that the Protectorate (including Uganda) consists of seven belts of country, which are strikingly unlike each other, but all parallel to the coast: the coast strip, the jungle belt of from seventy to two hundred miles, the volcanic plains, the Great Rift Valley, the Mau-Kamasia plateau, the basin of the Victoria Nyanza, and the valley of the Nile. This enumeration gives a good idea of the country traversed in going from the east coast to, say, Lake Albert, though it will probably occur to most who are practically familiar with the journey that the Kikuyu Hills, which are crossed between the volcanic plains and the Rift Valley, form, if not a separate geographical or geological zone, a very distinct wooded and fertile belt, contrasting markedly with the bare plains on either side. Also, although these zones are clearly marked on the route traversed by the Uganda Railway, it is not certain that they would be equally clear if one struck inland from other parts of the Protectorate, e.g. Lamu or Port Durnford.

Another statement of the physical configuration of the country would be that a volcanic upheaval has raised a great plateau some 300 miles broad in the regions between 200 and 500 miles from the sea. On the west this plateau slopes down to Lake Victoria, which is largely a collection of the waters which flow from it. On the east it slopes to the sea. The fact that the slope is only about 300 miles explains the absence of large rivers on the coast, as the great waterways of Africa, the Nile, the Niger, and the Congo, require a far larger space to accumulate their volume. On the north the plateau passes into the little known but relatively barren steppes inhabited by the Somali, Rendile, and other tribes in the neighbourhood of Abyssinia. In the middle it is divided by a huge cleft, the Great Rift Valley, which runs roughly north and south, and contains Lakes Naivasha, Nakuru, Baringo, and Rudolf, as well as smaller pieces of water and several volcanic hills. This valley, which appears to be the result of a subsidence consequent on a crack in the volcanic rocks, is in some places divided from the surrounding higher plateaus by precipitous walls (for instance, the Kikuyu escarpment), and in others by more gradual slopes. The general elevation is higher on the interior side, where the Mau is prolonged to the north-west in the vast plains of Uasin Gishu, but the outer or eastern side presents greater isolated heights in the chain of Settima and the great peak of Kenya (18,620 feet). Some small chains of hills run down towards the coast, and there are also several isolated mountain masses, of which by far the largest is Kilima-Njaro (19,200), though the Teita Hills, Kilibasi, and Kisigau are also of considerable size and remarkable appearance. The snows of Kenya form the river Tana, which discharges into the sea towards the south-east and contribute to the Waso Nyiro (more correctly E-uaso-ngiro), which runs north-east and disappears in the Lorian Swamp.

The history of the coast is a record of complicated quarrels neither easy nor interesting to recount. Arabic history in all parts of the world tends to degenerate into genealogy, and presents few questions of national importance. This tendency towards recurring petty feuds was naturally strong on a long narrow strip of shore where there was no room for any large State and no common interest to unite the various ports. In virtue of the advantages of its position, its good climate and fine harbours, Mombasa was the most important point, yet it cannot be said to have been a political centre for the surrounding country. It was simply the place which was most fought about and oftenest burnt. The native name, Mvita, means war, and never was name more justified by history. There can be hardly any town in the world which has been besieged, captured, sacked, burnt, and razed to the ground so often in so short a time. Mombasa was not so much the field where important issues were decided, as a seaport tavern into which every passing pirate entered to take part in a drunken brawl and smash the furniture, and it is only in quite recent years that it has begun to assume its proper position as an emporium and door for the interior.

The chronicle of these ancient squabbles may be summed up somewhat as follows. As far back as we can go the coast has been subject to Arab influence, but this influence was exercised at different times by different bodies of Arabs. The older settlements prior to the arrival of the Portuguese are quite distinct from the later lordship of Oman and Maskat, and the partial colonisation which it occasioned. When the Portuguese arrived in 1458 they found on the coast a series of independent towns, peopled by Arabs, but not united to Arabia by any political tie. Their relations with these Arabs were mostly hostile, but during the sixteenth century they firmly established their power, and ruled with the aid of tributary Arab sultans. This system lasted till 1631, when the Sultan of Mombasa massacred the European inhabitants. In the remainder of their rule the Portuguese appointed European governors, who were apparently most distasteful to the natives, for they invited the Arabs of Oman, who now appear on the scene for the first time, to assist them in driving the foreigners out.

The Yorubi, who were then the ruling family in Oman, expelled the Portuguese from all their settlements except Mozambique by the end of the seventeenth century. The real power on the coast passed into the hands of the Arab family called Mazrui, who, though at first merely governors and representatives of the Imam of Oman, soon became practically independent. But at the end of the eighteenth century the dynasty of Bu Saidi, who had succeeded the Yorubi as rulers of Oman, began to assert their rights over the coast, and in 1832 Seyyid Said broke the power of the Mazrui and transferred his capital from Maskat to Zanzibar, which then became the principal town of East Africa. At his death his dominions were divided, and the ruler of the southern or African portion became Sultan[1] of Zanzibar and of the coast. About 1880 the Powers of Europe, particularly Great Britain and Germany, began to take an interest in East Africa, with the result that the Sultan has now no practical authority on the coast (though he receives rent for part of it), and that the islands of Zanzibar and Pemba are a British Protectorate.

The Greek geographer Ptolemy (about A.D. 150) gives some account of East Africa as then known. He calls the country Azania, and speaks of the promontory of Zingis. These words may perhaps be connected with the Arabic name for the coast, Zanj, or in the plural Zunuj, which is no doubt the same as the Persian Zang, a negro. The old civilisation of the coast is sometimes spoken of as the Zang empire, though it does not appear that it was organised into a single State. It is probable that from very early times there was a regular migration of Himyarites from South Arabia to South Africa, who worked gold mines, and built Zimbabye and the other ruins of Rhodesia. It is also very probable that such localities as the Lamu Archipelago and Mombasa, which offer obvious advantages as ports, were repeatedly occupied before

[1] The ruler of Zanzibar is commonly called Sultan, but the correct title is still Seyyid. He is styled Jelalet in Arabic, Highness in English, and Hautesse (not Altesse) in French.

the oldest colonisation of which we have any record. It is said that the earliest settlements were made by the Emozeides (or Ammu Said) from Oman, but I have not been able to find any detailed information respecting this movement.[1] We have, however, a fair amount of tradition, if not of accurate detail, respecting the colonisation of the coast in the tenth and following centuries of the Christian era. The Arabic chronicles of Kilwa are published in the *Journal of the Royal Asiatic Society for* 1895, and another version can be found in Barros, *Da Asia*, Lisbon, 1778. The contents of the chronicles of Mombasa have been indicated by Strandes, Guillain, and Krapf. Those of Pate exist in MS. at Mombasa, but have not yet been published.

These chronicles ascribe the foundation of the coast towns to Arabs or Persians. The mingling of the two names is not surprising if one considers the relations between the two nations and how often the Arabs were in Persia or the Persians in Arabia. The presence of true Persians on the East African coast seems established. Burton discovered a Persian inscription near Tanga, and Persian coins have been found at Melindi. It is said that the ancient mosques in East Africa resemble Persian and not Arabian architecture. Makdishu has the reputation of being the earliest settlement, having been built, according to tradition, in A.D. 908. Then followed Kilwa about A.D. 975, and one or two hundred years later Mombasa, Kilifi, Malindi, and the settlements in the Lamu Archipelago, Pate (Patta), Siu, Faza, and Lamu itself. It would appear that these shores were also visited by the Chinese. Chinese coins dating between A.D. 713 and 1163 have been found at Kilwa and Makdishu, and a Chinese fleet is said to have visited the latter town in 1430. A family at Lamu claim descent from the Chinese, or Malays, who were wrecked there. The

---

[1] See Krapf, "Travels and Missionary Labours," p. 522 ; and Badger, "Imams and Seyyids of Oman," p. xii. The latter, quoting from the "Futûh-el-Buldân," says that Said and Suleiman, chiefs of Oman, withstood El-Hajjaj, Governor of Irak, who attacked their country in 684. They were ultimately defeated by him, and fled with their adherents to the "land of Zanj."

traces of Egyptian influence are slight, but an Egyptian idol has been discovered at Makdishu, and some of the inhabitants of Melindi assert that they are of Egyptian origin.

These Zanj coast towns apparently reached a considerable degree of prosperity and civilisation.   Ibn Batuta, the Arabic geographer, visited Makdishu in 1328, and describes it as an exceedingly large city.   He adds (Lee's translation, London, 1829, p. 57), "I remained some days the King's (of Makdishu) guest, and then set out for the country of the Zanuj, proceeding along the seashore.   I then went on board a vessel and sailed to the island of Mombasa, which is large, abounding with the banana, the lemon, and the citron.   They have also a fruit which they call the jammoom.   It is like the olive, with a stone, except that the fruit is exceedingly sweet.   There is no grain in this island.   What they have is brought to them from other places.   The people are generally religious, chaste, and honest, and are of the sect of Shafia.   After lodging there one night I set out by sea for the city of Kilwa.   The greater part of the inhabitants are Zunuj of the sect of Shafia, of religious and peaceful habits.   The King of the place at the time I entered it was Abu El Mozaffir Hasan, a person who had obtained great victories over the countries of the infidel Zunuj."

Vasco da Gama in his Journals gives a similar impression (*Journal of the First Voyage of Vasco da Gama*, Hakluyt Society, 1898).   Of Mombasa he says that it "is a large city, seated upon an eminence washed by the sea.   The port is entered daily by numerous vessels.   At its entrance stands a pillar, and by the sea a low-lying fortress.[1]   Those who had gone on shore told us that they had seen many men in irons, and it seemed to us that they must be Christians, as the Christians in that country are at war with the Moors.   The Christian merchants in that town are only temporary residents, and are held in much subjection, they not being allowed to do

---

[1] This can hardly be any of the existing forts, the date of whose construction is known.

anything except by order of the Moorish King. . . . Two men were sent by the Captain-Major to the King. When they landed they were followed by a crowd as far as the gates of the Palace. Before reaching the King they passed through four doors, each guarded by a doorkeeper with a drawn cutlass. The King received them hospitably, and ordered that they should be shown over the city. They stopped on their way at the house of a Christian merchant, who showed them a paper, an object of adoration, on which was a sketch of the Holy Ghost.[1] When they had seen all, the King sent them back with samples of cloves, pepper, and corn, with which he would allow us to load our ships."

Of Melindi he says: "The King wore a robe of damask trimmed with green satin and a rich touca. He was seated on two cushioned chairs of bronze, beneath a round sunshade of crimson satin attached to a pole. An old man who attended him as page carried a short sword in a silver sheath. There were many players on anafils and two trumpets[2] of ivory, richly carved, and of the size of a man, which were blown from a hole in the side, and made sweet harmony with the anafils.

"The town of Melindi lies in a bay, and extends along the shore. It may be likened to Al Couchette. Its houses are lofty and well whitewashed, and have many windows. On the land side are palm groves, and all around it maize and vegetables are being cultivated. We remained in front of this town during nine days, and all this time we had fêtes, sham fights, and musical performances."

The foundations of Portugal's power in Africa and the East were laid by Prince Henry the Navigator (1394–1460), the son of John the Great. This Prince, who appears to have been the first to grasp, or at least to try to execute, the great

[1] It has been conjectured that the merchant was really a Hindu, and the drawing a Hindu emblem and not Christian.
[2] Such trumpets may still be seen on the coast. There is a very fine one in the Sub-Commissioner's house at Lamu, which came from Siu.

idea that it was possible to sail round Africa and reach India, devoted his life to organising expeditions of discovery with this object, which, however, he failed to attain.   His captains explored the west coast of Africa as far as Guinea, but he died before any of them rounded its southern cape.   This was done in 1486 by Bartholomew Diaz, who reached Algoa Bay. John II., who was then on the throne of Portugal, realising the magnitude of the prospect thus opened, called the promontory the Cape of Good Hope, and selected Vasco da Gama to make the first expedition to India by the new route.   But fate was no kinder to him than to the Navigator.   He died before the expedition could start, and it was his successor, Manuel, who in 1497 despatched Vasco da Gama with four ships on his famous voyage.

Vasco da Gama, after touching at Mozambique, anchored off Mombasa on April 7, 1498, and found it to be a wealthy and prosperous town.   The Sultan was apparently disposed to give the strangers a good reception, but Da Gama, rightly or wrongly, suspecting treachery, inaugurated the long record of quarrels and bloodshed which forms the history of the relations of Portugal with the City of War.   He had some difficulty in entering the port, as his ship collided with the one astern of her, and the pilots confessed under torture that they had been ordered to wreck the fleet.[1]   For the moment no revenge was possible.   Da Gama went on to Melindi, where he met with a good reception, but would not land, and thence to India.   On his return the following year he did not touch at Mombasa, but stopped at Melindi, where he erected a stone pillar as a

---

[1] The whole of this story is difficult to follow or explain.   Da Gama says that when the pilots were tortured by dropping boiling lard on their flesh they confessed "that orders had been given to capture us as soon as we entered the port, and thus to avenge what we had done in Mozambique."   Correa (*Lendas da India*, translated by Stanley for the Hakluyt Society, 1879, p. 105) says that the Sheikh of Mozambique sent a message (a runner by land) to the King of Mombasa warning him that Da Gama was a robber, but he also says that after the Portuguese fleet had left, "the King, to conceal his treachery, quarrelled much with the pilots because they ran away, in the presence of the convict who had remained on shore (who was named Peter Diaz, and who afterwards came to India to our people and became a seafaring man so that they named him 'North

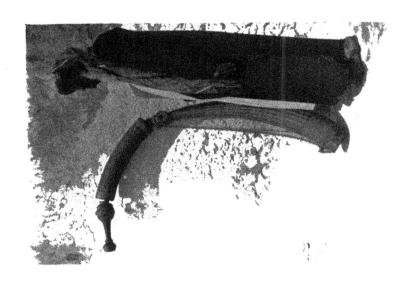

IVORY HORN FROM SIU.

SWAHILIS IN FULL DRESS.

token of gratitude for his escape. Camoens describes Vasco da Gama's doings in these parts in his "Lusiads," Books II.–V. In Book II. he relates the attempted treachery of the King of Mombasa, from which, thanks to the warnings of Mercury, Da Gama is delivered. In Books III.–V. Da Gama gives the King of Melindi a lengthy account of his voyage and of the state of Europe.

In the next few years poor Mombasa had to pay heavily for the accident to Da Gama's ship. It was sacked in 1500 by Cabral, and again in 1505 by Francisco de Almeida, the first Portuguese Viceroy of India. The Sultan became a tributary of Portugal, and about the same time the same fate befell the princes of Zanzibar, Kilwa, Sofala, Barawa, and Lamu. These possessions were organised as part of the Portuguese province of Arabia and Ethiopia, and placed under a governor-general. Somewhat later, about 1571, the vast oriental empire of Portugal was divided into three governorships: the central one extended from Cape Guardafui to Ceylon, with Goa as capital; the eastern from Pegu to China, with Malacca as capital; while the western division comprised the east coast of Africa, and was administered from Mozambique. Mombasa was attacked again in 1528 by Da Cunha with the assistance of the Sultan of Melindi, and was captured and burnt after a siege of nearly four months. After this there was an interval of about fifty years, in which practically nothing is recorded of it—doubtless while the town was growing up again.

According to native tradition, the Duruma tribe, who live

East'), and the King ordered the pilots to be beaten." If this story is true, it is hard to see what motive the King can have had except that he was sincerely sorry for what had happened. He had no reason to conceal his treachery, and if his original intention had been to attack Da Gama he would probably have killed Diaz. The fact that the King of Melindi gave the Portuguese so good a reception shows that the temper of the natives was not hostile. In my experience, when there is a misunderstanding between Europeans and Orientals it is generally the Europeans who are in the wrong.

Peter Diaz was one of the Degradados or convicts sent with Da Gama " to be adventured on land" in risky places.

immediately behind Mombasa, are descended from the Makwa tribe and from the people of Kilwa, who were brought thence to Mombasa by a personage called Bwana Kigozi. It is possible that there may lurk in this title the name of de Goez, a Portuguese general who defeated the Sultan of Kilwa, and deported him with many of his subjects to Mombasa in 1509.

Towards the end of the sixteenth century two new, though only transitory, powers make their appearance, and play their part in what is already becoming the monotonous drama of harrying the east coast—the Turks and the Zimbas. A Turkish corsair named Mirale Beque, or Ali Bey, arrived in 1585 and took tribute from Mombasa, Lamu, Faza, and Jumbo (Kismayu) in the name of the Ottoman Sultan. He ejected the Portuguese from most of their settlements, and when he returned to the Red Sea in the next year is said to have taken with him fifty Portuguese prisoners and about six hundred thousand pounds worth of plunder. The Viceroy of India sent a fleet from Goa, which burnt Mombasa as a punishment for having allowed itself to be plundered by Ali Bey.

The Zimbas were a tribe of fierce warriors, who came from the south of the Zambesi. Their name is possibly connected with Zumbo or with Zambesi itself, but little is known about their origin or affinities. It is said that Madagascar was invaded and occupied before the arrival of the Malays by a tribe called Vazimba, or Bazimba, who may be the same people. From 1586 to 1589 these Zimbas overran East Africa as far north as Melindi. They began by capturing Kilwa and massacring the inhabitants, after which they went northwards and besieged Mombasa. While they were thus occupied, encamped at Makupa on the mainland, Ali Bey and the Turks returned in 1588. They established themselves at Ras Serani, the end of Mombasa island which faces the sea, and built a fort there.[1]

---

[1] This was apparently on the same site where there is still a fort. First the Turks built a fort, then the Portuguese built a chapel, then the Arabs turned the chapel into a fort, the ruins of which remain.

Not long afterwards, in March 1589, Thomas de Souza Coutinho arrived with twenty ships, so that there were three rival powers more or less besieging the City of War.   At first the Zimbas appear to have made common cause with the Portuguese and to have attacked the Turks, who were expelled, Ali Bey and others being captured.   The Zimbas, it would seem, occupied Mombasa and attacked Melindi.   The Portuguese now proceeded to make war on the Zimbas with the aid of the tribe of Wasegeju, with whom they formed an alliance.   The Zimbas were defeated, and their power entirely broken.   Then the Portuguese sacked Kilifi (which was practically annihilated), and also Mombasa.   Ahmad, the Sheikh of Melindi, was appointed king of the latter town in the place of Shaho bin Misham, the last Sultan of the old dynasty.

This was in 1592.   The Portuguese, recognising the importance of Mombasa, appointed a Portuguese governor, and proceeded to construct the fort or citadel, which is still such a prominent feature of the town.   It was called the Jesus Fort, and was begun in 1593.   We also hear of blockhouses being constructed at Makupa as a defence against the Wanyika.   For some years no breach of the peace is recorded, but in 1612 the Sultan, Hasan bin Ali, quarrelled with the Portuguese governor, fled from the town, and after several adventures was murdered by the natives of Rabai.   The son of this Sultan, Yusuf bin Hasan, was sent to Goa and educated there as a Catholic, being baptized by the name of Jeronymo Chingoulia, and marrying a Portuguese lady.   His hypocritical professions of Christianity and loyalty procured his recognition as Sultan in 1630, but the next year he treacherously massacred all the Portuguese in Mombasa, and took possession of the fort.   Francisco de Moura was sent with a fleet from Goa to punish him, but Yusuf succeeded in escaping after capturing two ships, dismantling the fort, and, as usual, destroying the town.   For some years he caused the Portuguese much annoyance as a sort of buccaneer.   No more Sultans

B

were appointed. In 1635 the new governor, Francisco de Seixas de Cabreira, repaired the fort, which still contains two inscriptions, one recording these improvements, and the other the completion of the original building in 1595.

Then followed an interval of peace, but probably of tyranny, for we are told that in the middle of the seventeenth century the inhabitants of Mombasa and the other coast towns sent a deputation to Arabia begging the Imam of Maskat to assist them in turning out the Portuguese. Oman and Maskat, the history of which is henceforth closely connected with East Africa, were then ruled by the Yorubi (Yu'rabi)[1] family, who warred successfully with Persia and raided Salsette, near Bombay. The Ibadhi, or Bayazi, sect to which they belonged, held the view that any pious man, and not necessarily only members of the Prophet's tribe, could attain the position of Imam or religious head of the Moslem world, and in virtue of this doctrine, which is undoubtedly heretical according to the strict Sunni faith, the rulers of Maskat claimed to be Pontiffs as well as Kings. The secular title was Seyyid (less correctly Seid), prince or chief. The overtures from the East African Coast were well received, and the Seyyid Sultan bin Saif, who had expelled the Portuguese from Maskat, sent a considerable navy against their African possessions.

Between 1660 and 1690 there was much warfare and burning of towns after the usual fashion, and the cities of the Lamu Archipelago changed hands several times. But the advantage remained with the Arabs, who on March 15, 1696, entered Kilindini harbour and applied themselves to the siege of Mombasa, which lasted thirty-three months. The Europeans and 2500 natives, including the King of Faza, took refuge in Fort Jesus, while the Arabs occupied the town, Makupa, the chapel of Nossa Senhora das Merces at Ras Sarani, and Fort St. Joseph at Kilindini. They were able to prevent four Portuguese ships which arrived on Christmas Day from enter-

[1] Or Ya'arubah. See Badger, "Imâms and Seyyids of Oman," p. 53.

ing the harbour, and in January the already sore plight of the besieged was aggravated by an outbreak of plague. All the Europeans died, the commandant, Don Antonio Mogo de Melho, last of all, and in September 1697 the fort was held only by the King of Faza and a handful of men. Just at this moment reinforcements arrived from Mozambique and effected a landing, but though they protracted the siege for fifteen months more, their resistance was vain. The Arabs entered the fort on December 12, 1698, and put to the sword the scanty remnants of the garrison, only eleven men and two women. A Portuguese fleet arrived from Goa only two days later, but the admiral, seeing the Arab flag flying on the fort, did not attempt to land, and retired. The Arabs then occupied Pemba, Zanzibar, and Kilwa, and drove the Portuguese out of practically all their East African possessions except Mozambique. Walis, or governors, were established in the principal towns, Mombasa being entrusted to Nasir bin Abdullah el Mazrui, the first of that celebrated family[1] who have played so great a part in the destinies of the East African Coast down to the Mazrui rebellion of 1895.

The capture of Mombasa fort in 1698 marks the real downfall of the Portuguese power north of Mozambique, but it was reasserted for a couple of years from 1727 to 1729. After several unsuccessful expeditions the Portuguese were at last favoured by a quarrel between the Walis of Zanzibar and Mombasa, which enabled them to reoccupy the latter town and Pate. But in 1729 the people of Mombasa invited the Arabs to return; the Portuguese were driven out for the last time, and a fleet despatched by the Viceroy of India to their assistance was destroyed by a hurricane. An expedition sent from Mozambique to recapture Mombasa thought it more prudent to return without landing.

The results of the Portuguese occupation of the East African coast are very small, and consist mainly of a few buildings, of which the fort at Mombasa is by far the most

[1] Also called Benu Mazrua' or Mazara'.

considerable, and the presence of numerous Goanese whom the long-standing connection with Goa has brought over to Zanzibar and the mainland. There is no proof whatever that they penetrated inland, though they had apparently heard of Kilima-Njaro, as it was very natural they should do. They are generally accused of great tyranny and brutality towards the natives; but it is worthy of remark that they often had native allies, and that not only did natives go through the siege with them in Mombasa fort, but that during the siege the Wanyika spontaneously attacked the Arabs.

Except the Portuguese attempt at reoccupation mentioned above, little of moment occurred in East Africa during the eighteenth century. Bickerings of course there were, but of less importance than usual. As might be expected, the allegiance to Maskat became more and more shadowy, till about 1740 Othman bin Muhammed, the Mazrui governor of Mombasa, and the Nabahan King of Pate declared themselves independent, and proceeded to fight with one another for the supremacy of the coast, with no particular result. This declaration of independence was probably connected with a revolution in Oman, which had some importance for East Africa. The Yorubi were replaced as the ruling family by the Bu Saidi,[1] from whom the present Sultans of Zanzibar are descended.

For some time the Bu Saidi did not trouble much more about their African dominions than the Yorubi had done, but in 1785 the Imam Ahmad bin Said visited Mombasa and compelled the Mazruis to recognise him as their sovereign for the moment. The effect of the visit soon passed, but Said bin Sultan, the fifth of the line, took the decisive step of transferring his capital to Zanzibar. The result of this transfer was to increase the importance of East Africa generally, and of Zanzibar in particular. Hitherto that island had played a comparatively small part in the history of the coast. It is

---

[1] Sometimes called Albusaidi. Âl in this phrase is not the Arabic article, but a word meaning family.

very fertile, but has no good harbours, and is also unhealthy. It was first conquered for the Portuguese by the piratical Ravasco in 1503, and more definitely by De Lemos six years later. But the Portuguese clearly did not care for it as a residence. In 1635 the Sultan had become independent, though friendly to Portugal. Christians were at first tolerated, but about 1660 were massacred or expelled. After the Yorubi had conquered Mombasa, Zanzibar speedily passed into their hands, and was ruled by governors appointed from Arabia. When Seyyid Said established his residence there, the town is said to have consisted of a row of huts. He was doubtless guided in his choice of locality by the consideration that there were on the somewhat neglected island no old ruling families like the Mazrui of Mombasa or the princes of the Lamu Archipelago. Also, although the harbour is bad, the position of Zanzibar opposite the Coast renders it an excellent centre for a sovereign desirous to observe and control the whole littoral. Hence it soon became both commercially and politically the principal city in East Africa north of Mozambique, and expanded to imposing dimensions.

It was not till 1832 that Said[1] definitely settled in Zanzibar, but his reconquest of East Africa for Maskat, for it was nothing less, began ten years earlier, when at the request of the people of Pate, who had been defeated by their enemies the Mazrui, he occupied Pate and Pemba. A curious incident then occurred—the temporary British Protectorate of Mombasa. Suliman bin Ali, the Mazrui chief, fearing that Said was about to attack him, appealed to the British squadron, which happened to be then cruising in East African waters, and was granted British protection, subject to the confirmation of the British Government. Lieutenant Reitz (who gave his name to Port Reitz) was appointed Resident. Had this arrangement been

---

[1] This name is of course the Arabic Sa'id, but owing to the Swahili and European habit of neglecting to pronounce the letter Ain, the title and proper name Seyyid Said are often sounded in East Africa as if they were the same word repeated, and most incorrectly written as Said Said or Seid Seid.

accepted, the march of events in East Africa would have been much accelerated; but Said complained to the Bombay Government about the action of our vessels, and two years later the protectorate was terminated and the resident removed.[1]

Said then proceeded to attack the Mazrui, but his attention was distracted by troubles in Maskat, which prevented him from concentrating his attention and forces on Mombasa, which he besieged and occupied three times between 1828 and 1833, but each time returned with only a nominal victory. He finally achieved his object by treachery. The Mazrui Governor and twenty-six prominent members of the clan were enticed on board a vessel by false oaths and conveyed to the Persian Gulf, where they died in banishment. This broke the power of the Mazrui, and until their rebellion in 1895 little more is heard of them. They left Mombasa; the elder branch settled at Gasi to the south, and the younger at Takaungu to the north.

The latter part of Said's reign was largely occupied by troublesome operations against the islands of the Lamu Archipelago, where there were most complicated alliances and quarrels between the ordinary inhabitants, the Nabahan aristocracy and the Somalis. Though the people of Pate had invited his aid against the Mazrui, they now revolted, and Pate and Siu did not submit to Zanzibar until 1866.

Said died at sea in 1856, when cruising near the Seychelles Islands. He was without doubt the most eminent Oriental of modern times in East Africa. His reconquest of his ancestral dominions, though not unstained by treachery, showed energy and ability. He was intelligent, tolerant (as witnessed by his protection of Christian missions), not cruel, and disposed to encourage commerce. By his will he divided his dominions. Oman was left to his eldest son, Seyyid Thwain or Thuwayni; Zanzibar and the East African Coast to his younger son Majid. The brothers quarrelled, but the dispute was referred to the

[1] See Appendix B for particulars.

Viceroy of India, Lord Canning, who upheld the division, and declared Zanzibar independent of Oman.

From this period until the partition of Africa beween the European powers began in the eighties, few political events are to be recorded in East Africa. In 1875 Ismail Pasha, Khedive of Egypt, endeavoured to annex the northern part of the coast, and sent four ships under a Scotchman, who bore the somewhat mixed designation of M'Killop Pasha. This officer landed troops at Kismayu, and occupied the mouth of the Juba for about three months, but was recalled in deference to the representations of the British Government. But though the middle of the last century was happily barren for East Africa in military and political events, it was perhaps the most important period since its discovery by Europeans, for it was then that began the series of explorations which opened up the centre of the continent and removed the veil which had hidden for so long the Great Lakes and the sources of the Nile.

These great achievements need be only briefly noticed here, for few of them were concerned directly with the present British East Africa Protectorate, which remained practically unknown long after the more distant regions of the interior had been explored, as the earlier travellers often did not traverse the hinterland of the East Coast, and, when they did so, generally passed through what is now German territory. Indirectly, of course, by drawing attention to Uganda and other regions most easily accessible from the East Coast, the explorers had an immense effect on the territories of which I treat, and brought about the establishment of our protectorates and the construction of the Uganda Railway.

Three very dissimilar bodies of men contributed to this exploration of East Central Africa—slave-traders, missionaries, and geographical investigators. Infamous as the slave trade was, it tended to give those who practised it an acquaintance with the geography of the interior. It is clear, from the testimony of the earlier explorers, that the Arabs even at

Zanzibar had a far better notion of the general lie of the Great Lakes and the course of the Nile than the geographers of Europe.   Seyyid Said conceived the idea of making a chain of trading stations (curiously analogous to Krapf's idea of a a similar line of mission stations) extending from the coast to the Congo.   Bagamoyo was the usual point of departure, and Tabora the most important inland centre.   The Arabs used the waters of the Congo on their expeditions, and the Congo Free State was founded to protect the country from these eastern raiders.   Though the Arabs usually went inland through what is now German territory, because food could be obtained along the whole way and there were no hostile tribes, they were also aware of the other route through Masailand and to the north of Lake Victoria.   I have myself spoken to Arabs at Mombasa who professed to have reached the neighbourhood of the West Coast by this road.[1]

I have treated in another chapter of the exploring work done by missionaries, especially that eminent German, Krapf. He discovered Mount Kenya in 1849, a year after his colleague Rebman had discovered Kilima-Njaro.

The reader will find in Johnston's "The Nile Quest" (1904) a brilliant and interesting account of the various travellers who from the fifties to the eighties investigated the sources of the Nile and the adjacent equatorial lands. The journeys of Livingstone were mostly to the south of the regions with which we are here occupied; but in 1857 Burton and Speke made their way from Bagamoyo to Tanganyika.   Speke parted from Burton, and discovered Lake Victoria.   He subsequently made a second expedition with Grant in 1890 by the same route to Uganda, where he was well received by King Mtesa, and joined Sir Samuel Baker on the Nile.   In 1864 Baker discovered Lake Albert.   In the seventies Stanley and Cameron crossed equatorial Africa: to the former was due the foundation of the Congo Free State,

---

[1] After leaving the Nile they apparently took some route through Kanem and Sokoto.

and the commencement of our interest in Uganda, which ended in the establishment of the Protectorate. But it was not till the eighties that Europeans explored the territories between Mombasa and the Lake. In 1882 Dr. Fischer, a German naturalist, proceeded from Pangani to Kilima-Njaro, and thence across Masailand to Naivasha. There, however, he was stopped by the Masai, and had to return. In the next year Joseph Thomson succeeded in reaching Lake Victoria by the same route, and recorded his experiences in "Across Masailand," which is still one of the most valuable and entertaining works which can be consulted about East Africa. Though much impeded and harassed by the Masai, he not only penetrated from Mombasa to Taveta, and thence to Naivasha, but succeeded in continuing his journey to Njamusi (Njemps) at the southern end of Baringo, and thence crossed into Kavirondo over Kamasia and Elgeyo. He came upon Lake Victoria in Usoga, a little to the east of the mouth of the Nile, and then had to return on account of illness, but discovered Mount Elgon on his way home.

The last important discoveries in East Africa were made in 1887 by Count Teleki, a Hungarian, accompanied by Lieutenant von Höhnel. The best-known result of this expedition, which started *via* Pangani, Taveta, and Lake Nyiri, was the discovery of Lakes Rudolf and Stephanie, but incidentally Teleki was the first European to visit Kikuyu, which had been merely skirted by Fischer and Thomson.

In the early eighties German merchants began to be active in the coast towns, and made several treaties with the chiefs of the hinterland. In 1885 the German Government, who were anxious to inaugurate a colonial policy, gave the Society of German Colonisation, which had acquired these treaty rights, a charter of protection. From this date begins the partition of East Africa, and its administration by Great Britain and Germany. The period belongs to contemporary history: the events which it has witnessed affect so many individuals now living, and the main questions involved have so many personal aspects, that they cannot be profitably criticised by one who, like myself, has had a personal connection with our administration. I will therefore merely terminate this chapter by a brief recapitulation of the chief incidents which have resulted in the constitution of the present British and German territories.

Great Britain had not at this time any direct interest in the coast, but our influence was practically paramount at Zanzibar. It will be remembered that it was the Viceroy of India who settled the succession of Seyyid Said: in 1872 the British India Steam Navigation Company established regular communication between India, Zanzibar, and Europe; and in 1877 the Sultan offered to the chairman of that Company a concession of his mainland dominions. The British Government was not favourable to this concession, which fell through, but our official interest in Zanzibar was increased by the measures taken for the suppression of the slave trade. It became necessary to define the exact limits of the Sultanate of Zanzibar. Neither the Yorubi nor the Bu Saidi had ever organised their dominions or entered into any sort of international agreement. They had asserted their power in the coast towns wherever and whenever they could, but they had no control, either practical or theoretical, over the interior.

In 1886, by an agreement between England and Germany, the Sultan's dominions were defined as consisting of the islands of Zanzibar, Pemba, and the Mafia and Lamu Archipelagoes, and on the mainland of a strip of coast extending ten miles inland from Tungi Bay in the south to Kipini at the mouth of the Ozi River. To the north, the ports of Kismayu, Brava, Merka, Makdishu, and Warsheikh were also recognised as belonging to his Highness. The hinterland behind the ten-mile strip, between the Rovuma and Tana Rivers, was divided into two spheres of influence, German to the south and British to the north, the boundary being a line drawn from the mouth of the Umba River past the northern base of Kilima-Njaro to the point where the first degree of south latitude intersects the eastern shore of Lake Victoria.

It is to be observed that this agreement did not extend beyond the river Tana to the north, and complications soon began in Witu, behind Lamu. Certain refugees from Pate, under an outlaw called Fumo Bakari, had established themselves in this place. They were really little more than a band of robbers, but it suited the Germans to recognise them as an independent state, and to declare a protectorate over Witu. In 1887 Seyyid Barghash granted to the British East Africa Association a concession of his mainland possessions between the Umba and Kipini, and next year the association was reconstituted as the Imperial British East Africa Company, under a royal charter. From the initials of this title British East Africa has sometimes been known by the name of Ibea. The chairman was Sir William Mackinnon, a rightly honoured name, to whom a statue has been erected in the public garden of Mombasa. In the same year (1888) Seyyid Khalifa, the successor of Barghash, granted the Germans a similar concession of his territories south of the Umba. A complicated situation was created to the north of the Tana. The Germans had a protectorate over Witu, and demanded the cession of Lamu: the Sultan, on the other hand, offered to lease all his territories between Kipini and Kismayu to the British East Africa Company, in the same way as he had leased those below Kipini. The Germans protested, and claimed the country between Witu and the Juba.

These difficulties were finally settled by the Anglo-German Treaty of July 1, 1890, which dealt with several parts of the world, and ceded Heligoland to Germany. In East Africa, Germany renounced all claims to Witu and other territory north of the line drawn from the Umba to Lake Victoria, so as to leave Kilima-Njaro in her territory, and recognised a British protectorate over Zanzibar, Pemba, and the Sultan's mainland dominions between the Umba and the Juba. France also recognised our protectorate over Zanzibar in return for our recognition of the French protectorate over Madagascar. In 1891 an arrangement was made with Italy

as to the territory north of the Juba. A few months after
the signature of the Anglo-German Treaty of 1890, ten Germans were murdered at Witu, and a British expedition was
sent to avenge their death.

The history of Uganda is an important background to
the history of the Coast. Stanley first inspired European
missionaries with an interest in this country, and the Church
Missionary Society sent a party of pioneers in 1877, who
were soon followed by a Roman Catholic mission. The early
days of Christianity in Uganda were very stormy. The
missions met with alternate encouragement and persecution:
Protestants fought with Roman Catholics, and both with
Mohammedans. The rivalry between the first two sects was
particularly severe and practically political, since they represented the British and French parties. In 1890 the German
explorer Peters made a journey to the interior, during which
he made many treaties with chiefs in Uganda and elsewhere,
which would probably have created much trouble had they
not fallen through in consequence of the Anglo-German
agreement made in the same year.

In virtue of that agreement the British East Africa
Company proceeded to occupy Uganda, and sent Lugard
thither. He restored order in a manner which has won high
praise; but the Company found the occupation of Uganda a
heavier drain on their resources than they had anticipated,
and were anxious that Government should relieve them of
their burden. There was a strong feeling in many quarters,
particularly among those interested in missions, against the
abandonment of the country, and in 1893 Sir Gerald Portal,
then Agent and Consul-General at Zanzibar, was sent on an
expedition to Uganda to report " on the best means of dealing
with the country, whether through Zanzibar or otherwise."
In his report he deprecated the abandonment of Uganda,
for both religious and commercial reasons, and advocated the
establishment of an official administration and the construction of a railway. This was at the end of 1893, and

the rights over the various East African territories in the British sphere soon passed from the Company to the Government. In 1893 the Company retired from Witu, finding that the profits were not worth the trouble of a continual contest with the turbulent Sultan. In 1894 our Protectorate over Uganda was proclaimed, and in 1895 the Company sold their remaining rights to the Government for £250,000, and the East Africa Protectorate was constituted. An official notice of August 31, 1896, declares that "all the territories in East Africa under the Protectorate of Her Majesty, except the islands of Zanzibar and Pemba and the Uganda Protectorate, are for the purposes of administration included in one Protectorate, under the name of the East Africa Protectorate." It was decided to construct the Uganda Railway. The first rails were laid in 1895, and the first train reached the Lake in December 1901.

The transfer of these territories from the Company to the Government coincided with the Mazrui rebellion, which was not, however, in any way caused by the change, but rather by the activity of the missionaries and the interference with slavery, which for some time past had irritated the Arab population. The Mazrui, as related above, were the most important Arab family of the mainland, who had been continually in more or less open revolt against the rulers of Maskat, and had been subdued by Seyyid Said only by banishing the more influential members. As younger generations grew up, they several times rebelled against the Sultan, and as they were never properly defeated, they had an exaggerated idea of their own powers. The final outbreak was provoked by the appointment in 1895 of Rashid bin Salim as Wali of Takaungu, the residence of the younger branch of the family. Rashid was considered the safer candidate by the Company, in whose hands the nomination lay; but according to Arab ideas of primogeniture his kinsman Mbaruk of Takaungu had the better claim, and he took up arms. The revolt became serious when the elder branch of the Mazrui, resident at Gasi, decided to throw in their lot with their kinsman. Mbaruk of Gasi, the head of the clan, had a palace at that town, and a forest stronghold at Mwele, in the hills above. This latter was successfully stormed by a British expedition in 1896, and in the April of that year Mbaruk fled to German territory, where he still resides, and surrendered to the governor. The Mazrui rebellion is of importance as marking the definite substitution of European for Arab influence. Before the rebellion, the Coast was a protected Arab state: since its suppression it has been growing into a British colony.

I must mention a disastrous affair which occurred in 1897 —the Uganda Mutiny. The mutineers were the remnants of the force with which Emin Pasha had held the Equatorial Sudan against the Mahdists, and had been engaged to garrison posts in Uganda. They appear to have had real grievances as to pay and other matters, which could have probably been easily remedied by explanations and attention to just complaints. Unfortunately misunderstandings arose from the first, and when the mutineers were joined by the kings of Uganda and Unyoro the rising assumed a serious political character, and was not terminated till the end of 1899. Regrettable as it was, it had one good effect in contributing materially to the pacification of Uganda and Unyoro.

Most of the important events subsequent to this period will be mentioned in the following pages. In 1902 the Protectorate assumed its present limits by taking over from Uganda the two provinces of Naivasha and Kisumu.

CHAPTER III

THE COAST LANDS

ZANZIBAR—JUBALAND—TANALAND

IN the Coast Lands I here include not only the Coast strictly so called, but the nondescript country which lies between it and the plains of the interior. Politically, a strip of ten miles inwards from the sea is recognised as forming along the greater part of the Protectorate the dominions of the Sultan of Zanzibar; and in most parts, except perhaps in the neighbourhood of Witu, these ten miles indicate fairly well the more or less cultivated strip between the jungle and the shore. Except in Mombasa, which has become cosmopolitan, and where the Indian element is strong, the civilisation of the coast towns is still Arab, although since the Mazrui rebellion the Arab power is decadent and no longer a factor of political importance.

The headquarters of Arab influence are at the island of Zanzibar, the seat of the Sultanate, which lies about 140 miles south of Mombasa, opposite German territory. As I have related, the Sultan of Zanzibar formerly exercised a somewhat indefinite sovereignty over the Coast from Warsheikh (3° N.) to Tunghi Bay (10° 42' S.); but Germany has purchased his dominions south of the river Umba, and the British and Italian Governments occupy the more northern territories in return for an annual rental. Zanzibar, which, with the adjacent Island of Pemba, now forms a British Protectorate, is perhaps the richest and most beautiful spot in tropical East Africa. In few parts of the world will the traveller who stays one day, or even two, carry away such pleasant impressions of beautiful landscapes; but whether it is advisable to spend more than two days is doubtful, for the climate is by no means healthy.

The town, which lies on the western side facing the mainland, consists largely of square-built stone Arab houses, but an Indian influence is visible both in the population and the shops. A characteristic feature in the narrow streets is afforded by the heavy black doors of carved wood, which make a striking contrast with the white stone, and the vivid splashes of colour, where flame-coloured acacias glow like living fires in enclosed gardens. The island is almost entirely flat, and in its more accessible portions is covered with plantations of cocoanut and cloves. The latter are the chief source of its wealth, as they are only found here and in certain islands of the Moluccas. Interspersed with these plantations are native villages, and lakes covered with blue water-lilies, which make amidst the surrounding vegetation as pretty a landscape of the tranquil order as can be imagined.

A good road leads right across the island to Chuaka on the western side, passing through Dunga, an old palace of the Sultans, which is said to possess an authentic ghost, and which is situated in the centre of beautiful, if not very re-munerative, experimental plantations. Dunga is about the middle of the island, and marks a change in the scenery; for here cultivation comes abruptly to an end, and on the eastern side there are hardly any cocoanuts or cloves. The road runs under beautiful mango-trees; but there are few fields or gardens except in the immediate neighbourhood of villages, and the country is mostly covered with low scrub. The change in the people is also apparent. On the western side the inhabitants, if too black to plausibly call themselves Arabs, at least imitate the Arabs in their dress and manners, and have a certain liveliness of features. The inhabitants of the east are commonly known as Wahadimu, or serfs, and apparently represent the original African population of the island. Their unintelligent, prognathous physiognomy suggests a relationship with the lower Bantu-speaking tribes of the mainland coast.

Except in the cultivated western districts the island of Zanzibar is one of the most unknown parts of Africa, and few have penetrated into the remoter corners. It is said that Chuaka, which is now a most pleasant health resort, exposed to the breezes of the Indian Ocean, owes its foundation to the caprice of a former Sultan. His Highness, who was cruising about in a pleasure yacht, was wrecked on this spot, and found, to his annoyance, not only no accommodation but also no road back to his capital, and had to force his weary way through the jungle on foot. According to the legend, he said, with true Oriental logic: "This must not occur again. Build me a palace at Chuaka, in case I should be stranded there on any future occasion, and make a road from the palace to the town of Zanzibar, so that I may not have to walk through the jungle a second time." The European auditor who has now been appointed to supervise the finances of Zanzibar would perhaps hardly approve of such expenditure in the future, but who can say that the Sultan's proceedings have not been for the general good?

Except the eastern coast, nearly all the island is very unhealthy. It is curious that, though the fear of death is one of the strongest of human motives, it is the rarest thing in the world to find a town selected for its healthy site. Commercial and shipping facilities seem to be the main considerations which decide in what places humanity shall congregate; and though most people would pay a large sum down to insure ten extra years of life, few are willing to make the same payment in the form of sacrificing profits by living in a healthy place, where money-making is not so easy. Hence the population of Zanzibar crowds into the stuffy western port, and leaves the cool eastern shore to the winds and waves. The most pleasant and healthy places on the western side are two little islands in the bay of Zanzibar city. They have not cheerful names—one being called Grave Island and the other

c

Prison Island—and are not put to cheerful uses, as they are employed as a cemetery and quarantine station respectively; but if one can visit them when neither interment nor disinfection is in progress, one finds a pleasant scene and invigorating air.

Zanzibar acts as a great warehouse or distributing centre for the whole of the East Coast. It produces little for local consumption, the clove crop being sent entirely to Europe, but it is still the main port for the reception of European and Indian goods. It is also the headquarters and distributing centre of a considerable population who have come over from the West Coast of India—Goanese, Parsis, Hindus, and Indian Mohammedans. The Goanese number some large merchants in their community, but are mostly cooks, of which trade they have almost a monopoly. They are also extensively employed as clerks in Government offices. The Parsis appear to be excellent at clerical work, and act not only as clerks but also as contractors and lawyers. Much of the trade is in the hands of the other Indians, and many of them have acquired a considerable interest in land, having bought the shambas (plantations) of improvident Arabs.

The island of Pemba resembles Zanzibar in its main features, but is more mountainous, and therefore, oddly enough, more unhealthy. The moisture collects in the valleys between the elevations, and forms miasmatic swamps which outweigh the good that might be obtained by breathing pure air on the top of the hills.

Zanzibar is called Unguja in Swahili, the better known name meaning "land of the blacks." The orthography Zanguebar is due to the variation between Zang or Zanj, in dialects of Arabic. I have already sketched the history of the island, which attracted little attention before the nineteenth century, but became the most important place on the coast after Seyyid Said, the Imam of Oman, made it his capital. In 1890 Great Britain declared a Protectorate over the Sultan's dominions. Except for one incident the subsequent history of the island has been uneventful, and is mainly concerned with the suppression of the slave trade. The exception is that when Sultan Hamed bin Thwain (or Thuwayni) died, in 1896, his kinsman, Khalid, attempted to usurp the throne, and seized the palace with an armed force. As he would not surrender, the town was bombarded by the British fleet. Khalid escaped to the German Consulate, and thence to German East Africa. Sultan Hamud was placed on the throne, but died in 1902, and was succeeded by his son, Ali, who had been educated at Harrow, and was then a minor, Mr. Rogers, the First Minister, being appointed Regent. The Sultan is assisted in the government by several British ministers, but the exercise of authority is much hindered by the treaties which make the subjects of foreign powers, even when African by race, ex-territorial, and amenable only to the jurisdiction of their consuls.

Though I have started from the south at Zanzibar, I will, in making a survey of the coast districts of the mainland, ask the reader to accompany me to the extreme north of our territories and begin at Kismayu, the capital and port of Jubaland, about ten miles south of the mouth of the Juba River, and just below the equator. Though the inland boundaries of the East African Protectorate are not very clearly defined, the limits on the coast are definite enough, being the rivers Juba on the north and Umba on the south. Jubaland is practically a prolongation of northern Somaliland, and Gregory's division into seven zones does not apply here, the whole country from the shore inwards being a waste of sand and scrub, with occasional patches of pasturage and waterholes. The land on the banks of the Juba, however, is wooded and fertile, and yields cotton, among other products. The inhabitants of this cultivated strip, which is called Gosha, are runaway slaves, known as Watoro in Swahili, who collected here from all parts of Africa, and were able to successfully defy their masters. Another settlement of Watoro is at Fudadoyo, near the Sabaki River.

Outside Gosha the country is imperfectly known, and the
few names on the map indicate little more than water-holes
or halting-places for caravans.   I must warn the reader of
this peculiarity of African geographical nomenclature.   One
sometimes sees a desert strewn thick with names that suggest,
to the unwary, cities, or at least villages, but are really nothing
but camping-grounds, in no way distinguished from the surrounding solitude, where some enterprising traveller has spent
the night.   More important than these, but hardly more
conspicuous in reality, are the watering-places of the Somalis,
such as Afmadu, which has figured in despatches as if it were
a city like Mombasa, but is really nothing more than a collection of wells.   With the exception of Kismayu, and the
settlements on the river and the coast, there appear to be no
places of permanent habitation whatever in these regions from
the Juba to the hinterland of Lamu, and practically to the
Tana River.

The whole district is inhabited by those singular nomads
the Somalis, who combine the most opposite characteristics,
and contrive to be at the same time the wildest and most
civilised of Africans.   In race they are what, for want of a
better word, must be described as Hamitic, and, though dark,
are sharply distinguished from all negro tribes by their clear-
cut and often beautiful features.   Some of the young men of
the Biskaya section, whom I have seen near Lamu, might
have posed as very Apollos cast in dark bronze.   When the
Somalis come into towns they at once put themselves on the
same level of civilisation as the Arab, wear white robes, and
show a great aptitude for commerce, particularly cattle-trading.
In externals they are ostentatiously devout Moslems, and they
show a knowledge of European law, and a power of using it to
their advantage, which is without parallel among the natives
of East Africa, and is only rivalled among Indians.   Also they
are very quarrelsome.   But once back in their deserts, they
appear to drop all these town habits, and show no inclination
to raise their lives to a higher level of civilisation, but live as

cattle-herding nomads, chiefly remarkable for the extreme lightness of their baggage and celerity of their movements. Added to this, they are characterised by a pride, independence, and fanaticism most unusual in this part of Africa. It is to be hoped that in the future we may find some means of utilising this undoubtedly talented race. Hitherto our dealings with them have not been conspicuous for success, and have usually consisted of campaigns lightly undertaken, and terminating in elaborate explanations that we had gained a moral victory and achieved our real object, which proved to be quite different from what everybody had supposed in the beginning.

It is difficult to hazard even a vague opinion as to the value of Jubaland. The general impression left by the country is certainly that it is arid and unpromising. On the other hand, the banks of the Juba undoubtedly offer a strip of great fertility, and as the Somalis somehow manage to support very large herds of cattle on a very small supply of pasturage and water, it is possible that with irrigation a considerable cattle industry might spring up. But at present the whole region is so inaccessible, and for practical purposes so distant, even from Mombasa (there are no roads, and only a monthly steamer to Kismayu), and there are so many nearer and more promising localities in the Protectorate, that in estimating the economic possibilities of East Africa, and the best methods of using them, Jubaland may be left out of account. This conclusion might be upset by successful cotton cultivation. The banks of the Juba are certainly favourable for this crop, and if experiment proves that they are even more favourable than the banks of the Sabaki and Tana, it might be worth while to take the development of the country in hand at once.

At present our occupation of Jubaland is entirely military. There is no civil administration as in the other provinces, the necessary powers being exercised by the military officers. A garrison of 350 troops is maintained in the province, the headquarters being at Yente, on the Juba, about

18 miles from Kismayu.   This latter is a small town, with a
trading population of Somalis and Indians, gathered round
a central Arab fort.   There is no cultivation to speak of, but
some trade.   Hides and ivory are exported, and there is a
considerable importation of cotton stuffs and coffee berries, of
which the Somalis are very fond.   The harbour is not good,
but greatly superior to those on the Benadir Coast to the north,
where landing is exceptionally difficult, and at many seasons
of the year impossible.   The Italian Government have accordingly long been anxious to obtain a pier and custom-house at
Kismayu, and to lease a strip of land extending thence to
Jumbo on the Juba, so as to be able to take goods by this
route direct to Italian territory without paying duty.   But
the negotiations have not yet been brought to any definite
conclusion.

To the south of Kismayu the coast presents a series of
small islands, but no feature of importance, except Port
Durnford, a harbour of some size and depth.   It was formerly
a Government station, it being thought unadvisable in the
old slaving days to leave a long stretch of coast without any
officer ; but now that the slave trade has been abolished, this
station has been closed, though the buildings still remain in
the charge of a few police.   There are a few inhabitants, but
the scrub and sand begin immediately round the village, and
give one a good idea of the desolation of the district.

To the south of Jubaland lies the province of Tanaland,
which takes its name from the river Tana.   This considerable
stream rises from the snows of Kenya, and at first flows somewhat towards the north, almost reaching the equator, but then
makes a sweep round and proceeds south-east, entering the
sea about three degrees south.   The province consists of two
rather distinct parts : first, the banks of the river, which are
cultivated and inhabited for a short distance ; and, secondly,
the numerous towns, including Witu, which stud the mainland and the adjacent islands north of the river mouth.
This part may be considered first, since it comes first as

SIU FORT.

RUINS OF NABAHAN PALACE AND GRAVES AT PATE.

one descends the coast from Port Durnford. The first town is Kiunga, a small Government station with a police garrison. The climate is pleasant, and cocoanuts fairly abundant, but the inhabitants subsist chiefly by collecting cowries and such like marine industries. Kiunga is hidden by small islands which stretch in front of it, but lies outside the Lamu Archipelago, which begins to the south, and offers a remarkable specimen of a formation which is characteristic of the East African coast, namely, islands fitted very close in to the shore, so that they hardly appear as separate on an ordinary map. Other examples are Mombasa itself, Wasin, and Mozambique. The Lamu group consists of many such islands, the largest being Lamu, Manda, and Pata. They are all flat, and contain numerous inhabited or deserted towns, for their prosperity is somewhat fluctuating. The inhabitants of this coast have suffered much in the past from the raids of the Somalis. It is no doubt for this reason that so many towns have been built on the islands, as in this district the Somalis do not use boats; and a few years ago, when these raids recommenced, almost all the inhabitants of the littoral fled to the islands. Now, however, that tranquillity has been restored, a movement in the opposite direction has begun, and the islands are being deserted for the mainland shore, which is in some ways a pity, as they contain very fine plantations of cocoanuts.

This archipelago has witnessed at least three civilisations, the Bajun, the Arab, and the Portuguese, without counting the English and German. The Bajun, or Wagunya, a very light-coloured race, who inhabit the islands and the coast, claim to be of Persian descent, and the family of the Nabahans, who founded Pate, came, according to their traditions, from Persia.[1] But though this Persian influence seems to have been real, and to have left a memorial in a mixed race different from the Swahilis, we have not much material for its history or for

---

[1] Yet, the Benu Nebhan, er Nabhani, were a family of Oman, who were the ruling dynasty from 1154 to 1406.

fixing any dates.   More information will perhaps be forthcoming when the Pate chronicles, of which manuscripts exist, are published.

Many of the towns in the archipelago have odd little histories of their own.   A curious dual administration existed in the town of Siu until the middle of the last century.   The inhabitants invoked the aid of the Somalis in the seventeenth century to assist them against the aggression of the Nabahan princes of Pate.   The Somalis agreed, and the Nabahans were repulsed.   A government was then established, consisting of a Famao (a descendant of the Asiatic colonists) and a Somali sheikh, which lasted till 1842, when an energetic Famao named Mataka concentrated all authority in his own hands.   The Somalis applied to Seyyid Said ; but, though he attempted to reduce Siu, his efforts were not successful, and it was only after his death that the town submitted to the Sultans of Zanzibar in 1866.

Lamu is the headquarters of the Arab civilisation on the coast, and is a town of some importance, built on the island of the same name.   The situation, though not the sanitation, of the place is healthy, for the soil is sandy and porous, and an invigorating breeze comes in from the Indian Ocean.   All round are plantations of cocoanuts growing in the sand, and rustling with that pleasant murmur which is so unspeakably comforting to senses tortured by the buzzing of mosquitoes in windless swamps.   The town itself consists of a network of narrow lanes and closely-packed houses, crowded round an old fort now used as a prison.   Many of the buildings are solidly constructed, but all look dilapidated, and several seem to be in the last stage of decay and to threaten collapse.   It is interesting, though regrettable, to note that all the Arab towns in East Africa are totally devoid of that peculiar beauty and dignity which one associates with Mohammedan buildings in other countries.   The mosques are low, flat-roofed, inconspicuous constructions, with no ornament but a few roughly carved inscriptions, and bearing signs of no pious care or regard except an unwillingness to pull them down when they become dangerously ruinous. The minarets are low conical towers, which serve the purpose of the muezzin, but entirely fail to form a picturesque element in the landscape. The fact is, that in the better known Mohammedan countries, such as Turkey, Egypt, and India, the severity of Islam prunes and chastens the exuberance of Oriental art, and in favourable circumstances ends by combining purity and delicacy of outline with brilliant coloration. But here in East Africa, as probably in Arabia, one has merely the original uncompromising puritanism of the land of sands and rocks, revolting against all complexity and ornament which might seem in any way to modify the sublime but arid doctrine of the unity of the only God. Thus, no doubt, prayed Mohammed, in a mosque which was literally only a place for prostration (masjid), and not intended to raise or impress the spirits of the faithful by its outward form.

The greatest triumphs of Islam have been gained, not directly by the Arabs, but where they have been able to hand their religion on to another race, such as the Turks or Persians. Of the Arab character itself, it is perhaps rash to speak from an experience gained almost exclusively on the East Coast of Africa, but there at any rate it does not leave a favourable or hopeful impression on the observer. Of the great intelligence of many Arabs there can be no doubt, but one feels that the acute mind has not, as a rule, sufficient material whereon to exercise itself, and that it is liable to be blunted by an element of cruelty and sensuality which is rarely absent. They are quite unlike the Turks, whose remarkable history may be summarised as a power of seizing positions which they are totally incompetent to fill, a genius for conquest accompanied by incapacity for government. On the contrary, though intensely aristocratic and domineering, the Arabs seem wanting in both the patience and energy of military races. Intellectual, nervous, scheming, fanatical, yet withal sceptical, their minds find congenial employment in such subjects as genealogy, Mohammedan law, or even mathematics, but seem sterile in art, trade, government, or organised warfare, perhaps owing to an incapacity for self-discipline and the nemesis which makes the slave-owner incapable of being master of himself. For it must be confessed that it is as slave-owners and slave-traders only that the Arabs have cut a figure in East Africa. Nor were their enterprises, cruel and inhuman as they were, altogether ignoble. They had their good side in the courage and intelligence which enabled Arab caravans to penetrate to the interior of Africa, and actually cross it before the feat was accomplished by Europeans.

As long as the clove or cocoanut plantations in Zanzibar or on the coast-strip could be cultivated by a wholly disproportionate and unnecessarily large number of slaves, the Arabs were fairly prosperous, but they have not the instinct of either cultivators or men of business. They dislike the idea of paying wages, and are allowing their estates to fall out of cultivation rather than adapt themselves to new conditions. The real abiding influence of the Arabs in East Africa does not lie in anything that they have introduced or built, but in the fact that they have profoundly modified the race on the coast and produced the type known as the Swahili. This must be pronounced a most successful crossbreed, combining the physical strength and endurance of the African with much of the intelligence of the Semite.

It is remarkable that Mohammedanism has not been a greater force in East Africa, for the example of the North and West shows that it is congenial to African races. In the East almost the only people who can be called fanatical Mohammedans are the Somalis, and with them religion seems to be largely a matter of politics. The Swahilis are nominal Mohammedans when they are not Christians, but have very little respect for the observances of their religion, particularly prayers. It is, however, considered the correct thing and a sign of social distinction to belong to Islam, and when anything reminds them of its more convenient precepts, they are

second to none in fervour. I once imported some pigs to
Mombasa. The process of disembarkation was proceeding
satisfactorily, until some one who felt rather lazy said he was
a Mohammedan and could not touch pigs. Immediately
everybody began to say they were unclean animals, and that
no respectable, religious man could handle them. A deadlock
occurred, which was only terminated by finding two up-
country natives who had no religious feelings or social
pretensions.

Mohammedanism once gained a certain footing in Uganda,
but has not proved there a serious competitor of Christianity,
being recognised by the natives as standing on a lower level
of civilisation and education. It is remarkable, however, that
it has never had any appreciable influence on the Nandi,
Lumbwa, or Masai, who, as warlike tribes, ought to have
proved favourably disposed to its tenets. This must, I think,
be explained partly by a natural want of religious feeling, and
partly by the barrier of the coast jungle, which accounts for
so much in East Africa. The natives of the interior saw
occasional Arabs, as they saw occasional Europeans, but they
never made the acquaintance of a Mohammedan state, or
realised the power of the religion as a drill and discipline,
both social and military.

Most of the Arabs and Swahilis are Sunnis of the ordinary
type, but a few of the Arabs, particularly among the older
men, belong to the sect of Ibadhis,[1] who are distinguished by
their greater severity, and, among other things, will not smoke.
Though commonly known as Ibadhis, the members of this
sect would appear to be more correctly styled Abazi, from their
founder, Abdullah bin Yahya bin Abaz. They are also called
Beyazis. They are found in Oman and East Africa. In the
latter country, at any rate, they seem quiet and inoffensive, but
their views are not orthodox in the matter of free will, and they

[1] For details respecting this sect see Badger, " Imams and Seyyids of Oman,"
Appendix B. He is probably right in saying that non-smoking was originally
a Wahabi, not an Ibadhi, practice.

hold that any Moslem, not only a member of the Prophet's tribe, can exercise pontifical authority. Hence the Imam of Maskat. There are also a large number of Indian Shiahs, commonly known as Thenasheriyas (Ithnaashariyas) because they believe in twelve Imams. Many belong to the sect of Ismailiyas, the head of which is the Aga Khan, who generally resides in Bombay or Europe, but occasionally visits East Africa in order to collect offerings. He is the descendant of Ismail, the elder son of the sixth Imam Jafar-es-Sadik, who on account of his drunkenness was disinherited by his father in favour of the younger son, Musa-al-Kazim. The latter is accepted by most Shiahs as the true successor, but the Is-mailiyas attach a mystical meaning to the drunkenness of Ismail, and do not admit that he was rightly set aside. All these Indian sects are far more fanatical and quarrelsome than the Arabs, and are fond of bringing their religious disputes before the law courts, in which case they spare neither trouble nor money on litigation.

The costume of the Arabs is picturesque. On formal occasions, at any rate, the men wear a long gown of dark stuff with gold embroidery, which is called Joho. It is open in front, and displays a white tunic with a girdle, in which is a sword, the badge of an Arab gentleman. The ladies of Lamu surpass those of all other nations in retiring modesty, for they not only hide their faces, but walk about under a small tent, which requires the assistance of a servant to carry it. It is not surprising to hear that they have a very bad reputation for propriety; for in Africa female respectability is in inverse ratio to the quantity of clothes worn, and the beauties of Kavirondo, who imitate the costume of Eve, are said to be as virtuous as she was when there was no man but Adam in the world.

Lamu lies some little distance up a creek, at the entrance to which is the little port of Shella, with some remains of Portuguese architecture. Opposite this is the island of Manda. On the coast facing the sea are some ruins and a very pleasant

A LADY OF LAMU WALKING UNDER A TENT CARRIED BY SERVANTS.

ARABS

beach called Twaka (doubtless the same word as Chuaka in Zanzibar), which should make a good seaside health resort one of these days. The mainland around the Lamu Archipelago is very fertile, and, as far as the attacks of the Somalis have permitted, well cultivated. There is a considerable export of mangrove bark from the forests of this tree which line the shores, and there is every reason to hope that the cultivation of cotton will be successful.

Behind Lamu lies the curious little Sultanate of Witu, which once enjoyed the extraordinary honour of being a separate Protectorate. As I have explained elsewhere, this state originated in little more than a band of robbers collected by a Swahili outlaw, called Fumo Bakari, whom the Germans thought fit, for political reasons, to recognise as Sultan and place under their protection. The territory passed under British protection by the treaty of 1890, and we had to commence our administration by bombarding the town to avenge a massacre of Germans, so that altogether Witu has perhaps given more trouble in the world than it was worth. For the better preservation of peace and order, a clerk in His Majesty's Vice-Consulate at Lamu, who had claims to the succession, was proclaimed Sultan, and has given entire satisfaction.

Witu is about a day and a half's journey from Lamu. A voyage by boat through winding creeks to Mkonumbi occupies about an afternoon, and there remains a walk of some twenty miles along a good road, passing through the village of Pangani,[1] where there is a rest-house. We have at present no civil establishment at Witu, but a company of native troops with a European officer. The town is remarkable for the size and abundance of its pine-apples and mosquitoes, the advantage being hardly as great as the disadvantage. Both of these features are seen in full perfection in the Sultan's garden, which is a really beautiful park, though poorly kept

[1] Not to be confounded with the port of the same name in German East Africa.

up. The revenues of the state are largely derived from the sale of the vegetables grown therein. Almost more important than the Sultan is the mother of the heir-apparent, an old lady of much force of character. At a state audience with which she honoured me, an iron bed, surrounded with mosquito curtains of the thickest cloth, was placed in the middle of the room, within which she remained seated invisible. I am afraid that I offended against the court etiquette, or at least the good manners of the country, according to which a visitor is expected to dash at the curtains, saying that he must at any cost see the celebrated beauty they hide, and be dragged off by the attendants amidst the delighted screams of the old lady within,

Outside Witu are some Galla villages. This people, who were once the dominant race in this region, were driven southwards by the advent of the Somalis, and are now of little account, though distinguished from other natives by their Hamitic features. They are found on both sides of the Tana, but chiefly to the north. Among them live a hunting tribe called the Waboni (somewhat resembling the Dorobo of the Settima and Mau, and the Tumalods and Ramis among the Somalis), who seem to stand to them in some vaguely servile relation. The Wasania appear to be a somewhat similar tribe. The Galla village which I visited was stockaded, and more strongly built than is usual among African tribes. The ceremony of welcome includes a dance of warriors, who advance with their spears in position, and bring them within a few inches of the face of the person saluted, who is expected to show no concern.

Round about the town of Witu is the large forest of Utwani, rich in india-rubber, but very feverish. There is hardly any recent information as to the hinterland, which appears to be a plain covered with scrub and full of large game.

From Witu a march of about two hours across open, marshy meadows brings one to Kau, an old Arab settlement. This walk will always remain in my memory, on account of what appeared to be the astounding phenomenon of a snowdrift lying at a little distance in the rich tropical green. It proved to be a mass of pure white water-lilies, entirely covering a small pond, which was frequented by white egrets.

Kau is a small town on the Ozi, which practically forms the mouth of the river Tana, with which it is connected by the Belezoni canal. All the rivers of British East Africa, the Juba, the Tana, the Sabaki, and the Ozi itself, labour under the disadvantage of having large bars, due no doubt to the strong sea breeze which continually blows from the Indian Ocean and heaps up the sand. In the case of the Tana the original mouth is almost entirely closed, and the waters are diverted into the canal at Charra, about ten miles from the shore, and thence pass on into the Ozi, which has a broad stream and relatively good entrance at the port of Kipini. Though the water is shallow on the bar at low tide, vessels of some size can pass it, and it would not be difficult to remove the obstacle altogether, a course which may perhaps be adopted some day in view of the possibility of growing cotton on the banks of the Tana. The scenery on the Ozi is very beautiful, and somewhat resembles the upper reaches of the Thames. Forests of fine trees stretch down to the water's edge, and near the sea the climate is pleasant and mosquitoes absent. Above Kau the stream is narrower and surrounded by grassy stretches of marshy land, through which the above-mentioned canal passes to the Tana. It is said to have been dug by the Sultans of Witu, but has recently been dredged and improved, and dues are taken from the navigation passing through it. It is about three miles long, and has a strong current from the Tana. It is not improbable that the Ozi was originally a branch and second mouth of the Tana, the country between them being a delta, so that in the construction of the Belezoni Canal art has merely restored the original arrangement of nature.

The upper waters of the Tana are little known.   To the south of Mount Kenya, what is apparently the main stream is known as the Sagana or Kilaluma.   It receives several tributaries from the mountain, and from the south the important river Thika-Thika.   I have seen it in several places in this district, and found it a shallow and not very rapid stream (in August).   Further down there appear to be at least two falls, one where the river turns to the north, and the other at Hameye, near the equator.   Below this point it is navigable to the coast, a distance of about 200 miles, though, owing to the extremely tortuous channel, the actual course to be traversed may be considerably longer.   On the upper river the most important district appears to be Koro-Koro.   I have never visited it, but it is described as an open, healthy country, with fine scenery, and here and there good timber.   The river is dotted with numerous islands, on which maize and plantains are grown.   The district also produces a fibre from which excellent ropes are made.   The inhabitants are said not to be the same as the Wapokomo, who inhabit the lower parts of the river.   These latter are a Bantu race, speaking a dialect closely resembling Swahili.   They are a peaceful and fairly industrious tribe, and seem to be entirely under the control of the numerous Protestant missions established along the river. Both here and in Lamu German influence in religious bodies is strong, for missionary activity began before political divisions were created, and has not followed exactly the same East Africa lines.   Hence at the present day the missions in German East Africa are largely English, and those in Tanaland largely German.

The Tana, like the Nile, overflows and irrigates its banks, which are therefore very fertile.   The margin of cultivation varies from a quarter of a mile to three miles, one mile being perhaps the average.   Near the river are a good many trees, but beyond the limit of cultivation is open country and scrub. On the right bank is a constant succession of villages, but the left is almost uninhabited, the reason being that it was formerly exposed to the raids of the Somalis from the north, whereas the other bank was protected by the intervening river. These raids have happily now ceased, and the Wapokomo cultivate the left bank, but they have not yet ventured to build any villages there. As is generally the case with peaceful tribes who have no need to unite under a leader on warlike expeditions, they have no central authority, each village being independent. The chiefs and prominent men, however, belong to a secret society called the "Hyaenas," whose commands are obeyed with superstitious veneration under pain of death.

I have been four and a half days up the Tana—that is, a day and a half beyond the mission station of Kulesa. The lower reaches of the river, up to Ngao, are rich in cocoanut trees and other vegetation, and are probably capable of yielding fine crops of cotton and fibre with proper cultivation, but the country is decidedly unhealthy, being damp and, except the papyrus swamps of the Nile, more populous with mosquitoes than any land I have ever seen. A good deal of rice is cultivated near Charra, a village at the point where the Belezoni enters the Tana. Some distance above this is Golbanti, the seat of a Methodist mission, and an old settlement of the Gallas, whose name is probably preserved in the first syllable. Some years ago (I believe in the nineties) this mission was attacked by the Masai, and the resident missionary killed. This, I believe, is the northern limit of the raids of that tribe anywhere near the coast. Above Golbanti the next large village is Ngao, where there is a German mission. The climate here is better, and there is a small hill at a short distance from the river on which the missionaries' houses are built. I visited this place on Christmas Eve, 1902, and was very much pleased with the excellent singing of the native children, who have good voices, and have been taught by the missionaries to sing Christmas carols with great spirit and accuracy. In this part of the river's course there are several lakes, which are connected with the main stream in time of flood.   The largest is called Shakababo or Ashaka-baba. Above Ngao the climate is pleasant, and mosquitoes comparatively rare.   The banks of the river are raised and not swampy, although irrigation is easy and practised to a limited extent. The population appears to consist of about equal numbers of Wapokomo and pelicans.

CHAPTER IV

THE COAST LANDS (*continued*)

SEYIDIE—MOMBASA—TEITA

THE Tana River is a good dividing line in the East Africa Protectorate. To the north of it the country is little known, thinly populated, and the dominant influence is still Oriental; to the south it is much better known (though there are still large unexplored districts), the population is thicker, the Somalis cease altogether, and the dominant influence is distinctly European, not Oriental. It must be confessed that Tanaland is at present passing through a period of decadence, or, let us hope, of quiescence, for its natural resources are great. Formerly it was in some ways the most important part of the Protectorate; the Tana afforded a highway to the interior, and German missionaries and merchants collected in and round Lamu. But the construction of the Uganda Railway changed the centre of gravity; it became at once the natural and only road up country, and Mombasa was indisputably the principal port. Nevertheless, Tanaland is believed to offer such great natural advances for the cultivation of valuable tropical crops like cotton, copra, india-rubber, and fibre, that there is no reason why it should not regain an important commercial position, though it is hardly likely to rival Seyidie, the southern coast province, and its capital Mombasa.

Of course this southern part of the coast has been subject to Arab influence in its time as much as Tanaland, but the suppression of the Mazrui rebellion in 1895–96 was felt far more strongly in the south than in the north, and many better-class Arabs emigrated. This emigration almost coincided with

a large influx of Europeans in connection with the building of
the Uganda Railway, and it is no exaggeration to say that few
inhabitants of Mombasa are now conscious that it is an Arab
town. Melindi, Takaungu, Gasi, and other places still retain
this character, but even there I do not think one finds the
same number of Arab landowners and cultivators as in
Tanaland.

South of the Tana, Mambrui, Melindi, and Takaungu form
a little group of Arab towns whose importance in the future is
likely to depend on the fact that they form ports for a fertile
district where much grain is grown, and where there is also an
important forest producing good timber and india-rubber.
This forest, which appears to extend continuously from near
the Tana to Kilifi Creek, is very imperfectly surveyed, and
generally known by the names of Arabuko in the north and
Sekoki in the south, both designations being, as is often the
case with native names, rather difficult to define for practical
purposes.   There is a project, which it is to be hoped may be
realised, of building a railway from Mombasa to Melindi with
a view of utilising the riches of the district.   The latter town
is of some historic interest, and, like Mombasa, is mentioned in
"Paradise Lost," xi. 396, as part of the vision shown to Adam
of the future of the world :

> "Nor could his eye not ken
> Th' empire of Negus to its utmost port
> Ercoco and the less maritime kings
> Mombasa and Quiloa and Melind
> And Sofala, thought Ophir, to the realm
> Of Congo and Angola furthest south."

Vasco da Gama visited it first in 1498, after his unfortunate
accident at Mombasa, and again next year on his return
journey from India, when he erected a stone pillar, dedicated
to the Holy Ghost, to the south of the town.   It is not certain
whether the pillar which still stands on the spot is the same
one or a later substitute.   Da Gama mentions the fondness
of the inhabitants for fêtes and musical performances, and the

taste for them has continued. It is here that may be seen in full perfection ngomas or native dances, generally performed by women. The movements are not ungraceful, but the music is monotonous, and what would be tolerable for five minutes lasts five hours. Melindi would probably become a port of considerable importance had it a better anchorage, but the harbour is extremely shallow, and steamers have to lie a considerable distance from the shore. It has often been proposed to remedy this defect by the construction of a pier, but the funds have unfortunately never been forthcoming. To the north lies another Arab town, Mambrui, with some old buildings and also some good new ones, for the Wali, Sef-bin-Salim, has built himself a substantial house in European style, and also a hall for public meetings. A little way inland from Mambrui are the well-known Magarini shambas, considerable plantations of cocoanuts and other crops which were confiscated after the Mazrui rebellion, and are now leased by Mr. Anderson of Mombasa. A long account of these plantations is given in Mr. W. W. A. FitzGerald's book, "Travels in the Coastlands of British East Africa" (Chapman & Hall, 1898).

Between Melindi and Mambrui is the mouth of the Sabaki. Like the Tana, this river was better known ten years ago than now. It is formed by the junction of the Athi and the Tsavo, near the station bearing the latter name on the Uganda Railway. The country between this point and the sea has hardly been visited by Europeans of late years, but the river is believed not to be navigable owing to swamps and rapids. A little to the south of Melindi is the singularly picturesque inlet of Kilifi, where was formerly a town of the same name probably built in the eleventh century, but destroyed by the Portuguese in 1592. The inlet runs some distance inland to a large native village called Mtanganyiko, where we have recently built a pier to facilitate the export of grain, which is considerable. Three miles to the south of the Kilifi inlet is Takaungu, which was the headquarters of the junior branch of the Mazrui family. It was a dispute as to the governorship of

this town which brought about the Mazrui rebellion of 1895.
Between Takaungu and Mombasa lies the little port of Mtwapa,
which, like Melindi, has a poor and shallow harbour, though
there is a creek at the side which would be convenient for
shipping if trade increased.

To the south of this lies Mombasa, known to sailors by
three hills, called the Crown of Mombasa. As already mentioned, it is situated on an island, fitted closely into the mainland, from which it is separated only by a narrow arm of
water. Both to the north and south are extensive inland
harbours, invisible from the sea. The northern harbour, or
Mombasa proper, leads up to the old Arab town. Though it
is smaller and less convenient for steamers than the inlet on
the other side, the entrance is easier for sailing vessels, and
this circumstance probably determined the position of Mombasa. A prolongation of this harbour, known as Port Tudor,
is of considerable extent, but is not used by shipping. On
the continental shore of Mombasa harbour lies Freretown,
named after Sir Bartle Frere, a large and flourishing station
of the Church Missionary Society, founded in 1874, which
in its beautiful flowers and heavy close atmosphere recalls
Zanzibar.

The sheltered anchorage on the other side, called Kilindini
(the deep place), is not only much larger than Mombasa harbour, but, with its accessory waters, probably one of the largest
harbours in the world. It is practically certain that the great
shipping facilities which it offers will make it the business
terminus of the Uganda Railway, the port for all the up-
country trade, and the seat of the main custom-house. At
present it is used by the fleet and by about half the steamers
which frequent Mombasa. Out of its inner end opens on
one side the channel running round Mombasa Island, and on
the other Port Reitz, a fine deep arm of the sea, about a mile
wide and four miles long, called after Lieutenant Reitz, R.N.,
who was British Resident at Mombasa during our temporary
Protectorate early in the last century, and died there.

MOMBASA HARBOUR.

Mombasa itself, like most great ports, is very cosmopolitan, and shows at least three racial and social strata, the Arab-Swahili, the Indian, and the European, besides a number of ruins which commemorate the troubled rule of the Portuguese. The old Arab town is hidden at the end of the northern harbour. The large and solidly-built fort which commands this part of the town was, however, built by the Portuguese. All this quarter is hot and low-lying, but outside it towards the sea is a stretch of high ground exposed to an almost continual wind, and therefore cool and healthy, which has become the modern European quarter and is being gradually built over. More inland is a large Indian quarter, inhabited by Parsi, Hindu, and Mohammedan merchants. Conspicuous among them are the Bohras, an unorthodox sect of Shiahs, who wear a semi-European costume and small turbans of some material which resembles gold. They have a large mosque near the custom-house, and the city can also boast of a Parsi place of worship and a temple dedicated to the worship of the Lingam. A good road runs across from Mombasa to Kilindini, and is gradually becoming lined by European houses. This highway, like all considerable thorough-fares in Mombasa, is served by a system of trolleys—that is, small carriages running on rails and pushed by native boys, which is characteristic of the town, though it will probably soon have to give place—if it has not done so already—to electric tram-cars. The Uganda Railway starts from near the Fort, and, passing by Kilindini, crosses the channel at the back of the island by the Makupa bridge.

Vasco da Gama's description of Mombasa as " a large city situated on an eminence washed by the sea," though not con-clusive, seems to imply that the town as he found it faced the ocean, and was in the quarter now called Ras-Sarani. The spirit of war and destruction which brooded over the Coast for the next few hundred years naturally made the inhabitants of all ports, where it was possible, withdraw from the open sea into safer creeks and backwaters; and after reading the chronicles of Mombasa one can hardly be surprised to hear that ten years ago the town lay entirely to the landward side of the Fort. The heights which face the sea, wind-swept cliffs rising out of a surge which has rolled across the Indian Ocean, offer a site incomparably superior both in health and beauty; and if the buildings to be erected there are in any way worthy of their natural surroundings, the entrance to the harbour should take a high rank among the views not only of Africa but of the world.

Slightly inland of Mombasa are a number of mission stations, besides Freretown already mentioned. The Church Missionary Society are established at Shimba and Rabai, the latter of which is one of the oldest and most flourishing missions in the country. The United Free Methodists are at Jomvu, Ribe, and Mazeras, and the Lutherans at Jimba. All these missions are well attended, and have done much to spread European influence. To the south of Mombasa, however, there are still a good many Arabs, and, though Europeans are not the object of any hostility, they have not settled in this district to any large extent, in spite of its being perhaps the healthiest and most fertile part of the coast. A few miles inland runs the range of the Shimba Hills, which are well supplied with wood and water, and offer a climate which, though tropical, is very bearable. They begin almost behind Mombasa, and terminate towards the south in the beautiful hill of Mwele, where is a large village of the same name and a fine forest. This was the stronghold of Mbaruk, but his fortress was destroyed in 1896, when the Mazrui rebellion was crushed.

From the top of Mwele there is a wonderful view, taking in the island of Pemba on the one hand, and Kilima-Njaro on the other. On the eastern side is spread out the whole coast and sea as in a map, and to the west one looks across a wide, wooded plain, from which rise the lesser peaks of Kilibas and Kisigau, towards the snows of the great mountain. To the south are seen the hills called Jombo and Mrima. Near the latter are hot springs reported to contain sodium chloride.[1] Below the Shimba Hills is a very fertile coast strip, with large cocoanut plantations. The chief towns are Tiwi, Gasi,[2] and Vanga. Gasi was the peace capital of Mbaruk, and lies on the edge of the sea, about eighteen miles from his stronghold of Mwele, in the hills above. Somewhat to the south of it is the Ramisi River, where experiments are being made in the cultivation of tobacco. Vanga lies on the river Umba, which forms the boundary with German East Africa. This, together with the districts near the mouth of the Tana, is one of the few parts of the Protectorate which must be set down as dangerously unhealthy. It is low and damp, but fertile in cocoanuts, rice, and all vegetables which thrive in much moisture. The country reminded me of southern India, and it is much to be wished that Indians, who would probably find it a congenial home, would settle in it, for the climate is quite unsuited to Europeans, and cultivation suffers from a dearth of population. The Arabs took two out of every three children as slaves in the whole of this district, a tribute which was naturally terribly destructive to the native population, and after the Mazrui rebellion a great number of them emigrated, so that the country was deprived of both its aristocracy and proletariat. I am happy to say that, with the abolition of the slave trade, a distinct increase of population is beginning to be felt.

The name of Shirazi, a small town just to the north of the Ramisi, commemorates the settlement of a colony of Persians from Shiraz about 1200 A.D. A sultanate grew up in the Vumba district (the delta of the river Umba), which was once of considerable importance, and ruled the whole country from the neighbourhood of Tanga to Kilindini harbour. A

[1] "A rough analysis of the water shows that the contained salt is chiefly sodium chloride. A small proportion of alkaline carbonates and of calcium and magnesium chlorides also occurs."—Report by Mr. Walker, Government Geologist; Africa, 11 (1903).

[2] The name of this place is spelt with "Jim" in Arabic, not "Ghain," and is not connected with Ghazi, a conqueror. It perhaps means "hard."

remnant of this sultanate remained until a few years ago, in a personage called the Diwan of Vumba Kuu, who, though he had little temporal power, was much revered as a sort of pontiff. A drum stood outside his house, and any slave who wished to change his master could become the slave of the Diwan by beating on it twice. The Diwan had to be a descendant of Seyyid Abubakari, who ruled in Vumba from 1700–1742; but the appointment was, within these limits, elective, and largely depended on the wealth of the candidates, who had to perform various costly ceremonies. The last Diwan died in 1897, and his slaves, to the number of ninety-six, were all set free. No successor has been chosen, for, though there are candidates eligible by birth, none of them have the necessary means.[1]

Not far from the German frontier is Wasin, an island about three miles long and one broad, separated from the mainland by a channel which forms an excellent harbour. It contains an Arab town of the same name and some antiquity, which was formerly a trade centre of considerable importance, and is still the chief market for boritis or mangrove poles. The history of the place, could it be traced, would be of some interest, for it has probably been known to Arabic navigators since 500 A.D. The town contains three mosques, several stone houses and graveyards, but unfortunately the tombstones are said to be undated.

Behind the regions I have described, lies the Nyika, or jungle-covered plain, which stretches inland, gradually rising. Though it appears level, relatively to the isolated peaks which, here and there spring out of it, it is really, like most of the surface of East Africa, very uneven and broken up by fissures and undulations hidden under the all-covering scrub. It is sparsely inhabited by various tribes, called collectively

---

[1] A most interesting account of the Diwan and of all matters relating to Vumba will be found in "Notes on the History of Vumba, East Africa," by A. C. Hollis, in the *Journal of the Anthropological Institute*, vol. xxx. (N.S., vol. iii.), 1900, pp. 275–296.

Wanyika, of whom the principal are the Wagiriama, behind Melindi; the Waduruma, behind Mombasa; and the Wasegeju and Wadigo, further south. They are all in a low state of civilisation, except those who have come under mission influence, and merely cultivate such small patches as are necessary for the food of each village.

I have so often. used the word "scrub," and it is so important an element in East African geography and scenery, that I must describe exactly what it is. The chief constituents are thorny acacias, generally with flat tops and white stems. In dry weather they look gaunt, bare, and bony; in wet weather they are connected and partly covered with a network of creepers, and may even acquire a certain grace when draped with masses of convolvulus. Occasionally, too, one finds in the scrub flowering shrubs of marvellous beauty. But this is rare: what strikes one most about it is its formlessness, its utter want of distinction, and its terrible strength. It is the vegetable image of democracy. It grows no great trees and makes no fine views, but it has taken entire possession of the country, and you cannot turn it out. At present one merely regrets that so much land should be wasted, but before the construction of the railway the journey across the Nyika was the most formidable part of the march to Uganda, especially the forty miles between Samburu and Maungu, where there was no water. The horrors of the scrub are increased by the number of thorns, "the tyrants of the forest," as Krapf called them. The vegetation is spiny, spiky, and forbidding. Almost all the plants bear thorns: some bear nothing else, and exist solely in order to be disagreeable and obstructive. The "Wait-a-bit" thorn tells its own tale. Had it been desired to erect an artificial barrier for preventing the entry of civilisation into the interior, it would have been very hard to invent one more effective than that which Nature has provided.

There is one small but important district in East Africa —Teita and· Taveta—which is midway between the Highlands and Lowlands, partaking of the characters of both. It formerly was part of the province of Ukamba, but was detached and added to Seyidie in 1903, and I will follow this arrangement in treating of it among the Coast Lands.

A number of hills, as already mentioned, emerge rather abruptly from the scrub jungle at various points, but quite a cluster are found about a hundred miles from the coast, near the railway station of Voi, on a river of the same name. This river, which is often dry, flows between two rocky masses, of which the one nearer the sea is called Ndara, and the other is known by various designations in different parts, the most general name perhaps being Dabida. The hill-tops are rather thickly populated, but the valleys and plains are almost entirely uninhabited. For this there are two reasons. Firstly, all these plains were formerly raided by the Masai, and other natives were afraid to have either flocks or cultivation in them. Secondly, all the physical conditions combine to make the hill-tops the best part of the country. It is here that are the sources of the rivers and streams, which too frequently dry up by the time they reach the arid and porous soil of the valley, or else convert it into a temporary swamp in the rainy season. Also, the air on the heights is far better. This district rivals Rabai and the neighbourhood of Mombasa as an old centre of missionary activity. The Church Missionary Society have stations at Sagalla in Ndara and Mbale in Dabida; and the Roman Catholics a considerable establishment and grounds at the head of a valley called Bura, running up into the Teita Hills, about twenty miles from Voi.

These hill stations are beginning to be used as sanitoriums for Mombasa, and the movement is one which deserves to be encouraged. From Sagalla there is a magnificent view, comparable to that from Mwele, already mentioned; and the top of the mountain near Dabida is one of the most gratifying spectacles of native cultivation and irrigation to be found in East Africa. The ascent to Dabida is extremely beautiful, and, except for its precipitous character, reminded me of the

Valley of Tempe, as for a great part of the way the road lies along the banks of a stream, shaded by great leafy trees. Behind Bura is a district called Manda, which I have never visited, but which is described as excellent upland pastures.

A journey of about eighty miles from Voi, along a fairly good road, takes one to Taveta, the frontier station of British territory, just under the snows of Kilima-Njaro. The intervening country is known as the Serengeti Plains, but is really not much more open than the Taru jungle, and covered with scrub. Though there is no water for about fifty miles, game is plentiful, and some rare animals, including the strange, giraffe-like antelope known as Waller's gazelle (*Lithocranius Walleri*) are found here.

Taveta is a fairly large native village òr town—it is too big for the first name and too straggling for the second— near Lake Jipe. It is chiefly remarkable for · a forest containing very fine trees, which are probably the best timber in East Africa. Unfortunately, it is so situated that it is impossible to export them with profit, and bring the wood to either the railway or the sea at a moderate cost. There is a considerable traffic in cattle across the frontier, and, besides the road to Voi, a path much used by natives leads across the plains to Nairobi. It is a pity that the former road, which is practicable for wheeled traffic, was not made on the other side of the Teita Hills, along the Tsavo River to the Tsavo station on the railway. The distance by train to the coast would have been thirty miles longer, but this disadvantage would have been amply compensated by having a route passing through a rich and beautiful country, along the banks of a river instead of across a waterless plain. I once returned from Taveta to the Tsavo station along the right bank of the river, and was struck not only with the beauty of the scenery, but also with the excellence of the climate at a distance of two or three days' [1] journey from the railway, and an elevation

---

[1] I suppose the distance must have been twenty or thirty miles, but the jungle track which we followed was so winding that it is difficult to make an estimate.

of two thousand feet. There were no mosquitoes, and the temperature in January, which is the hottest month, was quite pleasant. The river here is broader than at the point where the railway crosses it, and is bordered with fine trees. The acacias formed veritable arbours or natural tents, in which one could sit bare-headed in perfect comfort in the middle of the day. In many parts mica was abundant, and flakes an inch or more long were found in the roadside stones. In one place the river flows under two rocky masses, called Theoka and Gulia, which somewhat resemble the cliffs on the Rhine. The whole country is uninhabited. The guides said that this was due to the former fear of the Masai.

THE TSAVO RIVER

CHAPTER V

THE INTERIOR AND HIGHLANDS

As I have already stated, the simplest description of the interior of the Protectorate is that it is a great volcanic plateau thrown up between Lake Victoria and the sea, occasionally rising into peaks of considerable elevation, and cleft down the middle, north and south, by a great fissure known as the Rift Valley. The greater part of this plateau possesses a temperate climate, and a vegetation which often superficially resembles that of European countries.

As might, however, be expected, the country immediately round Lake Victoria forms a distinct section, low and tropical in temperature and vegetation. The Lake appears to be fed by the streams which enter it from the surrounding mountains, and if one considers the enormous amount of rain which falls on the Mau range, its size is hardly wonderful. The chief rivers which enter it within the limits of British East Africa are the Nyando, the Kach, the Kuja, the Yalo, the Nzoia, and Sio, and many more are contributed by Uganda and the German territories. The shores are a low, fertile country, rich in crops and cattle, and inhabited by a peaceful and industrious race, but unfortunately they are unhealthy for Europeans. The drainage of swamps, and the various methods now known for destroying mosquitoes, may do much to improve this littoral in the future, but it is to be feared that it will be some time before we have even one perfectly healthy station in the immediate neighbourhood of the Lake, as the ill-defined marshy edges offer almost endless opportunities for the breeding of mosquitoes. Probably the best remedy would be to build a wall on the lake shore in the neighbourhood of stations, with a hard-beaten path behind it, so as to prevent the formation of any pools or backwaters.   It is said that the Germans have adopted this method with success.

Lake Victoria is less picturesque than Lake Albert, or the waters of the Rift Valley.   On the eastern side at any rate it is not surrounded by cliffs, and at the best-known points, such as Kisumu and Port Victoria, one sees not the main body of water, but a gulf or arm.   The finest views of it which I know are obtained from the hills of Lusinga, an island at the mouth of the Kavirondo Gulf.   On a fine day the blue waters as seen from these heights, and the clear outlines of the numerous little islands, recall the shores of the Mediterranean.

The best-known part of the Lake shore is naturally that traversed by the railway, which, after descending the Mau escarpment to Fort Ternan by precipitous curves, runs along the valley of the Nyando until it crosses it at Kibigori, and goes straight to Kisumu or Port Florence.   The former of these names is to be preferred as the designation of the town, for it is a real native name of importance which ought not to be lost, and the latter should be restricted to the actual port and pier. I may observe that African place-names give rise to many difficulties.   When, as often happens, the place which has become important under Europeans had not attracted the attention of natives, and was only vaguely distinguished by them from the surrounding country, the use of a new European name seems perfectly proper, such as Fort Hall.   When there is a definite and recognised native name, it is certainly desirable to preserve it ; but the difficulty is that each tribe has generally its own name for every remarkable natural feature, and as a rule it is mere chance, and not any consideration of the merits of rival claims, that decides which name finds a place on the map.   Thus, Mount Elgon is known as Masawa to most of the inhabitants in its vicinity, and Elgon appears to be an abbreviation of the Masai name Ol-doinyo loo-'l-goon, "The mountain of breasts."   Most accepted place-names in the interior of East Africa are, like this, Swahili corruptions of a native name picked up by Europeans from the porters who accompanied them from the coast. Thus Naivasha is for En-aiposha,[1] and Elmenteita for Il-muteita.

For twenty or thirty miles before reaching Port Florence, the railway travels under the Nandi escarpment across a level plain, which becomes swampy during the rains, but is very fertile in such native crops as millet and sweet potatoes, and also promises well for the cultivation of cotton. This plain was no doubt formed by the delta of the Nyando, but as a rule the low-lying district round the lake is narrow, and mountains begin to rise a short distance from the shore, though not rapidly or conspicuously. The country is remarkable as being one of the few thickly populated parts of East Africa. The natives, of whom more elsewhere, are generally known (as is also the district) by the name of Kavirondo. Linguistically they fall into two divisions; for the northern section speaks a Bantu language, and the southern (sometimes called Ja-luo) a Nilotic one, but both are similar in appearance and customs, particularly in the total nudity of the women. A characteristic but unlovely plant in all this country is the Euphorbia, a strange vegetable growth without leaves and somewhat like a cactus, with rows of vertical branches arranged like the arms and lights of a candelabra. The branches are easily broken, and secrete a copious white juice which is said to be very poisonous and to produce blindness if it touches the eyes.

To the north of the railway the Lake shore rises up into the Nandi country and the Uasin Gishu plateau. To the south is a little-known region lying between the Mau range and the Lake, various parts of which bear the names of Ugaya, Kossova, and Lumbwa. Ugaya is the part nearest to the Lake, thickly inhabited by Kavirondo and rich in cattle. Kossova or Kisii is a hilly district behind Ugaya, and is one of the least-known parts of the Protectorate. The inhabitants appear to be

[1] This is the pronunciation at the place itself, but near Kilima-Njaro the Masai call it En-aivasha. The first travellers in Masailand (Fischer, Thomson, &c.) came through Taveta, and wrote the name as they heard it pronounced there.

E

Bantu-speaking, and have a bad reputation for ferocity, but this may merely mean that they have a hereditary feud with their neighbours, who are not Bantu, and does not necessarily imply that they will be hostile to Europeans. Hitherto, we have had no relations with them. The Lumbwa country lies immediately west of the Mau and south of Fort Ternan. As far as I have seen it, in visiting Kericho and marching thence to Mohoroni, it is extremely beautiful, consisting of a series of meadows with numerous streams and strips of forest. Flowers and ferns, particularly the latter, are characteristic of the region. The inhabitants are closely allied to the Nandi, and speak almost the same language. They came from the north, and were formerly nomads, and have somewhat imperfectly adopted a sedentary life. Their houses are not built in villages, but are scattered all over the country, so that on looking round one generally sees two or three. This is very much the reverse of ordinary African scenery, for as a rule one marches long distances between villages, and perhaps this peculiar arrangement gives an exaggerated impression of populousness. The Lumbwa are very bad cultivators, and plant only a small grain called wimbi. The result is that they continually suffer from failure of crops, though the scarcity never amounts to a famine, as they have always large flocks of sheep and goats, whose skins they sell. With suitable crops and reasonably assiduous cultivation, there is every reason to believe that they would be most prosperous. The southern part of Lumbwa is called Sotik or Soti, but the character of the country and the inhabitants appears to be the same.

The whole of this district, bounded by the Mau and the Lake on the east and west, and by the railway and the German frontier on the north and south, is almost entirely unexplored, and the maps are not to be trusted. A party despatched by the East African Syndicate, who went through from Nairobi to Lake Victoria, keeping near the German boundary, reported that the indications of forests, plains, &c., on existing charts are erroneous, and gave on the whole a favourable account of the region.   The Commission which is at present delimitating the German and British territories will no doubt publish trustworthy information.   The researches of the East African Syndicate proved that there is a considerable amount of gold in this country, and that a reef apparently extends across the German border, but after further investigation it was decided that the metal was not present in paying quantities.

After having thus briefly described the country bordering on the Lake, we may turn to the most important part of the Protectorate, the high plateau divided by the Rift Valley. This valley is merely an unusually striking exemplification of a phenomenon which is characteristic of nearly the whole surface of East Africa—namely, the subsidence of certain portions on the cessation of volcanic activity.   Though one has often the impression of a level surface, compared with greater surrounding irregularities, as in the Athi Plains, the Taru jungle, and the floor of the Rift Valley itself, it will generally be found that these surfaces are extremely uneven owing to small sinkings of the strata in various parts.   In the Rift Valley this has happened on a titanic scale, but the cause is the same.   Towards its northern end the depression may be said to be double, as the valley containing Lake Baringo is divided by the Kamasia range from the valley of the Kerio River, which is closed towards the south by mountains, bounded on the west by the Elgeyo escarpment, and open only towards the north.

In considering the configuration of the temperate Highlands, it is most natural to approach them from the side of the sea.   A distinct change in the temperature, particularly at night, is noticeable after Tsavo station (mile 133), but the country continues covered with scrub, and does not show any open plains until considerably beyond 200 miles from the coast. All this western part of the Province of Ukamba is now little known or visited, for every one hurries through it in the train in order to arrive at the better parts beyond; but, though relatively inferior, it is not valueless, and it is greatly to be desired in the interests of the country, and particularly of the railway, that some use should be made of it, as it must be very disadvantageous for a line to pass for nearly 200 miles of its length through an uninhabited and totally unproductive jungle.   To the north of the railway is a range of mountains apparently following the course of the river Athi, and sometimes called the Yatta escarpment, and to the south are some isolated peaks, Theoka and Gulea on the left bank of the Tsavo River, and the Kyülü group further west.[1]   From an examination of the country which I caused to be made, it would appear that there is a fair amount of water, and that the slopes of the mountains offer good land for cultivation.   The late Mr. Walker, Geologist to the Protectorate, expressed the opinion that the neighbourhood of the Kyülü Hills had a very good soil, which would probably be excellent for agriculture.

Kibwezi, at mile 195 on the railway, though unfortunately unhealthy and in a belt of tsetse fly, is very fertile.   It was formerly a considerable centre, both for the Government and the Church Missionary Society, but both stations have now been removed.   A garden however remains, and a German firm are cultivating fibre, which is abundant here, as in all the district.   The end of this jungle country is roughly marked by Makindu (meaning palm-trees), a large station on the railway near the Kiboko River.   The climate, though still tropical, is quite tolerable for Europeans, and the prospects for cotton-growing, fibre, and other cultivation good.

After Makindu, the country begins to show more striking natural features, and is at once more open and more mountainous.   The stations of Simba and Sultan Hamud are celebrated hunting-grounds, and great quantities of hartebeest and other antelopes are visible at most times of the year. The defect of the district is a deficiency of water, though the presence of so much game is a testimony to the excellence of the pasturage.   The fact is that the railway, in order to follow

----

[1] These are the names as I took them from native Wakamba guides, but maps give different forms.

the easiest route, keeps at some distance from the Athi River, and avoids the land which is best watered and most suitable for agriculture.   Rather to the north of the line is a mass of mountains, culminating in the considerable peak of Nzaui. The hills to the south are smaller.   This side is a game reserve, and practically uninhabited.   Indeed, the whole of Ukamba has a singularly desolate appearance, and one may make the journey from Tsavo to Nairobi without seeing a village or a single native except a few who may have gathered round railway stations.   This apparent paucity of inhabitants is to a large extent real, for the country is very sparsely populated, but is also due to the habit of the Wakamba of living on the sides or tops of hills and concealing their villages as much as possible, a habit due, as in other places, to the former prevalence of raids.   Around Machakos, at any rate, there is a considerable population.

This station is, after Nairobi, the most considerable place in Ukamba, and was formerly the capital of the province and headquarters of the troops.   The name, in spite of its Spanish sound, is merely the *s* of the British genitive appended to the name of an African chief, and is short for Machako's village. Similar formations are Mazeras and Mumias, from Mazera and Mumia.   Machako, who was alive until recently, was a chief of great importance, and had a village on the top of a hill overlooking the European station, which is built on the lower ground near the water.   Owing to the railway having gone about twenty miles to the south, Machakos has lost much of its importance, and the troops have been moved to Nairobi. It is, however, still a trading centre, with a fair number of Indian shops, and has gardens in which fruit and vegetables are successfully grown.   Still more successful has been the garden of Mr. Stewart Watt at Engoleni, about eight miles distant, which produces excellent English fruit, particularly apples and apricots.   About sixty miles to the north lies Kitui, a name properly belonging to the district, but often given also to the Government station, which is more correctly called

Nengia.   There is a considerable trade, mostly in the hands of
Indians, between Machakos and this district, and it has been
found worth while to build a cable-way across the Athi River,
which in wet weather rises very high and is quite impassable.
From Nengia further trade routes lead to Mount Kenya and also
to Mumoni,[1] two strange castellated hills standing out like a fort
in the otherwise flat plain which extends to the Tana River.
The natives are said to be intelligent, but warlike.   Practically
nothing is known of the country either to the north or the
east.   I was told it would take about nine days to march
from Nengia to the falls of the Tana at Hameye; and somewhere to the south-east lies the German mission station of
Ikutha, about seven days' march from Kibwezi.

Ukamba is roughly divided into three districts, Kikumbuliyu, Ulu, and Kitui.   The first lies round Makindu, Masongaleni, &c.   Ulu extends from Machakos towards the coast,
and Kitui is situated to the north.   The part containing
Nzaui and the adjacent mountains is also sometimes called
Iveti.

The Highlands of East Africa, east of the Rift Valley, are
watered by two river systems, the streams from the Kikuyu
escarpment, which ultimately help to form the Tana, and the
Athi, which further east unites with the Tsavo, and is then
known as the Sabaki.   Between the Athi and the Tana is
marked on maps the little-known river called Nsao or Ndeo,
and the Gwaso-Nyiro (more correctly E-Uaso-ngiro) flows
northwards from Kenya.   For practical purposes, however,
the streams which water the good agricultural and pastoral
land are the Athi and the feeders of the Tana.   The former
rises in the extreme south of the Kikuyu Hills, and at first
follows a northerly course as far as the large mountain of
Douyo Sabuk (more correctly Ol-doinyo Sapuk), which forms
such a prominent feature in the view of the plains from

---

[1] From a distance Mumoni looks like a single mountain, but Mr. Walker,
who visited it, says it consists of two ranges of gneiss, separated by a tributary
of the Thika-Thika.

Nairobi. The railway crosses it at the station called Athi
River, which is a famous hunting-ground, where many sportsmen have slain lions, and some lions have slain sportsmen.
After rounding Douyo Sabuk the river turns sharply south-
east, and, as far as European knowledge is concerned, may be
said to vanish until it reappears near the Tsavo station, for
probably the only well-known point on its course is the
cable-way on the road to Kitui. It receives a number of
small tributaries from the direction of the railway, such as
the Machakos River, the Kiboko, the Kibwezi, and the Mtito
Andei or Nde[1] Rivers, but it is unfortunate that the route
taken by the railway has caused the districts furthest from
the main stream to be opened up first.

The plain lying to the north-east of Nairobi is watered by
an abundance of streams, falling into the Thika-Thika and
Sagana, which subsequently is known as the Tana. The
ways of nature and the wishes of mankind in the matter of
water do not coincide in East Africa. As a rule there is too
little, but here there is too much—not in the sense that the
country is too wet and marshy, for the streams are mostly
clean and quick-flowing, and carry the water off, but the
multitude of them impedes communication and renders roadmaking extremely difficult ; for water-courses which are
usually unimportant and fordable are apt to assume formidable dimensions during the rains, and will carry away anything but strongly-built bridges. The most ordinary form
of native bridge is formed by simply cutting down a convenient tree, and causing it to fall across a river. More
elaborate crossings are made with fibres, one on each side
to hold on by, and two or three below to walk on. These
constructions present great terrors to ordinary Europeans ;
but it is surprising to see how a native with a heavy load
on his head will step across the loose and swaying cords,

---

[1] This place is commonly but quite incorrectly called Mtoto Andei. It would
appear that it means "the wood of vultures." Andei, or Nde, is probably equivalent to the Swahili "ndege," a bird.

hardly touching the side-strings, and with no more sign of nervousness than a bird on a thin branch.

In mentioning these rivers, we have already arrived at the Kikuyu [1] Hills, one of the most beautiful, fertile, and economically important parts of the Protectorate. They consist of a number of undulating ranges, stretching up to Mount Kenya on the north and terminating in the south at the hog-backed mountain called Ngongo-Bagas.[2] On the west they are bounded by a clear-cut and precipitous descent into the Rift Valley, but on the eastern side the ascent is gentle and not very considerable, for the railway mounts only about 2000 feet in twenty-four miles. The fact that the hills are wooded, and thus sharply distinguished from the open Athi plains, where there are no trees after the station of Machakos Roads, generally produces an unduly strong impression that one has left the level country and entered into a new and mountainous region.

Nairobi is built just at the point where the railway enters the hills. The situation is unfortunate from a sanitary point of view, owing to the extreme difficulty of drainage; and it is regrettable that after the visitation of the plague in 1902, when many sites were moved, the whole settlement and railway station were not transferred a few miles higher up the line, where a far superior position could have been easily obtained. It is now probably too late to do this. At present the township consists of a semicircle of bungalows on a low ridge, and a huge railway station, houses for workmen, a few European shops, and an Indian bazaar, all laid out with rectangular symmetry on the plain. With the exception of a purple and yellow market, a monument of the public-spirited generosity of an Indian gentleman, nearly all the houses are

[1] The name Kikuyu is said to be derived from Kuyu, a fig. Fig-trees of various kinds are very abundant in the country.

[2] More correctly in Masai Eñg-ongu-e-'m-Bagasi, "the Eye or source of the Athi" (or perhaps of the Mbagathi). The explanation which makes it mean "the porter's eye," i.e. the point at which the caravan porter looks, appears not to be correct.

constructed of white tin, and somewhat resemble a mining settlement in the Western States of America. It must be candidly confessed that the result is not artistically satisfactory, and that the beauty of a view in Nairobi depends on the more or less thorough elimination of the town from the landscape. When this can be completely realised, and there are seen only two vast stretches of plain with Kilima-Njaro on one side and Kenya on the other, the effect is superb, and not spoilt by the spectacle of a distant train slowly crawling like an ant across the green-grey expanse.

The charm of the environs is some compensation for the unloveliness of the town itself. The plains in front have that grandeur which always belongs to large open spaces, but the wooded country at the back affords an unending succession of rustic landscapes which will bear comparison with the most beautiful parks and lanes of England. The energy of Mr. Ainsworth, who has so long and well filled the post of His Majesty's Sub-Commissioner in Ukamba, has constructed a series of roads about the town leading to Dagoreti and the Mbagathi River on the south, and Kyamvu and other localities on the north. This latter road is being continued to Fort Hall, and nearly all the land along it has been taken up by European settlers. It is just this fringe of the Kikuyu country which is the most picturesque part and most suitable for farms, since it combines agricultural land and pasturage, while it delights the eye with an alternation of forests and open glades. There are hardly any native inhabitants, for, from fear of the Masai raids which prevailed before the establishment of our administrations, they eschewed the neighbourhood of the plains and went further into the hills. There the ground is fertile indeed, but the scenery is less picturesque, as it consists of a succession of hills and valleys with a large cultivation of bananas and native cereals. There is also a good deal of European cultivation round Kikuyu railway station and Limoru.

The native inhabitants of this district are Masai and

Kikuyu. The former are now found chiefly round Nairobi and to the south, particularly near Ngongo Bagas and the river Mbagathi, and show a tendency to adopt a settled mode of life. Lenana, the great medicine-man of the tribe, lives in this neighbourhood. The Kikuyu (sometimes called Waki-kuyu, or more correctly, Akikuyu) are the inhabitants of the hills, and almost certainly the result of an intermixture of the Masai and a Bantu race. They are intelligent and fairly industrious, and live a semi-settled agricultural life—that is to say, they burn a clearing in the forest, build a village, and cultivate for a few years. As soon as the soil shows any sign of exhaustion they move on, burn another clearing, and repeat the same process. They extend right up to the slopes of Mount Kenya, and the population seems to be particularly dense in the neighbourhood of the mountain; though, owing to the habit of planting groves of bananas round the village, little can be seen but a mass of dead green leaves, showing no sign of human life to the unpractised eye. In the country between Kenya and Nairobi there are considerable gaps with no inhabitants. It would appear that they were depopulated during the famine of 1897, and have not since been re-occupied.

Besides Dagoreti, in the neighbourhood of Nairobi, the Government have two stations in the Kikuyu country—Fort Hall in Mbiri, on the Mathioya River, opposite to Mount Kenya; and Nyeri, lying more to the north-west, and connected with Naivasha by a tolerable road. Kenya is one of the shyest mountains in the world, and for the greater part of the day is, at most points from which it should be visible, covered by a thick mist. At Nairobi it can, not unfrequently, be seen for a few minutes early in the morning, or about four in the afternoon, but rarely for longer. During a stay of a few days at Fort Hall I never saw it at all, and was told that it is no unusual experience for it to remain veiled for months together. The best views are obtained from the neighbourhood of Nyeri. What struck me most in them was the immense breadth of the mass compared to the height. It seemed to block up all the northern quarter and shut off some mysterious hyperborean land. On the top is a curiously sharp, straight, snowy peak, almost like a flagstaff, and below it a glacier, but the expanse of snow (at any rate in January, which is equivalent to midsummer) is nothing like that on Mount Kilima-Njaro. The immediate surroundings and slopes of Mount Kenya have not been thoroughly explored. The natives are less friendly than in most parts of Africa, and the whole district being at some distance from headquarters, it has been thought well to use caution in opening relations with them. It would appear that there is a great belt of bamboo forest on the mountain, and below this a zone of cultivation. Two important tribes are the Embo to the east, and the Iraiini to the south. The latter name is said to mean swamps.

Like nearly all the northern interior of the Protectorate, the country to the north and east of Kenya is imperfectly known. Recent contributions to our knowledge of it have been by Tate,[1] Maud,[2] and Arkell-Hardwick.[3] The eastern side of Kenya is a cultivated country known by the general designation of Meru, and divided into the districts (going from south to north) of Makandini, Mnyiso, and Mzara. The soil is said to be extraordinarily fertile, and blessed with an ample rainfall. The inhabitants are unwarlike, and mostly Kikuyu or Kamba, who have migrated from the south, but between Mnyiso and Mzara there is a considerable settlement of Masai from Laikipia, who have taken to agriculture. North of Mzara the country consists of plains which are in parts grassy, but often strewn with boulders of lava or granite. Game, however, is abundant. To the west are several mountains, of which the best known is Douyo Girri-Girri, near Laikipia. The most important physical feature in the

[1] *Geographical Journal*, February 1904, "A Journey to Rendile."
[2] *Ibid.*, May 1904, "Exploration in the Southern Borderland of Abyssinia."
[3] "An Ivory Trader in North Kenya." Longmans, 1903.

whole district is, however, the river Gwaso-Nyiro, which receives the Gwaso-Narok from Laikipia, and the Gwaso-Marra from the direction of Kenya. It is apparently lost in the Lorian Swamp, but Mr. Tate thinks it really passes underground through Tabtu, Afmadu, Kumbi, and the Deshek Wama, to the Juba, the permanent water in those places being otherwise hard to explain. It is described as a stream of about fifty yards wide, turbid, but affording excellent drinking, and possessing a considerable volume of water, though navigation is rendered impossible by rocks and rapids.

To the north of Gwaso-Nyiro lies an undulating desert, covered with granite boulders and thorn bushes. There is no water in the rivers during the dry season, but it can be obtained by digging. Beyond this desert is Sambur, a district inhabited by Masai from Laikipia. They are said to have received the name Sambur (which means butterfly) on account of their habit of flitting about and changing their pasture lands. They appear to have intermarried with the Rendile, and to have lost their warlike qualities. Their country is described as dry, but affording sweet, nutritious grass on the uplands. North of it comes another desert, the Kohiti, and then the Rendile country, which is said to offer a bracing climate and fine grassy highlands sloping up to the Haldaiyan Hills (about 2° N.). Here is also Sogorti, a crater lake surrounded by thick woods of beech and juniper. The Rendile are apparently a branch of the Gallas, driven westward by the Ogaden Somalis. They possess considerable herds, both of camels and sheep, and in their general mode of life resemble the Somalis.

North of the Rendile, we come to the still less known Boran country, where the frontier between the British Protectorate and Abyssinia is very doubtful, but will perhaps be marked by the Goro escarpment (see Captain Maud's Map, l. c.). The Boran appear to be a tribe on about the same level of civilisation as the Somalis, but are not Moham-

medans. They are a pastoral people, and have large herds
of cattle, and also own horses, which is unusual in East
Africa. They are divided into two divisions, the Gona and
Subbu. Mixed with them are found tribes called Gubbra
and Gurre, who appear to be Mohammedan immigrants from
the Somali countries on the east.

Let us now return to the country south-west of Kenya,
and to the Rift Valley. All this region is very imperfectly
surveyed, and it is certain that the relative positions of even
important natural features are given quite incorrectly on the
official maps. It is therefore with some diffidence that I give
any general description of it. The reader will remember that
the Rift Valley is a huge trough, running first north-west and
then more directly north. The eastern side, in the general
sense, is a plateau sloping downwards towards the sea, on
which rise the Kikuyu Hills, running north and somewhat
east to Kenya. North-west of the Kikuyu Hills, and overlooking the Rift Valley, is the Settima (or O-Satima) range,
connected at its south-eastern end with Mount Kinangop,[1] or
Nandarua. A line drawn south-west from Kenya to Lake
Naivasha would probably pass through Nyeri station over the
Settima. This range, which is at least 10,000 feet high, is
probably the same as the Aberdare Mountains, though the
two are marked separately on some maps. To the north of
it, still on the top of the escarpment, and looking over Lakes
Hannington and Baringo, is the great plateau of Laikipia.
The equator appears to pass through the northern spurs of
Kenya, then just north of the Settima and across the southern
portion of the Laikipia plain into the Rift Valley near Molo.
The Laikipia plateau is entirely uninhabited since about 1890,
as are also the higher parts of the Settima range. The
mountains descend to the Rift Valley by a series of terraces,

---

[1] It is perhaps too late to change this name without being pedantic, but it
appears that the Masai call the mountain Kipipieri, and the plains at the foot
of it are known as Kinōbop, or Kinōkop, which perhaps means "the burning
country." Kinangop is an incorrect form, and does not mean "our land," as is
sometimes said. Nandarua is the Kikuyu name of the mountain.

which are used by the Masai as grazing-grounds, but are not permanently inhabited. The highest of these terraces below the main ridge of the Settima is called Angata-pus, the blue plains, or, less correctly, Engatabus. On it is a considerable swampy lake, called Elbolosoto (Elbolosat).

I have made the journey over the Settima by two routes. From Naivasha I ascended by the valley of the Morendat, by Lake Elbolosoto, to the top of the ridge, and thence down to Nyeri on the other side. From the summit there is a wide view over Laikipia, which appears as a plain dotted with a great number of green hills. The course of the Gwaso-Narok, which runs into the Gwaso-Nyiro, was also visible. In returning, I took a more direct route over the shoulder of Mount Kinangop. This road traverses considerable bamboo forests, which form two bands at an altitude of between 8000 and 9000 feet, and must be six or seven miles wide, if not more.

The East African landscapes, at from five to six thousand feet, recall English summer scenes. At seven thousand upwards they have a different and more austere character. The thermometer frequently falls below freezing-point at night, and it is only at midday that one is reminded that the sun is tropical. The open stretches of long grass mingled with bracken and blackberries often resemble a Scotch moor; but the vegetation, though not conspicuous, generally proves singular when examined. Belts of bamboo are common in all these regions, and in the unforested spaces are found shrubs which resemble heath, or St. John's wort, grown to the dimensions of a small tree. An occasional and very agreeable phenomenon is a kind of wild raspberry, which, like most of the characteristic plants, grows in belts. The fruit is large, above an inch long, and of a deep yellow colour. It tastes more like a mulberry than a raspberry. It is gratifying to add that in these higher regions one is almost entirely rid of the thorny plants which pervade the lower plains. At and above 9000 feet the most striking feature is the great stillness.

VIEW OF LAKE OLBOLOSAT FROM THE SETTIMA HILLS.

ANT HILLS NEAR BARINGO.

LAKE HANNINGTON AND FLAMINGOES.

There is hardly any animal life. One may see a few tracks of rhinoceros, a few pigeons, a few large butterflies fluttering languidly in the forest clearings, but the flocks of game, as well as the minor buzz and chatter of birds and insects, have altogether ceased.

The descent from these high regions to the Rift Valley is on the eastern side almost everywhere steep and sudden, though more gradual on the west. The valley is now often approached, and few more effective approaches could be found, by the Uganda Railway from Limoru. East Africa, as I have already indicated, is a land of great views. The combination of plateaus, isolated peaks, and great depressions offers opportunities for panoramas of size and grandeur unsurpassed elsewhere. Perhaps the impressiveness of these views is largely due to the fact that from the higher points one is often able to look down on the smaller hills, not merely to realise them as lower elevations, but to contemplate them from a real bird's-eye view as little knobs rising out of the lower level.

One of these views, though by no means the best, is afforded by the Uganda Railway. After leaving the station of Limoru, the train climbs in and out between the valleys and ridges of Kikuyu until it suddenly turns a corner and looks down on the Rift Valley, spread like a map below. In front lies the extinct volcano of Longanot, immediately below is the Kedong Valley and the curious round Kedong Hill; away to the south stretches the great trough in which are visible smaller depressions and elevations such as Mount Suswa. The valley extends to the north-west, but the view is blocked by a spur of Mount Longanot, commonly called the Saddle, which unites the mountain to the side of the escarpment. After making what seems a perilous plunge to the Escarpment station, the train runs along the side of the valley under Kijabe Hill until it surmounts the saddle, and the grey waters of Lake Naivasha lie in sight under the bluff upon which is built the Government station.

The Rift Valley in East Africa may be divided into three

portions—the southern, running down towards the German
frontier; the middle, extending roughly from Naivasha to
Nakuru; and the northern, going up towards Lake Rudolf.
The southern portion is little known, and appears to suffer, at
least at some periods of the year, from want of water. The
river Kedong, which rises somewhere near Kijabe, and flows
almost due south, does not do much to counteract the prevalent aridity, and, like so many African rivers, disappears
mysteriously.

The beautiful section of the valley is the middle one,
containing Lakes Naivasha, Elmenteita, and Nakuru. The
general direction of this part is north-west, but the view is
interrupted by a spur of the Mau escarpment, which projects
into the valley and forces the railway to make a considerable
bend. Between this spur and the western side of Lake
Naivasha (that is, the side away from the railway) lies the
beautiful little plain of Endabibi, which means clover in
Masai. It is described on some maps as a marsh, but this, I
think, must be wrong, though the neighbourhood of the river
Marmonet, which flows through it, may be swampy at some
times of year. From the Endabibi plateau, it is a day's march
over the pass at the top of the above-mentioned spur to the
Enderit River and the basin of Lake Nakuru. The views from
the summit of the pass are magnificent, for both Naivasha and
Nakuru look finer from the western side than from the eastern,
whence they are generally seen. Of the three lakes, Naivasha
is fresh, but Nakuru and Elmenteita are salt. By far the
most beautiful is Elmenteita. It is also the least known, for
it is not visible from the railway. The outlines of Naivasha
and Nakuru, though not unpleasing, are somewhat rounded
and monotonous, but the shores of Elmenteita project in
many capes and headlands, which I would fain see crowned
with a few castles or temples, though I fear the real old
African would think such erections a desecration of his
favourite wilds.

The rivers which enter these lakes have mostly the

deplorable African habit of dwindling as they get further from their sources, and hence bring down very little water in the dry season. Into Naivasha flow the Morendat and Gilgil, of which the former, at any rate, is a really beautiful stream in its higher reaches. The channel is cut so deep in the plain that the river is generally invisible until one is quite close, when one suddenly sees a deep green chasm, covered at the sides with trees and grass, and a fine flood rushing at the bottom. Into the south end of Nakuru enter the Magalia and the Enderit, whose name means dust. *Pulvis et umbra sumus!* One is accustomed to the sad reflection in the case of the animal and vegetable kingdoms, but in most parts of the world rivers are an exception to the melancholy rule. In Africa, however, it often does happen that when a river is marked on the map one finds in reality only a trench full of dust and a little shade. The Enderit, however, does not appear to deserve its name so much as other water-courses, for when I saw it, it possessed quite a respectable volume of water; and certainly the pasturage in the neighbourhood is excellent, as indeed it is almost everywhere in the Rift Valley. In most parts there is no vegetation except grass and a few flowers, but in some places, such as the Angata-oo-l-Käk,[1] near Gilgil, there are scattered low trees. Game is generally abundant, particularly Thomson's gazelle. A curious and pretty sight may often be seen, particularly near Naivasha, when these gazelles become surrounded by native herds and continue browsing among the sheep with perfect tranquillity. The valley still retains many traces of its volcanic origin. The interior of the crater of Longanot is said to be quite hot, and near the railway station of Eburu numerous jets of steam may be seen issuing from holes in the ground not far from the line. In the region between Eburu and Elmenteita, the low hills which rise from the floor of the valley assume the most fantastic forms, resembling sometimes castles, sometimes pyramids, and sometimes low walls.

---

[1] "The plains of small trees," also called, but less correctly, Rengata Elgek.

The northern portion of the valley, which runs pretty straight north from Nakuru, is less known than the middle part and less attractive, though by no means devoid of interest. It contains the extinct crater of Menengai, and Lakes Hannington, Baringo, Sugota, and Rudolf, Lake Stephanie apparently belonging to another system. For about twenty miles north of Nakuru the grazing appears excellent, and I am told that the same is the case for a considerable distance on the eastern side at the foot of the Laikipia escarpment, but a large part of the space traversed between Nakuru and Baringo is bare, hard soil covered with fragments of red rock. Still, though this tract is uninviting to the pedestrian, it is not devoid of vegetation, and the quantity of game testifies to the excellence of what grass there is.

A little to the south of Baringo lies Lake Hannington, eloquently described by Sir H. Johnston. Seen from the mountains which surround it, it appears to have a pinkish rim, which suggests that its waters have deposited some salt in great quantities. On coming near, one sees that this coloration is really produced by untold numbers of flamingoes, who feed and breed by the lake and sit in rows on its shores. They are so ignorant of the ways of that dangerous animal, man, or so engrossed in their own pursuits, that they can be approached without difficulty; but when a shot or two is fired over the lake, they rise and float for a few minutes over the water in clouds of rosy vapour. Another curious zoological feature which lends a characteristic aspect to the neighbourhood of Lake Hannington is the nests of the white ants, which here take a most unusual shape, being tall columns, ten or twelve feet high, and only a foot or eighteen inches broad. The interior of the pillar is hollow and generally crowded with white ants walking up and down the sides. I do not know whether they are the same species as the architects of the more usual form of nests, nor what is the object of the high aërial promenade which is apparently the only result of the pillar. We know, however, that white ants hate the light, and possibly the hollow column secures a maximum of air with a minimum of sunshine, since the sun's rays can descend into it only at midday.

The shores of Lake Baringo, which lies to the north of Lake Hannington, are marshy and unhealthy. At the southern end are two fairly large villages called Great and Little Njámusi. This name is preferable to the corrupt form Njemps, which has somehow got into books of travel and official. use. The inhabitants are called Njamúsi (the accent being on the first syllable for the place, and on the second for the people), and are agriculturists, but closely akin to the Masai. The mountains on the eastern side are wooded but stony, and bear little grass. The Government station, which was formerly on the shore of the lake, has been moved up into the hills, and a certain amount of cultivation has been successfully undertaken. Game is plentiful, and among other animals is found, though not too plentifully, that beautiful antelope, the greater kudu.

I have never visited the country north of Lake Baringo, nor have we any practical administration there. It is generally described as consisting of thorns, stones, and salt, yet there is a good deal of game, particularly near Sugota, which is probably as much a marsh as a lake, lying in a deep depression. The sides of the valley are perhaps less repellent, and Captain Maud, who marched from Lake Rudolf to Baringo to the east of Lake Sugota, and over the spurs of the mountains, gives a favourable account of the country. He says, "The hillsides were clad with every conceivable shade of green. Flowers brightened the landscape, which was the most beautiful we had seen since leaving Sidamo. To the south, long, easy, grass-covered spurs projecting far from the watershed. A long descent of three days' march, through country difficult to find a way, brought us to a smiling valley which we have called the Impala Valley." [1] This account tallies with what has been noticed in other parts of the Rift Valley, namely, that the richest portions are at the

[1] *Geographical Journal*, May 1904.

sides, where the rivers are still full and fresh.   All accounts, however, agree in describing the shores of Lake Rudolf as desolate and bare except at the extreme northern end, where the Omo enters it.   Yet the country seems to teem with game, which must find some vegetation for pasturage.   The inhabitants are the Suk to the south-east and the Turkana to the north-west.   They apparently belong to the same stock as the Nandi, and are closely related to one another, though hereditary enemies.   The Turkana have a reputation for ferocity, but we have had few dealings with them hitherto, on account of their great distance from our administrative centres. The Suk are inoffensive, and are chiefly remarkable for the huge masses of matted hair which they wear on their backs, arranged in a sort of chignon.

, The western side of all this great Rift Valley is formed by the Mau escarpment.   The elevation of the plateau on its summit is on the whole greater than that of the other side, but the descent is more sloping and less impressive, though the broad stretches of forest and grass are very pleasing to the eye.   Hence the more majestic views are those of the eastern side of the valley seen from the west, which are not those best seen from the railway.   The southern portion of the Mau is little known, and had apparently not been visited by Europeans for many years until I crossed it twice last spring, once from the Endabibi plain to the district known as Natít, on the western side, and once from Lake Nakuru to Kericho in Lumbwa.

The general characteristics of the country traversed on both routes were much the same as those noted in describing the Settima range: plains like Scotch moors, with bracken, blackberries, yellow raspberries, and patches of forest.   This latter was thicker and more abundant in the more southern part, but the timber was distinctly better in the regions above Nakuru.   Everywhere there was an ample supply of wood for fuel and building purposes.   I have not visited, nor have I any accurate information of, the extreme south of the Mau.

The name of Sosian which it bears on the maps appears to be correct.   Probably the country is much the same as that above Endabibi, and consists of a succession of woods and meadows.   It is uninhabited, but frequented by the Masai for pasturage, and the district of Natít on the western side was stated by natives to be a Masai country, and not part of Lumbwa. The country between Nakuru and Kericho is also uninhabited, except for a very few Wandorobo or hunters, and not even used for pasturage.   The Masai and Lumbwa are hereditary enemies, and mutually agreed to leave a space between them in order to avoid collision.   The district immediately above Nakuru is called Likyá : after that comes Mau-narok and Mau-nanyokye, or the black and red Mau, so called from the colour of the soil.   Then comes Tursoga.   The whole of this section is plentifully watered by streams, in rather deep valleys with steep, grassy sides, and appeared admirably suited for European residence and agriculture.   There is generally frost at night. As the land sloped down towards Lumbwa the temperature became appreciably warmer, and after passing through a thick belt of bamboos we found the vegetation considerably changed.

These remarks apply to the Mau south of the railway, which, though it naturally does not constitute a geographical boundary, yet follows a valley which roughly divides the part of the Mau which slopes down into Lumbwa from that which is continued to the north in the Nandi escarpment and the Uasin Gishu plateau.   This part of the range is much better known than the south, as the old caravan road to Uganda passed up the Molo, to the Ravine Station, about twenty miles to the north of the line, and thence through Nandi to Mumias. The present railway mounts the sides of the ridge near the river Njoro.   This district is thought by many persons to be the finest part of East Africa.   In its general features it resembles the belt of forest opening on the plains near Nairobi, which I have described above, but is on a grander scale. Lord Delamere has a large estate on the northern side of

the line, and several smaller holdings have been taken up
along the rivers Njoro and Molo.

The country to the north of the line resembles that to
the south in its essential features, but is rather more thickly
wooded, and perhaps for that reason damper. A road leads
from Londiani station to the Ravine, a truly beautiful spot,
but somewhat chilly to those accustomed to the tropics, and,
though it is almost exactly on the equator, much resembling
Scotland. The station is built on a small hill, and the name
of Ravine is derived from a curious fissure in the ground not
far off, which is apparently the result of volcanic disturbance.
Behind the Ravine is a great mass of mountains which
on the north-east sends out a range known as the Kamasia
escarpment and forming the edge of the Rift Valley, while
the more westerly part is properly called the Mau. The river
Tigrish runs from near the Ravine down to Lake Baringo.
Both in this river and the Njoro are found a considerable
number of opals, but unfortunately small and of little value.
To the north-west lies a wooded region bearing what ought
to prove good timber. It consists of a series of ridges and
valleys, the latter generally becoming swamps in wet weather.
The country is, however, not at all unhealthy, owing no doubt
to its elevation of from 7000–9000 feet. A journey of four
or five days brings one to the Uasin Gishu plateau,[1] which
is the chief physical feature in the north-west of the
Protectorate.

It is a vast open plain of grass, fringed on all sides with
trees. On the north it stretches towards Karamojo and
the little-known confines of Lake Rudolf. On the west it
descends to Mumias and the Kavirondo country by the
Kabras escarpment, while the escarpments known as Nandi

---

[1] The name is spelt in several ways, but as the plateau has attracted attention,
even in East Africa, only recently, there is no question of any orthography being
consecrated by usage, and the correct one may as well be employed. According
to Mr. Hollis ("The Masai," Clarendon Press, 1905, p. 259), the name means
"striped cattle," and should be spelt as above, an initial l, representing the article,
being omitted.

RUINS OF ANCIENT STONE KRAALS ON THE UASIN GISHU.

A BAMBOO FOREST IN KIKUYU.

and Elgeyo limit it abruptly on the south and east. To the west lies the somewhat flat but still imposing mass of Elgon, and to the north is seen a large mountain whose name is generally written Chibcharagnan, but which was called Kyap-kerangain by the natives whom I interrogated—probably a mere difference of dialect, Smaller elevations are the Karuna, Ossagati, and Ogwalal hills, all lying towards the north, and not interfering with the general character of the vast open plain, in which the only eminence is the Sirgoit Rock, about the middle of the eastern side. This mass of stone is about six miles from the Elgeyo escarpment, and really consists of four rocks, of which the largest, called Essirgoit, dwarfs the others, which are known to the Masai as Is-surutia, or ear-rings, a not very intelligible comparison to a European perhaps, but easily explained if one re-members the Masai habit of wearing a large round stone in the split lobe of the ear. There are several rivers, and no lack of water.

This plateau is the locality on which it has been pro-posed to locate a Jewish settlement. It is at present quite uninhabited, though traces of a former population are found in the ruins of stone kraals called Mokwan, which are said to have been built by a race called Sirikwa, who were driven out by the Masai. Many of the tribes on the Nile, such as the Madi and Bari, build huts which have the lower portion made of stone and the upper of some vegetable material; and perhaps the use of stone, otherwise so rare in East Africa, indicates a connection between the builders of the Mokwan and these tribes. The construction of the kraals, however, has not any resemblance of detail with the Nilotic huts. They consist of walls sometimes as much as five or six feet high, formed of stones quarried from the outcrops of rock on the plain, and laid one on the other without mortar. The walls enclose a square or oblong space, which was probably used for herding cattle, and the human part of the dwelling is represented by the bastions at the corners.

The Uasin Gishu Masai were exterminated from the plateau in consequence of tribal wars. Many accounts are given of these events, from which I select the following as the most detailed and plausible, though I am unable to vouch for its historical accuracy. A long time ago, when the old men of the present generation were boys (that is, probably forty or fifty years ago) the Uasin Gishu Masai went and fought the Masai of Naivasha. They defeated and expelled the latter, and the warriors remained at Naivasha, leaving the old men and women on the plateau. The men of Naivasha then went to the Masai of Kilima-Njaro, made an alliance with them, and together fell on the intruders at Naivasha, whom they dispersed to all quarters. Then the Nandi, hearing that the Uasin Gishu warriors were killed or scattered, fell upon the old men and women who had been left on the plateau, and exterminated them. This story explains how it is that small bodies of Uasin Gishu are found scattered in many places, e.g. Lumbwa and Nandi.

The southern edge of the plateau is wooded and known as Nandi. It is fairly thickly inhabited by a tribe of the same name, closely akin to the Lumbwa. I am afraid that the reader will weary of my recurring mention of fertile country and magnificent views; but such things are at least not monotonous in actual life, whatever they may be in literature, and one can stand a good deal of them. The praises of Nandi have been worthily sung by Sir H. Johnston, and I will only say that I agree with his estimate of this region as the most beautiful part of the Protectorate. The rolling downs, rushing brooks, the many trees and flowers, not forgetting cultivation and kitchen gardens, give one a sense of homely, comfortable, English summer-day beauty, while the spice of the magnificent is supplied every now and then by some gap which gives a peep over the Nandi escarpment into one of those spacious, airy views to which I have so often alluded—the black mountain masses of Kamalilo on the left, beneath them the low valley of the

Nyando, traversed by the railway, and far beyond it the green and mauve hills of Lumbwa.

But I must not leave this part of the Protectorate without mentioning the most surprising and magnificent of all views in East Africa, namely that from the Elgeyo escarpment (the eastern edge of the Uasin Gishu plateau) looking west over the Kerio Valley to the Kamasia Hills. My introduction to this splendid sight was most dramatic. When near the Sirgoit Rock we were told that we might see the escarpment, if we would make a short diversion to the right. This we proceeded to do, and, leaving our porters on the plain, began a rather difficult journey through swamps and a thick forest, where the greatest circumspection had to be used not to fall into the elephant pits which the natives of Elgeyo had made from time to time in the path. An elephant pit generally consists of a deep cutting, rather wide at the top but covered over and becoming narrower at the bottom, so that the unfortunate creature's legs get jammed when he falls in. After an hour spent in avoiding these perils, and climbing over or crawling under the fallen trees which often obstructed the route, we began to think we had lost our way, when suddenly we emerged, without the least notion of what we were going to see, from the dark twilight of the wood on to a grassy, sunny ledge looking over a valley perhaps twenty miles broad and five thousand feet deep. Opposite in the east stood the Kamasia escarpment, To the south a vast amphitheatre of rocks shut in the valley, and presumably divided it from the country north of the Ravine station. At the bottom we could see as in a map the Kamenarok Lake, and trace the course of the Kerio River flowing north on its way to Lake Rudolf and disappearing in the haze of dim, dreamlike plains. Immediately below us, on the sides of the Elgeyo escarpment, stood out green ledges or shelves, on which were native villages and cultivated fields, while in other places the precipice was carved into fantastic pinnacles like the roof of some Gothic cathedral.

Being open only to the north, and with difficulty accessible from the other three sides, this valley is little known. The inhabitants are tribes called Elgeyo, Muteyo, Margweti, and further north, Japtulel (or Ch'aptilel), who appear to practise irrigation and have a fair amount of cultivation.

NOTE.—Since writing this chapter I have received an interesting pamphlet published at Johannesburg, and bearing the title "A Report on the Pastoral and Agricultural Capabilities of the East Africa Protectorate," by John C. Bailie, T. C. Hinds, and F. R. N. Findlay. These gentlemen, who have formed a favourable opinion of the Protectorate, have selected a block of land on the Molo, Sigiri, Rangai, Alabunyata, and Larashat rivers, apparently just to the north of Menengai. Their choice is interesting, for it shows that valuable land may be found in districts like the northern part of the Rift Valley which have hitherto not been thought promising.

By the kindness of Mr. Hinde, H.M.'s Sub-Commissioner of the Kenya province, I am enabled to reproduce a sketch map made by him, and giving details respecting the natural features and tribes of the country round Mount Kenya, which I believe are not to be found on any map yet published.

CHAPTER VI

THE NATIVES OF EAST AFRICA

GENERAL

IT is perhaps rash to make any statements about East Africans in general. The large, popular divisions of mankind are not really homogeneous, and much error results from generalisation which assumes that they are so. A terrible amount of nonsense, for instance, is written and talked about Orientals, on the assumption that Turks, Hindus, and Chinese are all much the same. But, on the other hand, the inhabitants of a homogeneous area undoubtedly come under various common influences which develop common characteristics, however great the original difference in languages, race, and customs may be. In one sense Eastern Africa is not at all a homogeneous or uniform area. It exhibits, as I have explained elsewhere, great diversities of scenery, products, and climate. Still, the climate is such that mankind can go naked practically in all districts; the whole country is isolated from the rest of the world; the superior races, by sending offshoots such as the Somalis, may have influenced the languages and the physical type, but until the advent of Europeans the ordinary mechanical arts of civilisation were unknown; man was everywhere dwarfed by nature. In speaking of African natives in this chapter, I mean the natives of East Africa, excluding for most purposes such obvious immigrants as the Arabs and Somalis. I have not had an opportunity of visiting West or South Africa, but from what I have seen of negroes in the West Indies and the southern States of America, I should imagine that, except in the north of the Continent, African nature is much the same everywhere. It does not appear to me to be proved that there is any considerable difference between pure negroes and the Bantu races, as some authorities assert.

Most observers have remarked that quick excitability is the chief mental characteristic of Africans. They are dominated by the transient emotion or impulse of the moment, and neither remember what has preceded, nor look forward to what is likely to follow. On the whole, this is a happy and cheerful cast of mind; the African suffers little from the pangs of remorse or apprehension, and is always ready to be pleased by any agreeable trifle. The disadvantage of such a disposition lies in the negative side, that it is incapable of self-restraint, foresight, and fixed purpose or organisation. A typical African action is that of the caravan porter, who, after serving for weeks, perhaps months, and carrying laboriously a heavy load, deserts a day before he reaches home, regardless of the fact that he forfeits all his wages to gain twenty-four hours, whereas he would probably have worked an extra week without grumbling. The African does not care to be rich, or at any rate will not take the trouble to become so. If he is a chief, and his position allows it, he will accumulate wives and cattle; but the example of Arabs and Europeans has not inspired him with any desire to acquire money and property. This, I fear, can hardly be attributed to Arcadian simplicity, uncorrupted by the lust of wealth. The African is greedy and covetous enough, but he is too indolent in his ways, and too disconnected in his ideas, to make any attempt to better himself, or to undertake any labour which does not produce a speedy and visible result. His mind is far nearer to the animal world than is that of the European or Asiatic, and exhibits something of the animal's placidity and want of desire to rise beyond the stage he has reached.

Also in respect to decency—in the wide sense of the word —he seems to stand on a lower level than most races. This is particularly noticeable in the disposal of the dead, who in nearly all East African tribes are simply thrown into the jungle for the hyenas to eat.[1]   It is true that highly civilised races, such as the Parsis, have funeral rites which strike us as horrible, and that other nations might object to our own method of burial.   But all these proceedings are accompanied by ceremonies which show a desire to express respect and honour to the dead, whereas the East African throws his parent or child away without any sign of reverence or affection.   This is the more remarkable, because savages in other parts of the world have elaborate funeral rites which, however singular they may be, at least show a solicitude for the departed.   Similarly age, as such, inspires but little respect. Family affection is fairly strong, and children will look after their own parents, but alas for the old people, particularly widows, who have not got relatives to care for them.   Popular speech and proverbs testify to their helpless condition,

The want of decency, in the narrower sense of what we consider adequate clothing, is very remarkable.   Natives on the coast, who have any pretensions to be Mohammedans, of course, observe strict propriety in this respect, and some unknown influence introduced similar ideas into Uganda, which is the more remarkable as most of the neighbouring tribes are conspicuously nude.   But with these two exceptions, the native races of East Africa show an entire absence of the feelings which lead the European and Asiatic to cover their bodies.   The motive may, perhaps, not be quite the same in all cases.   The Masai warrior may have a touch of the sentiment of the Greek athlete, and pride in a well-developed form, but most natives appear to be simply in the state of Adam and Eve before the Fall, which is also that of the animals, and to have no idea of indecency.   It is noticeable that even the races who are more or less clothed, such as the Wakamba, wear their garments so carelessly that they by no means fulfil our ideas of propriety.   As a rule this nudity is confined to

---

[1] It is possible that this practice may be a remnant of unwillingness to defile the earth by burying a corpse in it, but inquiry made with the object of discovering such beliefs has hitherto led to no result.

the men, but in Kavirondo it extends to both sexes.   One would imagine that, if anything is primitive, this strange custom must be so, as it is difficult to imagine that women left off clothes.   On the other hand, neither the Bantu nor the Nilotic Kavirondo are particularly low in the scale of civilisation.

Another characteristic of most natives, which probably goes back to the infancy of the human race, is that they are more or less nomadic.   This is not only the case with the pastoral tribes, such as the Masai, but also with those who practise agriculture, such as the people of Kikuyu.   These have their plantations and villages, but they remain only a few years on one spot, and then wander on to another.   In case of want of rain, the scanty population moves to the banks of the nearest perennial water, much like the zebras and antelopes.   Even in Kavirondo, where there are settle-ments consisting of solid houses and surrounded by mud walls, the number of deserted villages testifies to the migrations of the inhabitants.   In spite of this mobility, most tribes are very careful how they go out of their own district, which is the only place where they feel safe.   I have known porters in Nandi (in the districts of Kakamega and Tiriki) march with loads for a whole day, and at the end return home at once rather than spend a night in a country which they did not know.   Most natives are timid and suspicious until they have learned to know a stranger, and if one considers the prevalence of raiding and the slave trade in the past, one can hardly be surprised.

It is not wonderful that natives, with the characteristics described, should have little in the way of social or political organisation.   For most tribes the family is the unit: a man owns a certain number of women and children, and that is all. The Bantu tribes have progressed very little beyond this con-dition.   There are rich and influential elders, but rarely, except in Kikuyu, a chief who can command obedience from any considerable body of people.   The Masai, and some of the other Nilotic tribes, have a military organisation based on a warrior caste; but though discipline necessitates the existence of chiefs, the chief does not appear to occupy a very exalted or enviable position, as he is obliged to retire from the ranks of the warriors and become an elder; nor does he appear to have much power of controlling or restraining the warriors, although he is obeyed as to the arrangement of expeditions.

More important than the chief is the medicine-man—to borrow a term from America which is not altogether satisfactory. This personage plays a considerable part in many of the tribes, particularly the Masai and Nandi, and appears to represent the highest type of intelligence which they attain. He is in communication with supernatural powers—though he has not anything so personal as a familiar spirit—and is implicitly obeyed on account of the evil as well as the good he can do. But though he attains to a greater position than any chief, it would seem that east of Lake Victoria there is nothing that can be called a tribal ruler or sultan, except among the Somalis, and even there the sultan's authority is not great. In Uganda and Unyoro, men like Mtesa and Kabarega deliberately ruled over kingdoms of which they were the heads, with lower chiefs beneath them, and made conquests with the definite idea of extending their authority. But even among the Masai ambition never took this form. They raided in order to carry off property, and though they certainly considered themselves superior to all other races, and took tribute from travellers, they never made the next step in political development—that of forming an empire of tributaries. Similarly the medicine-men, though their influence would probably enable them to assume a position like that of an Asiatic sultan, make no attempt at anything like continuous government. They receive a great many presents, and from time to time offer advice, which is obeyed—that is all.

This absence of political development is accompanied by a correspondingly rudimentary stage of religious ideas. There is nothing in any tribe which can be called a mythology or cultus. It is true that it is dangerous to argue that savage races have no religious ideas or ceremonies because foreigners notice none. In many cases secrecy may be a form of religious respect. But I think we now know sufficient of the East African races to say that they none of them possess any religious system comparable in development to the Juju of West Africa. Another indication of deficiency of religious feeling is the little progress made by Mohammedanism. The simplicity and directness of this form of theism make it attractive to most savage races who have any conception of a personal God, and its success in northern and western Africa has been remarkable. In East Africa it has never made any progress at all except on the coast, and even there the strictly religious side of its teaching seems to have remained without effect. The ordinary native who calls himself a Mohammedan regards himself as socially superior to others, and shows great anxiety in public about such matters as touching dogs or eating the meat of animals which have not been properly killed; but he rarely prays, and shows no trace of that fierce devotion and personal enthusiasm for Allah which is so common elsewhere, nor is there anything analogous to the practices of the dancing and howling dervishes.

The most definite religious beliefs seem to prevail among the Masai, who pray to God (Eng-aï) for children, rain, and victory, and believe in two deities, one black and benevolent, the other red and cruel, but fortunately also distant. Though their religious ceremonies seem deficient in order and ritual, they are remarkable as including prayers, addressed to a personal deity who takes an interest in the welfare of the tribe. The Bantu Kavirondo are also said to worship two deities, one good and the other bad, and to sacrifice animals to the former. The Nandi, Muteyo, and Kamasia are also said to pray to God, in some cases every day, and the same will probably be found true of other tribes related to them. It is noticeable that in all the cases mentioned the prayers are addressed to a benevolent deity. The idea that the world is ruled by a power who will do harm unless he is propitiated seems to be unknown, and no doubt its absence goes far to explain the simplicity of worship. The Masai (and probably the allied tribes) appear to believe that most people " die like cattle." Medicine-men and influential persons, however, are buried with more ceremony than others, and their souls are said to pass into snakes. Ancestor worship, even in a rudimentary form, is not recorded among these tribes. It seems, however, to have played a considerable part in the religions of the Baganda and their kindred, which have been largely superseded by Christianity, but were, as might be expected, more elaborate than any system found to the east of Lake Victoria.

Practically nothing is known of the religious ideas of the Bantu tribes in the East Africa Protectorate, but it seems clear that they play little part in their lives. In Kikuyu and Ukamba the Masai word for God, Ngai (Eng-aï), is used. It would appear that the Bantu equivalent, Mulungu, which is also widely used, originally meant ghosts, and that traces of ancestral worship are found among most of the Bantu tribes. Krapf says that the Wanyika laughed at the idea of God, but believed that the spirits of the dead (koma) haunt certain places and appear to the living. Burial is practised, but not regularly, bodies being often thrown to the hyenas; but when a corpse is buried offerings of food are sometimes placed on the grave. Krapf records vague ideas of immortality and also of metempsychosis. A belief in devils which can possess people (pepo) and in tree-spirits is also widespread. In Kikuyu there are sacred trees in every district, which are never injured, and under which goats are occasionally killed. These fragmentary and often inconsistent ideas possibly represent a degradation and distortion of some older inherited or borrowed system. Among the Wanyika of the coast and the Wapokomo of the Tana River there are secret societies, to which the chiefs belong, and which may have a quasi-religious

G

side, but the main object appears to be to secure obedience to the society's orders by spreading the idea that it can inflict death and misfortune, and the probability of anything like a real secret cultus has not been shown.   Most of the Bantu tribes appear to have a belief in witchcraft and witch-doctors. The latter (called Waganga) are not quite the same as the Laibons of the Masai, Nandi, Lumbwa, &c.   The Laibon can predict and to a certain extent influence the course of future events, and is much respected in consequence.   The witch-doctor's chief business is to detect persons, generally women, who are supposed to mysteriously cause the illness or other disasters of their neighbours.   Neither appear in the character of priests or the servants of a god—a vocation which is entirely unknown in East Africa.

Perhaps the most remarkable, as it is certainly the saddest, characteristic of the African races is the burden of suffering which they have borne.   It is far greater than that which has fallen to the lot of other uncivilised people, such as the aborigines of America or Australia.   Yet the African races, as a rule, are neither physically weak nor cruel.   But they are in the immediate neighbourhood of much stronger races, who long regarded them as the legitimate victims of the slave trade: they live in a country exposed to sudden natural visitations, but are not sufficiently civilised to prevent or in any way mitigate floods, epidemics, or droughts; their chief idea of activity is to wage wars in which mere plunder and destruction rather than conquest are the object, and there has rarely been an African potentate who did not wallow in blood. This is particularly remarkable in Uganda, where the continual massacres and wholesale mutilations ordered by Mtesa and Mwanga do not seem explicable by political necessity or any clear religious motive such as prompted the human sacrifices of the West Coast.   Hence it is that such fragments of native history as we get are chiefly the record of disasters—how this tribe was annihilated, why this district is uninhabited; this was the year of the great famine, that of the cattle plague; in a third, half the population died of smallpox or of sleeping sickness.

Against this catalogue of woes must be set the African's great insensibility, which is somehow compatible with quick excitability. There is a story that one of the early explorers who suspected a guide of treachery, threatened him with death, and in order to strike terror into him more effectively, had the knife sharpened and preparations for execution made before his face. The man, instead of being horror-struck, simply went to sleep. Without this sort of temper the African race could never have endured the killing and torturing which have fallen to their lot: on the other hand, indifference to one's own future sufferings is closely connected with indifference to the sufferings of other people.

That the African races will greatly improve under a civilised and beneficent rule, offering them adequate protection against man and nature, is clear; but it is not so clear what degree of development we may expect. The example of America shows that they have great limitations. In the northern States the negroes, though they speak the same language and enjoy the same political rights as white men, though they are the objects of no social or commercial persecntion, still manifestly remain on a lower plane than the whites, not only in such matters as art, science, and literature, but in business. Their powers of organisation, management, and controlling other men seem too deficient to allow them to conduct any but the simplest concerns. They can manage a shop, but not a bank. The most effective talent which they possess is eloquence: they make good preachers, and, I believe, good barristers. This reminds us of the East African's fondness for words. The simplest business transaction with native chiefs necessitates discussions lasting for hours and perhaps days.

Of the natives of eastern Africa the Baganda are incomparably the most intelligent and progressive. If they continue to advance at their present rate, they will rival the

Japanese in their power of assimilating European culture, and become a factor of the highest importance in the future history of the African continent. But it may prove that what happens in the individual will also happen in the race : that as the African child, after showing great quickness and power to learn, suddenly reaches a limit where development ceases and appetite seems to overwhelm the nascent intellect, so that the Baganda will find themselves unable to endure the strain of continual progress, and will stop or recede. Some years must elapse before events supply the answer to these questions. Though no other race shows the same desire for education as the Baganda, it must, I think, be admitted that all are, as a rule, surprisingly friendly and willing to learn. If one remembers that to kill a man of another tribe is universally regarded as a noble and glorious action, the wonder is not that some white men have been killed, but that the number of the victims has been so small. Also such incidents have nearly always taken place in the early stages of our relations. As soon as a tribe have a real knowledge of Europeans, they not only admit our superiority, but admit it in the friendliest way and without any sign of a grudge.

Except near the coast, few tribes have been long enough under European influence to receive anything which can be called an education ; but Swahilis who have been brought up in the mission schools make excellent clerks, and there are interesting cases of Masai from the Kilima-Njaro district, who have learnt to write in the schools at Taveta, corresponding with friends in their own language. The natives of Kikuyu and Ukamba are not only willing to cultivate for Europeans, but also do the greater part of the manual labour in the workshops of the Uganda Railway. The Masai have perhaps more intelligence than any other tribe, but their unfortunate prejudice against sedentary occupations retards their progress. They make good soldiers and policemen, and likewise act as stokers on the Uganda Railway, an employment which they do not consider as derogatory to a warrior, possibly as being analogous to tending cattle. Of the Nandi, Lumbwa, Suk, and Turkana, it is too early to say anything yet. The Kavirondo are willing to learn, and it was noticed that a couple of years ago they watched the proceedings of Indian agriculturists, and intelligently imitated their methods of irrigation. The least promising tribes seem to be those near the coast and on the Tana River. They have been in touch with Europeans and missionaries longer than any others, and show very little result.

The absence of any feeling for art in the African is remarkable. Its completeness will be realised by any one who tries to collect interesting or curious objects in East Africa. It will be found that anything ornamental is far harder to obtain than among such races as the South Sea Islanders or North American Indians. Carving is almost unknown, and what little there is in wood or ivory is executed in Zanzibar or on the coast, under Arab or Indian influence. Even in Uganda, where the standard of intelligence is so high, and where the power of the kings offered an opportunity for pageantry and magnificence, there is no attempt at beauty or ornamentation in architecture or costume, nor do even the rudiments of painting and sculpture exist. It is true that both nations and individuals who were deficient in artistic sense have done great things in the world; but the deficiency has generally been accompanied (and perhaps to some extent caused) by great energy in other directions. But in races which, like the Africans, have a tendency to listlessness, the absence of this feeling is not an encouraging sign.

(The relations between Europeans and Africans present in their extreme form the difficulties which may arise from the contact of advanced and backward races, and they are likely to form, in America even more than in Africa, one of hardest problems of this century. The case differs from other instances of such contact in two most important points :

the two races are too far apart to produce a successful hybrid, and the inferior race shows no sign of disappearing before its superiors. Such conditions occur elsewhere between races who are more or less on the same footing, as, for instance, Europeans and Chinese, but they are probably not found united in any other case where one race is so indisputably inferior. In Australia, New Zealand, and Tasmania the native race tends to disappear, or has disappeared altogether. In the Spanish and Portuguese parts of America a hybrid race has been formed. In North America the Indian tends to disappear, but also to some extent mingles with the whites, and a strain of Indian blood is not, like negro blood, regarded as a disgrace. Nearly all the races of modern Europe and Asia are the result of fusions between conquerors and con- quered, and the weaker elements have been eliminated by slaughter or breeding, or by both combined. But the African has hitherto shown no sign, either in his own continent or in America, of yielding to either process.

One result of this long contact without fusion is to offer the most remarkable contrasts in the methods which the superior race has felt justified in using at different times. After a period, when Africans were treated almost like beasts, and were certainly captured and shipped with less care than would now be bestowed on a consignment of valuable animals, came another period when they were suddenly declared to be the brethren and equals of the white man, and were given the same political privileges. There can be little doubt that the reaction erred by excess, and that the American negroes are not fit for the suffrage or for exercising the public offices to which they are theoretically eligible. This would seem to be the opinion of so liberal-minded and dispassionate a judge as Mr. Bryce.[1] In practice government in the southern States is only carried on by rendering the Constitution a dead letter, and by using various devices to prevent the negroes from

[1] "The Relations of the Advanced and Backward Races of Mankind."— *Romanes Lceture*, 1902.

exercising the influence to which their numbers entitle them. If they do exercise it, a revolt among the white population is the result. In 1898 a political combination was made in North Carolina, by which, in order to secure the negro vote, a certain number of judicial and municipal offices were distributed among negroes, with the result that in a few months all parties united to turn them out by force and to pass a law rendering such occurrences impossible in future.

On the other hand, in our West African Colonies negroes fill satisfactorily high judicial and administrative posts. But in these colonies the white population is small and largely composed of officials, so that, though negroes may hold high office, they exercise authority mainly over other negroes, and the general system of which they form part is subject to a firm European direction and control.

In considering the relations which should prevail between the two races, the main point to be observed is their relative numbers. In this respect our East African territories show great differences. The Kingdom of Uganda—and one may say the Uganda Protectorate as a whole—has a sufficient and fairly thick population. Also the climate of the greater part is not such as to attract Europeans. It is therefore adapted to be a black man's country, like our West African Colonies. But in the East Africa Protectorate the case is different. The native population is very small; only two districts (Kavirondo and Kikuyu) can be said to be thickly populated; large areas are uninhabited, and these areas, with others, are climatically and otherwise suited to European colonisation.

In other words, the interior of the Protectorate is a white man's country. This being so, I think it is mere hypocrisy not to admit that white interests must be paramount, and that the main object of our policy and legislation should be to found a white colony. To quote from Mr. Bryce's Romanes Lecture, to which I have already referred, "the matter ought to be regarded from the side neither of the white nor the black, but of the future of mankind at large." From that point of view,

those who believe that the qualities, ideals, and institutions of
Europeans are superior to those of African natives, can hardly
doubt that the establishment of a European colony in East
Africa will mark an epoch in the history of humanity, inasmuch
as it opens up to European civilisation a new and almost
unknown section of the world which has hitherto been a prey
to barbarism.

(To say that European interests must be paramount does
not mean that any violence or hostility should be shown to
natives; but it does mean that we must assist Europeans to
develop the fine land which the Protectorate contains, and
must not allow nomadic tribes to monopolise huge areas of
which they can make no real use.) (We must, of course, secure
for natives the possession of the space which they require, but
their present wasteful methods of abandoning land after they
have cultivated it for a few years, and moving on to another
place, cannot be allowed to continue. The district where the
land question is likely to present real difficulties is Kikuyu, as
here we have the combination of a climate and country suitable
to Europeans and a numerous native population. In other
districts I see no reason to apprehend difficulties, as either the
native population is very scanty or else the climate is unsuited
to Europeans, as in Kavirondo. (No one can doubt that the
rich and exceptionally fertile district of Kikuyu is destined to
be one of the chief centres of European cultivation, and the
process of settlement is facilitated by the fact that there are
gaps where there is no native population, though the land does
not seem inferior. The natives are willing to labour, and the
best solution would be for their villages to remain on the
estates of Europeans in order to supply workmen, the villages
and a sufficient amount of land round them being the property
of the natives and excluded from the area of the European's
property. In cases where this is not possible, and the natives
wish to move, they should be allowed to migrate to lands
reserved for their use, of which the Government should keep
a sufficient quantity in its own hands.

With regard to the Masai, I believe that it has now (October 1904) been decided to remove them from the neighbourhood of the railway (Naivasha and Nakuru), and place them in two reserves, one on Laikipia and one to the south of the Kedong.[1] This policy, if correctly stated, is far superior to that favoured by the Foreign Office at the beginning of the year, when it was proposed to make all the land in the Rift Valley along the railway a native reserve in which Europeans should not be allowed to settle—a proposal which was politically and economically disastrous and would have proved absolutely impracticable, for no one can doubt that it would have ultimately become impossible to exclude Europeans from the neighbourhood of the railway.

But though I have no objection to the removal of the Masai from the neighbourhood of the line, I think that great caution should be used in creating reserves, if by reserve is meant a district in which natives are left to themselves and allowed to do what they like. The most candid definition of a reserve which I know occurs in Mr. E. N. Buxton's "Two African Trips," page 40, where he says: "We have for good or evil interfered with the conditions established by centuries of intertribal war. I must confess to a hankering for some corner of the world where the struggle for existence may go on without let or hindrance from paternal government. We are establishing reserves in which all kinds of wild beasts are to be left to fight it out. Can we not extend such a measure to some of the human species to this extent that they shall govern themselves and the strongest prevail?" With this view of our duties and proper policy towards natives I entirely disagree. It utterly ignores the difference between mankind and beasts—a difference which, I admit, is minimised in Africa, but which still exists, and which shows itself, among other ways, in the fact that while most animals are incapable of develop-

---

[1] According to later information, the idea of the southern reserve has been abandoned, but the formation of the northern one is still under consideration.

ment or improvement, and cannot change their mode of life, mankind is almost without exception capable of such change and improvement. To wish to preserve intertribal war, or the military system of the Masai with its attendant immorality, appears to me to be little better than a proposal to protect cannibalism and human sacrifice. The existence of such practices is an interesting fact: one may even be glad if anthropologists have had an opportunity of accurately recording the circumstances in which they occur, but the most fervid votary of science would hardly propose to encourage or even permit their exercise.

(The only hope for the continued existence of these nomadic warlike tribes is that they should settle down and adopt fixed habitations and a peaceful occupation. To do all we can to bring about this result seems to me one of the elementary duties of religion as well as of good administration, and the fact that the change from a nomadic to an agricultural life has constantly occurred in Africa, and is occurring before our eyes, is distinctly encouraging.) In the neighbourhood of Nairobi there are Masai who live in villages and cultivate plantations. Reserves may sometimes be advisable in dealing with very strong native races, or, in the contrary case, where it is desired to prevent the extinction of a vanishing race; but in the case of races which are neither dangerous nor on the point of disappearing, I think that the sentiment which wishes to isolate them and arrest their possible improvement is false.

A race is not an entity like an individual; it is not even comparable to a species among animals. In the vast majority of cases, it is a hybrid and in a process of slow change. I can see no reason why we should attempt to stop this process of blending, which is nature's law. The Kikuyu, who are one of the most active and intelligent among the East African tribes, are almost certainly a comparatively recent hybrid between the Masai and a Bantu stock, and there is no reason why such hybrids should not continue to be formed in future, to the great advantage of the country.   Fusion between Europeans and negroes is of course out of the question ; but it is to be regretted that the Arabs have not introduced more of their blood into the country, as the hybrid between them and the negro (the Swahili) has many excellent qualities. There must be growing up at this moment a considerable number of children born of Indian fathers and African mothers, but, as far as I know, none are yet adult, and there are no data for saying whether the blend is satisfactory or not.   But among the Africans themselves it appears to me sound policy to encourage the intermingling of different tribes and the formation of a settled and peaceable population.

Excluding Europeans and Indians, the inhabitants of the East Africa Protectorate seem at the present day to fall into four principal classes—

(1) The Arabs and the hybrid race which they have formed with Africans, and which is known as Swahili or coast-folk.

(2) Tribes who, for want of a better name, must be called Hamitic, including the Somalis, the Gallas, the Rendile, and the Borans.   The aristocracy in Uganda were probably derived from an allied race.

(3) The Bantu - speaking population, comprising the Wanyika, the Wakamba, the inhabitants of Kikuyu, of the slopes of Mount Kenya, and of North Kavirondo, as well as tribes in the neighbourhood of Mount Elgon.   Linguistically the Swahilis belong to this division.

(4) The Nilotic races, comprising the Masai, the Nandi, the Lumbwa, the Suk, the Turkana, and the Ja-luo, or southern Kavirondo.

Perhaps one should add as a fifth class the hunting tribes known as Anderobo, Wanderobo, Dorobo or Torobo, found on the Mau and Settima and in the Rift Valley.   Perhaps, too, these may have affinities with the somewhat similar tribes in Tanaland known as Wasania and Waboni.   They all agree in living by hunting and in standing in some vague servile or dependent relation to a superior tribe, the Masai or Somali. Also they are sometimes, but by no means always, of dwarfish stature, and they may be allied to the pygmies of the Congo forest, and represent a hybrid between early unknown invaders and an aboriginal dwarf race. But at the present day even the Wanderobo do not represent one physical type, and it seems doubtful if they have one distinct language. The absence of such a language, however, would by no means be an argument against their relationship with the pygmies, as these latter also are said to have no language of their own, but to speak corrupt forms of the surrounding dialects.

Except for the coast districts, we have really no materials for the history of East Africa, and even there the record is brief, and extends back for only a few hundred years. It is pretty clear, however, that the present population, as in most other countries, is the result of a series of invasions, whose general direction has been, also as in other countries, from north to south. This is obvious in the case of the Arabs, and almost equally certain for the Gallas and Somalis. Also the Wanyika, who now inhabit the immediate hinterland of the coast from Melindi to Mombasa and Vanga, have a tradition that they came from the country behind Port Durnford. On the other hand, we hear that at the end of the sixteenth century the Zimbas came up from the country south of the Zambesi, and reached at least as far north as Mombasa. Professor Gregory thinks that the Wakamba may have come from the south, as there is a district called Ukamba to the east of Lake Tanganyika.

In the case of the Masai and allied tribes, although we have no historical record, the evidence of language and customs connects them decisively with the tribes on the Nile, such as the Dinka, Bari, and Latuka ; and their present distribution in the Protectorate is quite intelligible as the result of a south-easterly migration from the Nile basin. The Lumbwa tribe appear to have moved southwards from the higher plateaus to their present home within the memory of their traditions.

There remains the Bantu element. This term, as is well known, is applied to speech, not physical characters, and denotes the speakers of that great family of African languages which dominates the continent south of a line drawn roughly from the Cameroons along the Uelle to the north end of Lake Albert. It is a most remarkable fact that, whereas the languages spoken north of this line are very diverse and belong to many different families, there is south of it, if we exclude the tongues of the Hottentots and Bushmen, but one linguistic family. On the eastern side the southern incursions of Somalis and Masai have pushed the limits of the exclusive Bantu region a little farther to the south, but it remains the dominant form of speech as far north as the Tana River. One of the most interesting points in its distribution, however, is that, according to Sir H. Johnston, the most archaic forms of the language are spoken about Mount Elgon, which certainly suggests a wide-spreading wave of southward invasion from this quarter. But such speculation is the merest guess-work. After making allowance for the Hamitic and Nilotic migrations, which we can more or less trace, the distribution of the remaining population must still be comparatively recent compared with the career of the human race in Africa, and of the older fights and unions we have no hint or vestige left. It is certain from Greek and Egyptian sources that long before our era there were pygmies in the equatorial regions; but it does not follow that they were the only or the original inhabitants, neither does there seem to be any certain evidence as to whether their peculiarities are primitive or due to degradation.

As a mere attempt to present hypotheses in a united and coherent form, the following epitome of native history in East Africa may be given. All that can be said for it is that it is one explanation of existing conditions, and that it does not conflict with any data at present known. On the other hand, it may easily be upset by the discovery of new facts or may remain for ever undemonstrable.

East Africa was inhabited (it is dangerous to say originally, and useless to give even approximate dates) by tribes in a low state of civilisation, who have left no trace of distinctive arts or customs. They may have been connected with the pygmies, but there is no proof of it, nor, if they were, of what was the other factor in the hybrid. Over them came a great wave of Bantu speech (accompanied, no doubt, by an infusion of new blood), which spread to the south of the continent, and perhaps originated somewhere to the north of Lake Victoria. The Bantu area thus created was invaded by Hamitic races or hybrids of Hamites with negroes. The Hamites remained at first in the north, but formed in the west, in the region of the Sobat, a mixed race of negro and Hamite blood, now represented on the Nile by the Dinka, Bari, and Latuka. This race had a tendency to south-easterly migrations. It probably began by advancing to Karamojo and the Uasin Gishu plateau, whence the bolder elements (the Masai) detached themselves as conquering hordes, perhaps only a few centuries ago, and made themselves masters of the whole country between the Mau, the Tana, and the sea, and at least as far south as Kilima-Njaro. They were too rapacious to found any sort of empire, but they profoundly influenced the Bantu races, such as the people of Kikuyu, Ukamba, and Taveta, and in fact all except those quite near the coast. The Suk, Turkana, Nandi, &c., are allied stocks. More distantly but still definitely allied, both physically and linguistically, are the tribes on the Nile near Lake Albert, such as the Acholi, who may perhaps have some West African elements in their composition, and who spread as far east as South Kavirondo.

The kingdom of Uganda was also invaded from the north at an unknown date by a tribe known as Bahima. As these invaders imported a certain amount of civilisation and political organisation, and as they appear to have been clothed, it is probable that they were not part of the Nilotic group mentioned above, but Gallas or some kindred tribe from the north-east.   The fact that there is now no trace of them in the regions through which they passed, on this hypothesis, in order to reach Uganda, suggests that they moved south-west before the Nilotic tribes moved south-east.

The Masai-Bantu countries to the east were invaded in historic times from the north by the Gallas and Somalis. The Gallas somewhat checked the Masai, but were themselves dispersed by the Somalis.   They have had little influence in the better-known parts of the Protectorate, but are probably an important factor in the central northern districts.

The whole of the coast has been subjected to a strong, continuous Arab influence, which formed the Swahili breed but did not penetrate inland.

CHAPTER VII

THE NATIVES OF EAST AFRICA

SWAHILIS, SOMALIS, AND BANTU-SPEAKING TRIBES

In a previous chapter on the Coast Lands I have spoken of the Arabs and the part they have played in East Africa, and no more need be said here about the pure breeds. One of the most important factors, however, in East Africa is the mixed breed known as Swahilis, or Coast-men (from Sawahil, the plural of the Arabic Sahil, shore), who inhabit the coast of the mainland as well as Zanzibar, Pemba, and the Comoro Islands. As a matter of fact, there are few pure Arabs now on the mainland, and the name has come to denote a caste rather than a race, and is used by every one who has any share of Arab blood. The Swahili is as a rule quite black, and, though a characteristic physiognomy is not wanting, differs from the up-country native chiefly in civilisation and intelligence,

The special profession of the Swahilis in the past was that of caravan porter. Until the construction of the Uganda Railway, the interior could be approached, whether for slave-trading or other purposes, only by caravans, often numbering many hundred men; and, as animal transport was practically non-existent, everything had to be carried on men's heads, or, if they preferred it, on their backs. It is perhaps character-istic of the African to regard the head as primarily an organ for bearing burdens, and not for exercising the nobler func-tions with which Europeans associate it. But, though the African headpiece is put to menial uses, it must be confessed that it performs them surprisingly well. The Swahili porter wraps round his head a red blanket until it forms a sort of pad or solid turban, and then puts lightly on it a box or other load weighing 60 pounds, and often much more, and carries it with uncomplaining ease for four or five hours. Similarly the Swahili women perform astonishing feats of balance, if not of strength. You may often see one take an ordinary European bottle, almost throw it on her head, and walk off as if it were in the most natural and safest position in the world. The career of porter has, however, its prizes, which rise far above the simple trade of fetching and carrying, and culminate in the proud office of headman, or neopara,[1] who in a large caravan requires all the talent of a general and an explorer.

But the construction of the Uganda Railway has ruined the porter's trade, for, though large caravans still are necessary up country, they hardly ever start from the coast, and of recent years several thousand Swahilis have consequently been out of work. They have little inclination for agriculture or cultivation of any kind, though it may be hoped that they will take to it eventually, but have a fair aptitude for the smaller forms of trade and make excellent domestic servants. They are also passable as boatboys, sailors, policemen, and soldiers; but their honesty is rarely above suspicion, and they certainly are not first-rate military material. They are, nevertheless, a race of vigour, and, I doubt not, with a future, though, as they are the result of a continued mingling of Arab blood with native elements, and pure Arabs are likely now to visit East Africa in decreasing numbers, it is hard to say what changes the type may undergo. They have some records of their past history and an Arab pride in genealogy. The Swahilis of Mombasa divide themselves into ten tribes, according to the towns from which they are supposed to have come: Mombasa (or Mvita), Mtwapa (or Mtwafi), Kilifi, Pate, Shaka, Faza, Akatwa (or Somali), Gunya (or Bajun), Junda (or Jomvu), Kilindini, Tangana, and Changamwe.

[1] No derivation is forthcoming for this word. An educated native once told me he thought the true form was " mnyapara."

H

The chief claim, however, of the Swahili to attention is the Swahili language, which may be described as a cosmopolitan form of Bantu. As the Bantu languages seem preeminent among African tongues for their powers of expansion and conquest, so is Swahili pre-eminent among its Bantu brethren, and considering the area over which it is spoken, or at least in which it is useful, it may claim to be one of the great languages of the world. It is the chief means of communication in both British and German East Africa, and from Natal to Aden and from Mombasa to the Congo some one can nearly always be found who understands it. It thrives on the Coast at the expense of Arabic, and except the older men, who have themselves come from Arabia, very few persons speak Arabic except for the pride of being able to say they can do so. Even the late Sultan of Zanzibar habitually spoke Swahili in private life. Compared with kindred languages, the pronunciation is simple and easy, as it avoids the difficult sounds both of Arabic and other Bantu languages. The accent is almost invariably on the penultimate, the form of the words clear and well-defined, and a foreigner's efforts are easily understood. This comparative simplicity is partly the cause and partly the result of the cosmopolitan character of Swahili, but how real the practical advantage is will be appreciated by any one who tries to hold a conversation first with Swahilis and then with the inhabitants of Uganda. The language of the latter is allied to Swahili, and grammatically much the same; but it has a varying accent, and the words are so run together and the vowels so constantly elided, that even familiar words are often difficult to recognise.[1] The result is that a stranger has extreme difficulty in understanding or making himself understood.

Most readers are probably aware that the chief principle which guides the formation of Bantu language is that words are divided into categories distinguished by certain prefixes, and that words which are related grammatically are marked with

[1] Pilkington, "Handbook of Luganda," p. 91.

A NATIVE OF KAVIRONDO.

MACHAKOS FORT.

the same prefix.   For instance: wa-zungu wa-le wa-nne [1][2][3] wa-linunua mi-avuli mi-kubwa mi-nne, vi-su vi-kubwa vi-nne [4][5][6][7][8][9][10] na ki-lemba ki-kubwa ki-moja, means: Those four Europeans [14][11][12][13][2][3][1] bought four big umbrellas, four big knives, and one big turban.[1] [4][7][6][5][10][9][8][14][13][12][11] It will be seen here that the words which agree together grammatically begin with the same prefix, and, so to speak, bear the same label or ticket.   *Wa* indicates human beings; *mi*, trees or similar objects (including umbrellas); while a large class of words denoting inanimate things begin with *ki* in the singular and *vi* in the plural.   Thus, in the above example, one knife would be *kisu kimoja*, and four turbans *vilemba vinne*.   Of course, the concord is not always as obvious as in the words cited, as the identity of the prefixes or tickets is not absolute, but the principle remains the same.   The beginner finds it rather difficult at first to get hold of the essential part of a word.   One is familiar with the idea that the end of a word can change, and that *bonus, bona, bonum* all mean " good "; but it seems more perplexing when the beginning changes, and the alternatives are words of such different appearance as *mwema, mema, chema, njema*, and *vema*—all meaning " good," whereas the common part, *ema*, is unmeaning Similarly, the possessive pronoun, *my*, can assume the forms *wangu, changu, yangu, zangu*, and *langu*.

When spoken or written with accuracy, Swahili is a terse and vigorous language, well adapted for simple statements and business transactions; but one may perhaps doubt if too great a strain is not put on its resources in its more modern developments, which are mostly due to missionary influence, and make one wonder, as one does in the case of Finnish and Turkish writers, who try to render German philosophy and French novels in their own tongues, whether the language is not being used for higher purposes than it was intended to

---

[1] The corresponding words in English and Swahili are marked with the same numeral.

serve. On the other hand, nothing can be more absurd than the idea of many ignorant Europeans, that missionary Swahili is too correct and artificial. It is true that there is a grammarless jargon, spoken by up-country natives and Europeans, which is understood by Swahilis just as we can understand pidgeon English; but the jargon is not used by Swahilis among themselves, nor will it go very far, even in simple business transactions.

I would, however, enter a protest against the use of Swahili grammatical forms in English; for instance, Kiswahili, as the name of the language. If I rightly understand the matter (and I have no claim to be an authority on Swahili) Kiswahili means, the Swahili style or language, or in the Swahili style or language. It is closely analogous to such a phrase as "po russki" (in the Russian style) in Russian. Now, it is perfectly natural to say in Russian, "govorit po russki"; but it would be perfectly absurd to say in English, "speak po russki," instead of "speak Russian"; and it seems to me almost equally unreasonable to say, "speak Kiswahili." Similarly, I think one should be as sparing as possible in the use of the Swahili prefixes—*U* to denote a country, and *Wa* to denote a tribe. Such words as Uganda, Ukamba, Wakamba cannot now be rejected; but I should avoid forms like Wanandi, Wamasai, Waswahili, and forms in *M* to denote the singular of the same words. To talk of an Mswahili[1] (sing.) and the Waswahili (plural), as many people do, is to import Swahili grammar into English, and as inappropriate as to speak of Italiano and Italiani, instead of Italian and Italians.

Besides the modern missionary literature, Swahili has produced a certain number of compositions written under Arab influence, but does not seem likely to develop in this direction.

---

[1] The accepted orthography of Swahili in the Roman character uses *M* to represent a syllable. This seems to me a mistake. One would suppose "mtu," man, to be a monosyllable. As a matter of fact it is not only a dissyllable, but the accent is on the first syllable, as if it were "*ŭ*mtu." It is true that the *u* is not the usual vowel represented by this sign (that is, English *u* in full), but a sort of vocalic nasal, analogous to the vocalic *r* of some languages.

The Arabic alphabet is still sometimes used to write the language, for which purpose it is extremely ill adapted. It is perhaps fortunate that the habit of using not only Arabic letters but the Arabic language for official and legal documents prevailed, as otherwise Swahili would probably have become as overburdened with Arabic words as Turkish. As it is, a very just mean has been preserved, somewhat analogous to the use of Latin words in English. Slightly modified Arabic words are used where there is no native expression handy, but they have not driven out the original vocabulary. Most Swahili compositions are handed down orally, and not in writing. They consist chiefly of tales and poetry, a selection of which has been published by the Rev. E. Steere.[1] There are also a certain number of chronicles carrying back the history of the Coast towns for several centuries; but they are, in most cases at any rate, written in Arabic. The tales seem mainly borrowed from the "Arabian Nights," or similar sources, though local colouring is introduced. The poetry consists mostly of either songs for dances, or Moslem religious verses, called Utenzi. Steere mentions, as examples of these latter, an account of a contest between Mohammed and Moses, and a poetical paraphrase of the story of Job. As is common in Oriental languages, Swahili poetry avoids the speech of everyday life, and uses an artificial dialect which is hardly understood by ordinary people. An extreme case is the Kinyume, an entirely unnatural and invented language, formed by taking ordinary words and putting the last syllable first, as, for instance, mbengo, zimbu, ndapu, pantaku, pisiku instead of ngombe, mbuzi, punda, ntakupa, and sikupi.[2]

Like most languages which have little literary cultivation, Swahili is broken up into many different dialects, every town, and sometimes even the quarters of a town, having special

---

[1] "Swahili Tales," 2nd ed., 1889 (Society for Promoting Christian Knowledge).
[2] It will be noticed that *mb* and *nd* are treated as single sounds. "Punda" becomes "ndapu," not "dapun."

peculiarities. On the coast the dialect of Lamu is generally considered the best by natives, but it is not that used by the missionaries, and hence not that generally learnt by Europeans. The variety in common use is the dialect of Zanzibar, to which most text-books refer.

After the Arabs and the mixed breed of Swahilis, we must consider the Hamitic races, the Gallas and Somalis. These tribes are allied to one another, and, according to tradition, both crossed from Arabia into North-East Africa, and moved southwards; the Gallas first subjugating the natives, and the Somalis subsequently crushing the power of the Gallas. In the time of the Portuguese, the Galla appear to have been the dominant race from Abyssinia to the sphere of Arab influence, and Swahili tradition relates that at the end of the sixteenth century they attacked and slew the Sultan of Umba, the present southern border of British East Africa. Mr. Hollis[1] thinks that the sultan was killed by the Zimbas; but, even if this can be proved, the fact that native tradition ascribes the disaster to the Gallas shows that their power must have reached far to the south.

In the middle of the last century they were still considered the principal race on the East Coast. Krapf (1858) went out as "a missionary to the Galla," and conjectured that their total number amounted to between six and eight millions. This was probably even then an exaggerated estimate, but to-day there are only a few hundreds of them in the accessible parts of our Protectorate, though no certain statement can be made about the northern interior. They could not withstand the Somali invasion, and were simultaneously attacked by the Abyssinians, who are said to still consider all Gallas as their slaves. Their power on the Coast was finally destroyed in 1872, when the Chief of Kau, on the Ozi, with whom they were at war, combined with the Somalis, and inflicted on them a crushing defeat. At the present time they appear to be of no importance for the

[1] Notes on the "History of Vumba," p. 281.

political and economic life in the Protectorate, and are found
chiefly in small scattered communities in Tanaland. They
have no central government, and, though the tradition of the
kingly dignity survives, no one is rich enough to defray the
expenses of the coronation feast and accompanying ceremonies.
They have considerable pride in their origin and past, and
relate a story to the effect that they once possessed a sacred
book, like the Bible or Koran. The precious volume was,
however, eaten by a cow, and whenever a cow is killed they
are said to look in the stomach to see if a copy is not there.
The name Galla is commonly restricted to the tribes of this
race in Tanaland, but the Rendile and Borans of the northern
interior appear to belong to the same stock.

Far more important are the Somali tribes, who stretch
from the Red Sea across the Juba to the interior of Tanaland.
According to their tradition, their ancestor, Sherif Ishak,
crossed to Africa from Arabia about five hundred years ago.
The Somalis below the Juba River represent the southernmost
extension of the movement ; and though they keep up relations with the other tribes in the north, they are in many
ways separate from them. Whatever overtures were made to
them by the Mad Mullah during the recent war met with no
practical result, and they were by no means anxious that
he should come southwards.

The chief tribal divisions in Jubaland are the Hertis and
Ogadens. The former dwell near the Coast and at Kismayu.
They are more or less settled, and, finding it disadvantageous
to be on bad terms with Europeans, are loyal to the Government. The Ogaden are wilder and more nomadic. They
have given considerable trouble, and it would even now not be
safe to depend on them, though their excesses in the past
were probably due more to motives of private revenge and a
hereditary habit of fighting intruders, Arabs and others, whenever they dare, than to any deliberate political movement
which can properly be called rebellion, They are divided
into several tribes, of which the best known are Rir Mohammed,

Mohammed Subeir, Abud Wak, and Olihan or Aulihan. They had until lately a sultan, but he appeared to exercise little authority outside his own tribe. In the troubles of 1900–1 he was taken prisoner, but escaped, after which he was not recognised by the British authorities, and, owing to family feuds, could not exact obedience from his own people. He wrote a curious letter after escaping from prison to the authorities of Kismayu, saying he had found a change of air absolutely necessary for his health. "By-the-bye," he concluded, "I left a wife and a Koran behind. Don't trouble to return them."

The Somalis of Tanaland are generally known as Biskayas. Their regular residence appears to be inland, and it is only on raiding expeditions, which have been stopped of late years, that they reach the banks of the Tana or the shores of the Lamu Archipelago. They are governed by a chief or sultan, called Hasan Burjan, who appears to be a man of great authority. It is a common native story, that when messengers went to him for any negotiation he would warn them that he could make his subjects do whatever he ordered, and as a proof would bid some one lick the dust of his sandals, which was done unhesitatingly.

We have had on several occasions considerable trouble with the Ogaden, and have rarely been successful in inflicting punishment, but it may be hoped that an era of peace has now commenced. At the end of 1900 some of their chiefs surprised Mr. Jenner, the Sub-Commissioner of Jubaland, when he was travelling, and murdered him. The murder was probably due to personal motives, and I think it would have been better to have treated it as a crime, rather than as an act of political revolt. The latter course was, however, adopted; war was declared against the Ogaden, and a costly expedition was despatched. It gained no success proportionate to its size and expense, for it was unable to capture or force a battle on the light-footed nomads, who vanished before it in a scrubby wilderness, well known to them, though pathless to strangers, while it was, on the other hand, exposed to sudden attacks from fanatical desperadoes.

A small expedition of about 200 irregulars, conducted in the south by Mr. Rogers, Sub-Commissioner of Lamu, and now Regent of Zanzibar, met with much greater success, and demonstrated the greater efficiency as well as the much greater cheapness of this method of warfare. After about £140,000 had been spent in about six months, it was decided that for financial considerations the campaign could not be continued on such a scale, and active operations were replaced by a blockade to be continued until a fine of 5000 cattle should be paid. This measure, which would have been the cheapest and easiest to enforce in the beginning, proved successful, and the whole amount was paid up in about a year. An even more important result was that the Somalis were impressed with the idea that it lay within the power of the Government to stop their trade and deprive them of the luxuries which they value, such as cloth and coffee.

The future of the Somali race is to my mind one of the most interesting and difficult of the problems presented by East Africa. For the present, I advise that we leave them alone, or at least avoid as far as possible the task of attacking them in their own territory. They are naturally isolated, and, if our officers will only avoid getting killed, can do little harm by quarrelling with one another in Jubaland. Our real task at present is rather to see that they do not encroach to the south, and to prevent them from raiding the Tana River and the Lamu Archipelago. But we can hardly avoid in the future the further task of making a permanent settlement in Jubaland, and the delimitation of the Abyssinian frontier may perhaps precipitate that settlement.

It is certainly to be desired that we should utilise the Somalis. There can be no doubt that they are the most intelligent race in the Protectorate, though it may be urged with some justice that they are also proud, treacherous, fanatical, and vindictive. Too much stress, I think, is often laid on these bad qualities, and it is certain that the average Englishman has little sympathy for the Somali. He tolerates a black man who admits his inferiority, and even those who show a good fight and give in; but he cannot tolerate dark colour combined with an intelligence in any way equal to his own. This is the secret of the almost universal dislike of the Babu, and it reappears in the unpopularity of the Somali among East African officials. The Somali are not willing to agree to the simple plan of having a fair fight and then shaking hands when defeated, but constantly indicate that they think themselves our equals or superiors, and not unfrequently prove it. Whenever it is worth our while to occupy Jubaland, and let them see a few hundred white men instead of half-a-dozen officials, which is literally all that they know of us at present, I anticipate that we shall not have much difficulty in getting on with them. The attractions of civilisation are so great for them, and our superiority in this respect so incontestable, that there can hardly be any doubt as to the result. What will happen in the wider limits of Somaliland, north of the Juba, it is hard to predict, but the area to the south is sufficiently small to offer an easy field for the extension of European influence when it is commercially and financially worth while. But meanwhile I think we had better let the Somalis alone, and avoid these conflicts between a lion and a swallow.

The Bantu-speaking tribes of the Protectorate (besides the Swahilis) are the Wanyika, or inhabitants of the jungle, behind the Coast line; the Wapokomo, on the Tana; the people of the Teita Hills and Taveta; the Wakamba, whose centre is about Machakos and the Nzaui peak, but who appear to extend from the Sabaki River to the district of Meru on the east of Kenya; the Kikuyu or Akikuyu, inhabiting the Kikuyu country and the slopes of Kenya; and the Bantu Kavirondo, on the north-western shores of Lake Victoria, with whom should perhaps be classed the little-known tribes of Kisii or Kossovo.

It does not seem necessary to assume that there is any

racial as opposed to linguistic unity among these peoples. At any rate the burden of proof lies with those who make the assertion. It would appear that the Zulus and other warlike tribes of South Africa are very different from the Wakamba and Wanyika; and unless the unity of physical type can be proved, I should be inclined to think that the stock, or the many mixed stocks, who have produced the natives of East Africa have merely adopted a Bantu language.

The Wanyika are found all along the Coast, and the Wapokomo probably belong to the same stock; but from living on the banks of the river, and largely depending on it for their livelihood, they have become expert boatmen, and adopted various new customs. According to their own traditions, the Wanyika represent a southern migration, and came originally from Digi and Kirau in Shungwaya, the country behind Port Durnford. One of their tribes, the Wasegeju, claim to be descended from the Somalis. The principal sections are the Wagiriama, the Waduruma, the Wadigo, and the Wasegeju, but there are many others, and every tribe is divided into clans, and every clan into families. Being so near the coast, they have naturally received in some cases a tincture of Arab influence, either directly or through the Swahilis, and it is perhaps due to this that they seem to have had occasionally chiefs who became small sultans; but their original customs, like those of most East African tribes, show no trace of political organisation, though we often find Kayas, or meeting-places, where the elders assemble and discuss matters of general interest. Like most East African tribes also they migrate readily, and in the severe droughts to which the Nyika is subject from time to time, they generally move to the banks of the Sabaki or some other river.

I once visited a Wanyika village, probably of the Waduruma, two or three miles from Samburu station. Had we not been taken thither by guides we should never have discovered it, for it was surrounded by a vegetable wall formed of trees, entwined with creepers, which made it look merely like a thicker part of the jungle. This careful concealment, and the obvious timidity of the population, all told of the old slave-raiding days. The women ran away and hid, and could not be induced to speak to Europeans. All the Wanyika are agriculturists, and live chiefly by cultivating maize. Their languages seem to be closely related to one another, and to Swahili, and to differ chiefly in pronunciation. Though one must be thankful for scientific reasons to the missionaries who have registered these dialects and preserved them in translations of the Bible, one cannot help thinking that for practical purposes it would be better to extend the knowledge of Swahili than to perpetuate somewhat small differences.

The Wakamba are one of the largest and most important tribes of East Africa, and inhabit the basin of the Athi River for some distance on each side. They are found as far east as the neighbourhood of Rabai. According to one theory, they came to their present territory from the south. They have been influenced by the Masai, though not so strongly as the Kikuyu. Their country is divided into three districts : Kikumbuliyu in the south, being the sparsely populated jungle, with occasional hills, about Makindu, Kibwezi, Masongaleni, &c.; the Ulu Hills and Machakos in the centre; and Kitui to the north, both the latter districts being fairly populous. It is said that within the memory of man the Masai occupied much of the land about Machakos, but were driven out by the Wakamba after a severe struggle. In most parts of Ulu and Kikambuliyu the villages are still built on the hills, and the plains left uncultivated, owing to the fear of Masai raids, which were a very real danger until a few years ago. The Wakamba do not now appear to be a warlike race, though the inhabitants of Mumoni and some parts of Kitui are said to be more energetic than the other sections. As a tribe they seem inferior both in vigour and intelligence to the Kikuyu people, and drunkenness is terribly prevalent among the older men. They have no political system and no considerable chiefs, at least in the better-known parts of the country. The villages are mostly small, and founded on the polygamous family system.   If the sons become rich enough during their father's life to be independent—that is, if they have acquired sufficient cattle, wives, and children to start a village of their own—they usually leave the parental village and build another elsewhere. Social life is based on the proprietary family system, young males and all females being regarded as the absolute property of the head of the family as much as cattle are.

Although they are not at all unkind to their wives and children, family and sexual relations seem devoid of all touch of sentimentality.   Wives are the recognised sign of wealth, and girls are regarded simply as calves which can be sold for a certain price.   Most bad customs have a good side, and this view of the destiny of daughters prevents infanticide and the exposure of female infants which is so common among un- civilised races ; but it may be doubted if the Wakamba see any difference between selling their daughters in marriage and selling them as slaves.   It is characteristic that the legal owner of a woman is regarded as the owner and father of her children, whoever the real progenitor may be.   The Wakamba have no respect for maidens, and regard a pregnant girl as the most eligible spouse, exactly as if she were a cow in calf. During the time of the famine a great many Wakamba women went to live with the Indian coolies who were working on the railway, then in process of construction.   Their object was simply to obtain food, not to gratify an illicit passion, and their male relations offered no objection to the proceeding. But when the famine passed, and children began to be born of these unions, the husbands came to the Indians and said they were ready to leave the women, but wanted the children.   The Indians naturally wished to keep the children on the ground that they were the fathers, and not the Wakamba.   But the latter could not understand this claim, and argued that the owner of a woman was the owner of any offspring she might produce, whoever the father in the ordinary sense of the word might be.

No detailed information as to their religion is forthcoming, but if they possess any system of ideas or practices which can be dignified by that name, it is, as is usual in East Africa, obscure and secretive. The belief in witchcraft and the detective powers of the witch-doctor flourishes, and has developed an organisation for purposes of terrorism and money-making. About harvest time the witch-doctor goes round the villages, and hears what complaints there may be of misfortunes which have occurred, including deaths, which are rarely ascribed to natural causes. Every one knows that he will lay the blame on some woman. Those who wish to keep scandal from their door propitiate him, while the jealous or revengeful secretly suggest the names of probable culprits. Finally, he mentions a name to the Wazee or elders of the village. It is generally that of a woman whose relatives have offended or not paid him, or, if he is not swayed by any personal motives, some poor creature who has no near relatives. Nothing is said to the woman, but she is gradually more and more shunned by the others till she perceives her coming doom. It is a happy thing that negroes are not sensitive or nervous, but the position for a European would be terrible. After some time all the people go out of the village, leaving her there, till a man comes and spears her from behind, pinning her down into the ground. In this position she is left still alive until the others come back and beat and stone her to death. This custom is called Kinyolla. It is said that as many as forty women were killed in this way in the neighbourhood of Machakos within one year.

The language of the Wakamba resembles Swahili in its construction, and appears to be intelligible to the neighbouring Kikuyu tribes. Phonetically, it differs from Swahili considerably, and the sound of the two languages is unlike, owing to the prevalence in Kamba of *th*, *ts*, *dz*, and also of the modified vowels, *ö* and *ü*. The plural prefix for human being is *a*, not *wa*, and the people really calls themselves Akamba, Wakamba being a Swahili form. There are at least two dialects recorded in Mrs. Hinde's vocabulary,[1] the Ulu and the Nganyawa, spoken in part. of Kitui.   Few Arabic words are used.

Next door to Ukamba on the west lies the Kikuyu country.   The inhabitants, who calls themselves Akikuyu, speak a Bantu[2] language resembling that of the Wakamba, and like it characterised by the plentiful use of *th*, which entirely replaces *s*, at least in some dialects.   The consonants *p* and *f* are also entirely avoided.   As a physical type, they are probably hybrids between the Masai and a Bantu race, but their resemblance to the Masai is largely the result of direct imitation.   Their warriors regard the Masai Elmoran as the ideal of chivalry, and copy their arms, manner of dressing the hair, &c.   We know that sections of the Masai have a tendency to adopt a sedentary life when they become separated from the rest of the tribe, and also that the Bantu languages have great powers of expansion at the expense of other tongues. In the famine of 1882 Masai settled among the Kikuyu tribes, and took Kikuyu wives, and in some cases they entered the service of Kikuyu chieftains as a sort of mercenaries.   The geographical position of Kikuyu, as a fertile strip on the borders of the plains frequented by the Masai, makes it eminently probable that from one cause or another Masai would settle from time to time in the district where life was so much easier, adopt the Bantu language, and introduce Masai blood.

The character of the Kikuyu people is quite in keeping with such a hypothesis.   Like the Bantu tribes generally, they are essentially agriculturists and cultivators, but they still have a warlike strain in them which shows itself in continual

---

[1] "Vocabularies of the Kamba and Kikuyu Languages of East Africa," by H. Hinde (Cambridge Univ. Press, 1904).

[2] There can be no doubt on this point, particularly after the publication of the Kikuyu vocabularies of MacGregor (Soc. for Promoting Christian Knowledge) and Mrs. Hinde (both 1904).   Professor Gregory was misinformed in stating ("Great Rift Valley," p. 352) that the language is not Bantu, and allied to Masai.

robberies, raids, and intertribal quarrels. They have not one head, but their chiefs are of greater importance than those of the other Bantu tribes, and such men as Kinanjui, near Nairobi, and Karuri, near Nyeri, are important allies for the Government, to which they show perfect loyalty, for they can each put several hundred men in the field. There are also a multitude of smaller chiefs, and, as the country is much split up by valleys and ravines, the various clans and sections tend to become isolated and hostile to one another. A feeling that continuous interbreeding in these small sections might impair the qualities of the race has resulted in a curious custom by which, at certain times of year, bodies of warriors go round the country and meet with a hospitable reception in all the villages, whether friendly or hostile. They stop three days, and are introduced to all the women judged capable of child-bearing.

The Kikuyu country is, as elsewhere described, the high, fertile, wooded strip extending from Ngongo Bagas northwards to Kenya. The number of natives is estimated at from 200,000 to 300,000.[1] It is, at any rate, one of the most thickly inhabited parts of East Africa, the population being specially dense near Mount Kenya. Between that point and Nairobi there are several areas which were deserted during the famine of 1897, and have not been reoccupied, though the soil appears to be rich and likely to repay cultivation. It is probable that the inhabitants of the slopes of Mount Kenya, at least on the south and east, are Kikuyu or closely allied tribes. They have hitherto been somewhat hostile, and have been deliberately left alone until we have better connection by road and telegraph with the whole district. Some persons, how-ever, who have visited the country and have a right to speak with authority, think that some of the tribes to the south-east, particularly the Embo, are of a different stock. They are said to fight with stone knobkerries and to speak another

---

[1] The last official report ("Africa," 15, 1904) thinks it cannot be far short of 1,000,000.

language. Near the Embo live the Mbe, who are a mixture of Akamba and Akikuyu. To the north-east of Mnyiso are the Embi, who are said not to be true Akikuyu, and to speak a language not easily understood by their neighbours. There appear to be about four dialects of the Kikuyu language, but they have no names.

The last division of the Bantu races of the Protectorate to be noticed are the Bantu Kavirondo. The distribution of tribes round the eastern shores of Lake Victoria is not easy to explain. The shores of Kavirondo Bay, at the head of which is the railway terminus, are inhabited by a race who speak a Nilotic language. They are often called simply Kavirondo, but it is perhaps well to distinguish them by the name of Ja-luo, which they themselves use. To the south is the Bantu tribe often called Kosovo, but apparently calling themselves Aba-Kisii, in which *Aba* is equivalent to the Swahili prefix *Wa*. To the north of the Ja-luo, and occupying the valley of the Nzoia, are the Bantu Kavirondo, and other Bantu-speaking tribes are found to the west of Mount Elgon. Except in language the Ja-luo and the Bantu Kavirondo are much alike, and one is not conscious of any material change in the customs and appearance of the people in passing from one sphere to the other. There are not yet any data to warrant a dogmatic explanation of this distribution. The Ja-luo are linguistically allied most closely to the Aluru and Acholi of the southern Nile, near Lake Albert, and it would be natural to suppose that in their south-western migration they came to Bantu-speaking lands and were partly assimilated linguistically, though influencing the customs of the Bantus in the valley of the Nzoia, while to the south, for reasons which are obscure, they preserved their language as well as their customs. On the other hand, if it is maintained that the country down to the south of Kavirondo Bay was originally inhabited by Nilotic tribes, and that the Bantu are the intruders, I do not see how the contention can be disproved. Still, the fact that Bantu languages are spoken from Mombasa to the Rift Valley, and on both sides of Lake Victoria as well as to the north, does lend a *primâ facie* support to the idea that there was once a continuous stretch of Bantu population into which a wedge of Nilotic folk has penetrated.

The Bantu Kavirondo are peaceful, industrious people, whose most remarkable peculiarity, shared with the Ja-luo, is that both sexes go stark naked. The married women some-times wear a minute apron, but mature females, who are pre-sumably matrons, can sometimes be seen (perhaps more among the Ja-luo than the Bantus) without a scrap of clothing. They have the reputation of being a highly moral and respect-able race, but their nudity is not artistic or pleasing, and is one of those African customs which I would fain see done away with, and there is little doubt that it will be a thing of the past in a very few years. This absence of clothing has not, however, extinguished the love of ornament. The Kavirondo women load themselves with as many beads and necklaces as they can get, and the men have a fancy for elaborate head-dresses, in which feathers and sections of hippopotamus teeth, cut or filed to the thickness of a knife, play a prominent part. These customs do not throw much certain light on the origin of the race. It is true that entire nakedness among the men is characteristic of the Nilotic tribes, but their women are carefully dressed. On the other hand, the Bantu negroes, though they may wear more clothes than the Nilotic, have little notion of decency according to our ideas; and it is said that at the court of the King of Uganda women were allowed to be naked, although the men were obliged to be completely clothed.

In other ways the Kavirondo people by no means stand on a low level of civilisation, and compare favourably with the inhabitants of Kikuyu and Ukamba. Their houses are well made and their villages surrounded by a wall of clay or a moat. For sanitary, or more probably superstitious, reasons they frequently move their villages, and in northern Kavirondo it is no uncommon thing to find close together the old disused site, with its wall and moat still intact, and a new village. This custom may be partly due to the fact that the dead are buried in their huts, which are not used afterwards. After a certain time all the huts become thus converted into cemeteries.

The Kisii people are practically unknown to Europeans, but are said to be brave and warlike, and appear to hold their own against the Lumbwa, with whom they have a chronic feud. The Bantu Kavirondo, however, are peaceful, and essentially agriculturists. They grow a good deal of maize, sorghun, and other grains, and the amount of cultivated land which one sees round their villages is unusually large for Africa. They are amiable and intelligent, but all the older men are terribly given to the use of native intoxicants and hemp-smoking. These vices seem to have a worse effect on them than on other natives, and, in interviewing their chiefs, I have always found that nearly every one over thirty was a decrepit, tremulous old man, incapable of transacting business. The more important chiefs can command the allegiance of a large number of people, and make some attempt at policing their districts. One of the best known is Mumia, who has given his name to the large station Mumias, near the Nzoia, which is practically the capital of Bantu Kavirondo. On the whole, they would be one of the most promising populations of the Protectorate, if it were not for their aforesaid vices.

Their language is divided into a number of dialects, such as Luwanga, Lurimi, and Lunyara, vocabularies of which are given by Sir H. Johnston.[1] They are said to be more archaic than the eastern Bantu languages, and to be connected with those spoken in Uganda and Unyoro. Remarkable in them is the frequent use of *kh*, which is eschewed by the Eastern languages. Igizii (the language of the Kisii) would appear from these vocabularies to have some resemblance to the Kikuyu tongue.

[1] "The Uganda Protectorate," p. 890 ff.

CHAPTER VIII

THE NATIVES OF EAST AFRICA

MASAI, NANDI, ETC.

THE significance of the name Nilotic as applied to certain tribes in the East Africa Protectorate must not be unduly pressed. It merely means that these tribes are connected with other tribes which now live on the southern Nile, but the evidence before us is hardly sufficient to prove that the tribes on the Nile should be regarded as a homogeneous unit, or that those which hang together with one another and with the tribes of East Africa have any special claim to be regarded as the characteristic population of the river banks. It would seem that the Madi, who are one of the main elements in the riparian population between Gondokoro and Wadelai, belong to another stock, at least linguistically, with possible West African affinities, and the East African tribes show indications of two separate sub-groups. The Masai are linguistically most nearly allied to the Bari and Latuka, living at present in the neighbourhood of Gondokoro, while the Nilotic Kavirondo or Ja-luo are clearly connected with the Acholi dwelling to the north-east of Lake Albert; and apparently both are more distantly related to the Dinka and Shilluk, who inhabit the country north of Gondokoro on the banks of the Sobat. These relationships may be regarded as fairly certain, as they are based on the triple bond of resemblance in physique, language, and customs. Physically the Nilotes are generally tall thin men, with features which are not characteristically negro and often almost Caucasian. Their languages are sharply distinguished from Bantu. Grammatical forms are built up chiefly by adding suffixes, and in some of them at any rate there is an article.   There is also a considerable general resemblance in vocabulary and phonetics.   In customs there is such general agreement as might be expected among kindred peoples practising very different modes of life, and among all the men go completely naked, though the women are clad. Other remarkable customs found both on the Nile and in East Africa are the habit of resting standing on one leg, the extraction of the middle teeth of the lower jaw, shaving the heads of women, drinking the warm blood from living animals, and the toleration of free love between the warriors and unmarried girls.

Some of these tribes now extend as far south as German East Africa; but, though there is no historic evidence of the fact, it can hardly be doubted that they have come from the countries west and north-west of Lake Rudolf, such as the neighbourhood of Gondokoro and the Sobat.   They are probably a mixed race, representing a fusion of the negro with some superior type, which we must confess to be unknown, though the neighbourhood of Egypt and Abyssinia affords support for many hypotheses.   Sir H. Johnston thinks that the other and superior factor may have been the Gallas or Somalis, which is not impossible.   Baker states [1] that the appearance of the Latuka indicates a Galla origin, and that Gallas are found on the east bank of a river known to the natives as Chol, which is only fifty miles east of Latuka. He says that these Gallas have frequently invaded the Latuka country, and on their expeditions were always mounted on mules.

Of these Nilotic tribes in East Africa the best known are the Masai,[2] who in the past have perhaps been the most interesting and important race in the country, though they have not the qualities which offer much promise of progress and increase in the future.   They are mostly warlike nomads,

[1] " The Albert Nyanza," p. 205.

[2] For my information about the Masai I am much indebted to Mr. Hollis, whose valuable work, " The Masai: their Language and Folk-Lore," is being published by the Clarendon Press, and will probably appear before this.

with a social system based on military ideals, who were long the terror and scourge of all their neighbours, their raids having extended from the middle of what is now German East Africa to the Tana River and the vicinity of Mombasa. Their present haunts are the Rift Valley (including parts of the Settima and Mau ranges), the plains, excluding the scrub country, as far east as Kilima-Njaro and the parts of German East Africa immediately south of these districts to about lat. 5° south. In the Rift Valley there are not many to the north of Nakuru.

The Masai are divided into two sections, L-Oikop and the Masai proper. The former name is given to those who have settled down and adopted an agricultural life. They are found chiefly in German territory, near Lake Natron and south of Mount Meru. In our Protectorate similar tribes appear to be the Njamusi, who inhabit two large villages at the south end of Lake Baringo, and various scattered settlements recorded as existing at the south end of Lake Rudolf and in the countries to the north of Kenya. The people of Kikuyu and Taveta, who are agriculturists, have also a good deal of Masai blood and many Masai customs, but speak Bantu languages. In these cases, however, it would appear not that a section of Masai have settled down, but that a settled Bantu race has become strongly influenced, by intermarriage and otherwise, by the surrounding Masai. The settled Masai are often called by their nomadic brethren Lumbwa, which appears to be a term of contempt. The name is confusing, because it is also applied by the Masai to another large tribe akin to the Nandi, who call themselves Sikisi, and has passed into European parlance as the popular and official name of this people and their territory.

The Masai proper, whose name should be more accurately written Maasae, are pastoral nomads, who recognise only two things as worthy of their care and interest, namely, cattle and warfare. Of late years circumstances have tended to change their practice, if not their ideals, but formerly every man's

youth—that is, till he was about twenty-seven or thirty—was
spent in fighting or cattle-raiding. These expeditions were
directed either against the surrounding tribes or against other
sections of the Masai. The quarrels among themselves account
for the disappearance of the Uasin Gishu Masai, and perhaps of
others. Merker, in his recent work "Die Masai" (Berlin,
1904), divides the whole people into three provinces—Kisongo
to the south of Kilima-Njaro, Elbruggo in the Rift Valley,
and Loita between the two, which perhaps roughly represents
the principal divisions as known to Europeans; but it would
appear that the Masai divide themselves into five districts,
namely, Kaputiei (the Kapite plains), En-aiposha (Naivasha),
Kisongo, L-uasin-gishu, and L-Aikipiak (Laikipia), of which
the two latter have practically ceased to exist, the remnants
of the inhabitants being mixed with other tribes. L-Oita and
Purko (Elbruggo or Elburgo) are both subdivisions of the
En-aiposha district. Each district has a chief (ol-aunoni),
who must be a retired warrior; but far more important are the
Laibons (properly Ol-oiboni) or medicine-men, by whose advice
all matters of public concern are directed, and who have
acquired an almost royal position in consequence. This office
is hereditary in a family of the Sighirari subdistrict, and the
holder of it, Lenana, more correctly Ol-onana (the gentle one),
resides near Nairobi. He is the younger son of a famous
medicine-man called Mbatian, who preferred him to his elder
brother Sendeyo. According to another story, Mbatian intended that Sendeyo should succeed him, and bade him come
next day and receive the insignia of office, the chief of which
was an iron bar or club. Lenana, knowing of this, acted like
Jacob, and presented himself before his father very early in
the morning. The old man, who had but one eye, and whose
sight was dim with age, thought it was his eldest son, and gave
him the insignia, saying, "Be thou great among thy brethren
and among all people." Sendeyo refused to accept Lenana as
Laibon, and was supported by the Loita section. It so happened that the division of parties corresponded roughly with

that between German and British territory, with the result that Lenana came to be regarded as chief of the British and Sendeyo of the German Masai. In 1902, however, Sendeyo and his people became dissatisfied with the German administration, and, after making peace with Lenana, came over into our territory, and now dwell in the southern part of the Kedong valley.

The male Masai are divided into "ages," according to the date on which they were circumcised, a ceremony to which great importance is attached. It usually takes place between the ages of thirteen and seventeen, but may be delayed if the youth's family is poor and cannot afford the necessary feast. When the proper time arrives, a circumcision feast is held every year for four years in succession, and all the boys who undergo the operation belong to one age. Then follows an interval of about three and a half years in which no feast is held, and then another age commences. Each age has a name, and is called alternately right and left. Thus those who were circumcised in 1896 and the following years are right hand and are known as Il-Kishon (lives) or Il-Kitoip (the lucky ones), while those who were circumcised at the beginning of this year (1904) are left hand, and called Il-Meitaroni (the unconquered). Two ages are considered equivalent to a generation, and the names are known for more than a hundred years back.

After circumcision a Masai, who has previously only been a Laioni or youth, becomes a warrior, commonly called Elmoran (strictly speaking, Ol-murani in the singular, Il-muran in the plural), and remains so until he marries. The warriors do not dwell with the rest of the tribe, but have separate kraals, where they live with the immature unmarried girls. It is extraordinary that a custom which must be disastrous for the physical well-being of the race, and is doubtless responsible for its decrease in numbers, should be tolerated among a people whose ideal seems to be in other respects a strenuous and almost ascetic life of untiring military activity. According to their own traditions, the practice was permitted because it was found that the girls, if kept apart from their own warriors, allowed themselves to be courted by the enemy and betrayed the interests of the tribe. It is to be hoped that in time this evil custom will be suppressed. As far as I know, it continues unabated among the Masai; but among the inhabitants of Taveta, who had borrowed it from them, the influence of civilisation has partially abolished it.

A Masai warrior is rather a fine-looking creature, though generally so smeared with oil and red clay that it is better to interview him out of doors and at a slight distance. The hair is grown as long as possible, and plaited into a short pigtail. On full-dress occasions a helmet is worn made of a lion's head and mane, which is effective and imposing, and the face is surrounded with a circle of ostrich feathers. The body is absolutely naked except for a short cloak hanging down the back, and is often elaborately painted. Bracelets, anklets, and ear-rings are also worn, the latter often of enormous size. The lobes of the ear are slit in childhood, and gradually distended by forcing objects into the opening. In modern times a jam-pot has become a favourite form of ear-ring, but the older fashion is to wear a large round stone weighing between two and three pounds. Ear-rings of chains are also commonly worn. The arms are a sword, a club carried behind, a spear with a very long blade, and an oval shield bearing figures in red, white, black, and grey, which indicate the clan and age to which the bearer belongs.

At about twenty-seven or thirty, a Masai becomes an elder (Ol-moruo), and marries. Formerly he was not allowed to do this until he had been on several raids; but in these more peaceful times the tendency is to quit the ranks of the warriors earlier, for their life, though glorious and not without its pleasures, is subject to many restrictions. An elder, on the other hand, may get drunk and smoke, eat and drink what he likes, and generally takes his ease. An expressive saying, meaning "Don't give yourself airs," says "Don't lie on your back with your feet against a post, like an old man with many sons," this being the way in which the Masai paterfamilias takes his ease while his family do the work. Polygamy is usual, though most men content themselves with two or three wives, and do not imitate the connubial extravagancies of other tribes.

The women have a pleasant expression, but are rendered hideous according to the ordinary ideas of beauty by shaving their heads—a rare habit which is said to also prevail on the Nile. Unlike the men, they are carefully and decently dressed in skins, and also wear an extraordinary profusion of iron ornaments. Coils of iron wire are wound round the arms and legs until they form veritable sleeves and trousers ; circles of similar wire are worn round the neck like an Elizabethan ruff, and large wheel-like rings hang from the ears. The whole costume is monotonous and dark, and when one sees these shaven heads, leather garments, and masses of burdensome and totally unornamental metal, one can only wonder at the trouble the good ladies take to make themselves hideous. Civilised costumes are not over sensible, but the lower races of mankind seem to fall below the animals in the senseless mutilations and unwieldy ornaments with which they afflict themselves.

As the Masai never kill game, and do not cultivate the ground, their diet is somewhat limited. Warriors are bound to subsist solely on meat, milk, and blood, and when they eat beef retire to special huts in the forest. Women and elders are not under the same restrictions, but take little vegetable food. The somewhat horrible habit of drinking blood is prevalent among most of the Nilotic races. It is a common practice to tie a leather thong round an animal's throat and shoot an arrow into the jugular vein. The blood is collected in gourds as it gushes forth, and is drunk warm. A Masai riddle, which throws a curious light on their social customs, asks what it is that is pushed against the wall of a hut. The answer is, a widow when blood is drawn from cattle. All the people crowd round the animal for a drink ; but the widow,

MASAI WARRIORS.

IN THE SETTIMA HILLS.

who has no one to help her, is pushed out of the way and cowers against the wall.

The language of the Masai is sharply distinguished from the surrounding Bantu tongues, and shows no trace of their influence, being, as mentioned, connected most closely with Bari and Latuku. Now that its grammatical structure is properly understood, it seems to be fairly easy, and the pronunciation presents no great difficulties, as there are few combinations of consonants. The words are, however, long, and a European's first impression is that they are confusingly like one another, owing to the continual repetition of the article (ol, il : en, in),[1] without which a substantive is as a rule unintelligible. The large part played by the article is very remarkable, and, with the exception of the verb, it appears to be the only part of the language which has any vigour and flexibility, the substantive by itself being helpless and incapable of expressing case. By a curious use the article is prefixed elliptically to a genitive to form what in most languages would be a derivative substantive. Ol-le-'ng-aina, the-of-the-hand, or the elephant. This expression is exactly equivalent to the Sanskrit *hastī*, the handed (animal), from *hasta*, a hand. Ol-le-lughunya, the-of-the-head or the brain, is like the Greek ἐγκέφαλος. Words are formed by both suffixes and prefixes. The former are the more frequent, prefixes being chiefly used to mark the persons of the verb.

As might be expected, literature is not the strong point of this warrior race. They appear to have nothing like epic or heroic poetry, but a good number of fairly dramatic stories. A man-eating devil is a frequent character in these tales, and the great powers of medicine-men and the danger of neglecting their advice are often illustrated. Beast stories are also frequent. As a rule the hare is the clever animal, and takes the place of the fox or jackal in other countries. One story

---

[1] Unlike the Bantu languages, Masai has no fondness for *nd*, *ng*, as initial sounds. Words like Ngongo, ndito, Ndabibi are Swahili corruptions, and should be Engongo, endito, Endabibi.

relates with some humour how the lion went to law and claimed the ostrich's chicks as his own young, and no one dared to dispute his power of laying and hatching eggs. Prayers and warlike poems seem to be exclusively for singing, not for recitation. They are short, and consist of alternate solos and choruses, each of one line.

As is the case with nearly all East African tribes, the religious ideas of the Masai are vague, and little has been developed in the way of a cultus or mythology. I should, however, mention that Merker, in his recent work already referred to, reports as current among the German Masai a great number of traditions analogous to those of the ancient Hebrews and Babylonians. It would be rash to assume that a people coming from the north and the neighbourhood of Egypt and Abyssinia cannot have brought with them such traditions; but Hollis reports that similar legends are not known in British East Africa. I cannot help suspecting that, if they are known in German territory, they must be due to European and Christian influence. It is true that the Masai have by no means shown themselves amenable to missionary influence; but a certain number of them have learned to read and write in the old-established mission at Taveta, and they may possibly have got hold of some distorted version of the biblical account of the early history of the world.

The Masai are not afflicted with the belief in witchcraft, which causes so much unhappiness among the Bantu tribes. Their Laibons or medicine-men do not detect witches, but are diviners, who foretell the future by such methods as casting stones, inspecting entrails, interpreting dreams, and prophesying under the influence of intoxicants. They can also, according to popular stories, perform miracles, such as changing fruit into children, and, in particular, they can bring rain; but no explanation of their power is given. The deity is known as Eng-aï (that is, the word *aï*, with the feminine article, not *Ngai*, as it is sometimes written), which appears to be used either in the definite sense of a personal God, or very indefinitely of any remarkable phenomenon, such as rain, sky, or a volcano. In the former sense it is said there are two gods, the Black God (Eng-aï narok) and the Red God (Eng-aï nanyokye). The former is benevolent and sends rain, though the stories published do not contain many references to his intervention in human affairs. He lives immediately above the earth, whereas the Red God lives higher still. The Masai say that when loud claps of thunder are heard the Red God is trying to get down to earth in order to kill men, whereas the distant rumbling is the voice of the Black God saying, "Do leave them alone: do not kill them." There is also a quasi-divine personage called Naiternkop, who lives on Mount Kenya and who, if not the creator, played some part in making the present arrangements of the world. The chief characters in the Masai Genesis are this deity, a Masai called Le-eyo and a Dorobo, that is, one of the tribe of hunters often called Wanderobo. There are various versions of the story, but the gist of it is that the deity let cattle down from heaven by a cord, and that by one means or another the Masai cheated the Dorobo out of his share and got all the animals; the object being to explain how it is that the Masai have all the cattle, while the Dorobo live by hunting.

Naiteru-kop told Le-eyo that when a child died he was to throw away the body and say, "Man, die and return: moon, die and stay away." Unfortunately the first child that died was some one else's, and Le-eyo was so selfish that he would not use the right formula, but said, "Man, die and stay: moon, die and return." Shortly afterwards one of his own children died, and he tried the correct words, but in vain. Naiteru-kop told him that he had spoilt matters for ever, and hence the moon comes back, but the dead remain dead.

Le-eyo had two sons. When he was dying he asked the elder what part of his property he would like. He replied, "I want something of everything in the world." So his father gave him a few cattle, a few sheep, a few goats, a little grain, and so on.   He then asked his younger son what he wanted, and the son replied, " The fan which hangs from your arm."   Le-eyo said, " My child, because you have chosen this fan, God will give you wealth, and you will be great among your brother's people."   The elder son, who wanted something of everything, became the ancestor of the Meek (Bantu tribes or barbarians); but the younger, who had chosen the fan, was the father of all the Masai.   It will be observed that the setting of all these stories seems to be in East Africa, and not in the earlier home of the Masai.

We may therefore conclude that their southward migration is ancient, though we have no data whatever for fixing even approximately the time at which it happened.   What we know of the history of the tribe refers entirely to the last century, and chiefly to the latter half of it.   Their southward advance was successfully resisted by the Wagogo and Wahehe; and in the north, though they raided on the Tana as late as the nineties, they were kept in check by the Gallas and Somalis.   But the main feature of this period seems to have been a series of wars between the agricultural and pastoral Masai, which were disastrous to the race as a whole and resulted in the Uasin Gishu plateau being entirely depopulated. The division between the two sections cannot be ancient, for both of them speak the same language, and it is quite possible that the nomads may in some cases have abandoned a settled life.   About 1883 peace was solemnly restored between the two at Sangaruna Ford, on the river Pangani, by the ceremony of exchanging cattle and children.   But the agriculturists suffered severely, and the remnants of them who were spared by their kinsmen were often destroyed by hostile tribes, like the Segelli (more correctly L-osegela), who settled in the Nyando valley, but were annihilated by the Nandi and Lumbwa (Sikisi). .

The nomadic section indeed prospered for a time, but it was a prosperity based on robbing their neighbours and bound to disappear with the introduction of any sort of civilisation. In 1859 they actually sacked Vanga. They resisted the Arab slave-dealers with success, and forced all travellers to pay hongo or tribute. Nor were Europeans treated at first with more respect. Thomson had to pay tribute in 1883, and speaks of "the atrocious life one is compelled to live among the Masai savages. They ordered us about as if we were so many slaves."[1] But shortly afterwards a series of disasters overwhelmed them and the flocks on which they depend—famine, repeated attacks of cattle-plague, and smallpox. The Wakamba and other enemies attacked them, and the increase of European influence stopped the raids on which they depended to make good their losses. Their attitude towards us has, however, been friendly. This is generally ascribed to the advice[2] of the old medicine-man Mbatian, the father of Lenana, who when dying summoned the tribe, and, after foretelling the epidemics which would destroy men and cattle, said that white men would come, of whom the Masai were to make friends. This wise advice is doubtless emphasised in the minds of the Masai by the consideration that among the other natives every man's hand is against them, and were they to go to war with the Government they would have no allies.

The future of these people is not an easy problem. They resemble the lion and the leopard, strong and beautiful beasts of prey, that please the artistic sense, but are never of any use, and often a very serious danger. Even so the manly virtues, fine carriage, and often handsome features of the Masai arouse a certain sympathy; but it can hardly be denied that they have hitherto done no good in the world that any one knows of; they have lived by robbery and devastation, and made no use themselves of what they have taken from others. There are, however, two hopeful points for the future.

[1] "Through Masai Land," p. 336.
[2] There seems to be no doubt that shortly before his death Mbatian summoned the tribe and made an impressive dying speech, but the account of this advice about Europeans is open to suspicion. Mr. Hollis could not find confirmation of it.

Firstly, the Masai perform well whatever occupation they consent to engage in. They make good herdsmen, policemen and soldiers, though it must be remembered that there is some danger and inconvenience in keeping alive the warlike sentiments of the race in their own country. Secondly, the example of the pastoral Masai speaking the same language as the nomads shows that as a race they oscillate between the two modes of life, and the idea that they may be induced to settle down and take to agriculture is confirmed by the fact that many Masai near Nairobi and Taveta own plantations. It would appear that when once they begin to cultivate they do not return to their nomadic life.

The remaining Nilotic races are the Suk-Turkana, the Nandi-Lumbwa, and the Ja-luo of Kavirondo. All these resemble the Masai in the nudity of the men, and the first two at any rate have the same institution of a warrior class, though the system is less developed and less strictly carried out. They differ from the Masai, however, in being more or less settled, and more or less agriculturists, though in many cases it is clear that they have only recently abandoned a nomadic life and imperfectly adopted sedentary habits. Many of them, like the Masai, drink blood, but unlike them hunt game.

The Turkana and Suk appear to be nearly allied, though, to judge from Sir H. Johnston's vocabularies, their languages are very different for practical purposes. They agree, however, in counting up to five, and then saying five and one,[1] &c., though they have the widespread word *tomon* for ten. I have never come into contact with the Turkana, who are reported to be of gigantic stature and extremely fierce. This latter quality is, however, generally attributed to tribes of whom we know little; and recent information makes it probable that the Turkana have been so harried by the Abyssinians

---

[1] It would appear that all this group of Nilotic languages had originally numbers only up to five. Up to that number the words show some resemblance in the different languages. For the higher numbers are used either expressions like 5 + 1, &c., or else new and perhaps borrowed words.

that they would welcome closer relations with the British authorities. Unfortunately, the distance and aridity of their country makes it difficult and unprofitable to introduce an effective administration at present.

The Suk, who inhabit the Rift Valley north of Baringo, are also a warlike race, and the hereditary foes of the Masai, but quite friendly to the British Government. As far as I have seen them, they are tall men, but hardly gigantic, with an intelligent and amiable expression. They have two remarkable customs, which strike every one who sees them. The one is their fashion of hairdressing, which cannot be called cleanly or beautiful, for the naturally short hair is pulled to make it as long as possible, and then mixed with clay and fat, the whole mass being put into a bag which hangs down their back. The other is their habit of always carrying about an absurd little stool, about six inches high, on which they seat themselves on every possible occasion. They have extremely elaborate dances, in which they imitate with great accuracy and spirit various animals, such as birds and baboons. In the western districts they are said to cultivate industriously, but in the country about Lake Baringo, though they do not show the Masai's disdain for agriculture, they produce few crops, owing no doubt to the poor nature of the soil.

The Nandi, properly so called, occupy the district which bears the same name; that is, the wooded southern edge of the Uashin Gishu plateau and the great mountain mass of Kamalilo, above Fort Ternan. They appear to be practically the same people as the Lumbwa of the Nyando Valley, and are also closely related to the Kamasia, who inhabit the north-west escarpment of the Rift Valley, and to the Muteyo, Elgeyo, and other tribes of the Kerio Valley. Both the Nandi and Lumbwa are warlike, and the hereditary foes of the Masai. They keep considerable herds of cattle, but also cultivate, though in this respect the Nandi are far superior to the Lumbwa, who are very bad agriculturists, and frequently threatened with famine owing to their lazy and careless habits.

K

The correct name of the Nandi appears to be Nandiek, and that of the Lumbwa Sikisi or Kip-Sikisi, Lumbwa being the designation for them used by the Masai, from whom it passed to Europeans. According to their tradition, they descended into their present country from somewhere near the Uasin Gishu plateau, and have only recently adopted a settled life. Both they and the Nandi have several chiefs of importance; but, as among the Masai, more important still are the medicine-men or Laibons, who appear to decide what the action of the tribe will be in all serious matters. According to the common story, they killed some time ago a celebrated medicine-man, called Poyisia, and were straightway visited by every imaginable misfortune, including famine, smallpox, and defeat by their enemies. This was clearly the vengeance of Poyisia's angry spirit, and in the hope of averting further disaster they show the greatest respect to his three sons, Kibalés, Koitalél, and Kipchambér. For a long time it seemed impossible to get into touch with these Laibons, who remained a mysterious and hostile power; but lately Mr. Hobley, to whose ability and knowledge of the country our administration owes so much, has succeeded in having interviews with them, and found them, like nearly all natives, well disposed to Europeans, when once they had made their acquaintance. It is a curious instance of how different from ours are an African's ideas of showing respect, that when Mr. Hobley entered the assembly, convened for the meeting, there was nothing to show which was the Laibon, and no one was willing to point him out. This was really due to extreme deference, and a similar feeling makes the native avoid mentioning his name or alluding to him except in a whisper.

Both the Nandi and Lumbwa have rather a bad name with our officials, and our relations with them have been somewhat unsatisfactory, but I think the fault is at least as much ours as theirs. As I have explained elsewhere, they are sorely tempted by the telegraph and railway lines which we have built in their country, and which by an unhappy coincidence offer wire for female apparel and bolts as male weapons. Their cupidity was first excited by the construction of the telegraph in 1900, and their thefts became so persistent and considerable that an expedition was sent against them, and was meeting with fair success when, in consequence of very injudicious orders given by an official on tour, it was suddenly stopped. Now, I am opposed to punitive expeditions if they can possibly be avoided, but if they are once begun the only thing to do is to make them thorough and successful. To stop them in the middle must mean, as it did in this case, that the natives think we cannot go on and that they have the best of it. The thefts of iron continued, and in 1903 a small expedition was necessary against the people of Taptangale in Kamalilo, who had been endangering the safety of the line. In this expedition, I am glad to say, we had the assistance of some of the Lumbwa, and those of the Nandi who were not implicated in the thefts did not actively assist the people of Taptangale. Since that time matters have been better, and a new Government station has been opened at Soba, near Kamalilo, with excellent results.

Of the Kamasia there is little to be said. They are not many in number, or well known, and, as in their weapons and manner of dressing the hair they imitate the Masai, they are often not distinguished from them. Their language, however, appears to be closely allied to Nandi, and they are agriculturists and hunters. They are considered by the other natives to be skilful medicine-men, and specially expert in the art of producing rain. Like all this group of tribes, they are probably of mixed origin, and show very various physical types. I have been much struck by seeing in assemblies of warriors held at Londiani or the Ravine faces which seem to reproduce the features of the ancient Egyptians as shown on their monuments.

The last and least characteristic section of the Nilotic tribes are the Ja-luo, also called Nyifwa, or Nilotic Kavirondo, who inhabit the shores of Kavirondo Bay, including the valleys of the Nyando and Yala. They have retained their language, and carried to an extreme the habit of nudity, but otherwise have assimilated the peaceful habits of the Bantu Kavirondo. Almost the only noticeable difference is that whereas the villages in the north are surrounded with mud walls, those of the Ja-luo are protected by a thick-set hedge of euphorbias and aloes. They are industrious agriculturists, and are said to have profited of late by the example of the Indians settled near the Kibos River, from whom they have learnt how to irrigate. They are also good fishermen, and capture fish either by spearing or in large wicker traps. They hold in great esteem a certain kind of blue glass bead, which is occasionally found in the ground in North Kavirondo and believed to fall after a thunderstorm. The interest of the matter, however, is that these beads are apparently of very ancient workmanship, and possibly come from Egypt or Nubia. It seems probable that they were buried in the ground and are occasionally exposed by violent storms.

The language shows a great resemblance to Acholi, the numerals and pronouns being almost identical.

I have several times alluded to the Wasania, Waboni, Wanderobo, and Kunono, who are often spoken of as servile or helot tribes, and correspond to the Tumalods (smiths) and Ramis (hunters) of Somaliland. These all appear to be the remnants of older tribes who have accepted a position of inferiority under the victorious invaders. The servile relation is plainest in the case of the Kunono, who are the smiths of the Masai. As these haughty warriors will not do any manual labour, they require workmen to make them arms, and have a special class living among them for this purpose. They will not intermarry with the smiths, or even touch a piece of iron which a smith has held without first oiling their hands. The Kunono language is said to be different from that of the Masai, but merely a corruption of it, and not an independent tongue.

The Wanderobo, who are more properly called Dorobo, are wandering hunters who are found among the Masai and are tolerated by them, on condition of paying a percentage of the ivory which they obtain. Though not dwarfs, they are usually somewhat mean-looking men of low general intelligence, but they show surprising boldness and cunning in hunting. They have great skill in making poisoned arrows, armed with which a man will go into the forest and attack an elephant single-handed. The flesh round the poisoned wound is cut out and the rest eaten. As a rule they wander about until they kill some large animal, and then settle round the carcase until it is consumed. They will remain like this round an elephant for many days, long after the stench has become intolerable to Europeans.

Of the Waboni and Wasania I have no certain information. They inhabit the forests of Tanaland, and are said to be hunters like the Dorobo.

CHAPTER IX

EAST AFRICA AS A EUROPEAN COLONY

HEALTH, CLIMATE, FOOD SUPPLY, ETC.

HOSTILE politicians have long poured contempt on East Africa as a land of swamps and deserts. It may be hoped that a better idea of its character and possibilities is now prevalent among well-informed people, but there is still a good deal of scepticism. It must be admitted that it is intrinsically improbable that there should be a country on the equator resembling Europe in many of its features and suitable as a residence for Europeans. Indeed the fact is explicable only if we consider that altitude to a certain extent counteracts latitude. Our ordinary notions of equatorial lands are derived from accounts of Brazil or West Africa—that is, of equatorial climates on or but little above the sea-level. It is only in a few rather distant places, such as East Africa and Bolivia, that we meet the much rarer combination of equatorial position and an altitude of six thousand feet and upwards.

Viewed as spheres for the activity of European races, the parts of the globe which lie near the equator can be divided into two classes, those where Europeans can live permanently and bring up their children, and those where they can work as men of business or officials, but always as strangers and sojourners in a foreign land, and on condition of sending their children to Europe and revisiting it from time to time themselves. The former class—that is, the lands suited for permanent residence—is much the smaller, and a rare exception between twenty degrees north and twenty degrees south of the equator. Perhaps one ought to make a third class of tropical climates—-those where Europeans cannot live at all. It is certain that there are places where they cannot thrive for long.

The lower parts of East Africa may all be described as planters' countries—that is, countries where Europeans can live and supervise plantations without any great inconvenience to their physical well-being, but where they cannot reside permanently. From the point of view of health, the coast of the East African mainland (with a few exceptions) is the best of these districts. Zanzibar and Uganda must be pronounced inferior, though still habitable. The worst parts are the shores of Lake Victoria and some swampy places on the coast, such as Vanga and the lower part of the Tana River, in both of which the number of mosquitoes and the absence of proper accommodation are very trying to Europeans. But the greater part of the coast, particularly Mombasa and Lamu, must be given a high rank for healthiness among tropical countries, and is, I think, superior in climate to Bombay, Calcutta, or Madras. This is due largely to the dryness of the soil, and above all to the constant fresh breeze from the Indian Ocean. Taking into consideration the possibilities of going up country by rail for an occasional change, Mombasa must be pronounced a very tolerable residence for Europeans.

The Highlands of East Africa, in which one may include the Teita Hills, are more than this : they are a country in which Europeans can thrive and breed, as is shown by an experience of some years. This, of course, does not mean that the climate has no faults. Europeans, though not critical of any climate near home, become exceedingly exacting in their demands as to the tropics. To my mind, the worst climate I have ever experienced is that of New York, which presents alternately the disadvantages of the arctic and the torrid zones, but I never heard of any one being deterred from going to America by climatic considerations. In East Africa there is no doubt a certain amount of fever. Whether it is ever actually caught above five thousand feet may be doubted. Perhaps the victims are always persons who have got it into their system elsewhere.   But it is certainly not more prevalent and not more dangerous than influenza in England, and the prospect of it need not deter any intending visitor or settler. To the best of my belief, there have been no instances in the Highlands of dangerous forms of fever such as black-water.

It may be reasonably asked, if the highlands of East Africa are really a healthy and fertile country, how does it come about that they have been hitherto scantily populated, miserably cultivated, and almost totally unproductive? The answer is, that until recently they were practically closed to all but African natives, as neither the Arabs nor the Portuguese could advance inwards from the coast.   The African tends to frequent hot, low, luxuriant regions like the shores of Lake Victoria : he can stand the climate, and finds more easily the plants or animals on which he subsists.   Not only were the higher regions less attractive, but many causes tended to depopulate them.   They were specially accessible to the slave-raiders ; they were devastated by intertribal wars and raids; the want of communications turned local droughts into disastrous famines ; there were no means of preventing or arresting the spread of epidemics.   The introduction of a little civilisation clearly changes all these conditions ; but still it must be remembered that in Africa the forces of nature are powerful, and, though they can be conciliated, they cannot safely be defied or neglected.

No doubt the great requisite for preserving one's health in East Africa, as elsewhere in the tropics, is good accommodation.   This can easily be shown in East Africa by comparative statistics of deaths among officers who have had to move about much or live in distant stations, and those who, like the railway officials, live constantly in centres where proper houses are available.   Though the climate is perfectly healthy, the sun is strong and the rain violent.   If people expose themselves to the sun, or even if they live in houses with too thin a roof, they run a great danger of sunstroke or some similar malady.   If, on the other hand, they get wet or allow the rain to enter their houses, they catch a chill, which is more dangerous in the tropics than in temperate climates. But in an ordinary solid house both dangers can be effectively avoided. Perhaps the danger of catching a chill is greater than any which comes from the heat.

In Nairobi and the Kikuyu district the average temperature appears to be about 66° F. in the cool season and 73° F. in the hot. The coolest time is in the early morning, when the thermometer often falls to 45° F. At midday it often reaches 80°. Nevertheless at Limoru, a railway station in Kikuyu about 7000 feet above the sea, I have seen the whole country enveloped in mist at midday and have felt the need of a greatcoat. In the Rift Valley the mornings up till ten are delightful, and the middle of the day not unpleasantly hot; but near Naivasha and the Kedong a strong wind often rises about 4 P.M. On the Mau escarpment and the Settima range the climate is similar to that of Nairobi, but cooler; and at stations like the Ravine the impression of cold is increased by the mist which may be seen creeping in the surrounding forests. Both on the Settima and Mau I have seen ice about a sixth of an inch thick, and felt at least one degree of frost at 6 A.M. The seasons are, of course, the opposite of those to which we are accustomed in Europe. The hottest period is from December to April, and the coolest from July to September. The great rains fall from March to June, and the smaller in November and December. Showers are not infrequent between June and November, but January, February, and the beginning of March are quite dry. The average rainfall for Ukamba is given as 40 inches per annum. At Machakos the average for six years was 34.76, and at Kikuyu 36.14. More accurate and continuous observations are, however, to be desired; for, though the rainfall is not deficient, the precise time of the rainy season is less accurately known than is generally supposed. Rain is usually expected at the end of March, but is often delayed, and for agricultural purposes more definite statistics are desirable. The rainfall on the Mau and round Lake Victoria is apparently heavy, but statistics are not yet accessible, though I believe that observations are now being taken.[1]

There have been in the past considerable famines—one in 1897 and another in 1882; but it would appear that the drought was only partial, and that food was always obtainable in abundance near Lake Victoria and Mount Kenya. Were a famine like that of 1897 to recur now, it may be hoped that, with the facilities of transport afforded by the railway, there would be little or no loss of life.

It may be practicable in the future to guard effectually against droughts by making reservoirs in Kikuyu and elsewhere. The question is almost entirely one of money, for there is always a large unused volume of rainwater which runs off as soon as it falls, and Kikuyu is little more than a series of valleys filled in the wet season by rushing torrents which might easily be held up by a dam. Unfortunately the cost of a dam of sufficient strength has hitherto proved prohibitive for the slender resources of the Protectorate. Also, if one takes into consideration the rainfall, the catchment area, the rate of evaporation, and the amount of water which can be accounted for, it is clear that there remains a very large volume of which no account can be given. The only plausible hypothesis is that it sinks into the ground, and flows in a subterranean layer down to the sea. It is permissible to hope that it may be possible to reach this layer by sinking wells, and at present boring operations with this object are being undertaken in the Taru jungle, near Voi. The discovery of water in such wells would enable us to cultivate a large part of the Protectorate which is at present useless jungle, but the crops which are now produced in Kikuyu and other districts are a proof that irrigation is not required there.

---

[1] Since the above was written the following statistics have been published :— Rainfall from April 1903 to April 1904 : Mombasa, 33.84 inches ; Rabai, 35.18 ; Shimoni, 42.51 ; Nairobi, 42 ; Fort Hall, 51 ; near the Lake, 60–80. The figures for the coast are rather below the average.

It would seem therefore that, as far as climate, temperature, and rainfall are concerned, the Protectorate is shown to be suitable for European residence. It also yields in abundance the articles which Europeans require for their sustenance and comfort. Meat, milk, and butter are plentiful, cheap, and really excellent. The mutton can compare with that of Wales. Fowls, though common at the coast, are neither plentiful nor stout up country, but there is no reason why these deficiencies should not be remedied by the larger introduction of foreign birds, which have been found to thrive. Except in Lake Victoria, the fresh-water fish, though abundant, are only moderate in quality, being small and bony. Large and good fish, however, can be obtained at Kisumu, and the sea fish at Mombasa is excellent. With a little organisation there ought to be no difficulty in delivering both at Nairobi. European vegetables, particularly potatoes, flourish in such profusion and excellence that it has been hoped that they will form one of the staple exports of the Protectorate. European fruit, especially apples, apricots, and pears, is grown with success. It would appear that the varieties which thrive best are those which are not imported directly from Europe, but have been previously acclimatised in non-European temperate countries such as Tasmania and Japan.

Such being the climate and produce of the country, it will no longer sound incredible to state that European children can be reared there without danger or difficulty. The number of fat rosy infants to be encountered on an afternoon's walk at Nairobi is quite remarkable, and though our experience of Nairobi as a European residence is rather short, it extends in the case of Machakos to nearly fifteen years.

Before leaving the subject of health, I had better say a word about two epidemics which have visited the country— the plague and the sleeping sickness. The appearance of the former at Nairobi in 1902 was a perplexing phenomenon, which has given rise to considerable medical discussion, inasmuch as no cases occurred at Mombasa or elsewhere. It would appear, however, that the outbreak was due to the introduction of ordinary bubonic plague from India, and not to the presence in Ukamba of the endemic variety of the disease, which is said to exist to the west of Lake Victoria and in German territory. At that time there were a large number of coolies working for the Uganda Railway, who had been allowed to congregate in crowded and ill-kept quarters, and the plague was probably introduced among them in a consignment of infected goods from India. Heroic measures of disinfection, including the destruction or removal of a great part of the town, were adopted, and the disease was entirely stamped out after sixty-three cases and nineteen deaths had occurred. No Europeans were attacked, and the outbreak may be regarded as an isolated event having no bearing on the general health of the Protectorate. Indeed it was not an unmixed evil, for it brought about many salutary changes in Nairobi for which we might otherwise have waited long.

The sleeping sickness is a far more serious and more permanent phenomenon, though it need not occasion the least alarm to any Europeans who may be thinking of settling in the Highlands, since it is confined to Uganda and the Kavirondo country on the littoral of Lake Victoria. As this latter district is divided from the rest of East Africa by the cold and uninhabited Mau, the infected area is absolutely isolated, for natives are practically unable to cross the mountains except by the railway, where they can be examined. Besides, the people of Kavirondo have no connection with the eastern provinces or motive for visiting them. It was formerly said that the victims of the disease did nothing but sleep and eat until they died, but this account of the symptoms is a little too summary. The sleep is not so conspicuous a symptom as might be supposed from the name ; but the patients are certainly lethargic, and have a difficulty in standing or maintaining any position which requires an effort. The disease is known in West Africa, and has either come across the continent or possibly arises in various localities from unknown causes.

I do not know whether authorities are yet definitely agreed on its character and origin, but the investigations conducted in Uganda by Colonel Bruce appeared to conclusively prove that its distribution coincides with that of a fly (*Glossina palpalis*) allied to the tsetse, and that both this fly and the infected patients are infested with a species of trypanosoma, a genus of protozoa known to produce various diseases in animals in other countries. From experiments performed on monkeys, the inevitable inference seems to be that the fly injects the trypanosoma into the blood, from which it passes in time to the spinal fluid and thence to the brain, when death ensues. No remedy has yet (September 1904) been discovered. The disease has inflicted terrible ravages on the shores of the Lake, but in Kavirondo at any rate it shows signs of dying out. Europeans are susceptible to the infection, though, owing to their clothes and more careful habits of life, they are far less exposed to the attacks of the fly than natives, and only one or two cases have occurred among them. The very few instances of the disease which have occurred in East Africa have been natives of Uganda, who have developed it after arriving, for one of the great difficulties attending the prevention of this pest is that hitherto no method has been found for detecting it in its early stages, though it is now thought that a swelling of the glands of the neck is characteristic. It is very important to prevent the entrance of infected persons into the country east of Kavirondo, for *Glossina palpalis*, or a closely allied species, exists in some parts (*e.g.* near Kibwezi), and should it receive the trypanosoma by biting an infected patient, it would doubtless be capable of transmitting it. It would appear that these malignant flies are found in trees or bushes near water, but not in rushes or papyrus. Within the infected area, swampy districts with no trees were found to be free both of the flies and the disease.

CHAPTER X

EAST AFRICA AS A EUROPEAN COLONY (*continued*)

MINERALS—VEGETABLE PRODUCTS

HAVING seen that the Protectorate is not wanting in the conditions necessary to insure to Europeans a comfortable and healthy life, we will now inquire what occupations and prospects it offers. The industries which it is possible to exercise in East Africa fall into three classes—those concerned with minerals; those concerned with vegetable products, including not only agriculture in the strict sense, but the cultivation of cotton, and the export of timber and rubber; and those concerned with the pasturage of sheep and cattle, to which perhaps may be added ostrich-farming.

The prospect of finding valuable minerals is one of the strongest incentives which attracts Europeans to distant lands, and it is not surprising that more investigations have been made in the mineralogy of the Protectorate than in more promising directions of inquiry. The results have been negative, or unsatisfactory. All the districts likely to contain precious metals have been examined by the East African Syndicate, and by the late Government Geologist, Mr. Walker, who, however, died before he had time to complete his survey. It is true that the investigations made cannot be accepted as absolutely conclusive, for the more northern parts of the Protectorate, with the exception of the area west of Lake Rudolf, have been left untouched, and in many other regions the scrub and grass were so thick that it was difficult to get any general idea of the soil; but the agreement between the opinions of practical miners and scientific explorers is remarkable, and offers little ground for anticipating the discovery of rich deposits. This is not surprising, if one remembers that the whole of the centre of the Protectorate, including the Mau, the Rift Valley, Mounts Kenya and Kilima-Njaro, is covered by a huge lava cap which hides, and probably renders inaccessible, whatever mineral wealth there may be underneath.

There is no confirmation of the reports that gold is to be found about Mount Jombo (near Vanga) or Makindu, but it is undoubtedly present on the eastern shores of Lake Victoria. Discoveries on both sides of the German frontier show that a reef runs northward from German territory across the boundary through Kamagambo, and possibly reappears some-where in Kabras or the neighbourhood of the Sio River. Un-fortunately, the gold appears to be found in such conditions that the working of it is difficult or unremunerative. As far as I know, the East Africa Syndicate has published no de-tailed report of their operations in this district; but they stopped work in December 1903, and it was certain that they did not think the prospects good enough for them, though opinions differed as to whether a firm in a smaller way of business might find it worth their while to prosecute the search. A prospecting expedition was sent to the north-west corner of Lake Rudolf, but was unsuccessful.

A little silver has been reported from behind Mombasa, but not in considerable quantities. Many spots in the Rift Valley seem to offer all the conditions favourable to the formation of diamonds, but, unfortunately, the diamonds themselves are wanting. Opals and agates are found in great quantities in some rivers—as, for instance, the Tigrish and the Njoro—but the stones do not appear to be of any value. It has been constantly asserted that there is a carboniferous belt behind Mombasa, extending from the German frontier towards the Tana, but, though search has been made, no coal has yet been discovered.

Iron is found in great abundance and in several ores, which the natives are able to smelt. Mica is conspicuous in several parts of Ukamba, particularly along the Tsavo, and the flakes appear to be of considerable size. Graphite is also reported from the banks of the same river. Good building-stone is common, and marble is reported both from the north of Mount Elgon and from the Teita Hills. Limestone is also very generally distributed. Valuable clays have been found in the Rift Valley, and the Industrial Mission have established a manufactory of tiles and pots at Jomvu, near Mombasa, with satisfactory results. The East Africa Syndicate investigated a large deposit of soda at Magadi, in Ukamba, near the German frontier. It was said that the quality of the deposit was well reported on, but I believe that they have not yet been able to find a market sufficient to warrant the expenses of working. Good bricks are made both at Mombasa and in Nandi.

Although it is notorious that the discovery of mines is often a matter of surprise, and not according to scientific forecasts, it will be seen from the above that there is no reason to think that minerals will play an important part in the future of East Africa. The country possesses in abundance such simple and useful materials as stone for building, clay for pottery, and easily-smelted iron ore, but, as far as we know, not much more. It is much to be regretted that coal cannot be found.

It is in the vegetable rather than in the mineral kingdom that the strength of East Africa lies. It is a double strength, for the wild indigenous products are of considerable value, and many important exotic plants can be cultivated with success. Among the former are india-rubber, copra, fibre, timber, and castor-oil berries; among the latter, cotton, vanilla, tobacco, coffee, cereals, European vegetables, and fruit.

According to the reports of the Agricultural Department, the soil varies from coarse gravel to rich deep loam, and is seldom either clayey or sandy. The greater part of the country is covered with a deep layer of reddish light loam, and there are limited areas of rich deep soil. The eastern plains, in the

Ukamba and Kenya provinces, are covered with a black, heavy, tenacious loam. Experts report that the blacker soils are the richer, but more difficult to bring under cultivation. As a rule, the soil is very friable and easily cultivated when the old turf has been removed. A rather heavy plough is said to be necessary for breaking up the land, but light plough cultivators or drag harrows are recommended as sufficient for subsequent work.

The indigenous rubber of East Africa is a creeper called Landolphia, of which two species are found—*L. florida* and *L. Kirkii*. The latter is the more valuable. An allied genus, named Clitandra, has been discovered on Kilima-Njaro, and probably occurs within the limits of the British possessions. None of the tree rubbers are known to be indigenous, but Colonel Sadler reports that the Para (*Hevea brasiliensis*), the Central American (*Castilloa elastica*), and West African (*Funtunia elastica*) varieties are being cultivated in Uganda with encouraging results. They could therefore probably be cultivated equally well in those parts of the East Africa Protectorate which have a similar climate. The largest areas which have been ascertained to produce indigenous rubber are on the coast. It grows about Mwele (to the south of Mombasa), around Takaungu, in Gosha, and in the Utwani forest, round Witu; but the best known rubber-grounds, though there is really little reason to believe that they are more productive than the others, are the forests known as Araboko and Sekoki, between the Tana River and Kilifi Creek. The more northern part is called Araboko (or Arabuko), from a village of that name, and the southern, Sekoki; but the application of the names is somewhat arbitrary, and it is doubtful if native and European usage are in accord. The centre of the forest appears to consist of thick-growing timber, while the vegetation on the edges is somewhat more open and scattered. It is in this margin that the Landolphia grows best. Landolphia will probably be found in most parts of the Protectorate where there is anything that can be called wood or forest, as opposed to mere scrub. It occurs along the Voi River, on the Nandi escarpment, and on Mount Kinángöp. It has not yet been discovered on Kenya, but the analogy of Kilima-Njaro makes it highly probable that it exists there. Hitherto, the collection of rubber has not been much encouraged, as it was entirely in the hands of natives, who were under no supervision, and used the most ruthless methods, so that a large demand was likely to mean the extinction of the crop. A creeper like the Landolphia is more likely to suffer than any form of standing tree, for the reckless native collector simply cuts through the stem and lets it bleed at both ends. Recently, however, concessions for indiarubber tapping have been given to Europeans in Arabuko, Sekoki, and Mwele; and it may be hoped that, with proper supervision of the tapping and replanting, the yield will considerably increase.

Copra is exclusively a coast product, for, though the cocoanut grows near Voi, it cannot be made to bear fruit far from the sea. The regions where the palm thrives cannot be called suitable for European colonisation; but I mention this industry here because any danger to health which there may be in superintending such plantations is materially decreased by having a climate like that of Nairobi, twenty-four hours from the coast. Also in many places, certainly near Lamu, the cocoanut plantations themselves are far from unhealthy. The palm grows all along the coast, but the best localities are said to be the Lamu Archipelago and Tiwi, south of Mombasa. The copra is said to be of good quality, and might either be collected by Europeans from Arabs and natives, or grown by them on their own account. Most of the cocoanut plantations are owned by Arabs; but owing to the abolition of slavery, and their inability to adapt themselves to changed conditions, the proprietors are mostly in a bad way, and many would be glad to sell. It is said that the Lamu copra contains 85 per cent. of oil: that from Mombasa and Zanzibar 78 per cent.

The most recent information on the prospects of the copra industry will be found in Mr. Whyte's report [1] on the

---

[1] " Africa," No. 3, 1903.

sea-coast belt of the Protectorate. Mr. Whyte was head of the Agricultural Department, and has had a lifelong experience of tropical agriculture in other countries. He was of opinion that East Africa offers as good a field as Ceylon for the cultivation of the cocoanut palm; and also recommended the cultivation of indigo, as one of the most valuable of indigo-producing plants (the *Indigofera arrecta*) is found wild in considerable abundance.

Fibre-producing plants, particularly the Sanseviera, are common in the Protectorate, and are almost the only thing of known economic value found growing in the scrub. They are abundant, not only in the temperate and better-known parts of Ukamba, but also about Voi, along the Tsavo River, near Kibwezi and Makindu, and along the Tana. It is therefore probable that they are to be found in the whole area of the great jungle behind the coast. A German firm are working fibre on a large concession near Kibwezi. The quality of this product exported from most parts has been well reported on, and very fine samples have been received from the little-known districts of Korokoro, on the upper Tana. An American firm have taken up an area for fibre cultivation on the Tana, and are investing a considerable amount of capital. The fibre when properly prepared is quoted at about £30 a ton. Sisal hemp and Mauritius hemp have also been proved to grow well. The latter fetches about £24 per ton in the European market. Other native plants which are said to produce excellent fibre are Mogumo (*Ficus* sp.), Mogiyo (*Triumfetta rhomboidea*), Mondoe (*Abrutilon glaucum* and *Dombeya* sp.), the wild banana, Wali (*Raphia*), several species of Hibiscus and Chokochare.

There is an abundance of timber suitable for fuel, house-building, and making furniture, and probably some of the woods will be found to make a profitable article of export. Some of the finest trees, unfortunately, grow in rather inaccessible districts, such as Taveta, Mount Kinangop, and the southern Mau, in all of which may be found tall, straight trunks, rising fifty feet or more before they branch; but, owing to the difficulty of transport, it is hard to see how this wood can be used for anything but local purposes. There are, however, at least two fairly accessible districts producing an abundance of timber which has probably a commercial value, namely, the coast and the forests on the Mau through which the railway passes, particularly those to the north of the line. From many parts of the coast, notably Lamu and Vanga, there is a steady export of mangrove poles for building purposes, and trees of greater value yielding ornamental woods are found in the Mwele Hills and in the Arabuko and Sekoki forests. These trees comprise ebony, trachylobium, bambakofi (an afzelia), and mrihi (an albizzia), and it is thought they would be acceptable on the London market. Shipment would be easy if a railway were constructed, or a series of short tram lines, connecting the forests and the ports. On the Mau are vast forests of juniper and olive. The trees are of fine growth, and untouched, as the country is not inhabited. A concession for the export of this timber is now in process of negotiation, and it is hoped that, if sufficiently low rates can be obtained from the Uganda Railway, it will take a favourable place on the market.

The timber on the Kikuyu escarpment will hardly prove suitable for exportation, but is excellent for local building and furniture. The predominant trees are cotton, olive, two or three kinds of fig, juniper, and podocarpus. Bamboo occurs in belts at various places above 6500 feet.

The scrub jungle, from Mombasa to Makindu, contains various kinds of acacia suitable for fuel which supply firewood for the Uganda Railway, but not much timber which can be used for other purposes. Ebony, however, is found in the lower parts.

The castor-oil plant grows in great abundance in many parts of Ukamba and in Kikuyu. The beans are worth about £2, 10s. a ton locally, and are said to fetch from £8, 5s. to £9, 10s. in the English market. They could probably be considerably improved by cultivation. There is a good local market for this product, as both the railway and steamers use considerable quantities.

There is an increasing export of mangrove bark, which goes almost exclusively to Hamburg. It is at present collected chiefly at Lamu and in the Vaneza district, but the tree is abundant in most parts of the coast. The quality is reported to be the best in the European market, and the superior varieties called Mkuko and Msindi produce 50 and 60 per cent. of tannin respectively.

Sugar-cane grows freely in many parts, and is cultivated by the natives, but has not been exported.

· Maize and beans are very abundant, but being low-priced products have not received the attention they merit, as their cultivation is likely to pay only if practised on a large scale. There is a good market for maize in South Africa, and it is grown both in Kikuyu and on the coast. Good crops have also been obtained from rain and without artificial irrigation in the parts of the Taru jungle near the line. The quality of the native seed is poor, but better varieties are being introduced. There is a great demand both in Europe and South Africa for the long red native bean of Kikuyu and Kavirondo, which can be cultivated without difficulty.

If we turn to the exotic plants which can be grown in the Protectorate, those respecting which we have the most certain information are European vegetables and coffee. Both of these have been cultivated for some time in Kikuyu with success, and vegetables have been grown at many other points, such as Machakos, Naivasha, the Ravine, and Nandi Boma. The coffee is good, and as yet free from disease; and the only question is whether the state of the market is favourable for an increase of the world's production of this article. The excellence and abundance of vegetables is indubitable, and local needs must create an increasing demand. It is, however, a matter for serious consideration whether a permanent trade in this article to South Africa can be established, as

many persons have hoped. The essential, but as yet unful-
filled, condition for such a trade is the establishment of some
agency able to buy up potatoes and other vegetables, and to
arrange for them the whole journey from Nairobi to Mombasa
by rail, the sea voyage to Delagoa Bay, and rail again to
Johannesburg. The fact that some consignments have fetched
remunerative prices without such supervision is encouraging.
but many others have been spoiled on the way, and it cannot
be said that the trade has yet been put upon a satisfactory
basis. From an imperial point of view, we should not forget the
possible importance of East Africa as a victualling station where
our fleet could be supplied with fresh vegetables in case of need.
Experts consider that in an ordinary season a profit of at least
£2 per acre should be realised on each crop of potatoes.

But far more important than vegetables, as a possible
article of export, is cotton. Though it has not yet been
cultivated to any considerable extent, the data in our possession are most encouraging. The plant grows wild in many
parts—in Gosha, Tanaland, and near Voi—and it seems to
be an accepted maxim that land which will produce bad
cotton will also produce good cotton if better seed is
sown. Also we know that ten or twelve years ago, before
the British Protectorate had been established, and when
Lamu was still in the German sphere, a German firm
experimented in that district with imported seeds. It is
not known whence the seeds were obtained, but the reports made by experts in Liverpool, Naples, and Germany
on the cotton produced have been preserved, and are most
satisfactory. The samples were priced at from 7d. to
9d. a pound, and were classified as resembling lower quality
sea-island, and between Tahiti and sea-island. Recently an
expert has been sent out. to examine the country, and his
report was equally favourable. It would appear that the
Sabaki, the Tana, and probably the Juba, present much the
same conditions for cotton-growing as the Nile; but that,
considering the difference in the price of land, an acre of

cotton in East Africa ought to be grown for about £6 less than in Egypt, which leaves ample margin to cover the increased freight. As possible cotton lands we have the islands of the Lamu Archipelago, which seem to present exactly the conditions required by the sea-islands variety; the banks of the Tana, Juba, and Sabaki; the shores of Lake Victoria, and a number of places in or near Ukamba, notably Voi and Makindu. Near the Lake, in Kavirondo, cotton is already being grown by Indians, and encouraging experiments have been made near Nairobi. Cotton grown up country and sent down by train would always be handicapped by the railway freight, but that grown on the coast and large rivers could be shipped without difficulty.

Experiments which have been begun in cotton-growing are probably already bearing fruit, and there seems to be no reason why East Africa should not become one of the great cotton-producing countries of the world. Samples grown from Egyptian seed near Nairobi and in Kikuyu have been examined by the British Cotton-growing Association, and priced at 5½d. and 6d. per lb.; but no report has yet been published of the experiments conducted by Government in the much more favourable districts on the coast and round Lake Victoria.

With regard to tobacco, the prospects are less certain. A coarse variety of the plant grows wild in Ukamba, and experiments in the cultivation of a superior quality are being made on the Ramisi River, to the south of Mombasa. The results are not unsatisfactory, and it would seem that an article sufficiently good for internal consumption can be obtained. But long and costly experiments in German East Africa have not been successful in growing from imported seeds any of the higher varieties, and though an apparently excellent leaf has been obtained, it has not developed the precise qualities required by the trade. It is true that the British territory is not absolutely similar to the German, but this negative result in the latter is not encouraging.

Native cereals, such as maize and millet, grow in great

abundance, and even in the scrub behind the coast two or more rain-crops of maize can be obtained in the year. Both Kikuyu and the coast are veritable granaries, where the natives sometimes suffer from a too abundant harvest, for they store a plentiful crop, and do not trouble to sow another. With regard to European cereals, the data are not so full as one could wish. Oats thrive in Nandi. Barley grown in Ukamba was valued in London at £1, 12s. the quarter, and wheat from the same locality was classed on a par with American wheat. There seems to be no reason why the great plains of Ukamba, the Mau, and the Uasin Gishu should not produce wheat in considerable quantities, and more experiments with these crops are desirable.

Two other crops which are being tried are ramie fibre and vanilla, the former in Kikuyu, the latter on the coast. The former is said to have yielded good results; the latter, which takes some years to grow, is not yet mature, but, judging by the example of Zanzibar, is likely to thrive. Sesamum and groundnuts also do well, but chiefly in the hot districts. It will, however, prove profitable to induce the natives to grow them and buy up the crops.

Experiments in the rearing of silkworms have been carried on in the Kenya province during the last two years. The silk produced has not yet been valued, but the conditions seem favourable. Several hundred Japanese mulberry-trees have been planted, and are found to produce three or four good crops of leaves per annum, so that a farmer might have, say, three yields of silk a year against one in southern Europe. The worms have thriven well, the mortality being only 1 per cent.

The official report on the experiments of the Agricultural Department just published (January 1905) says that the year under review (April 1903–April 1904) has been abnormally dry, but that "maize, millet, wheat, barley, lentils, fenugreek, linseed, and native beans have been pre-eminently successful; cotton, clover, ryegrass, lucerne, and Egyptian clover moderately so." The unusually dry weather no doubt accounted for the moderate success of the latter crops.

CHAPTER XI

EAST AFRICA AS A EUROPEAN COLONY (*continued*)

PASTURAGE—LAND QUESTIONS—ZIONISTS—INDIANS

THE prospects for pasturage in East Africa are as promising as for agriculture. Cattle are kept by most of the tribes, and even the apparently barren Somaliland affords subsistence to large herds. In the neighbourhood of the railway are several extensive plains which are either used by the natives as grazing lands, or frequented by troops of antelope, which is generally considered a sign that cattle will do well. One stretch of plains begins soon after Makindu, and reaches to Nairobi. In the more eastern part there are a few scattered trees, but to the west the grass lands are quite open. An extension of these plains stretches northwards from Nairobi towards Mount Kenya. The small meadows interspersed with coppice near Ngongo, to the south of Nairobi, afford excellent grass to cattle owned both by natives and Europeans. Some of the best grazing land, and certainly that which is best known and most seen by the public, lies in the Rift Valley, on either side of the railway. Beyond the limits of the valley rise on the east the pastures of Settima and Laikipia, and on the west the great plateaux of the Mau and Uasin Gishu gradually sloping into the partly wooded but still pastoral districts of Nandi and Lumbwa. Of these pastures the last two are used by the tribes of the same name, and caution would have to be used in settling Europeans there. The Uasin Gishu and Mau are uninhabited, but the grazing prospects have been well reported on both by official experts and private inquirers. The chief need in this case is to improve the communication, and make roads to the north and south of the railway. If a large timber concession is granted for the Mau forests, it may be hoped that a branch line will be constructed northwards towards the Uasin Gishu. It would serve the double purpose of providing the necessary transport for timber, and rendering the plateau accessible to colonists.

The Athi plains right down to Sultan Hamud and Simba are practically uninhabited, and could be taken up freely by Europeans. New Zealanders have expressed the opinion that the grazing near the two stations named ought to be suitable for merino sheep. It may be hoped that in time it will pay to construct a branch line northwards from Nairobi to Kenya, as the country offers a good combination of agricultural and forest land, opening out into plains. With regard to the Rift Valley, Settima, and Laikipia, there is no doubt as to the quality of the grazing, which is excellent; but the question of how much land can be used by Europeans depends on how much land is reserved for the Masai. It is certain that this tribe straggle over a far larger area than they require.

The proposal to make a native reserve along the railway seemed to me disastrous, for it would prevent Europeans from utilising the advantages created by the line, and leaves them in the hands of nomad tribes, who do not appreciate them, and would far sooner have no railway. Fortunately the Government are said to have abandoned this idea. The practical alternatives are either to settle the Masai in a limited extent of ground in the Rift Valley, or to remove them altogether to a distant reserve, say on Laikipia. I believe that the Government have now decided on the second of these alternatives; but even if the Masai remain about Lake Naivasha, there can be no reasonable doubt that there is room for Europeans in the Kedong Valley, in the Endabibi Plain, on the Enderit River, at the north end of Elmenteita, and generally to the north of Lake Nakuru, where the grazing is said to be excellent at the foot of the eastern escarpment, and the country is uninhabited. Should Laikipia not be required for the Masai, it will probably afford superb land for European graziers. If

A Path in the Woods near Kericho.

Nyeri Hill.

it is made a reserve, the Rift Valley and Settima should be available for Europeans.

According to the reports of the Agricultural Department, the soil of the Rift Valley is uniformly fair, not rich, and affords a stretch of good dry grazing ground. The district is better suited to raising stock than to agriculture; but in the wet season wheat, maize, potatoes, and ordinary crops might be successfully grown. It is considered that at present the land will carry two sheep per acre of clear grazing, but that with development it could be stocked more heavily. The herbage differs in various parts of the valley. Round Lake Naivasha there is a close sward of stargrass (*Cynodon dactylon*); but in the basin of Lake Nakuru this is replaced by a rougher growth of hard tufty grass, which provides an enormous quantity of rough fodder.

The quality of the pasturage in the Rift Valley is due to the fact that it has been continuously grazed by native cattle during many years. The northern Mau has not been so grazed, and therefore the pasture is rougher, but, on the other hand, the soil is richer and the rainfall heavier. When the land has been improved by close, confined grazing, it is probable that this district will prove superior to the Rift Valley. It is calculated that the farms in this part of the Mau should carry three sheep per acre.

The southern Mau is reported to possess superior grazing properties. The drier districts are, in the opinion of experts, suitable for merino crosses, and the moister for the hardy Cheviot sheep and Ayrshire cattle. The soil is deep rich loam, inclined to wetness, but easily drained, as the country is a series of slopes and narrow valleys, with streams at the bottom. It is reckoned that farms in this district should carry three wool sheep and a small head of cattle per acre.

When I left the Protectorate in July there were practically no wool-bearing sheep in the country, only a few having been introduced for experimental purposes; but there was already a considerable export of the hides of native sheep and goats.

I see no reason why there should not in the future be a great export of wool and preserved meat as well as of hides. The best cattle seem to be those which come from Somaliland, Kenya, and the shores of Lake Victoria, and the few bulls imported from England have thriven. Cattle, however, when moved from one district to another are very liable to sickness, and when foreign animals are introduced in larger numbers it is probable that there will be many disappointments from the same cause. Pigs and poultry appear to do well. Of imported stock Guernsey cattle and Lincoln and Welsh sheep are reported to do best, but it is thought that crossbreeds of English and native animals will prove preferable. They resist disease better than either of the parent breeds, and crossbred cattle show a great improvement in the first generation. But it is estimated that it will take five or six generations of cross-breeding to produce a wool-bearing sheep of the merino type.

Horses do not do well on the coast, though the Arabs own a few. There are hardly any at Mombasa, as the trolley system renders riding and driving unnecessary. It was formerly very difficult to obtain horses up country, owing to the belts of tsetse fly to be passed on the way. This fly, however, ceases beyond Kibwezi, and horses can make the journey in safety by train. There are now a considerable number in Nairobi, where races are held twice a year. In 1901 several were carried off by an outbreak of horse sickness, for which it was difficult to account, but which was probably partly attributable to bad stabling. Since then they have thriven better. Donkeys and mules do well.

It has been proposed to utilise some of the indigenous animals, such as the elephant, zebra, and ostrich. I shall speak of these animals in the chapter on game. Though the zebra can be domesticated, and used either for riding or driving, it would appear that we have not yet succeeded in obtaining a serviceable animal suitable for everyday work either from the pure-bred zebra or from any hybrid. The African elephant is also probably capable of domestication, but the market is so small that the experiment would not be commercially successful. For ostrich-farming, on the other hand, the prospects are good. The birds are abundant, and, according to South Africans who have examined them, grow feathers of the right quality. The districts where they are most numerous are the Athi plains, and in the Rift Valley.

It will now, I hope, be clear that East Africa provides for a European family the climate and food they require, as well as profitable occupations. Nay more, it is a country which has a singular charm for Europeans, to which they become attached, and which inspires a passionate longing for return in those who leave it. It cannot at present be recommended to persons without money as a place to seek a fortune, for there are as yet hardly any openings for white men who are not prepared to buy land or to carry on some definite business, as the country is not sufficiently developed to offer any positions for overseers or working men which could be filled by Europeans. But those who have about £500—and the more above £500 the better—ought to find no difficulty in buying and working a farm. The quality and quantity of labour obtainable varies. It is cheap (about four or five rupees a month) in Kikuyu and Ukamba, and fairly plentiful; plentiful also in Teita and Kavirondo. In the Rift Valley the Masai make good herdsmen and watchmen, but will not at present undertake much other work, which, however, does not matter, as the country is almost entirely pastoral. In the uninhabited districts, such as Mau and Uasin Gishu, Masai would probably be willing to serve as herdsmen; but it would be necessary to import agricultural labour from Kikuyu or elsewhere, unless it were found that at these higher altitudes Europeans could work in the fields, which is doubtful. Our experience of native labour since we have occupied the Protectorate is encouraging; for the natives have of late shown a docility and aptitude which was hardly anticipated, and have proved that they can and will work not only in the fields, but at various mechanical crafts in the railway workshops.

Conditions change so rapidly in East Africa that it is hard to give any advice as to the best place to settle. For general agriculture Kikuyu perhaps bears the palm. Almost all temperate crops can be raised there; labour and water are abundant. Agricultural land and pasturage are found close together for those who like variety, and they can also try their hand at ostrich-farming or silkworm-raising. Cotton can also be grown and india-rubber collected in some parts. Perhaps a better field for such industries as cotton and fibre is found a little further down the line, near Makindu. As a climate, Kikuyu is preferable; but Makindu, though warmer, is quite tolerable, and in the opinion of experts [1] offers a richer soil than Kikuyu, and greater scope for enterprise to a settler with a fair amount of capital. Fibre plants are plentiful, and cotton, tobacco, maize, rice, water melons, chillies, and wheat are cultivated. Graziers should turn their attention further west to the pastures which I have described, but Nandi and Lumbwa, as well as parts of the Mau, offer possibilities for agriculture as well as pasturage. Mr. Linton has also expressed the opinion, in which I concur, that the country round the Tsavo is of great promise both for agriculture and stock-raising, though a place for the capitalist rather than the ordinary settler.

I fear it cannot be denied that the Government have been somewhat behindhand in assisting and encouraging colonisation. In theory they desire it, and have invited immigration; but there has been a woeful discrepancy between theory and practice. Considering the strict economy which regulates the administration of the African Protectorates, it would perhaps have been unreasonable to expect that the machinery for arranging colonisation should have been made ready before the colonists were actually forthcoming. The Masai proverb says, "Don't make a cloth to carry the child before the child is born," but European babies and European settlers expect to

---

[1] Mr. Linton, head of the Agricultural Department, in Agricultural Report on the country between Voi and Kiu ("Africa," No. 5, 1904).

find things ready for them. At any rate, now that it is demonstrated that Europeans are willing to take up the land, it is not creditable that many should have left the Protectorate because they could not obtain plain and businesslike answers to their applications. If a man asks, "Can I have this piece of land or not?" he may rightly expect to be told Yes or No; and if an administration invites immigration, the immigrant may reasonably expect to be told where he can have land, and to be shown it in an accessible spot. Yet in East Africa it was often difficult to get an answer to such questions.

The fault does not lie in the land regulations, which are sufficiently liberal, but in the absolute lack of administrative organisation, which must occur in a growing country where the authorities refuse to allow any considerable change in a detailed scheme of expenditure prepared six, twelve, or even seventeen months before. Such programmes of expenditure are bound to require variation in East Africa; for not only are unforeseen developments sure to occur, but those who prepare the estimates are not even allowed to anticipate contingencies, and there is no chance of any item being passed which cannot be shown to be actually and immediately necessary. The advent of European settlers at the beginning of 1904 was, in many ways, a sad failure; because not only was there no provision for receiving them under the Budget of 1903–4, which was in force until April 1904, but the Foreign Office were not even willing to revise the Budget for 1904–5, made in November 1903. The consequence was that the staff of the Survey and Land Department was totally inadequate for the work thrown upon it: there were no police, no guides, very few roads, no hotels to speak of, and colonists went wandering about asking to be shown land which they could take up and were unable to find it, in spite of the thousands of square miles all round needing nothing but owners. To complete the confusion the Foreign Office, owing, as I hope, to some misunderstanding which will be removed, suddenly ordered some of the most important concessions to be cancelled and the part of the country best adapted for Europeans to be declared a native reserve.)

(It is no use lamenting the past and the lost opportunity, but it is most earnestly to be hoped that when the Protectorates are taken over by the Colonial Office next year, or even before, the land question in East Africa may be put on a business footing.) The first essential is to have as complete a survey of the country as is compatible with rapidity, so that both the public and Government may know the amount and quality available. Besides the surveyors charged with the technical work of mapping the country, there should also be in the Land Department officials of some colonial experience able to judge of the size of the grants to be made, and the terms on which they should be made. The conditions and quality of the land vary so much in different parts, that a general rule seems hardly possible. The plan which has hitherto been followed is to give leases for ninety-nine years. The area for agricultural holdings has generally been 640 acres (one square mile), and has not exceeded 1000 acres unless there were special reasons. The ordinary size of a grazing area is 5000 acres, but those who have been willing to go some distance from the railway, and open up really new country, have been encouraged with larger grants. The greatest variation has been in the matter of granting freehold, for while ordinary holders were only allowed to have 1000 acres on this tenure, the East African Syndicate were given the right of purchasing 500 square miles (320,000 acres). It is desirable that all these points should be considered by experts in land settlement, with a view to local conditions.

Besides the question of native reserves, forest reserves must be considered. It is most necessary to maintain them in order to prevent the country from being deforested and to insure an adequate fuel supply for the railway; but otherwise they should interfere with colonisation as little as possible. More roads should be made, especially on the southern Mau, as this large tract is at present practically inaccessible.

We may, I think, rely on the natural influx of immigrants
to take up most of the land along or near the railway; but
a well-considered colonisation scheme for settling fifty or a
hundred British families in some of the more distant parts, on
the Mau or beyond the Settima range, would be a distinct
advantage.   Such schemes have, I believe, been tried in New
Zealand and elsewhere with success.   In these more distant
regions the best land is not always that which joins on to the
nearest inhabited settlement, and single individuals or families
are naturally averse to being quite alone in the wilds.   Something of this kind is attempted in the concession given to the
East Africa Syndicate, but provision is there made for settlement only on a very small scale.

Another colonisation scheme which has attracted considerable attention is the proposed settlement of Zionists on
the Uasin Gishu plateau.   When the proposal was first made
in the autumn of 1903, I gave it a very qualified assent, as it
appeared to be a means of introducing capital into the country
and not open to any particular objection, since the locality
selected was remote from all other European settlements.
But the scheme was not executed at once, and meanwhile a
rush of Europeans arrived at the beginning of 1904, who were
willing to take up, and some of whom actually did take up,
land round the plateau.   It is practically certain that in the
near future all this surrounding area will be occupied by
people of British race, and, that being so, though I am no
anti-Semite, I greatly doubt the expediency of putting in the
midst of them a body of alien Israelites.   To do this is to
reproduce that distribution of population which has been the
bane of Eastern Europe and Asia Minor, namely, enclaves of
races with business capacity, such as the Jews and Armenians,
who differ in language, religion, and manner of life from the
surrounding Russians and Turks, with the result that racial
hostility is almost inevitably produced.   Neither can I see
how the scheme is likely to benefit the Jews.   The amount of
population who could be accommodated on the Uasin Gishu

would not materially relieve the congestion of the Russian and Polish towns, and a considerable personal experience of both Africa and the Jewish parts of Eastern Europe makes me think that the proposed transfer would be too abrupt and defeat its own ends. I have never myself seen a case where Jews are really agriculturists. But admitting that they can become so, their agricultural capacities are certainly not highly developed, and considering how many ordinary conveniences are wanting in East Africa, and how much immigrants are thrown on their own resources, it would seem to be a country rather for those who have hereditary and personal experience of agriculture than for those who are new to the pursuit.

Another proposed form of colonisation deserves mention, namely, the settlement of Indians. There is a large Indian population in East Africa, composed of Hindus, Mohammedans, Parsis, and Goanese, partly established since some time owing to the old commercial connection with India, and specially Goa, and partly reinforced by new arrivals of late years owing to the construction of the Uganda Railway, which employed 20,000 coolies and attracted a large number of merchants and contractors. Sir Harry Johnston once expressed the opinion that East Africa ought to be the America of India. I hardly feel able to agree with so broad a statement, for the various districts of East Africa differ so much from one another that generalisations are dangerous, and the fact seems to be that India does not require an America. The Indian Government do not encourage emigration, and, though Indians are ready to seek new markets, they do not really settle in foreign countries. They trade there, but they desire to return to India; and it is to India that they send their money, instead of spending it in the land of their residence. Still, Indian cultivators would be welcome on the shores of Lake Victoria and on the coast, where it is not likely that more white men will live than those who are required for the general supervision of estates and business. The style of cultivation practised near Vanga, and about the mouth of

NAIVASHA.

MASAI CATTLE.

UASIN GISHU PLATEAU FROM THE SIRGOIT ROCK.

the Tana, is suitable to their aptitudes, as is also trade with the natives; and, as the Arab element does not seem to be on the increase, there is room for them. Similarly, they are likely to do well in Kavirondo. A small settlement of time-expired railway coolies has been made on the Kibos River, about ten miles from Kisumu. They are chiefly occupied with the cultivation of cotton, and, though they are not perhaps drawn from the class best suited for agriculture, the results have been sufficiently satisfactory to warrant the continuation of the experiments, especially if Indians of the real agricultural classes can be attracted.

But I do not think that it would be wise to let Indians acquire land to any extent in the cooler parts of the Protectorate which are suitable for Europeans. The intermixture of races in a seaport like Mombasa does not much matter. Such towns become cosmopolitan, and, though instances like the Armenian massacres of 1896 at Constantinople are not encouraging, the different races generally manage to get on together. But it would be a very different thing to allow two races so dissimilar, and yet so much on a level, as the Indian and British to compete in colonising East Africa. It may be doubted if the Highlands are really congenial to Indians. The coolness of the climate is not appreciated by them, and the agriculture is not of the class to which they are most accustomed. But they are keenly alive to the advantage of acquiring valuable property, and the example of Zanzibar, where large numbers of plantations belonging to impoverished Arabs have passed into the hands of Indians, shows that as landowners on a large scale they are not a blessing to the country, inasmuch as they do not spend money on improving their estates, but merely bleed them in order to send it to India. There are indications that this danger exists in East Africa, and that some of the poorer Europeans have borrowed money from Indians on mortgages. I therefore, when Commissioner of the Protectorate, discouraged all acquisition of land by Indians in the Highlands, except in the immediate vicinity of towns.

CHAPTER XII

ADMINISTRATION

PRESENT ARRANGEMENTS—WAYS AND MEANS

Our East African possessions consist of the two Protectorates of East Africa and Uganda, the former comprising all our territories to the east of Lake Victoria, the latter those lying to the north and west. The Uganda Protectorate must not be confused with the kingdom of Uganda, from which it takes its name, as it includes, in addition to that kingdom, the adjacent Bantu countries of Unyoro and Usoga, the upper waters of the Nile and its right bank in the north, and Toru, Buddu, and Ankole in the south. Formerly the provinces of Naivasha and Kisumu, to the east of the lake, were included in the Uganda Protectorate, and the boundary was practically the Kikuyu escarpment; but, as the railway advanced, this division was found to have many inconveniences, and was superseded by the present frontier, which starts from the north-west corner of Lake Victoria, follows the river Sio, crosses Mount Elgon, and follows the course of the Suam and Turkwel to Lake Rudolf.

It is, however, generally agreed that it would be advisable to amalgamate the two Protectorates, and if this is to be done, it certainly ought to be done soon, for the longer they remain apart, the more they tend to become different in their administrative system and regulations, which is what should be avoided. There is no great diversity of interests between the two territories. If it were possible to detach the districts inhabited by Somalis, it would be an excellent thing to form them into a separate government, as they are different in population, economic and physical conditions from the other provinces; but, unfortunately, they are too small to form a separate administration, and the adjoining Somali territories are not British. It would be possible and advantageous, if it suited the Egyptian Government, to detach the northern part of the Nile province from Uganda, at least as far south as Nimule, and add to it the territories of the Sudan. But the central portions of the two Protectorates are naturally connected together; they feed the same railway, and the same steamers on Lake Victoria; in the case of military operations they have to assist one another; the postal, telegraph, and medical departments are already fused, and it is most desirable that the process of union should be continued, and that all common interests and tasks should be directed by some central authority on the spot. Sir Harry Johnston's proposal that there should be a Chief Commissioner for the whole territory seems to me the best one, and he should be assisted by three Deputy-Commissioners—one for the Coast, one for the Highlands and the Kisumu province, and one for the present Uganda Protectorate.

Another reason for uniting the territories is that, compared to East Africa, Uganda has comparatively few healthy stations. In the interests of the Service, it would be well if there was a freer and more frequent change from unhealthy to healthy posts than is possible at present.

Though the present East Africa Protectorate is commonly spoken of as one territory, and is so for many purposes, it is hampered by a most inconvenient political division, a large part of the Coast being legally the dominions of the Sultan of Zanzibar. When the British and German spheres were divided, the Germans bought theirs outright, but we agreed to lease from the Sultan, for an annual rental of £17,000, such parts of the Coast as were then recognised as his Highness's dominions—that is, the Lamu Archipelago, a strip extending from the sea ten miles inland from the German frontier to Kipini at the mouth of the Ozi River, and an area with a ten-mile radius round Kismayu. This unfortunate arrangement can be explained, but cannot be really excused, and the sooner it is terminated the better. Its inconvenience is not that we are burdened by an annual payment, or that the Sultan interferes with our administration, for his sovereignty is purely nominal; but that as long as this nominal sovereignty exists the country must be regarded as subject to the same treaties and disabilities as Zanzibar, and that therefore the British authorities, as representing the Sultan, have no juris-diction over foreigners, including natives of German East Africa who may happen to cross the boundary, and the native servants of such Europeans as are not British subjects, and no power to tax them. I must say that during my stay in East Africa the foreign representatives were most considerate in the use they made of these rights in Mombasa; but as long as the rights exist legislation is often hampered, and many desirable improvements, such as the creation of a municipality at Mom-basa, are impossible. Inasmuch as the whole system of the Sultan's mainland dominions is now a mere theory and legal fiction, it is to be hoped it may soon be brought to an end, which could be done in several ways. The Powers might renounce their rights, which is perhaps the most probable solution, or the Sultan might formally cede all his territory except certain buildings, for which he might continue to receive the same rent as at present, so that he would suffer no loss.

The whole of both our East African Protectorates are within the zones in which the free importation of arms, as well as of spirituous liquors, is forbidden. Greater vigilance in preventing the entrance of firearms is desirable, for it cannot be denied that somehow or other a good many old weapons find their way, though through what door is not quite clear, into the hands of natives. The prohibition both to import and to manufacture spirituous liquors is, I think, satisfactorily enforced as far as European beverages are con-cerned; but it has not yet proved possible to restrict the manufacture by natives of the many intoxicating drinks made from palms, sugar-cane, honey, &c., which they were found

using when we undertook the administration of the Protectorate. It is extraordinary what Africans will drink. A
native of Kikuyu once saw a friend of mine, who had a bad
sore throat, using a gargle, which happened to be particularly
strong. Heping to cure him of his drunken tastes, my friend
let him help himself to the gargle, which he did liberally.
No physical evil, but also no moral good, was occasioned.
The native came back next day for another drink of the
liquor, which he said he thought excellent.

The northern boundary of the Protectorate also presents
political problems, as it is not fixed for a great part of its
length. As far as our territory is coterminous with the Italian
sphere, it is clearly bounded by the river Juba, but between
Lugh and Lake Rudolf there is a great gap where we have
no frontier of any sort with Abyssinia. The line drawn on
most maps, which is generally about 6° N., is quite imaginary.
We have no pretence of administration or authority in this
district, and the Abyssinians have advanced far to the south
of our supposed limits.

This southward movement of the Abyssinians is a serious
matter. We know that they have appeared on the Turkwel
River in the west, and in the neighbourhood of El-Wak in the
east, and that they have a post at Erero. King Menelik and
his government disclaim all responsibility and knowledge of
these raids, but the superior chiefs do not keep the smaller
chiefs quiet, and the advance continues. The Abyssinians,
though not nomadic, are, like the Turks, very destructive, and
soon strip a country bare; and as their southern districts are
occupied chiefly by military bands, the process of exhaustion
is accomplished with unusual activity, and a new looting-
ground is soon required. It is true that all this region is
very distant. People hardly think more of it at Mombasa
than they do in London, and an expensive extension of our
power and responsibilities, which would probably not be commercially profitable, is to be deprecated. But, on the other
hand, there is no mistaking the rapidity and significance of

this southward advance. If it continues at the same rate which it has maintained during the last six years, the Abyssinians will in another six years be on the Uasin Gishu plateau and the slopes of Mount Kenya. Also, though we need have no aggressive land-hunger in these distant regions, it is decidedly desirable to keep the Abyssinians as far as possible from the civilised part of the Protectorate, and avoid the cost of any elaborate system of defence in the future, while it is not wise to cede any territory on the assumption that it is desert.

Hitherto our experience in East Africa has not been one of disillusion. As a rule we have not found that supposed valuable lands were deserts, but rather that supposed deserts were valuable lands. A visit of inspection was paid to the frontier last year (1903) by an expedition under Mr. Butter, and we may hope that an amicable arrangement will soon be concluded by which the Abyssinians will be kept as far to the north as possible. We cannot any longer expect to keep them above 6° N., but possibly a line between 3° and 3.50°, following the natural features of the country, would be acceptable to both parties. There is said to be an escarpment running through this part with an uninhabited unhealthy strip at the bottom. This would make a good frontier, for if the escarpment were left to the Abyssinians they would have little temptation to advance beyond it. Unless it is thought essential to have a strip affording right of passage round the head of Lake Rudolf, it would appear to be immaterial where the frontier cuts its eastern shore, as the whole of this district is reported to be desolate and devoid of vegetation.

If the frontier is once arranged with King Menelik, it would be desirable to secure its observance by establishing two or three military posts of native soldiers and a few British officers between Lake Rudolf and the Juba. Though the country is not rich, it would probably repay, at least to some extent, the expense of these establishments; for it has been ascertained that in return for effective protection against the Abyssinians, the inhabitants would gladly pay a property tax of ten per cent. in cattle, and we could also direct to Kismayu a considerable volume of trade in ivory, hides, &c., which at present crosses the Juba from our territory, and is shipped from the Italian sphere.

The southern border of the Protectorate has been accurately delimitated only as far west as Kilima-Njare. To the west of this it is formed by a line drawn from the end of the frontier on the mountain, where a pillar has been erected, to the point where the parallel 1° S. intersects the shore of Lake Victoria. Fate loves to raise difficulties about frontiers, and create circumstances which render the clearest expressions ambiguous. In this case, parallel 1° S. cuts the shore at three points at least, since at the place of its intersection a hatchet-shaped cape projects into the lake, and, of course, the angle which the line makes with Mount Kilima-Njaro, and consequently the amount of territory which it includes, will depend on which point is ultimately accepted. This portion of the frontier is at present being delimitated by an Anglo-German Commission.

I gladly testify to the cordial spirit of co-operation which the German authorities have always shown in dealing with questions concerning the two Protectorates. It is a pity, however, that there is as yet no extradition treaty, or some less formal arrangement to the same effect, between the two territories, and that an offender who commits a crime in one has only to go over the border into the other in order to be scot free. The local authorities are perfectly willing to assist one another by delivering up criminals, and the only difficulty is legal. One cannot help thinking that the law, in its anxiety to be an exact science, sometimes frustrates its own objects. In the present case it is held that the sovereign rights of the Crown over a Protectorate are not sufficient to justify extradition.

The territory comprised within these boundaries is divided into seven provinces, besides the unorganised territories in the north near Abyssinia. These provinces are Jubaland, Tana-land, and Seyidie on the sea; Ukamba and Kenya inland, but to the east of the Rift Valley; Naivasha, comprising the Rift and part of the Mau; Kisumu, on the shores of Lake Victoria, including Nandi and Lumbwa. Jubaland is under military government, and as long as communication is so bad the administration must be more or less unsatisfactory. The remaining provinces are each administered by a Sub-Commissioner, who resides at the provincial capital. These towns are, following the order of the provinces given above, Lamu, Mombasa, Nairobi, Fort Hall, Naivasha, and Kisumu, Besides these there are seventeen other Government stations. Four are on the coast—Kipini, Melindi, Takaungu, Shimoni (combined with Wasin). Actually on the railway are only the four provincial capitals of Mombasa, Nairobi, Naivasha, and Kisumu; but within twenty miles of it are Rabai, Mwatate near Voi, Machacos, Dagoreti in Kikuyu, the Ravine, Kericho in Lumbwa, Soba, and Nandi Boma in Nandi. Taveta, on the German frontier near Kilima-Njaro, Kitui in Ukamba, Nyeri in Kenya, Baringo on the shore of that lake, Mumias on the Nzoia River, and Karungu, on the shore of Lake Victoria near the German frontier, are the only stations at any distance from the line. Besides this, we have military stations with one or two officers at Witu and at Mohoroni, on the line near the lake. Voi, Makindu, and Nakuru are important railway stations where there are a considerable number of Goanese and Indians, and a few Europeans.

The administrative officers under a Sub-Commissioner are known as collectors and sub-collectors, or occasionally as district officers and assistant district officers. When possible, both a collector and a sub-collector are placed at every station, but the paucity of the staff often makes this impossible. In theory their chief duties are to collect revenue and administer justice. In practice a young man of between twenty-five and thirty often finds himself in sole charge of a district as large as several English counties, and in a position which partly resembles that of an emperor and partly that of a general servant. In theory such matters as the Post, Public Health, Public Works (including one's own house), and Police are directed by the corresponding departments of the central administration, but in practice the supervision naturally falls to the lot of the man on the spot. The accepted ideal is that each department should control its own ramifications in the provinces, but where those ramifications hardly exist the officer on the spot will often show himself a surprisingly efficient Jack of all trades. One cannot justify the building of bridges which by all laws of construction ought to collapse, but, for all that, in distant places one is thankful to walk over them instead of wading through rivers.

The central departments are nominally located at Mombasa, but really to a large extent at Nairobi. At the former are the Law Courts, Custom House, Post Office, Treasury, Port Office, Audit and Transport Offices. At the latter are the headquarters of the Military, Railway, Medical, Forestry and Agricultural Departments, as well as of the Land Office. The Police and Public Works may be said to be distributed between the two towns. In a country where there are only three posts a week this arrangement is extremely inconvenient, for public business must be unduly delayed unless the departments likely to be concerned in a given matter can consult one another within a day. The best plan is that adopted in India, where the Government spend the cool weather on the coast, and move up country when it grows hot. If this is too expensive for Africa, the next best arrangement would be to make Nairobi the official capital, and leave at Mombasa only those offices which are inseparably connected with the coast, such as the Customs and Port Office. It is impossible to concentrate the Government at Mombasa, because for various reasons the headquarters of the Military and Railway Departments, as well as of the Land Office and of all the officials who have to deal with questions of colonisation, must be at Nairobi, and it is extremely inconvenient for them to be separated from the Commissioner and his financial and legal advisers.

I need not give a detailed account of the administration. Particulars will be found in the official reports on the Protectorate which are published from time to time. But two general criticisms suggest themselves. The first is that the administration is undermanned; the second, which is partly a consequence of the first, that it is too much concentrated along the line of the railway. Of course we must avoid inconsiderate expenditure and mere speed in progress without knowing where we are going. Of course, too, we must advance from well-known to less-known places, but the time has certainly arrived when, for both political and financial reasons, we ought to extend our influence as much as possible. In the relation of European and African tribes, it is not true that familiarity breeds contempt. The hostile natives are almost invariably those who know nothing about Europeans, and kill some stragglers out of mere bravado. With the possible exception of the Somalis, who cannot be classed as ordinary African natives, every tribe appears to accept the white man as a superior and not unfriendly creature the moment he appears as the representative of regular government, and it is surprising how small a force of police is sufficient to support our authority. But when natives receive their first experience of the foreigner by chance contact with traders, particularly Indians, who fail to inspire respect and at the same time provoke resentment by arbitrary acts and forcible appropriation of supplies, then trouble often occurs, and as a rule it is found that those who are most aggressive are least capable of defending themselves.

The conclusion to be drawn is that the establishment of effective administration should as far as possible anticipate private immigration to a district, or at least accompany it. Also, in order to make the Uganda Railway pay—that fundamental and recurring problem of East African finance—it is absolutely necessary to provide feeders for its traffic. In most of the parsimony that characterises our expenditure lurks the fallacy that a railway will pay for itself without any effort being made to render the country through which it passes productive. It is clear, however, that in order to provide traffic for the Uganda Railway, we must begin by creating a production of exports and a market for imports, not only in the immediate margin of the line, but in all the inhabited country round it. In my opinion this can be done, and done without much difficulty, but it cannot be done without increasing the extent and efficiency of our administration. To cover the cost of such increase we need not look to an ultimate improvement of trade which will increase the Protectorate revenues in the indefinite future. It can be proved that additional officers and stations pay for their salaries and up-keep in all districts which are at all prosperous. What costs money is the central administration: it is expensive and not directly productive. On the other hand, a sub-collector receives a salary of only £250, and, including all the travelling, transport, and miscellaneous expenditure which he may occasion, does not cost the Government more than £500 in all. Against this, he probably makes £900–£1000 in revenue derived from fees and taxes; and it must be remembered that an extra officer means extra revenue, for it means that he visits districts which would otherwise be neglected.

I have so often alluded to the question of expense, and it is of such great and obvious importance, that it will be well to examine here the state of the Protectorate finances. The figures for the last two years are roughly as follows:—

	EXPENDITURE.	REVENUE.
1902–3 . . .	£311,460	£95,284
1903–4 . . {	Not audited, but roughly £351,000 [1]	Not audited, but roughly £109,000
1904–5 . . {	Estimated £376,967	Estimated £121,692

[1] This is the figure indicated in "Africa," 10, of July 1904. "Africa," 15, 1904, published in January 1905, gives it as £418,877, "including some arrear charges." I do not understand these figures.

The revenue for 1904–5 will probably largely exceed this estimate. The increased expenditure is mainly due to new military arrangements.

The difference between the revenue and expenditure is made up by an annual grant in aid from the home Treasury. The figures since 1895 are to be found in the official publications, but I do not give them here because, though they are of course correct in a literal sense as a piece of accountant's work, they are puzzling and even misleading without elaborate explanations to explain their fluctuations. The Protectorate took over two provinces from Uganda in 1902, and expenditure on behalf of the railway has sometimes been included in the Protectorate budget and sometimes made a separate account. From time to time there has been heavy extraordinary expenditure, such as £56,000 for two steamers on the Lake. All that can be said is that, taking everything into account, there is a steady increase in revenue. The chief items of revenue are customs duties, licences and taxes, posts and telegraphs, and the proceeds of the sale and rent of land. The customs duties, being collected at seaports within the Sultan's dominions, have to conform to the treaties which bind the Zanzibar Government. They consisted until recently of a uniform *ad valorem* duty of 5 per cent. on imports, and export duties of from 5 to 15 per cent. on various articles. It has, however, been found compatible with the international obligations of Zanzibar to make the following changes, which were brought into force in April 1904. The import duties are raised to 10 per cent., but at the same time most of the export duties are abolished, and articles likely to conduce to the development of the country, such as agricultural implements and stock for breeding, are admitted duty free. On the whole, this will probably cause an increase of about one-third in the customs revenue, but we have not a year's figures before us as yet. An increase of the postal and telegraph revenue is also certain if European immigration is encouraged.

At present the chief item in the receipts from licences

CROSSING THE ATHI.

and taxes is the hut tax, derived from a small annual payment of two or three rupees per hut by natives.[1] This impost
occasions no hardship, and cannot be considered excessive if
one considers how great and direct are the advantages which
natives have derived from the establishment of our rule and
the abolition of the slave trade. The tax is collected without
difficulty, and the missionaries, who were consulted before it
was levied, offer no objection to it. It brings in at present
about £16,000, but the amount is increasing every year, as
the influence of Government becomes more extended. The
increase in the census must also have a favourable effect on
the receipts. In some districts, particularly on the coast, the
slave trade was a terrible drain on the population, as more
than half the children were taken away. Now that this
scourge has been removed, we may hope to witness a very
material rise in numbers, and I see no reason why the hut
tax should not gradually increase to about £35,000 in the next
few years. At present the taxation of Europeans is extremely
light, though some of the forms which it assumes, such as
game licences, cause irritation and complaint. In fact, there
is probably no country in the world where the incidence of
taxation per head is so small, as there is no income tax,
house tax, or land tax. A larger and more established white
population may, however, find it to their own interest to
contribute more largely to public funds.)

The chief items of expenditure were as follows in 1903 :[2]—.
£58,000 for civil administration, including police ; £33,000
for public works ; £64,000 for military ; £62,000 for the
working of the Uganda Railway ; and £17,000 as rent and
interest paid to the Sultan of Zanzibar. Of these figures it
may be hoped that the annual deficit on the working of the

[1] The reason of the difference is that the tax was fixed at two rupees per
hut for East Africa, but in Uganda, where the people were richer, at three
rupees. When two of the Uganda provinces were incorporated in 1902, it was
thought better to maintain the old rate in them.

[2] I have distributed the cost of transport, which is shown separately in the
published official figures.

railway will disappear in a year or two, and that the line will at least pay its way. But most of the other expenditure is bound to increase. I could wish myself to decrease the military expenditure, which I think unnecessarily high, and to increase the police force, but this is a topic to which I shall presently recur in more detail.

The gist of this survey of revenue and expenditure is that even if the country does not make any sudden rapid progress —which is not improbable, and, in my opinion, will happen under proper management—the expenditure should in the next few years decrease, owing to the disappearance of the deficit on the working of the railway, and the revenue increase by about £10,000 a year. This provides a sound margin out of which a somewhat more liberal expenditure may be met without increasing—or even while diminishing—the annual grant. It is, however, my own conviction that if the administration were conducted on rather broader lines the revenue would augment very rapidly, and the country would cease to be a charge on the home Treasury.

CHAPTER XIII

ADMINISTRATION (*continued*)

SUGGESTIONS FOR THE FUTURE

IF, then, we may hope to attain by natural progress and better management the means of providing for a somewhat more liberal expenditure without increasing the cost of the Protectorate to the mother country, let us consider what are the improvements and extensions of administration most needed. They fall into two classes, those concerned with natives and those concerned with Europeans. I have treated elsewhere of various questions raised by our relations to the native element, and will here confine myself to one. It may be assumed that every one will agree that our object should be to bring all the natives of the Protectorate under our influence, and not allow the more distant parts of the territory to remain ignorant and hostile, as they are, to some extent, at present.

We may set aside as a problem to be considered separately the administration of Jubaland, where at present we merely maintain a garrison.

After Jubaland, the most neglected province is Tanaland, in which there are only three civil administrative officers, the Sub-Commissioner, with an assistant, at Lamu, and a collector at Kipini, who is in charge of the whole of the Tana River. There is also a company of troops with one European officer at Witu, and small detachments of native police, without any Europeans, at Kiunga and Port Durnford. This utterly inadequate arrangement is supplemented by the native civil administration, dating from the times of the Sultan's direct government and comprising a number of governors (liwalis [1]

---

[1] Liwali is a Swahili corruption of the Arabic Al-Wali (the Governor).

and mudirs) and judges (kadis), but the staff is still insufficient. At least two more officers ought to be appointed, one for the Lamu Archipelago and surrounding districts on the mainland, and one for the upper waters of the Tana. At present the important and productive district of Korokoro is entirely neglected.

The province of Seyidie has perhaps the best distributed staff in the country, and may be said to be adequately administered on the assumption—often, alas, not correct—that all the stations are really supplied with the officers who are nominally posted there. It often happens that the illness or leave of officers, or sudden and urgent need elsewhere, gives no alternative but to let a station remain vacant for some time. Much the same is true of those parts of the up-country provinces which lie near the railway or Lake Victoria. The latter region, in particular, ought to receive special treatment, because, though it is rich and very populous, it is also unhealthy for Europeans. Some rules, which need not be discussed here since they are a detail of internal discipline, should be elaborated on the basis of giving officers only a short term in this province or more frequent leave. Either system has inconveniences, but I think an effort should be made to introduce the second; for, though the frequent change of officers may be good for their health, it is not good for a district to be always administered by new men. Further, the sanitation of Kisumu should receive attention, and a sanatorium ought to be built in Nandi, or at the nearest suitable point, to which officers could repair frequently and recruit for a few days.

There are, however, two important and populous districts up country, which have hitherto been left alone and which now require attention. These are, first, the country west of the Mau, between the railway and the German frontier—that is, Lumbwa, Sotik, and Kossova or Kisii; and, secondly, the slopes and immediate neighbourhood of Mount Kenya. Both these regions are rich and populous, and both present a certain danger if they are neglected, for the Lumbwa might attack the railway, and the less-known tribes round Mount Kenya do attack those who are better known. These latter have welcomed our administration, and we are consequently bound to protect them. It would therefore be well to take these districts successively in hand, and definitely establish our influence in them. About a year ago (towards the end of 1903) it seemed as if it would be best to begin with the Lumbwa-Kossova country. It was reported that gold had been found there by the East Africa Syndicate, and the thefts of railway material by the Nandi were troublesome; but the Syndicate decided not to work the gold, and better relations have been established by Mr. Hobley with both the Lumbwa and Nandi.

The second question, therefore—that of the Iraiini, Embo, and other tribes round Mount Kenya—seems to me the more important. The country is one of the most fertile and pleasant in East Africa; many Europeans, colonists as well as missionaries, have been attracted by it; wherever we have opened stations, as at Fort Hall and Nyeri, we have found the natives friendly, ready to assist us and to pay hut tax. But those who do not know us are hostile and suspicious, and there is great danger that if we do not establish our influence among them by firm but peaceful methods, some day a catastrophe will occur. Some missionary will be murdered or a caravan will be cut up, and the incident will be made the occasion of a costly punitive expedition. I therefore recommend that we advance into the country with an adequate force of troops and police, and establish two Government stations, from which we can begin negotiations with the natives. I see no reason why the foundation of these stations, to be placed in positions selected by local experts, should be attended by any more hostility than the foundation of Nyeri. The first columns must be prepared to defend themselves against possible attacks from natives, but it is not likely that the attacks will be repeated or that any serious operations will be necessary. On the other hand, prudence requires that we should put ourselves into communication with our base; and for this purpose I recommended the construction of a telegraph from Nairobi to Fort Hall, the headquarters of the Kenya Province. I have every belief that if some such scheme is carried out, all the country round Mount Kenya will within a year be peaceful and accessible to Europeans.

When this has been done, it will be well to deal with the Lumbwa-Kossova country on the same lines. Here, too, I anticipate little difficulty if we follow the good policy of making our first appearance firmly, peacefully, and in sufficient strength to overawe resistance, for which only a force of two or three hundred men is required. The unknown element in this district is the tribe of Kisii or Kossova, to which I have several times referred. Practically all we know of them is that they are Bantu-speaking, brave, and that they fight with the Lumbwa; but it by no means follows from this that they would be hostile to Europeans. If they did prove intractable we should have the Lumbwa as allies against them; but judging from the analogy of other cases where we have had to deal with two tribes mutually hostile, but neither overwhelmingly superior to the other, the chances are that the two parties would fully appreciate the position, and both endeavour to obtain our good graces.

If we had two new stations in Kenya, and two more in Lumbwa and Kossovo, I think our administration would be adequately represented up country. We might perhaps have another in western Nandi and another in northern Ukamba, but these are less necessary than those first indicated. I may add that I think the country to the north of Mount Elgon requires attention, as it has become the resort of a dangerous riff-raff, composed of Swahilis and low-class Europeans. The territory belongs to Uganda, but it is on the borders of the two Protectorates, and both are interested in maintaining order.

In the coast districts of Seyidie and Tanaland the old Arab civil administration is continued, and the various governors and judges receive small salaries from the Government; and it may be asked how far we should attempt to introduce a similar native administration among the up-country tribes. No fixed rule can be laid down in such a matter, for native systems of government—if indeed such a term can be used—vary greatly in the development that they have attained and the authority that they wield. But taking the tribes east of Lake Victoria, and excepting the quasi-civilisation of those on the west, I should say that, though it is advisable to subsidise the principal native chiefs and secure their friendship, it is not at present desirable to entrust them with more administrative power than can be helped, particularly in cases where there is any question of collecting taxes. They are inclined to exaction on their own account, and for some time to come our main object must be to accustom natives to Europeans. If possible, taxes ought to be in all cases collected by Europeans only. The employment of Swahili tax-collectors in the Kisumu Province has led to complaints.

In suits, either between natives or between a native and a European, the special native courts regulations are found to work well. Under them cases are heard by European officers with native assessors, and the latter are most efficient in producing the person who is ultimately admitted by every one to be the culprit, though their methods are not exactly in conformity with the European law of evidence. The law administered in these native courts is the Indian Penal Code, with such alterations as may be necessary. It must be admitted that it often seems unreasonable to apply civilised law to simple savage life. The difficulty in East Africa has more than once taken the form that it appeared impossible to punish legally an admitted culprit.

A curious case occurred a few years ago, when four men

committed a murder at Melindi. They were practically known to be the criminals, and when questioned confessed their fault. They were then sent to Mombasa for sentence and execution, and various circumstances rendered it most desirable to make an example of them. But the Mombasa court gave them an advocate, who made them plead not guilty, as the Indian Code, for reasons which are no doubt excellent in India, takes no account of confessions to the police. No other evidence was forthcoming, and to their immense astonishment they were acquitted. The situation was serious, for the example of an unpunished murder was bound to have a disastrous effect, and the only theory by which the native mind could explain the course of the law was dangerous to the public peace. They argued thus: "The law of the Europeans requires a life for a life; therefore, if one man murders another, the murderer is shot. But if four men kill one man they are let off, because it would not be fair to take four lives for one." Finally, as the four murderers could not be executed, they were deported to Kismayu, it being in the Commissioner's power to remove individuals in this way when he is satisfied by sworn evidence that their presence is dangerous to peace and order.

Another curious case occurred in the Kisumu Province just at the time when it was transferred from Uganda to East Africa in 1902. A few days before the transfer a man was sentenced to death by a native tribunal held under European supervision. This form of court was at that time legal in Uganda, but not in East Africa. Unfortunately, the man was not executed before the transfer of territory took place. When it had once been accomplished, the execution seemed altogether illegal. He could not be executed by the authorities of East Africa, for, according to the law of that country, he had not been condemned. Nor could he be executed by the authorities of Uganda under their law, for the place had ceased to be Uganda territory. To let him go free would have been a scandal to the natives; to go through the process of trying him again before another court hardly less scandalising and mysterious. It was the man himself who helped us out of the difficulty. In ignorance of his security he tried to escape, and was shot by a warder.

Not less important than civil administration among the natives is the question of the military force to be maintained in the Protectorate. On this point I do not share the views of the home authorities. They were impressed by the fact that in 1901 and previous years it had been necessary to borrow considerable numbers of troops from India, at great expense, to aid in the Ogaden punitive force, the suppression of the Uganda mutiny, and other expeditions; and they decided that, rather than incur such debts in future, it would be better to maintain a reserve battalion constantly in Africa at the charge of the four Protectorates. The question is really entirely one of money. If we are to expect a succession of fairly serious military operations, with which the troops already in the Protectorate could not deal, it would be more economical to keep supplementary troops on the spot and avoid the expense of transport. But if, as I believe, there is or ought not to be any prospect of such a series of operations, then the policy of increasing the number of troops seems doubtful. If the Protectorate is administered with a desire to preserve peace, it appears to me that one battalion ought to be sufficient for its needs, provided that the police force is increased and kept in a state of efficiency, and that a volunteer corps of Europeans is formed.

The military operations which are likely to occur in the Protectorate will be, if not unnecessarily exaggerated, either very small or, on the other hand, very serious. All the steps which I foresee as probable in Kenya or Lumbwa can be accomplished by two or three hundred men, who can, at least in part, be police. The only serious danger which I can imagine is a campaign against the Somalis. It ought, in my opinion, to be avoided; but, should it prove inevitable, it must be conducted either with a small force and a few hundred native irregulars, who can move easily in the jungle, or else with a very large force, which can occupy and hold the whole country. But the experiment of 1901 showed that a moderately large force of a few thousands is useless in this curious scrub-covered region as a means of offence against nomads. They cannot be forced to deliver a stand-up battle, and they cannot be prevented from harrying. I have little apprehension of a general rising of natives against Europeans. The natives are united by no ties of government or religion, and are divided by a hundred tribal animosities. We have often used the Masai against other tribes, and were it necessary to operate against the Masai, which I do not anticipate, it would be equally easy to use other tribes against them. Also it is clear that if a general combination of natives against Europeans were possible, it would be very dangerous to rely on native African troops. Whatever causes could lead to rebellion could also lead to mutiny. We ought as soon as possible to abandon the employment of native irregulars, or at any rate subject them to a much stricter discipline. They are invaluable on account of their local knowledge and their power of moving freely in bush and scrub, which perplex other troops; but though they cost nothing at the time, we pay dearly for their services by encouraging a warlike spirit and a love of raiding, which we should try to extinguish.

I believe myself that in the future we ought to have hardly any punitive expeditions in East Africa. A lamented official in the Protectorate service used to say that every military officer on landing at Mombasa ought to be presented with two decorations; after the first punitive expedition in which he took part he would be deprived of the first, and if after that he took part in a second expedition he would lose the other. By the irony of fate, this official was killed by natives, and his death gave rise to one of the most serious punitive expeditions which the Protectorate has ever witnessed; but his observation was no doubt just. If there were no decorations, there would be fewer of these little wars. Every administrator ought to regard a punitive expedition as an evil, and in some ways an admission of failure, and ought to take care that the love of decorations, or even the worthier desire of giving the troops some practice and experience in military operations, is not allowed to override the greater claims of justice and good policy.

What is wanted is to impress the natives with our strength and our omnipresence, or at least our long reach.   This is best done by sending frequent patrols through disturbed districts, which need not cost a single life, and by establishing numerous posts with as many European officers as possible.   Unfortunately here the arts of war and peace present a real diversity of interests.   The military men rightly want to concentrate the troops as much as possible in headquarters, in order to form them into a serviceable and coherent military unit.   Detachments naturally interfere with the realisation of this ideal. The men get out of practice, and lose the habit of working in large bodies.   But, on the other hand, the well-trained troops which military officers desire are unsuited for administrative purposes, being only intended for use in an emergency.   No objection could be taken to this were it not for the fact that the East African administration does require a large amount of quasi-military work, while, as I hope, it gives little opening for real military enterprise.   I would therefore propose not to have more than a thousand regular troops in the country, and to devote the economy thus made to considerably increasing the police force, who should have sufficient military training to enable them, if necessary, to fight with naked savages only armed with spears and arrows.   Also, it either is or very soon will be necessary to have a small white police force.   As European settlement continues, the advent of a certain number of rough characters is inevitable, and it would not be wise to attempt to use natives for arresting white men.

In discussing the military position, I have considered only East Africa in the political sense, and excluded Uganda, which is perhaps a somewhat artificial limitation.   In that territory the density of the native population and perhaps the temper of the northern tribes may necessitate the presence of larger garrisons and greater readiness for serious operations. Also, the natives of the kingdom of Uganda at any rate are sufficiently civilised to see to the policing of their country themselves.

I have also dealt with the finances of East Africa as separate from those of Uganda, which they are under the present arrangement, although for convenience all import duties for either Protectorate are taken at Mombasa and credited to East Africa. Financially, Uganda is a very uncertain element in the future. For the period April 1903 to April 1904 the revenue is quoted as £49,501 and the expenditure as £186,884.[1] But this Protectorate presents a feature totally absent in East Africa, namely, a large native population which is assimilating European ideas and is anxious to purchase European goods. At present the purchasing power is wanting, but if any plentiful and paying article of export can be found, or if by some other means, such as the employment of workmen on the construction of regulators for the Upper Nile, money comes into the hands of the natives, a great increase in imports and revenue will certainly result. It is gratifying to see that in 1903–4 imports have increased in value by £60,651.

Hitherto I have inquired what improvements in administration are necessary in connection with natives, and found the chief desiderata to be an increase of Government stations, European officials, and police, which might be counterbalanced by a decrease of military expenditure. Even more obvious is the want of a larger and more efficient organisation for dealing with European immigration and settlement. I am treating of many aspects of this question in other chapters, and will here confine myself to the purely official questions of what modifications are desirable in the machinery of government.

The modifications required are, I think, radical and im-

[1] " Africa," No. 10, 1904.

portant. It is true that, in some ways, we want more officials to deal with white immigrants—that is, more surveyors and more men capable of managing the practical details of land settlement; but, on the other hand, East Africa has distinctly suffered from a too bureaucratic and meddlesome form of government in some matters and an utter absence of government in others. This is the result of the place having been called, and in the time of the Arab power properly called, a consulate. Now, a consulate is a British official agency established in a foreign country to protect the interests of British subjects. In Oriental countries, such as Zanzibar, its functions are considerably enlarged, and include the administration of justice and a certain control over legislation in as far as it affects British subjects. But it is in all cases assumed that there is a foreign power behind which is doing the work of government, and the action of the consulate is at the most regulative. This was more or less the case in East Africa before the Mazrui rebellion; but after that rebellion things changed, and the fiction of a consulate in a foreign country ought to have been done away with and replaced by some more living system of administration. Unfortunately it remained, and, like so many legal fictions (*i.e.* the Sultan's mainland dominions), had most powerful effects in practice. The persistent idea that East Africa was a consulate has shaped the policy of the home departments, though they would sincerely and indignantly deny the statement. Hence the continual demands for reports followed by no action: hence the superfluity of regulations about details, particularly such official matters as leave, precedence, pensions, &c., and the absence, inadequacy, or at best unconscionable dilatoriness of legislation on really important questions such as land settlement.

The cure, or at any rate the first treatment, for this evil is, in my opinion, very simple—namely, the institution of a council to assist the Commissioner, composed of both official and unofficial members. Such a body exists in most of our foreign possessions, and it would be hard to maintain that its introduction into British East Africa is premature, since it already exists in German East Africa, where the European element is certainly not stronger than with us. I am an official by training, and am well aware of the advantage of official procedure and the necessity of many things which seem to the public merely pedantry and red tape. But it cannot be denied that the bureaucratic genius is regulative rather than inventive: we are inclined to keep people quiet rather than to raise possibly fruitful controversies; to let well, or even ill, alone and to feel happiest when the day's work has been successfully distributed between those two great solaces of official life, the waste-paper basket and the pigeon-hole. But this temper is not sufficient of itself to manage the destinies of a full-grown and active country. Still less can it supply the life and vigour required by a young and developing country, which can be profitably managed only if the governing powers endeavour to ascertain what are the real and legitimate wants of the public and do their best to satisfy them.

To many of my readers it will probably appear that I am dilating on the most ancient platitudes; but every one who has been acquainted with East Africa in the last few years will admit that such principles were by no means platitudes there. The difficulty was for the public to let the officials know what was required, and then for the officials to obtain the assent of the home Government. The institution of a council should go far to improve this state of things, particularly if the council is allowed some discretion in the allocation of public expenditure. Hitherto one of the greatest practical difficulties in East Africa has been that the Commissioner was obliged to make in November a detailed statement of the revenue and expenditure for the twelvemonth beginning in the subsequent April. It was not even permissible to revise the figures in February or March when, more accounts being to hand, a more accurate forecast was possible. Prevision of this kind is only possible in countries where revenue and expenditure have settled down in certain regular lines; it is not possible in a growing country, where some unforeseen contingency is almost sure to occur within twelve months. In April 1903 there were hardly any applications for land in the Protectorate. Nine months later they were numbered by hundreds, and about forty intending immigrants arrived by every steamer. It is not altogether easy to devise a plan which would combine in a practical manner elasticity with the legitimate expectation of the financial departments, that expenditure will be kept within the limits fixed; but the local administration would find things easier if lump sums could be assigned to certain heads, such as public works or survey, with only general instructions as to the manner in which they should be applied, and of course on condition of a strict account being rendered.

At present the great question affecting European interests in East Africa is land settlement. Discussion and difference of opinion as to the best form of tenure and size of holdings is possible; but there can be no doubt that whatever decisions are taken on such points, it is necessary to have an adequate survey of the country, and also to decide what land can be given and what must be reserved for natives, forests, and other purposes. At present land is granted subject to survey, and not only is there much uncertainty, but delay is inevitable, because the staff of surveyors can hardly get through a tenth of the work before them. Hitherto it would perhaps have been premature to appoint a large Land and Survey Department, before it was certain that there would be a demand for the land; but now that we know that the land is valuable and appreciated by Europeans, it is essential that such departments should be established on an adequate scale. Not only will they speedily repay their cost, but without them the country must go to confusion and ruin.

Other questions of importance are the game laws, the

currency, the construction of roads, and education. Of the game laws I have said something elsewhere. The present currency consists of rupees, annas, and pice, for which it is proposed to substitute the decimal system of Ceylon—that is, rupees and cents. This is certainly more logical and convenient than the present division of the rupee; but it may be questioned whether even more radical changes should not be made. The existing system was introduced because the chief foreign connection of East Africa was with India, and if that connection is to maintain its importance, the Ceylon coinage is probably the best. But if the dominant element in East Africa is to be not Indian but European, and if the connection with India is likely to lose its importance, the propriety of introducing British currency should, I think, be considered. In any case the introduction of notes, if possible in terms of pounds sterling, is an urgent need, on account of the extreme inconvenience caused by a heavy coin of small value like the rupee to travellers and to those who wish to remit large sums by post.

More and better roads are much needed, and in most places they involve the construction of bridges, as the numerous water-courses and other deep clefts are practically impassable for wheeled traffic. At present no one but the Government is in a position to undertake roadmaking; but in German East Africa I believe this task devolves on the various communes, and the arrangement seems good if European settlement is sufficiently advanced to render it feasible. The municipality of Nairobi has made considerable progress in roadmaking within its limits.

Education, which among the Germans is recognised as being partly the business of the Government, is entirely in the hands of missionaries, with the exception of a small European school at Nairobi belonging to the railway. Perhaps this arrangement will be found sufficient for some time to come, for the missions are many and the native population scanty. But the education of natives is a matter of so great

THE ATHI RIVER.

importance that, as communications and funds increase, the Government will probably give it attention.   The establishment of more native hospitals is also desirable, not only from motives of humanity, but for better understanding the diseases and medical needs of the country.

CHAPTER XIV

THE UGANDA RAILWAY

PROBABLY the Uganda Railway is to the general public the best-known feature in East Africa. Never perhaps has a railway been so prominent, and so completely dominated all surrounding interests. And rightly so. It is not an uncommon thing for a line to open up a country, but this line has literally created a country. As a civilised territory and a possible residence for Europeans, East Africa may be said to have come gradually into existence at exactly the same rate as the rails advanced, and at present the most important question that can be asked about any locality is, How far is it from the line ?

The whole enterprise offers the most extraordinary example of the pluck and luck which characterise the British race, and also of our happy-go-lucky methods. It may probably be said, with justice, that every other nation would have shrunk from the task, but also that every other nation would have executed it in a more business-like way. Yet whatever criticisms may be made on the circumstances of construction, and especially on the cost, no one can deny that the result is successful and useful.

It is a curious confession, but I do not know why the Uganda Railway was built, and I think many people in East Africa share my ignorance. It is a little hard to believe that the only motive was purely philanthropic—namely, the suppression of the slave trade—nor are the strategic advantages of the line very obvious, for though it certainly might be used as an alternative route for sending troops to the Sudan, no attempt has been made to open up communication on the higher waters of the Nile, and the journey would in any case be long. It is most remarkable that at the time when the construction was decided on, there appears to have been no idea of the value, or even of the existence, of the high temperate region to the east of Lake Victoria. On the other hand, there was probably an exaggerated idea of the riches and fertility of Uganda, a country of great interest, with a large and exceptionally intelligent native population, but in most parts at any rate not suited for European settlement, and not as yet proved to yield any produce which would approximately repay the cost of the line. Yet, looking at the completed railway to-day, I think even hostile critics will admit that it justifies its existence. The slave trade has disappeared so entirely that one is apt to forget that only a few years ago it was a real horror and scandal which called for energetic suppression. The line is found to pass through a healthy and fertile district which ought to soon become a considerable European colony with good commercial prospects. Above all, the completion of this route has had the most remarkable effects in opening up the countries of Central Equatorial Africa, and dissipating the cloud of ignorance by which they were concealed. What may be the whole consequences in the future of this sudden illumination of the Dark Continent, no one can predict, but one remarkable result is our control of the sources of the Nile, and the grandiose plans now set forth for regulating the water supply of Upper Egypt.

It is perhaps not superfluous to repeat that the Uganda Railway is not in Uganda at all, but entirely in the East Africa Protectorate, the whole breadth of which from the sea to Lake Victoria it traverses. It is as if the line from Charing Cross to Dover were called the French Railway. In some of the earlier reports it was described as the Mombasa-Victoria Railway, a far more correct name, which has, however, been entirely dropped in favour of the shorter title. It consists at present of a single line, which starts from Mombasa Island, crosses over to the mainland, and terminates at Kisumu or Port Florence on the Kavirondo Gulf, an arm of Lake Victoria, where two steamers run in correspondence with .it. .The total length is 584 miles, and the direction westerly, with a strong trend towards the north, as Mombasa is a little south of 4° S., and Kisumu a few miles below the equator. To be more accurate, the direction is north-west as far as Nakuru, and then nearly due west across the Mau range to the Lake.

The final arrangements for the Mombasa terminus have not yet been made, but it is almost certain that considerable wharves and warehouses will be constructed at Kilindini (the large harbour about two miles from Mombasa), which will thus become the starting-point of the line for all but purely local purposes. It has also been proposed to make another terminus on the shore of the mainland, where steamers could load and discharge. This would save a few miles of railway, and be in many ways an advantageous arrangement, but it is doubtful if the formation of the coast, which rises rather suddenly and steeply, will permit the project to be executed. At present the line starts from Mombasa town, and, running past Kilindini, crosses the Makupa Creek at the back of the island, and climbs up to Mazeras, about 530 feet high. This first portion of the line is also one of the most beautiful. The vegetation is tropical and luxuriant, and the steep ascent affords from time to time views over the Mwachi River and the various arms of the sea around Mombasa.

After Mazeras begins a long and most uninteresting stretch, extending nearly 200 miles to Makindu (mile 209), in which the railway passes through thorny scrub, which is specially thick up to Voi (mile 102), and then presents more frequent clearings. I believe that this part of the railway, though far less sensational than the engineering works in Kikuyu and Mau, really offered greater difficulties of construction. The thick vegetation rendered survey and alignment difficult, and until after Voi it was exceedingly hard to obtain a general view of the he of the land. Added to this, there was no water at all for a stretch of forty miles, and not a superfluity in

other parts: the climate was most unhealthy, and the continual attacks of lions often threatened to totally demoralise
the workmen. I have often heard it said that in no part of
the construction were the indomitable courage and per-
severance of Sir G. Whitehouse, the chief engineer, more
conspicuous or more useful than in driving the line through
this monotonous, unhealthy scrub.

On reaching Makindu the railway, though not making any
noticeable ascent after Mazeras, has gradually mounted over
3000 feet, and proceeded nearly two degrees northwards. It
is now on the edge of the cool and healthy districts commonly
known as the Highlands, and proceeds across the plain to
Nairobi, rising about 2270 feet higher in 120 miles. This
section was not as easy to lay as might be supposed, for, though
the country is open and healthy, the plains are not so level
as they appear—as even a pedestrian soon finds out—but
present a series of undulations and depressions which
necessitate continual deviations from the straight direction.
Also there are a considerable number of water-courses, which,
though of little importance in dry weather, become dangerous
and rushing torrents during the rains. Wash-outs and inter-
ruption of the traffic have been frequent in these regions.

Nairobi is the headquarters of the railway administration,
and possesses not only a large railway station, offices, and
dwelling-houses for the staff, but also extensive workshops,
which are really remarkable in so remote a place. In them
can be made everything necessary for a railway except loco-
motives. It is interesting to observe that considerable and
increasing use of native African labour is made in these workshops. At first Indians were almost exclusively employed, but
it is now found that the Wakamba and Wakikuyu make very
good workmen under European or Indian surveillance.

After Nairobi begins the most picturesque part of the
railway. The line mounts the Kikuyu Hills, and rises about
2000 feet in 24 miles, Limoru station being 7340 feet high,
though not quite the highest place in this section. On reach-

ing the summit, a few miles further on, it descends suddenly and rapidly to the Escarpment station, situated on a ledge overlooking the Rift Valley on the western side of the Kikuyu escarpment. This point has a double interest. Firstly, it is perhaps the finest view on the journey. The almost instantaneous change of landscape when the train, which has been meandering through the cultivated fields of Kikuyu and the swamps beyond Limoru, suddenly rushes round a corner and begins to descend into a huge wild valley with the Kedong hill and river at the bottom, while Mount Longanot towers on the other side, is one of the most remarkable transformation scenes in the world. Secondly, it was at the Escarpment station that began the celebrated "inclines," whose remains may still be seen, and whose memory still evokes a tremor in the nervous system of many East Africans. The history of these inclines is that when the rails reached the escarpment it was found that the proposed permanent line, which was to run along the side of the Rift Valley *via* Kijabe, would require about eight large viaducts. These were not ready, and could not be received for some months. Sooner than wait and stop progress, it was decided to run a temporary line straight across the plain, from the Kedong River to the saddle of Mount Longanot—a prolongation of that mountain stretching across the Rift Valley and to some extent closing it. This was easy enough as soon as the Kedong was reached, but there was a precipitous descent of about 1500 feet, which no ordinary line could make, but which was effected by a rope incline—that is to say, a stage hung on an iron rope which descended the most appalling precipice, and, though it somehow or other adhered to the rails, seemed to be suspended on the perpendicular hillside. It was in vain that engineers explained that the apparatus was peculiarly safe—in fact, not nearly so dangerous as an ordinary express: when the rope shook and the stage waggled in mid-air, the boldest heart trembled. Yet though some people were known to walk down rather than take the incline, even the most timid and the most critical made use of it to go up. So great is the power of laziness.

Now that the permanent line has been made, the railway avoids the Kedong River and keeps to the side of the mountains, running over its imposing viaducts to the dusty, gusty station of Kijabe—the name means " wind," and is very appropriate—and thence to Lake Naivasha, and onwards up the Rift Valley. Its direction at this time is almost north, but the configuration of the mountains and of Lake Elementeita obliges it to make a sudden loop to the south; then it turns north again along the side of Lake Nakuru, and, running across its northern shore, takes a westerly direction, although with many curves and wrigglings, across the Mau. This section of the railway in the Rift Valley is said to have been the easiest and the best laid from the first. The section on the Mau escarpment, if not really the most difficult to construct, is certainly the most impressive, on account of the great elevation (7940 feet at Molo), the wide and varying views, and the huge viaducts. There are twenty-seven of these latter, measuring altogether 11,845 running feet in 73 miles, the largest being 881 feet long and the greatest height 111 feet above the bottom of the ravine crossed.[1] They were constructed by an American firm. On this section is the only unfinished work on the railway, which is perhaps already (August 1904) complete—namely, a tunnel about mile 525, which will materially assist traffic, and remove a difficult piece of line which has been the cause of several small mishaps.

After Fort Ternan—a point which is seen in the distance long before it is reached by devious curves and long-legged viaducts—begins the last section (536–584 miles), which, though it is comparatively flat, was perhaps the most difficult of all to construct, owing to the spongy, unstable character of the soil. Luck favoured the first construction, for there was a protracted spell of dry weather in these regions at the end of 1901 almost amounting to a local drought; but about April

[1] Final Report by the Uganda Railway Committee ("Africa," 11, 1904, page 18).

1902 it began to rain, and it is hardly an exaggeration to say that it rained for eighteen months. By dint of continual attention and reconstruction, the line is now really open to traffic; but even as late as 1903 floods, stoppages, and derailments rendered communication very uncertain and precarious.

Another difficulty experienced in this section near the Lake arose from the continual thefts of railway material by the natives, chiefly the Nandi, which often threatened to destroy communication and occasion serious accidents. It must not be supposed that the Nandi had any idea of cutting our communications, or even of committing acts of political hostility. Their operations were simply burglarious. A railway line appeals in the strangest way to both sexes of African natives. Telegraph wires are regarded as a most ornamental and desirable article of female attire, and the male sex find, in various bolts and rivets used to secure the rails, perfect weapons obviously intended for braining their enemies. One can imagine what thefts would be committed on a European railway if the telegraph wires were pearl necklaces and the rails first-rate sporting guns, and it is not surprising that the Nandi yielded to the temptation, but rather that within a comparatively short time they were broken off the habit.

The railway at present terminates at Kisumu, also called Port Florence. It would perhaps be best to call the whole township by the native name, and restrict the European designation to the railway station, pier, and surrounding quarter. There was an alternative proposal to carry the line through the high Nandi country to Port Victoria, in the northeast corner of the Lake. The greater expense of this route was a sufficient reason for preferring the other, but it offered many advantages, and one cannot help regretting that it could not be adopted. It would have opened up the Nandi country —one of the finest districts of the Protectorate, which is now unfortunately left somewhat on one side—and it would have secured a somewhat better port on the lake. Port Florence lies at the end of the Gulf of Kavirondo, a long shallow bay which hardly offers sufficient depth for large shipping, and which has the further serious and ever-increasing danger for the public health, that it becomes very easily fouled, and has no movement to speak of to refresh its sluggish waters.

The railway was built almost entirely by coolies brought over from India; and though the cost of transport and of providing the food to which the men were accustomed was considerable, I do not think the necessary labour could have been provided in any other way. After nearly nine years the natives have become so far familiarised with the railway, and the idea of working for Europeans, that they are able to perform the class of work required for maintenance; but it may be doubted if even now they could be used for purposes of construction, and it certainly was out of the question when the railway commenced. The jungle which surrounds the first part of the line is practically uninhabited, and to have brought labour down from Uganda would probably have been a more lengthy and difficult task than to bring it from India, to say nothing of the difference in efficiency.

Everybody is probably aware that the Uganda Railway has been the object of much criticism. It must be confessed that it was built with great technical skill, but otherwise in a somewhat singular and unbusinesslike manner. The construction was supervised by a committee sitting in the Foreign Office, and composed of distinguished gentlemen of wide experience, but in most cases that experience did not embrace railway work. Now, as one who has had an official connection with the Uganda Railway, I will venture to say that I have never known any class of questions as to which a man without technical knowledge is more hopelessly at sea than those presented by engineering and railway management; and it appears to me that the only practical method of building a railway is to leave such matters entirely in the hands of experts, subject to certain general limitations as to cost, direction, &c. The Uganda Railway Committee, however, had no mistrust of their own powers or diffidence in interfering, and did not even

avail themselves of the valuable local assistance which was at
their disposal.   By a most unfortunate arrangement, the local
administration of the railway was made entirely separate from
the administration of the Protectorate, although it included a
great many things which really had nothing to do with railway construction, such as the policing and sanitation of the
whole line and of the most important stations on it, and the
management of the railway zone, a tract of one mile on each
side of the line.   The Committee in their final report blandly
remark that their arrangements insured harmonious working
between the authorities of the Protectorate and the officers of
the railway.   As a matter of fact they insured a permanent
squabble between the two administrations, which was most
disadvantageous to the public interest and most unnecessary.

I may observe that I was not Commissioner of the Protectorate at the time this arrangement was made, and that my
criticisms are more or less impartial.   The Protectorate was
then administered by Sir A. Hardinge (now H.M.'s Minister in
Persia), an officer of most exceptional ability and brilliancy,
whose advice on non-technical matters connected with the
railway would have been of great value.   Not only were the
two local administrations distinct, but the Uganda Railway
Committee was not the same as the African Department in
the Foreign Office; and it was said that the differences of
opinion between the two were real and important.   The result
of all this was that whenever there was a question affecting
both the railway and other interests in the Protectorate, there
was no common authority who could settle it except the
Secretary of State.   And, as the Secretary of State had clearly
only time to acquaint himself with questions of the utmost
gravity, this meant that no one quite knew who decided all
the questions of moderate importance.   Hence much confusion.

The most serious criticism passed on the Uganda Railway
is that it was unduly costly.   Elaborate defences have been
made to prove the contrary, but I think that every one who

has an adequate knowledge both of the country and of the history of the construction is agreed that the line ought really to have cost about four millions sterling, whereas "the total expenditure out of Parliamentary grants up to the date the Committee ceased to control the outlay" (which is not quite the whole expenditure) was £5,317,000."[1] The expenditure on accessories was, no doubt, very ample; on housing the officials and the subordinate staff, on building whole towns, on the medical and police departments. I do not find fault with this expenditure, but Africa would be a very different place from what it is if everything were done on this scale, and I think it would have been more natural and more advantageous to have enlarged the corresponding departments of the Protectorate administration instead of creating duplicate departments.

But, no doubt, the chief assignable cause of the excess in expenditure was the enormous amount of temporary work on the line. A German official, who travelled over the railway shortly before its completion, said, on returning, "I am ashamed of my country. We have not built one railway to the Lake yet, and the English have built two." For a large part of the line this was hardly an exaggeration. Even now the traveller sees everywhere traces of temporary bridges and temporary lines, and sometimes two of the latter, making three lines in all, before the final route was laid. The most striking example of this method is perhaps the inclines to which I have already alluded. First of all was constructed a temporary line in connection with the inclines, running straight across the plain; then followed the permanent line along the side of the escarpment *via* Kijabe; but, as this involved the erection of a number of viaducts, there was a preliminary stage, with a second series of temporary lines and "reverses," until the viaducts were erected. All these arrangements have been defended on technical grounds; but when the ordinary man reflects on the undoubted fact that other railways do not

[1] Final Report by the Uganda Railway Committee ("Africa," 11, 1904).

show this amount of provisional lines and bridges, and that so great a specialist as Colonel Gracey, after officially inspecting the line, expressed the opinion that these numerous temporary diversions resulted in extra cost without materially advancing the progress of the work,[1] he can hardly avoid the conclusion that greater economy was possible.

Though the line as a whole has now assumed its final form, it may still be worth while to make some alterations in the steep ascent from Makupa to Mazeras, and render the gradients easier. It appears that at present trains have to be composed of fewer carriages than is advantageous, merely on account of this piece of line, and that the ascent could be rectified so as to allow the passage of longer trains at a cost which would be covered by the saving effected by the improvement.

Taking the railway as it stands, almost the only criticism to be made on it is that it does not pass through many of the richest districts of the Protectorate. It would have been preferable, for instance, if it could have gone through the Kenya province and Nandi. But such a route would have been much more expensive, and, as I have already pointed out, the peculiarity of this railway is that it was not built, as is generally the case, in order to connect a series of known points, but was driven through an entirely unknown country. Hence it does not so much traverse the best districts, as supply a series of points from which those districts may be easily reached. If the hopes of the Protectorate's progress in the near future are justified, it is not improbable that a branch line will be built by some private company from Nairobi to Mount Kenya. One such company has already seriously under consideration the possibility of building another line along the coast from Mombasa to Melindi.

It is a pity, however, that the railway did not pass through the Government station of Machakos, where there is

---

[1] Correspondence respecting the Uganda Railway ("Africa," No. 6, 1901), pp. 9, 10.

a considerable population and cultivation, instead of going straight across the picturesque but barren Athi plains. It is also to be regretted that Nairobi was chosen as the site for the railway headquarters. Though the surrounding hills are healthy, the plain on which the railway station, the works, and the workmen's quarters are situated offers great difficulties to drainage, and it will be hard to ever make it satisfactory from a sanitary point of view.

At present the Uganda Railway has not only cost between five and six millions, but is run at an annual loss. For 1903–4 the deficit on the working was about £60,000, and for the current year it is estimated at £45,000, but will probably be less. The revenues derived from the railway zone —that is, a mile on each side of the line for nearly the whole of its length, but not including Mombasa and the neighbourhood—are paid into a special account, and set against the capital cost. This arrangement is, I think, a pity, for it will in all probability be a very long time before the revenues of the zone can be in any way compared with the expenditure on construction, but they would form a useful addition to the revenues of the Protectorate. They consist chiefly of rents, and at present amount to rather more than £1000 a year. I am afraid that this figure, as a contribution to paying off six millions, will create a smile, but it is bound to largely and steadily increase. At the same time, except in the improbable event of precious minerals being found within the railway zone, it will clearly take many years before this revenue accumulates sufficiently to balance the cost of the line. The best chance of increasing it is to find some use for the land between Makindu and the coast, a strip of 200 miles, which is at present absolutely unremunerative.

Though it is not likely that we shall see the capital cost of the railway repaid, there is every reason to hope that the deficit on the working will disappear, and that the line will shortly pay its way, and even bring in revenue. The traffic depends not only on East Africa, but also on Uganda, and perhaps the prospects of increase in the immediate future can be judged best from the Uganda trade returns, as nearly the whole of this trade passes up and down the line, while a certain amount of the East Africa trade is distributed along the coast. In his last report,[1] Colonel Sadler reports that the trade of his Protectorate shows an increase of 86 per cent., as compared with the previous year, the imports having practically doubled, and the exports risen over 64 per cent. The increase of imports is chiefly due to the growing demand among natives for cotton goods, corrugated iron (for roofing houses), and European groceries ; tea, biscuits, and jam' being much appreciated. In exports the chief increase is in skins and hides. A trade in fibre is commencing, but owing to the prevalence of sleeping sickness in the Sese Islands and other places where rubber is grown, the export of this article has declined. It will thus be seen that the remarkable growth of trade is by no means due to accident or an exceptionally favourable year, but rather to circumstances whose operation may be expected to continue and produce even more striking results when the public health improves.

The increase of traffic in the East Africa Protectorate is likely to depend entirely on the encouragement given by Government to European settlement and colonisation. If European immigration is discouraged (as it practically has been) no large increase of trade or railway traffic can be expected to occur in our possessions to the east of Lake Victoria, because the native element is small, and shows little inclination to use European goods. If, however, a considerable white community is established up country, there is no reason why the trade should not increase by leaps and bounds as that of Uganda is doing. It would be of special advantage to the railway if some permanent industry involving the regular export of heavy goods (such as timber from the Mau or soda from the deposits in Lake Magadi) could be established.

[1] General Report on the Uganda Protectorate for the year ending March 31, 1904 ("Africa," 12, 1904).

I have unfortunately no figures which enable me to make a trustworthy calculation as to the proportion which increased railway revenue bears to increased general trade in the two Protectorates; but I should say that the very favourable statistics quoted from Uganda, and the more intelligent régime which I believe is prevailing in East Africa, afford a reasonable hope that the railway will be able to cover its expenditure in about two years, and after that be worked at a profit. The more recent accessible statistics refer to the year April 1903–April 1904, and the chief fact to be gathered from them is that exports are increasing. Hides amounted to 1316 tons against 171 in 1902–3, potatoes to 1216 against 354, and grains and foodstuffs to about 1500 as against 600 in the same period.

Two other feeders for the railway traffic are the Congo Free State and German East Africa. The former exports hardly anything but ivory by the Eastern route, but this route is beginning to be used both for the Belgian officers and the importation of stores. In the event of any considerable works, railway or other, being commenced in the neighbourhood of Lake Albert, the Uganda Railway would probably prove the cheapest and quickest road for importing materials.

The Uganda Railway also takes most of the trade from the German territory lying round the southern part of Lake Victoria, where there are several Government stations, as it is naturally quicker to send goods by water to Kisumu, and then by rail to the coast, than to carry them the whole way by caravan in German territory. We have at present two steamers on the Lake, and have undertaken the task of surveying the southern or German part. I hear that trade is so promising (December 1904) that a third steamer is about to be constructed, and that the Germans also think of having one. It is reported that the earnings of the steamer traffic in 1903-4 amounted to £6000,[1] but the prospects for the current year are very much better.

At present (July 1904) the journey from Mombasa to the

[1] " Africa," 10, 1904.

Lake takes about forty hours, but will probably soon be shortened. The journey from Kisumu to Entebbe takes about seventeen hours, and a trip round the Lake in the railway steamer about a week.

The chief practical question for the Uganda Railway at present is whether it would not be advantageous to reduce the freights. I will not venture to give an opinion on a subject which involves so many technical considerations, but I observe that the German line in Usambara is said to have increased its receipts by reducing its charges.

CHAPTER XV

TRADE

ZANZIBAR, as the centre of the Arab power, and connected by many ties with India on one side and Maskat on the other, has dominated the trade of East Africa since the middle of the nineteenth century. The island contributes little to the commerce of the world except a considerable and very valuable export of cloves, but it acts as a gigantic go-down or store-house for the whole East African Coast, where both imports and exports are received and distributed. In 1902 the value of its imports was £1,106,247, and of its exports £1,080,277, whereas the corresponding figures for the East Africa Protectorate were only £426,267 and £113,206. This position is not likely to be maintained, as steamers touch more and more frequently at the mainland ports; but even as late as 1903, 32.5 of the exports of the East Africa Protectorate went to Zanzibar, and their further distribution in Europe and India could not be traced, though, of course, Zanzibar is only a consumer on a very small scale. The imports are easier to trace, and it would appear that in 1903 about 28.5 came from the United Kingdom and 33.4 from India, the next largest importer being Germany with 11.4. According to the last statistics our share has slightly decreased, the United Kingdom sending 28.1 of the total amount of imports, India 28.4, and Germany 12.7.

An inspection of the figures [1] for imports and exports between 1899 and 1903 gives the singular result that whereas the exports have regularly increased and more than doubled

---

[1] Taken from bluebooks " Africa," 10, 1904, and " Africa," 6, 1903. There are some discrepancies in the published figures.

(£71,145 in 1899 and £165,060 in 1903), the imports have remained at much the same figure during..the whole period, with a tendency to decrease (£472,370 in 1899, £426,267 in 1902, and £443,032 in 1903). The figures are, however, misleading. Those for exports represent the natural growth of the Protectorate, but those for imports represent the result of a struggle between two sets of causes. On the one hand, the permanent European element in the Protectorate and the extension of our influence among natives, leading to a larger demand for European goods, have both increased. On the other, while the Uganda Railway was under construction about twenty thousand coolies, as well as numerous contractors and engineers on temporary service, were in the country, who nearly all departed in 1902 and 1903. At the same time, the industries of the Protectorate began to develop, which occasioned a heavy fall in some articles of importation, notably provisions and building materials—rice, for instance, which had previously been imported from India, being now grown in the Protectorate. Taking all these causes together, it would appear that the permanent purchasing and consuming power of East Africa has really increased.

In the future the volume of the East African (as distinguished from the Uganda) import trade is likely to depend mainly on the increase of the European population. The native population is small, and does not show much inclination to adopt a higher standard of comfort, though clothing is becoming far more general, and there is likely to be a steady and somewhat increasing demand for blankets and cotton goods commonly known as Merikani.[1] Should the Somalis show any inclination to adopt a more settled and civilised mode of life, they have sufficient intelligence and commercial aptitude to become a very important factor in the trade of East Africa but the future of this enigmatical people, about

---

[1] *i.e.* American material. American merchants were early to the fore in East Africa, and the United States was the first power to establish a Consulate at Zanzibar (in 1836).

whom I have said more elsewhere, is a problem not easily solved. What proportions the European population will ultimately assume is, of course, the main question for East Africa from every point of view, and probably to double it would be almost equivalent to doubling the imports. A larger settled population would feel the need of many things which pioneers can do without; but, on the other hand, the process by which imported articles are replaced by African home products is bound to continue in the case of such items as grain, rice, vegetables, building materials, furniture, and perhaps tobacco.

If, however, we include Uganda in East Africa, as is natural, we may legitimately look forward to a large native market in the future, as the population on the western side of the Lake is numerous, intelligent, and anxious to adopt European inventions. In the house of one of the Regents at Kampala I saw electric bells; and the people have by their unaided efforts reached a stage in architecture, cultivation, roadmaking, and the arts of life generally, which makes them able to appreciate not only the ordinary native trade goods, but also substantial articles like furniture and machinery. The opening of this market to any large extent is much delayed by the inland and inaccessible position of Uganda, the apathy of merchants, and above all by the want of purchasing power among the natives, who, though rich in all the necessaries of African life, have not yet discovered in abundance any valuable export which is easily convertible into currency. A development of the india-rubber, cotton, and coffee industries will perhaps change the position, and the construction of works to regulate the flow of the Nile, as proposed by Sir W. Garstin, would also have the effect of introducing money into the country.

The most recent figures for Uganda trade [1] are distinctly encouraging, as the value of the trade in 1903–4 was £176,047, showing an increase of 86 per cent. over the present year. Imports have practically doubled, and exports have increased

[1] Colonel Sadler's Report ("Africa," No. 12, 1904).

64 per cent. There is an increasing demand, not only for cotton goods, but for corrugated iron, with which the natives are roofing their houses, and for such groceries as teas, jams, and biscuits. They also buy enamelled hardware and boots.

The figures for the value of articles exported from the East Africa Protectorate are—1898–1899, £71,145; 1899–1900, £121,686 (this represents a year of famine, when the natives were obliged to sell what they could get to obtain food, and the exports of ivory, rubber, and hides rose considerably); 1900–1901, £89,858 (this represents a year of plenty, when the natives were disinclined to sell or work); 1901–1902, £113,206; 1902–1903, £165,060. The increase in this last year is mainly due to an increase in the amount of ivory, copra, and hides exported. These, with the addition of rubber and grain, are the most important articles of export at present. The ivory trade is somewhat fluctuating and precarious, and is likely to continue so in the future. Its proportions must depend very much on the regulations adopted in the future for preserving elephants, and the question is largely one of business *versus* sentiment. One cannot help regretting that an intelligent creature should be slaughtered in order that creatures not much more intelligent may play billiards with balls made out of its teeth; but, on the other hand, there are undoubtedly many more elephants in Uganda than are wanted, or are good for cultivation. It is probable that the establishment of a practical frontier with Abyssinia, protected by military posts, will increase the export of ivory from Kismayu, by diverting thither much merchandise which now goes to Italian ports, though produced in our territory. The export of the other articles mentioned can be almost indefinitely increased, if the cultivation or production is systematically organised. Of hides there is already an abundant supply, which could be augmented if animals were kept on a large scale, and arrangements made for tinning the flesh as well as utilising the skin. The production of copra increased in a marked manner between 1902 and 1903, and there is no reason why india-rubber should not do the same, now that the business is being taken up by responsible firms. Beeswax is said to be an important export from German East Africa, and there is no reason why it should not also be exported from our territory, as it is easily procurable.

It is quite possible, however, that the export trade of the Protectorate in the future will depend mainly on industries which are now in their infancy, such as cotton, wool, timber, and fibre. I have discussed the prospects of these in another chapter, but no figures are as yet to hand. In any case, good shipping facilities are available at all the important ports, with the exception of Melindi, where the extreme shallowness of the harbour makes loading and unloading difficult. As far as anchorage is concerned, Mombasa, with its two harbours, communicating with the accessory waters of Port Tudor and Port Reitz, is one of the most favoured ports of the world, and would doubtless become one of the most important were it supplied with fresh water and coal.

The island of Mombasa contains no springs, and the only water is either rain collected in tanks or a brackish fluid of indifferent quality drawn from wells. Fresh water could be obtained from the Shimba Hills on the mainland without much difficulty, and brought in by pipes at a cost of about £100,000; but it is a question whether such an outlay would pay at present, as it may be predicted with certainty that the native population would refuse to pay for good water if they could have bad water gratis, and any attempt to fill up the present wells or stop their use would probably cause a riot. If, however, the initial difficulties of constructing waterworks could be surmounted, the ultimate advantage of making Mombasa a port of call for the big liners and a resort of the fleet would be great. Its position would be further improved if coal could be found in the interior. Many maps mark a "carboniferous area" as extending from the German frontier through the Taru jungle to the Tana River, but no real trace of coal has yet been discovered, though it is only just to say that most of the area is covered with scrub, which renders geological investigation difficult. A company, which realised the great possibilities which would be opened if Mombasa could be supplied with water and coal, offered to construct the waterworks in return for certain commercial advantages and the right to prospect for coal in the above-mentioned carboniferous area; but when I left East Africa the concession had not been arranged.

An important aspect of the East Africa trade is the competition between English and foreign merchants, particularly Germans. The number of German compared with British firms in Mombasa, Nairobi, Entebbe, and Lamu is remarkable; and though the presence of some of them may be explained as a relic of the times before the present German sphere was marked out, yet it cannot be said that there are British firms in the German sphere in the same way that there are British missionaries there. It cannot be denied that the Germans are making a great effort to secure commercial preponderance on the East African coast, including Zanzibar, and that they are likely to succeed unless our merchants show more energy and enterprise than they have done in the last few years.

I am aware that nothing is more unpopular, nothing creates greater indignation, than to hint that British commercial houses are deficient in these qualities; but an experience in many countries has convinced me that the criticism is true. The contention of the British merchant is, as a rule, that his goods are better than any others, that foreign countries ought therefore to buy them in preference to any others, and that if they do not do so this is the fault of the nearest representative of the British Government. I remember that some years ago, when I was Chargé d'Affaires in Bulgaria, British merchants complained that their excellent and solid goods found no sale, whereas inferior and perishable German articles of the same kind were bought with avidity. It was pointed out that the Germans found out exactly what the Bulgarians wanted, and what they would pay, and then advertised accordingly. The

British merchants said, finally, as a pathetic *reductio ad absurdum*, "You surely don't expect us to have labels printed in the Cyrillic alphabet!" Yet it was precisely this spirit, which failed to realise that the Cyrillic alphabet is as natural and necessary a medium for the transaction of business in Bulgaria as the Latin alphabet is in Manchester, which cost those merchants the loss of the Bulgarian market. Again, the British merchant is inclined to disdain all enterprises which do not bring in ten, or at least five per cent., and to argue that, if he can get that return for his money in certain parts of the world, there is no reason why he should take less elsewhere. This argument is incontrovertible, but it is clearly the reasoning of old-established firms, who do not want to seek or retain new markets, and those who use it cannot be surprised if they find that such markets are in other hands when the small despised beginnings have developed into big concerns.

The German, on the other hand, is far more inquiring, more adaptable, more ready to experiment and undertake small speculative businesses, and (let me say at any rate one thing which will not be unpalatable to the British merchant) much more strongly supported and even pushed by his Government. In German East Africa experiments have been made by Government on the most lavish scale, with a view of ascertaining what products are likely to be successful and commercially profitable, and the German, Austrian, and French lines of steamers are all subsidised.

The result of this is that about half the trade of British East Africa was carried in foreign bottoms in 1903. In that year the British India had a direct service from England, though only once a month, whereas the German line had a fortnightly service, and gave rebates to those who confined shipments to them, which they were able to pay out of their subsidy of £85,000 per annum. But in 1904 the British India found they could not continue to run through the Suez Canal, and adopted the route round the Cape, with the consequence that the majority of the cargo now goes in German vessels. The main connection of the Coast with Europe is kept up by the German line running to Naples, Marseilles, and Hamburg, and the Austrian Lloyd running to Trieste, while the Messageries Martitimes (which, however, touch only at Zanzibar) take a considerable part of the passenger traffic. The British India Company has a bi-monthly service between Mombasa and India, one monthly steamer from Aden, and one from England round the Cape of Good Hope. This is the only British line which at the present serves the Coast, and the arrangement clearly dates from the time when the commercial interests of the Protectorate lay mainly with India. In view of the fact that the subsidies given to foreign lines are not merely protective, but practically aggressive, and imposed in the hope of capturing a rising trade, it is generally recognised that the East African Coast offers an exceptional case where subsidies, even if condemned by our financial policy as a general rule, may be adopted as a defensive measure. It is to be hoped that some line of steamers of established reputation may receive a subsidy which will enable them to institute at least a monthly service of cargo and passenger steamers through the Suez Canal. The total gross tonnage which entered Mombasa in 1903–4 is given as 636,235, representing 246 vessels, and showing an increase of 52 steamers over the previous year. Of this tonnage, 274,101 is said to have been British, 291,658 German, 60,906 Austrian, and 9570 Zanzibar. The total tonnage for all the Protectorate ports is given as 754,156.

CHAPTER XVI

SLAVERY AND MISSIONS

IF one asks what are the special and peculiar qualities of the African races, what actions or modes of life distinguish them from the other breeds of mankind, what characteristic part have they played in history, I fear that the answer is to be found in the one word "Slavery." Many other nations have supplied slaves, but none in such a wholesale manner, and none of the great divisions of mankind has ever been so definitely and complacently relegated by the others to an inferior position: "a servant of servants shall he be unto his children." This disastrous destiny is due no doubt to the great individual strength of the negro, which renders him an efficient if not industrious labourer, and to the weakness and defencelessness of all negro social organisations, which rarely assume the proportions of a state or are capable of resisting the attacks of the slave-raider. It has also been unfortunate for the negro race that, though their continent is proverbially unknown and mysterious, it is close to the strongest nations of the world, who have long regarded it as a human hunting-ground, whereas the other inferior races, who might have shared with the Africans the unenviable burden of servitude, have mostly been hidden in out-of-the-way corners and also been wanting in robust physique. It must also be admitted that the negro acquiesces in slavery. We may agree that the oppression of ages has left him little chance of developing a sense of independence and dignity; but still, as far as we can see, African society, when uncontaminated by extraneous influences, is based on the right to own and sell women and minors as if they were cattle, and it is certain that the chief ambition of liberated slaves is to have slaves of their own. It suits the thriftless, indolent nature of the African to depend for subsistence on another person, and, though capable of vanity, he has no pride to be offended.

The East Coast of Africa seems to have been left to Mohammedan slave-traders, whereas the West was the market for Christians, and supplied labour for North and South America. The Arab traders of the East were men of energy, and not only raided the hinterland, but penetrated by land to the basin of the Congo on the other side, and even approached the West Coast through Kanem and Bornu. It does not appear, however, that there was any route for the slave trade between Egypt and Uganda or the neighbouring countries. The caravans of slaves were brought down to the Coast, and were either kept there and in Zanzibar or despatched to Arabia, whence many found their way into Turkey. It is probable that the lot of slaves consigned to domestic service in the Mohammedan East was better than that of those who had to work in the American plantations; but Christian slave-owners were at least innocent of the manufacture of eunuchs. British prudery has prevented this abominable trade from receiving the public opprobrium which it merited; but as practised by Oriental slave-raiders it occasioned the most appalling mortality, and sensibly increased the sum of human misery.[1] But whether on the east or west of Africa, it is almost impossible to exaggerate the horrors and cruelty of the slave trade. The subsequent lives of slaves may in some cases have been no disadvantageous change from the barbarism of their original haunts; but the processes of capture and conveying to the market seem to have generally been as barbarous as was compatible with not killing the human merchandise.

The suppression of the slave trade was far more difficult on the East than on the West Coast. There it was a special

[1] It is only due to Mohammed to say that according to the "Traditions" he prohibited the making of eunuchs.

and not over creditable industry, looked at askance by the religious and philanthropic, even when it was legal, and not practised by ordinary merchants or on a small scale. Hence, as soon as the trade was forbidden, it was comparatively easy to seize slave-ships. But on the East Coast no moral stigma whatever attached to the traffic; every one engaged in it without shame, and it was the ordinary practice to add a few slaves to a cargo of other merchandise. Hence the trade long survived formal prohibitions, which had no real effect. Treaties made with the Imam of Maskat in 1822, and with the Sultan of Zanzibar in 1845, forbade the export and import of slaves; and in 1890 the Sultan of Zanzibar was a party to the General Act of the Brussels Conference by which he, as well as the Powers of Europe, agreed to introduce certain practical measures, such as restrictions on the importation of arms, with a view of stopping the slave trade. Nevertheless, it is only with the advent of this century that it can be said to have really ceased.

The position of our East African possessions with regard to slavery is somewhat peculiar. They are founded on the suppression of slavery: our interest and activity in this part of the world largely originated in our desire to put down the slave trade: the establishment of our rule, by effectively terminating that trade, has been one of the greatest philanthropic achievements of the later nineteenth century; and yet, by a strange combination of circumstances, the East Africa Protectorate is severely, and not altogether unjustly, criticised for maintaining and tolerating slavery at the present day.

The facts of the case are that, owing to the promises which we made to the Arabs when we took over the Coast, slavery is recognised as legal within the Sultan's dominions— that is, in a strip ten miles wide along the Coast, with the exception of Kismayu, where it was abolished by a decree of Sultan Barghash in 1876. It is important not to exaggerate the evil. In all the rest of the Protectorate slavery is as absolutely forbidden by law as in the British Isles, and in the ten-mile strip trading in slaves is absolutely forbidden. No slave can be bought, sold, or otherwise acquired; and every child born since 1890 is free in virtue of a decree of Sultan Ali, published in the August of that year, so that the institution is bound to die out in time. But in the case of persons who were in slavery before 1890, the status of slavery is legally recognised; that is to say, if a master and slave appear in court, the law takes cognisance of their position as such, instead of setting aside the relationship as a thing unknown to British law. Every care is taken to protect the interests of slaves, and it is not often that one comes into a British court without being freed. Slaves who complain of the cruelty of their masters are almost invariably manumitted, and in bad cases an offending master is obliged to free all his slaves. But the court will support a master who claims a right to the services of a refractory slave, and will probably require the slave either to return to work or pay his master a certain sum per month out of the earnings he makes elsewhere. He will not, however, be required to return to his master if he objects.

It cannot be denied that the situation is regrettable. Great Britain has always adopted an anti-slavery policy, and inconsistencies and anomalies in a policy which professes to be based on motives of morality, and not on expediency, cannot be allowed without a certain loss of sincerity and moral prestige. They are peculiarly inconvenient when they can be explained by interested motives. In this case, slaves are allowed to claim their manumission as a right in Zanzibar, and the Zanzibar Government, in whose finances the British Treasury is not directly interested, are obliged to compensate the master for the loss of his slave. In the East Africa Protectorate, in whose finances the British Treasury is directly interested, freedom cannot be claimed as a right, and the British Government will not compensate masters.

The contrast is certainly unfortunate, and illustrates what foreigners call our hypocrisy. This is a charge which we are never able to understand, nor will anything shake the confident belief of the average Briton that as a nation we are far more honest and truthful than the other peoples of Europe. Nevertheless it does no doubt happen that we sometimes pursue with vehemence a policy of disinterested justice, and suddenly make an exception when we find that our own interests are involved. In the present case, I am bound to say that I think that this unfortunate contrast between Zanzibar and the Protectorate is not due as a matter of fact and history to a disinclination to spend money, but rather to the conflict between our principles and our promises. Both are equally sacred, and we must remember that, though there would be no excuse for any one who should promise to tolerate Arab customs, including slavery, nowadays, things were very different at the time when the promises were made. Before the Mazrui rebellion in 1895, the Arabs were really an independent power under our protection, but by no means amenable to our orders in internal matters. We could not have suppressed domestic slavery, and it might have been dangerous to interfere with it. But still it is unfortunate that we undertook to tolerate it.

Admitting the evil, I think it must also be admitted that it is one which touches principles and sentiments rather than practical life. In practice the harm done by the continuance of slavery is not great. As no slaves can either be born or acquired, slavery must in a few years die out, and meanwhile the tie of servitude is becoming slighter and slighter. I am not one of those who think that domestic slavery is a harmless institution, or so interwoven with the habits and customs of the country that it cannot be dispensed with. Even if we admit that the improvident negro races are best off when they are under an obligation to work, there is no reason why individuals should be bound to particular masters; and the system by which a man who works outside his master's estate has to pay him a portion of his earnings must be condemned. Also it cannot be denied that the Arab character is prone to deliberate cruelty, and is not to be trusted with irresponsible authority over persons of inferior race. But in spite of all this, the fact remains that slavery is now so shadowy and decadent a system, that it may be wondered if it would really be worth while to take energetic measures to sweep it out of the way before it dies a natural death. In and near Mombasa there are no real slaves, though doubtless there are a good many persons who are not legally and technically free. I knew, for instance, an officer whose cook was a slave of the Wali of Takaungu. This did not prevent him from entering the service of a European, and behaving in every way like a free man, nor, I believe, did he make over any portion of his wages to the Wali. But he occasionally paid him a complimentary visit, and presented him with offerings of fruit. Had he been out of work or in distress, he would have undoubtedly looked to the Wali to maintain him.

Many slaves cultivate land for their masters, and live to all appearance like freemen. They are expected to devote five days a week to their master's plantations, but on Thursday and Friday may work on their own land, which is given them by their master. Slaves who are engaged in trade are assisted by their masters, and pay them a percentage of the profits, but never more than half the sum earned. Carpenters and masons pay nothing, but work for their masters at half price whenever required. An interesting and important class of slaves are the captains of dhows. Almost all the trade of the Coast is in their hands, and they are rarely freemen. They receive a quarter of the earnings of their vessel.

About Melindi, Witu, and Lamu there are large Arab establishments in which many slaves are kept; but it may be doubted if there are any who are really anxious for their freedom and unable to obtain it. In a vast number of cases the slave would look upon the severance of his connection with his master as simply equivalent to the loss of a place, and would wonder what he should do for a living. I doubt myself if the legal abolition of the status of slavery would produce much visible change.   As things are, about 100 manumissions take place a year.[1]   In 1902–3 there were no prosecutions for cruelty, and one was reported last year.   The increasing number of Europeans, with the greater publicity given to everything that happens in the Coast towns, is a great guarantee for the cessation of abuses.

Outside the ten-mile strip of the Sultan's dominions, slavery has no legal existence, nor do I think that any tribes of the interior capture or keep slaves.   I made this remark in my official report for 1903, and a critic, who justly noticed that I also said that there are several tribes of whom we know little or nothing, questioned whether in these circumstances we had sufficient warrant for denying the existence of slavery. The criticism struck me as worthy of attention, but still I think that both my statements are justifiable.   It is true that we know next to nothing of such tribes as the Kisii, the Sotik, the Elgeyo, the Turkana; and yet I think we might safely affirm that they are none of them cannibals, merely because cannibalism, even if only practised in secret, is always known, and arouses in other natives, if not exactly moral detestation, at least a very lively dread of those who practise it.   The same may be said of slavery.   Any race which raids for slaves and keeps persons of other tribes in servitude is at once known, dreaded, and avoided.   I do not think that any tribes in East Africa have this reputation.   The only slave raids in recent years have been made by the Abyssinians, who, according to report, have carried off many both of the Turkana and the Boran as slaves.

In denying the existence of slavery, I, of course, merely deny that East African tribes hold in servitude other natives not belonging to the family, and kept in an inferior position. It cannot be denied that, as mentioned above, their family relations partake of the nature of slavery and property in human flesh.   It would probably be impossible to explain to a native of Ukamba or Kikuyu that there is any difference

[1] 121 manumissions are reported for 1903–4.

between his wife and a female slave whom he had bought, though perhaps it would be more correct to say that he would regard a female slave as a wife rather than *vice versâ*.   But though brides are bought and sold, it would appear that in some tribes at any rate they have some choice in their destiny, and are not made over to men against their will; and it need hardly be said that, though our law is obliged to recognise native marriages, it does not recognise the right of a native to sell his relatives.   Still, the family and social relations of natives are based on such low moral ideas, that they cannot become satisfactory without the introduction of profound changes.   It is for the missionary rather than the Government to introduce those changes, for they can only be brought about by education, but meanwhile we must be on our guard to prevent possible abuses.   There have, for instance, been cases of natives attempting to sell girls for prostitution, where the transaction, had it not been discovered and prevented, would have hardly been distinguishable from a sale into slavery.

Certain backward tribes, such as the Wadorobo, Waboni, and Wasanya, are often spoken of as helots, and as standing in some kind of servile relation to a stronger tribe such as the Masai.   It is, I think, a total misrepresentation to regard their position as really analogous to slavery.   The backward tribe is, as a rule, obviously inferior and wilder than the superior race, and the relation between the two, though not exactly analogous to anything now existing in Europe, is feudal rather than servile.   The inferior tribe secures immunity, and is perhaps protected by the superior, and in return renders certain services, such as manufacturing weapons.   Another singular custom which has been described as slavery, though really not analogous to it, is that among some tribes a convicted murderer, and perhaps his family, is obliged to serve the family of the murdered man for a term of years.   The theory underlying this is that murder is equivalent to robbery, inasmuch as the relations of the murdered man have lost a labourer. If the murderer cannot give adequate compensation, he must make good the loss he has occasioned by filling the place of his victim.

I would fain see the stain of slavery removed from the Coast; but, with this one exception, I think we have every reason to congratulate ourselves, without undue self-laudation, on the accomplishment in East Africa of one of the greatest works of humanity which the world has seen. It is only ten or fifteen years since the whole country from the ocean to the Congo groaned beneath oppression and bloodshed. On the Coast the Arabs took two children out of three from every family as slaves. From Lake Victoria almost to Mombasa the Masai harried the whole land. The valleys were deserted, and no one dared to keep cattle for fear of exciting the cupidity of the raiders. In Uganda, Mtesa and Mwanga put to death tens of thousands in apparently aimless fury, to say nothing of tortures and mutilations. The caravans of slave-traders traversed the whole country seeking for their victims. Every tribe was at war with its neighbours, and nature augmented the misery wrought by man by causing from time to time terrible famines. If East Africa is not yet a paradise, we may at least congratulate ourselves on having changed this scene of human suffering. The slave trade is at an end, and even sporadic cases of kidnapping are not heard of any more. Massacres are equally a thing of the past; and if raiding and intertribal wars still continue, they continue only in the remoter districts, and it may be hoped that with the extension of our effective administration they will disappear altogether. Africa has not yet become civilised, but it has become possible to think of civilisation.

Although the slave trade, massacres, and other forms of barbarism could only have been abolished by force and the strong arm of Government, we must not forget the immense debt which Africa owes to gentler methods, to moral influence and missionary enterprise. It is regrettable that many white residents and many Government officials are in incomplete sympathy with missions, and under-estimate the value of the humanitarian work which they perform.... One may doubt whether the attempts to evangelise countries which have old and philosophic religions of their own, such as India and China, are likely to meet with much success; but I must say that in all parts of the world where I have come in contact with missions, I have found that their labours, if judged by an entirely unsectarian standard merely as contributions to the welfare of mankind, are deserving of the highest praise. Before living in Africa, I had made the acquaintance of two bodies of missionaries—namely, the American Missions to Armenians in Asia Minor, and the various missions in Samoa. The former have perhaps done more to help that unhappy people than all the Governments of Christian Europe, and have set a good example of the right way to influence the religious feelings of a civilised race, namely, by making little attempt at direct proselytism, but by trying to understand and sympathise with all that is good in their ancient Church. In Samoa the relatively high civilisation of the natives is entirely due to the missionaries; and the troubles of 1899, though they took the form of a contest between a Protestant and a Roman Catholic chief, were certainly not due to religious causes.

In the East Africa Protectorate I can give the missionaries nothing but praise and thanks. This encomium cannot, perhaps, be extended unreservedly to Uganda, where politics mingled with religion, and the Roman Catholics became the French party opposed to the Protestant and English party. But this difference is now a thing of the past, and one can only say that, if formerly religious zeal in Uganda overstepped the bounds of law and order, the harvest of this somewhat violent sowing has been rich and abundant beyond comparison; for there is probably hardly any other instance where a heathen country has adopted Christianity and education with such enthusiasm. Also, if the beginnings of Christianity in Uganda were somewhat mixed up with politics, it must be admitted that the result is politically important and satisfactory. Mohammedanism is not dead in Africa, and can still give the natives a motive for animosity against Europeans, and a unity of which they are otherwise incapable. Had Uganda become Mohammedan, which was at one moment quite possible, the whole of the Nile Valley and of east central Africa might have been in the hands of Mohammedans, ready to receive and pass on any wave of fanaticism which might start in the north, and perhaps to start one themselves.

It is, however, to be hoped that the evil of Uganda—the rivalry of two Christian sects—will be avoided elsewhere. In a savage country the juxtaposition of religions which are not in mutual harmony cannot conduce to edification, and is very likely to lead to strife. But this strife appears not to have infected East Africa. In Mombasa and Teita there are Roman Catholic and Protestant missions in close proximity, and I have never heard of any quarrels. Neither is there any whisper in East Africa of the scandals which are alleged to prevail elsewhere. I have never heard of trading missionaries or missionaries with native families. The opening of a new mission station has seemed to me to be generally as efficacious for the extension of European influence as the opening of a Government station, and there are districts in East Africa, such as Teita and the lower Tana, in which European influence has hitherto been represented almost entirely by missionaries, but which have made as great progress as the regions which have been taken in hand by Government officials.

The most practical missions are, I think, those which are industrial. It is hard to say what amount of dogmatic Christianity is really imparted to African brains by the most successful teachers and preachers. Perhaps not much; but they certainly teach those natives who frequent them to lead a better life than their pagan brothers, and it facilitates that better and more civilised life if natives can engage in some form of trade or occupation which causes them to more or less break with their old associations and come under

Q

Christian supervision. From this point of view I think it is a great mistake to isolate natives or place them in reserves, if such a course can be avoided, for such isolation inevitably confirms them in their old bad customs and cuts them off from contact with superior races which might improve them. Hitherto the only industrial missions have been those of the Roman Catholics; but I am glad to say that recently one has been started in Mombasa in conjunction with the Church Missionary Society, and is doing well. One of the principal industries is pottery and tile-making, but much good might be done by teaching the natives to cultivate cotton, india-rubber, and groundnuts.

Missions abound in East Africa. About ten denominations—or at any rate separate religious institutions—are represented, including Americans, Quakers, and the Swedish Church. The largest establishments are those of the Church Missionary Society, the Roman Catholic Church, and the German Lutherans. The chief stations of the first named, as of all the older societies, are near the coast at Freretown, Rabai, and Jilore; but they have also paid peculiar and successful attention to the district of Teita and Taveta, and since the construction of the Uganda Railway have been active in Kikuyu. These missions are under the Bishop of Mombasa, whose diocese also includes part of German East Africa. The Roman Catholic missionaries mostly belong to the Society of the Holy Ghost, and are commonly known as the Black Fathers, in contradistinction to the White Fathers, an Algerian society whose headquarters are in Uganda. They are under a bishop resident at Zanzibar, and in Mombasa and Nairobi have large congregations, owing to the number of Goanese in the Protectorate. They have not, however, made the same progress amongst the natives as in Uganda, though they have a large industrial mission, with considerable cultivation, at Bura, between Voi and Taveta. The German Lutheran missions recall the time when German influence was strong in what is now the British Protectorate. At one period, before the present political spheres were defined, British commercial and missionary activity seemed to radiate chiefly from Zanzibar, while the Germans were active in Tanaland. The missions have still preserved this distribution, and both the Universities' Mission and the Church Missionary Society have numerous establishments in the parts of German East Africa which are, roughly speaking, opposite Zanzibar and Pemba, while Lutheran missions remain at Jimba, near Mombasa, at Nengia, Ikutha, Myambani, and Mivukoni, in the little-known wilds of Ukamba and in Tanaland. On some parts of the Tana River the natives actually speak a little German.

One of the most interesting figures in the brief annals of East Africa is connected with these Lutheran missions—Ludwig Krapf, who, with his colleague Rebmann, must be regarded as one of the greatest pioneers not only in evangelisation but in geographical discovery, since it is to them that we owe our first knowledge of Kilima-Njaro and Kenya.

Krapf was the son of a farmer, and born near Tübingen in 1810. His talents and application gained him admission to the Anatolian School in that learned city, and, combined with his energy and piety, rendered him most suitable for the career of a scientific missionary which he adopted and adorned. He was first of all sent to Shoa in Abyssinia, but subsequently, finding that his labours were impeded by political difficulties, he shifted the sphere of his activity to Mombasa in 1844. During his whole life he had a singular mania for the Gallas; he baptized the country between the Tana and Juba Ormania, or Gallaland, a designation which has not endured; and, in discussing " the probable mission of the Gallas in the providential scheme," he stated that he " considered them destined by Providence after their conversion to Christianity to attain the importance and fulfil the mission which Heaven has pointed out to the Germans in Europe." It is only just to say that these strange fancies did not diminish his energy in other directions; when, as was often the case, he found no Gallas handy, he was unremitting in his efforts both as a religious

teacher and a student of other native races. He was a man
of large ideas; and another of his ambitions, more practical
than the creation of an Ormanian empire, was to build a chain
of missionary stations right across Africa, and thus connect the
east and west coasts.

Krapf belonged to that class of travellers who appear
ludicrously deficient in all the physical aptitudes necessary in
wild countries, and yet accomplish journeys which would try
the endurance of most soldiers and sportsmen. His riding
animals generally ran away, extraordinary accidents happened
to his gun, and the most striking article of his equipment
seems to have been an umbrella, which is frequently mentioned
in his narratives, and which once, when opened suddenly,
scattered a band of robbers in panic. But he had a knowledge
of native languages which was worth a horse and a gun, and,
more than that, knew how to feel and how to inspire sympathy.
Seyyid Said, the Sultan of Zanzibar, introduced him to his
governors as " a good man who wishes to convert the world to
God," and he settled under the protection of the authorities at
Rabai, where he laboured with Rebmann. His evangelical
work met with little immediate success, as he candidly con-
fesses: "This morning," he writes on 9th March 1848, "two
old Wanika women, as self-righteous as any person in Europe
can be, paid me a visit. When I spoke of the evil heart of
man, one of the women said, ' Who has been slandering me to
you? I have a good heart, and know of no sin.' The other
woman said, ' I came to you to ask for a garment, and not to
listen to your discourse.' A Mnika said, ' If I am to be always
praying to your Lord, how can I look after my plantation?'"
Krapf's literary labours, however, laid a very solid foundation
for future mission work. He compiled a Swahili dictionary
and grammar, and translated the whole of the Bible and other
religious works.

Nevertheless, the apathy of the people of Rabai weighed
upon him and his colleague, and in 1848 they decided on
starting an inland mission. It was arranged that Rebmann

MOUNT KENYA FROM THE FOOT OF THE SETTIMA HILLS.

SIMBA: A HUNTER'S PARADISE.

KIMAA.

should go due west, and Krapf somewhat to the north in quest of his **Ormania**. As a matter of fact, Rebmann made three expeditions to Chagga,[1] on the southern slopes of Kilima-Njaro, and established the existence of that mountain, of which the Portuguese had some notion; while Krapf, after visiting Usambara, made two journeys to Ukamba, for which he conceived nearly as much enthusiasm as for Gallaland. He had a special friend in Kivoi, the chief of Kitui, who was unfortunately killed on a journey in his company; and Krapf returned to the coast only with great difficulty and many hardships, as Kivoi's people held him responsible for the murder, which they thought he ought to have prevented. He fully describes Kenya, or Keguia, which he first saw on 3rd December 1849, "and observed two large horns or pillars as it were rising over an enormous mountain to the north-west of the Kilima-Njaro, covered with a white substance." It is a curious example of the worthlessness of much vehement criticism, particularly criticism based upon theories and applied to facts, that the existence of the snow-capped mountains seen by Krapf and Rebmann were discredited in many quarters, even by Livingstone, and most unmerited abuse was showered on the explorers.

On returning from Ukamba, Krapf went to Europe, and after a short rest wished to return to Rabai in 1854, but on the way out was taken seriously ill in Egypt, and had to abandon missionary work in Africa. In 1860 he published his "Travels, Researches, and Missionary Labours during an Eighteen Years' Residence in Eastern Africa," a most instructive and readable book. The interest which it created induced two English and two Swiss missionaries to proceed to Mombasa, whither they were escorted by Krapf, who introduced them to the country. Owing to political difficulties with the Arabs, only Wakefield remained at the station of Ribe, near Rabai, where he was afterwards joined by New. Both of them did

---

[1] Krapf always speaks of this place as Jagga, just as he calls Tana and Taveta, Dana and Dafeta. It is most curious that this able philologist should not have overcome the Teutonic inability to distinguish hard and soft consonants.

good work in geographical exploration. Wakefield investigated the Tana and the Pokomo country, and New ascended Kilima-Njaro and actually handled the snow.

In 1872 Sir Bartle Frere was sent on a special mission to Zanzibar, to negotiate with the Sultan a more effective treaty for the suppression of the slave trade, which was finally signed by Sir John Kirk. On returning, he urged on the Church Missionary Society the importance of establishing at Mombasa a settlement for the reception of liberated slaves. This was agreed to, and the settlement, called Freretown in his honour, was founded in 1874 by the Rev. W. S. Price, and in a year's time about 500 rescued slaves were housed and instructed there. A large church was opened at Rabai in 1888, and there also considerable numbers of slaves congregated. This, however, nearly led to serious trouble, as the Arabs of Mombasa contended that many of these slaves were mere runaways from domestic service, who had no right to their freedom.

A disturbance seemed imminent, but the danger was happily averted by the generosity of the British East Africa Company, who paid the ransom of all the runaways, and on January 1, 1890, papers of liberation were presented to 950 persons.

From the centre thus formed at Freretown and Rabai missions were sent to other parts of the Nyika, and to the Teita-Taveta district, which may be said to have received a special missionary civilisation of its own. Mr. Wray, who is still there, founded the mission at Sagalla in the Ndara Hills in 1883. He had at first some trouble, and in 1887 the mission was attacked by natives, who accused him of occasioning a drought. It is a curious example of the workings of the African mind, that the operation of washing clothes and hanging them out to dry was regarded as a piece of maleficent magic intended to prevent rain. The Taveta mission, connected with the name of Mr. Steggall, was originally founded in the Chagga country, but removed to its present location within the British territory in 1892. Since the

Uganda Railway opened up the interior, stations have been founded in the last few years near Nairobi and in Mukaa near Kiu, also at Thunguri in Kenya.

The Universities' Mission have a bishop and a cathedral at Zanzibar, and stations in the more southern parts of German East Africa, but no connection with the East Africa Protectorate.

CHAPTER XVII

THE NEIGHBOURS OF BRITISH EAST AFRICA

THE East Coast of Africa is at present divided between Italy, Great Britain, Germany, and Portugal. France's interests are limited to Madagascar and the Comoro Islands,[1] and the other colonising powers, such as Holland and Spain, never paid any attention to this side of the continent. The Italian sphere is the northern part of the East Coast down to the mouth of the Juba : the British possessions extend from the Juba to the Umba on the Coast, and their interior boundaries have been discussed elsewhere : German territory comes next, running down south to the Rovuma River and Cape Delgado, and stretching inwards to Lakes Tanganyika and Nyassa : then comes Portuguese territory, divided in the middle by the Zambesi, and bounded on the south and west by Lake Nyassa and British possessions.

Of these four spheres, it may be safely said that the Italian is the least attractive. It would be hard to imagine anything less inviting than the fort-like promontories, without a blade of verdure and generally enveloped in sand-storms, of which the traveller catches an occasional glimpse from the steamer as he rounds the Horn of Africa. In the interior it is said that there are fertile valleys, particularly along the banks of

---

[1] It is probable that these islands, which lie at the northern entrance of the Mozambique Channel, were occupied by the Arabs very early, and that the name signifies "Islands of the Moon." The principal islands are Grand Comoro, with a volcanic peak 8500 feet high, and Mayotte. The French occupied Mayotte in 1841, and their protectorate was extended to the rest in 1886. The Archipelago has an old connection with Zanzibar, and many natives divide their time between the two. Much inconvenience is caused by their claiming French protection in Zanzibar. The Comoro islanders are of a very mixed race, but those who visit Zanzibar speak good Swahili.

the Webi Shebeli, yet this considerable river is so exhausted by evaporation and absorption by the thirsty soil that it terminates in a marsh before it reaches the sea. The produce of Italian Somaliland—as the district is often called—is, however, considerable, and consists of cattle, sheep, goats, hides, ivory, and various gums. Commercially it labours under the great disadvantage of having no good harbour, and the Coast is always inaccessible during a great part of the year for ships of ordinary strength, which cannot face the fury of the monsoon. Mogdisho or Makdishu, the principal port, is one of the hardest places in the world either to land at or to spell. The above orthographies give an idea of the ordinary pronunciation; but at least ten others may be found, some of which, being based on Portuguese and Italian methods of representing the sound which we render by *sh*, are very perplexing : such are Magadoxo, Mogadiscio, and Moguedouchou. The correct but unused form is said to be the Arabic Maq'ad-ush-Shat, " the sitting place of the sheep," in reference to a local legend.

Politically Italy occupies this region by a double tenure ; she has a protectorate over various small sultanates such as Obbia and Mijertein, and leases from the Sultan of Zanzibar the four towns of Brawa, Merka, Mogdisho, and Warsheikh, from which this portion of the littoral is often, though somewhat ironically, known as the Benadir or Harbour Coast. This arrangement is similar to that by which we occupy the Sultan's dominions in the East Africa Protectorate, but the Italians are anxious to replace it by the purchase of the four ports. No agreement, however, has yet been come to on the matter.

Hitherto the Benadir Coast and Hinterland have been administered not directly by the Italian Government, but through a company ; and it may be said without international discourtesy that this administration was profoundly unsatisfactory, for nowhere has it been criticised more severely than in Italy, and it would appear that there were serious differences of opinion between the officials of the company and the Italian officers in their employ. I believe that, as the result of a commission of inquiry held recently, a more direct Government control will be established. Hitherto the company practically followed the methods of the Zanzibar government, and confined their administration to the four ports and a few posts on the Juba River. It was hardly safe to go a few miles into the country without an armed escort, and last year (1903) Bardera on the Juba had to be abandoned. Further, it was alleged that the motives of this company being exclusively commercial, the worst abuses, such as the slave trade, were tolerated for fear of creating trouble which could interfere with trade. It is to be hoped, in British interests, that a more effective system of government may soon be established on the Italian bank of the Juba. As is well known, a river is not a good frontier, because it tends to unite rather than divide population. As the natives are constantly crossing from one bank to the other, the valley of the Juba practically forms a single district, and it is difficult to establish order on one side as long as lawlessness prevails on the other.

I have no personal acquaintance with the Portuguese possessions in East Africa; but, to judge from all accounts, though they are far older and richer than those of Italy, they have not attained a much higher development, and effective administration is almost confined to the seaboard. The Makua tribes near Mozambique are only now being brought under subjection, and it is said that the Angoche country, which lies between Quilimane and Mozambique, has not yet been conquered, and is largely in the hands of chiefs descended from Zanzibar Arabs. Historically, these Portuguese colonies represent stages on the road to India: they were founded as part of an attempt to create an Indian Empire, and the various settlements were maintained in order to establish regular communication with fixed ports of call. The African territories themselves were a matter of very secondary importance, and when they ceased to serve their original purpose received but scant attention. They appear, however, to be rich, and to yield in abundance such products as ivory, cotton, copal, rubber, and various valuable drugs. The trade of the coast is said to be mostly in the hands of Indians, and large tracts of the country are let to chartered companies. Much of the interior consists of prazos da coroa or crown lands, mostly leased to half-caste planters.

In the eighteenth century an attempt was made to colonise the country systematically, and a number of Portuguese women were sent out to Mozambique and received lands on condition of marrying Europeans. This condition was not observed, and other stipulations respecting the size and tenure of the crown estates were also neglected. The result was the rise of a class of half-breed landowners, many of whom became practically independent of the Government and terrorised considerable districts. In the last century efforts were made to abolish this system, but without success; and the Government has in the end had to conciliate the occupants of the prazos, and give them a quasi-feudal position by recognising them as its agents. It is said that very great evils, including the practical enslavement of the natives, result from this system.

The coast and the banks of the Zambesi have the reputation of being very unhealthy. Of the hinterland little is known, as the only railways are built rather for communication with the Transvaal than for opening up the colony. The interior, however, contains salubrious uplands, like most parts of East Africa, and the Namuli Highlands, to the north of the Zambesi, are highly spoken of for their beauty and excellent climate.

German East Africa offers more points of interest than the Italian and Portuguese possessions, on account of its resemblance to our own territories. The physical features are much the same, the boundary being quite arbitrary. It was acquired at much the same time as our Protectorate, and is administered with roughly the same objects and by the same methods, though with sufficient differences to make comparison curious and instructive. The country has a longer coast-line than

British East Africa, with a series of considerable ports and more navigable rivers, though none of any very great size. It also possesses the splendid peak of Kilima-Njaro, with its fertile slopes and upland pastures, which, as is well known, the German Emperor insisted on retaining as a *sine quâ non* condition of any delimitation. Perhaps, too, the mineral wealth is greater than in our territory. But, on the other hand, the climate as a whole appears to be less healthy: much of the interior is reported to consist of arid steppes; the communications are very imperfect, and perhaps the natives are a greater obstacle to colonisation than in our sphere.

The territory is divided into twenty-one administrative districts: Tanga, Pangani, Bagamoyo, Dar-es-Salaam, Kilwa, Lindi, Songea, Mahenge, Kisaki, Kilossa, Mpapwa, Iringa, Langenburg, Kilimatinde, Tabora, Ujiji, Bismarckburg, Mwanza, Bukoba, Kilima-Njaro, Usambara. The first six of these districts are on the coast. Tanga is the starting-point of the Usambara Railway, and, next to Dar-es-Salaam, the most important port, but Bagamoyo is likely to be long a considerable commercial centre. It was formerly the chief point of departure for the interior, and, being directly opposite to Zanzibar, it has a lively trade with that island, as native craft are able to make the journey at all times of the year. It may be doubted whether the Germans do wisely in endeavouring to attract all the trade to Dar-es-Salaam, for the natural ease of communication and long-established custom, which is always a strong force in Africa, tend to attach the native merchants to Bagamoyo.

Dar-es-Salaam (the abode of peace) has an excellent harbour, though somewhat difficult of access, and a dock. It is the best-built town on the coast. It was laid out with a lavish disregard for cost, and its wide tranquil streets bordered with flowering trees, its parks and gardens, its comfortable residences, its magnificent hospital, and other buildings give it somewhat the appearance of a German Kurort transferred to the tropics. It labours under the disadvantage of being, unlike Mombasa, a new and European creation. Fifteen years ago it was merely a village, and, though it is a fine port, it does not yet appear to be recognised as the natural emporium for the merchandise of the interior.

Kilwa and Lindi, the southern maritime districts, have a considerable export of grain, and communicate with the interior by the rivers Rufiji and Rovuma. Both are navigable for large craft as far as two hundred kilometres during four months of the year, and for about fifty kilometres during the rest. There are two towns called Kilwa—Kilwa Kivinje on the mainland, and Kilwa Kisiwani, about twenty-five miles to the south, on an island, opposite to the proposed terminus of the Nyassa Railway. This latter, often written with the Portuguese orthography as Quiloa, is the oldest historical site on the coast respecting which we have any authentic records. Two Arabic chronicles of the town are extant, one of which was published in the *Journal of the Royal Asiatic Society* for 1895, pp. 385–430. It is said to have been founded about 975 A.D. by Ali, the son of Hasan-bin-Ali, king of Shiraz, who had a dream warning him to leave the country with his whole family, which they accordingly did in seven ships, of which the sixth reached Kilwa. The dynasty founded by Ali ruled for about five hundred years, and extended its dominions along the coast. In 1502 Vasco da Gama stopped at Kilwa, on his second voyage to India, and exacted from the Sultan a yearly tribute. As this was not paid with regularity, the town was stormed and occupied by the Portuguese in 1505; but as it was some distance from the gold mines of the south, and of little use to ships going to India, it was abandoned in 1512, and left to the rule of independent chiefs. It is said to have contained 300 mosques, of which two now remain. The German Government are taking measures to preserve these and other ancient buildings in the town.

Opposite the mouth of the Rufiji are the Mafia or Monfia Islands, seven in number, of which Mafia and Chole are the best known. They are very fertile, and, besides yielding copra

and similar tropical produce, support a considerable number of
cattle. They were annexed by the rulers of Kilwa about 1000
A.D., and, like that town, contain some interesting ruins.

Like the British East Africa Protectorate, the interior of
German East Africa is said to consist of a series of zones; but,
instead of a gradual and persistent rise, we have on the best-
known route—Bagomoyo, Mpapwa, Tabora, and Ufiji—a
mountain barrier at a short distance from the coast, followed
by a descent. This configuration, by keeping off the moist sea
breezes, perhaps accounts for the greater aridity of the upland
plains. The first zone is the coast strip, behind which are the
Usagara Mountains, about 6500 feet high. Next come the
Ugogo plains, from 3500 to 4000 feet high, the western part
of which, known as Mgunda Mkhali, is a rocky and waterless
desert, apparently somewhat resembling the country to the
north of Mount Kenya. The fourth zone is the tableland of
Unyamwezi, with the town of Tabora, about 4000 feet above
the sea-level. Until the rise of Nairobi and Entebbe, Tabora
was the only city of any eminence in the interior of East
Africa, and, though not very ancient, is anterior to the European occupation of the country, having been a residential
centre for the Arab slave-traders. As all the roads from the
coast, Tanganyika, and Lake Victoria converge towards it, it is
a commercial and strategic centre of the greatest importance,
and in the number and size of its buildings is said to far surpass any of the native coast towns. The Arab domination in
Tabora was disturbed by the revolt of a native chief called
Mirambo, who during many years, until he died in 1887,
carried on a successful warfare against them. The population
of the district is said to exceed 300,000, and the inhabitants
are celebrated as being the best porters in East Africa. The
fifth zone—after the coast strip, the Usagara mountains, the
Ugogo plains, and the Tabora plateau—is formed by the allu-
vial lands round Lake Tanganyika. Here is situated Ujiji, a
town probably destined to commercial importance in the future,
but described as being at present squalid and unhealthy.

The southern districts call for little remark. The principal export seems to be india-rubber. In Iringa are the important native states of Uhehe and Usanga. The Wahehe formerly gave a good deal of trouble, and cut up a considerable force of Germans in 1891, but have been quiet of late. The northern provinces are Bukoba, on the boundary of Uganda, and Mwanza, Kilima-Njaro, and Usambara on that of the East Africa Protectorate. In Bukoba is Lake Kivu, said to be of singular beauty, and surrounded by fertile country. Mwanza comprises the rich cattle country of Usukuma, but also a large extent of barren plains. Gold has been discovered in this district, near the British frontier, but is probably not to be found in paying quantities. The trade of Mwanza is of considerable interest to us, as it is now mostly carried by the Uganda Railway, and the Lake steamers which run in conjunction with it and call at Shirati and other ports on the Lake. The district of Kilima-Njaro is called after the mountain of the same name. The southern slopes of this huge mass of volcanic rock are said to be exceptionally fertile, and to offer as good a locality for European colonisation as any in East Africa; but owing to the want of communications, and the hostility of the natives, little has been done in the way of settlement. The chief town is Moschi. It is stated that quite recently (autumn of 1904) a number of Boer families from South Africa have been given land in this district. It has often been suggested that a branch of the Uganda Railway should be built in this direction to the German frontier. This could hardly be recommended financially at present, but there is a very fair road from Voi to Taveta, which with a little improvement might be made practicable for motors. With colonisation, the production of Kilima-Njaro must become considerable, and it would be worth while to attract its trade. Usambara would appear to be the most progressive and best developed district in the colony, owing to its accessibility and excellent climate. It is traversed by the navigable river Pangani, and a railway has been constructed

from Tanga as far as Korogwe. In it are the Usambara and
Pare mountains, with a pleasant and healthy climate. Several
plantations, particularly of coffee, have been started.

The differences in the administration of German and British
East Africa are mainly due to the fact that, whereas we have
devoted our time and attention chiefly to the construction of
the Uganda Railway, and shown extreme parsimony and indifference in other respects, the Germans have done little in
the way of railway construction, but have devoted themselves
to the methodical development of the colony with a systematic
thoroughness characteristic of the race, and a lavishness due
to the determination to establish a colonial empire at any
price. In the financial year 1900–1 the expenditure on
German East Africa was £617,950, and this apparently did
not include subventions to steamers. In the British East
Africa Protectorate the expenditure during the same period
(exclusive of the accounts of the Uganda Railway) was
£193,438. Since then, the German expenditure has decreased. It was £414,190 in 1903–4, and is estimated at
£471,718 for the current year.

These large sums have been partly expended on the fine
buildings already mentioned at Dar-es-Salaam and elsewhere.
In this matter it would seem that the right course is a *via
media* between the methods of the two nations. The palaces
and fortresses erected by the Germans can hardly be defended
as necessary expenditure. On the other hand, many lives
would have been saved if British officers had had better
accommodation in the early days of our Protectorate. The
German method has generally been to make provision for all
possible needs and accidents; we, on the other hand, have
rarely sanctioned any expenditure (except in connection with
the railway) until experience, often dearly bought, proved it
was necessary. The cost of the public works executed by the
Germans must have been very considerable. Five lighthouses
have been erected on the coast, and a dock constructed at
Dar-es-Salaam. Carriage roads of considerable length have

been made, and it is possible to drive from Dar-es-Salaam to Tanganyika and Lake Victoria, from Tanga to Kilima-Njaro, and from Kilwa and Linda to Lake Nyassa.

As might be expected, the scientific departments, which have been almost entirely neglected in the British possessions, have received great attention. Elaborate and costly experiments have been made, with a view of ascertaining what products are likely to prove a success, and the Government plantations, especially at Kwai, in Western Usambara, are said to be on an extensive scale. There is a museum at Dar-es-Salaam, meteorological observations are recorded at about twenty stations, and considerable progress has been made in surveying and mapping the country. In this respect we are deplorably backward. When I was Commissioner of the Protectorate, I habitually consulted a German map, which took some account of the districts on our side of the boundary, and nourished myself, so to speak, on the crumbs which fell from the Teutonic table. They were better than any repast which our own cartographers could provide.

The expense of the military and civil administration is about equal (each about £116,000). About two thousand troops are kept, which is not excessive in a country with few communications and many wild tribes; but large forces of irregulars are said to be maintained at various points of the interior.

There are a considerable number of military officers and non-commissioned officers occupying civil posts, which probably results in a more rigorous enforcement of regulations than is usual with us. Some British subjects, who were attracted by the reports of discoveries of gold in Mwanza, returned complaining of the number and severity of the restrictions imposed, and saying that, for the first time in their lives, they found their own officials tolerable by comparison. On the other hand, there are district councils on which the merchants and planters are represented—an example which our authorities would do well to follow.

The Germans are said to deal with natives more severely than we do, and to be less popular with them. The most definite instance of this unpopularity is that Sendeyo, the Masai chieftain, came over from German to British territory about two years ago, in spite of the fact that by so doing he had to abandon his claims to supremacy in favour of his brother. On the other hand, natives are said to immigrate into German territory from the Congo Free State and the Portuguese dominions, so that they cannot find the régime very distasteful. Probably the German inclinations in favour of an inflexible system and military discipline are less agreeable to the African than the happy-go-lucky methods of British administration. There can be no doubt that disorders are suppressed with rigour, and that the Germans have a reputation for ferocity. A curious story is told to the effect that some years ago several rebels were executed on Kilima-Njaro, and, as specimens were wanted for the craniological section of the museum at Berlin, their skulls were destined for this purpose, and prepared by boiling. The impression produced on the native mind was inevitable and ineradicable—namely, that the flesh was eaten by the authorities.

Domestic slavery is tolerated, though the slave trade is, of course, forbidden, and stringent instructions are issued to officials to prevent its secret practice. The report published by the Foreign Office on the German colonies for 1902–3,[1] and based on the Imperial Chancellor's Memorandum on the development of the German colonies in Africa and the South Seas, says:—

"The effect of the Imperial Chancellor's Ordinance on the subject of domestic slavery, of November 29, 1901, is shown by the fact that the official liberations increased from 444 in 1901–2, to 965 in 1902–3. The provisions of this Ordinance have rapidly become known among the native population, and every slave is now aware that he can purchase his freedom by payment of a comparatively small and easily-earned sum.

[1] October 1904, Annual Series, No. 3296.

That more slaves have not taken advantage of this (723 in the year under review, as against 646 in the preceding year), shows that the condition of domestic slavery in East Africa is not one of great hardship. The above-mentioned Ordinance has prepared the way for the complete abolition of slavery, which will be initiated by decreeing that all persons born after a certain date are free, as soon as the means of communication in the Protectorate have been so far improved as to make it possible to replace slavery by free labour."

More attention is paid to education than with us. Whereas there are no Government schools in British East Africa, instruction being entirely in the hands of the missionaries, the Germans have eight, at Dar-es-Salaam, Tanga, Bagamoyo, Mwanza, Bukoba, Kondoa, Iranga, and Mpapwa, besides several communal schools. The results achieved by these establishments are officially reported as satisfactory ; but it is noticeable that Indians and Goanese are largely used as clerks, and that the half-civilised Swahilis seem to be the only African race who can cope with the intricacies of the German language. There is an amusing story which relates that some spot in the interior was christened Wilhelmshöhe, and a discourse made to the assembled natives on the august significance of the imperial name. When subsequently asked if they could remember what the place was called, they replied, " Yes, Whisky-soda."

Against all the advantages which arise from lavish expenditure and systematic thoroughness, must be set the want of communications. The published figures, giving the amount of hut tax collected in each district, leave the impression that only about half the area is effectively administered, and this is doubtless chiefly due to the difficulty of moving about. The navigable rivers do not extend far inland, and the example of British East Africa shows how little effect a waterway (such as the Tana or Juba) has in opening up a country compared to a railway. Further, the colony is peculiarly unfortunate in having on each side of it a better route to Lakes Victoria and Nyassa than it can itself afford, so that it loses the vivifying effect of the traffic. The Uganda Railway taps the shores of Lake Victoria and the north-western provinces of German territory, and in the south the roads from Kilwa and Lindi to Nyassa cannot compete with the Zambesi route. The only railway, that from Tanga to Korogwe, affects practically nothing but the plantations in Usambara. This state of things will, no doubt, be altered when a railway is built into the centre of the Protectorate. A private company propose to build a line from Dar-es-Salaam to Mrogoro, and the Reichstag have sanctioned a guarantee for the payment of interest. A route across the Pugu Hills has been surveyed, and the total length will probably be about 140 miles—that is, about the distance from Mombasa to the Tsavo—though, owing to the different arrangement of the zones, the country immediately behind the coast is probably more valuable than in our territory.

In looking at the British and German colonies, one is involuntarily led to ask which method of management is the better. It is as yet too early to judge by results; we are hardly past seedtime, and certainly not come to harvest. Some years must elapse before we can offer a definite opinion on the commercial prospects of the Uganda Railway, or say whether the large outlay made by the Germans on such things as Government plantations will prove remunerative. But, as far as one can judge by present temporary conditions, it does not seem likely that the German territories will make more rapid progress than our own. The revenue has for some years been about £150,000, whereas that of the British East Africa Protectorate has in the last five years advanced from under £70,000 to about £110,000, and may perhaps amount to £140,000[1] at the end of the current year. Considering the greater expenditure of the Germans, the greater length of their coast, and the fact that they have had the 10 per cent. duties for several years, whereas, owing to international stipulations,

---

[1] The increase is largely due to the increase of the Customs duties from five to ten per cent.

we have only just been able to introduce them, the difference is less than might have been expected.

Such a question as the comparative extent and success of colonisation can only be decided by actual results. Though we can draw upon a population with greater aptitudes for colonial settlement, German merchants and planters have been quite as much to the fore in British East Africa as our own people. Still, although the Germans have done all in their power to encourage colonisation, and we have done nothing to speak of, and practically discouraged it, it would appear that there are more genuine settlers in our territory than in theirs. The most hopeful point in the British position is that we may legitimately expect great and sudden progress in the next few years, whereas in German territory there is no present reason for expecting more than very gradual improvement. I would not, however, have us lay any flattering unction to our souls and congratulate ourselves, as we are wont to do, on managing everything better than all other nations. It would be very odd if we had not some return for the six millions spent on the Uganda Railway.

CHAPTER XVIII

ANIMALS

ONE of the striking and unique features of East Africa is the extraordinary abundance of large game. Taking the animal kingdom as a whole, it cannot be said to show extreme exuberance. Snakes, centipedes, and scorpions are less heard of than in most tropical countries; though mosquitoes and flies are a nuisance here and there, they are local, and large districts are free from them. One does not feel, as in some parts of South America, that one is surrounded on every side by the brilliant fluttering life of birds and butterflies, and that every flower and plant is teeming with insects. Water-birds are very plentiful on the banks of lakes and rivers, and the Coast offers a fair show of bright plumage; but the dense forests of the Highland hills are remarkable for their deep, dead stillness, unbroken by any sight or sound of living things. Much the same may be said of all Uganda and the countries by the Upper Nile, except on the banks. High grass grows everywhere, and the cover which it affords creates an impression, in this case undoubtedly erroneous, that it contains few animals.

But in the uplands of the East Africa Protectorate, particularly in the Rift Valley and the plains between Nairobi and Makindu, all the conditions are favourable to spectacular effect. The animals are large, and, as there is hardly any vegetation except short grass, nothing interrupts the view. Beasts which are generally thought of as the rare possession of some fortunate zoological garden, here walk about in flocks as numerous as ordinary cattle, and not much more disturbed by the passing trains. The reports of telegraph officials are full of complaints about the injury done to their wires, because monkeys will swing on them, or thoughtless giraffes walk across the line without making allowance for the length of their necks.

Africa south of the Sahara, excluding the northern part of the continent, but including southern Arabia, forms the zoological district known as Ethiopian, and characterised both by the absence of many well-known families, and by the remarkable development of some groups of mammals. Bears, tapirs, deer, wild sheep and goats, and typical swine are entirely, or almost entirely, absent; and the same is the case with several less conspicuous classes, such as shrews and beavers. On the other hand, apes, carnivora, and some classes of ungulata are represented very largely, and often by forms unknown in other parts of the world. Peculiar to Ethiopian Africa are the two great anthropoid apes, the gorilla and chimpanzee, as well as a host of smaller monkeys and baboons. Among the carnivora, lions, leopards, cheetahs, hyenas, jackals, wild cats, and wild dogs occur in inconvenient abundance. But most remarkable and conspicuous of all are the huge and sometimes beautiful ungulata—the elephants, rhinoceros, giraffes, hippopotami, zebras, buffaloes, and all the host of antelopes. As these latter are sometimes erroneously called deer, it may perhaps be well to remind the reader that deer, which do not occur in the Ethiopian region, have antlers, which are usually branched, and which periodically fall off and are renewed, whereas the antelopes have simple permanent horns of quite a different structure, which never fall off.

Explanations of zoological distribution are peculiarly speculative, and therefore changeable. In order to account for the habitat of the existing fauna of the world, naturalists have turned the ocean into dry land, and submerged or fished up continents and islands as often as suited their theories. The main facts connected with the Ethiopian region are that its fauna presents marked resemblances to that of south-eastern Asia, as, for instance, the presence in both of the lion, elephant, and rhinoceros, and marked differences from that of Madagascar. The idea that there was once a continent where is now the Indian Ocean seems to be abandoned, and the hypotheses now in favour to explain the above coincidences and differences are two, the first that Equatorial Africa was the centre where many prominent types, particularly the larger ungulata, were developed, and whence they radiated; and the second the exact opposite, namely, that these forms were originally developed in Europe or Asia and penetrated to Equatorial Africa, where, owing to their being relatively unmolested by man, they survived longer and in greater numbers. This latter theory was originated by Huxley, who had not before him all the data now available, but saw his way to his conclusions with the prevision of genius, and the tendency of the most recent biological research, influenced specially by the discovery of various extinct mammals in the Libyan desert, is to revert to it rather than to the hypothesis of equatorial origin. It is, in fact, thought that there are only three primary zoological regions, Australia, South America, and the third comprising all Europe, Asia, Africa, and North America. In this latter region, the original productive centre was in the northern rather than in the southern hemisphere, and the peculiar fauna of Madagascar is explained on the supposition that it had already been severed from the mainland when the larger apes, carnivora, and ungulata migrated into Africa.

In many parts of Africa indiscriminate destruction has rendered game scarce and shy, even where it has not been actually exterminated, and, as far as I know, it is only in the East Africa Protectorate that one finds this remarkable combination of numbers, fearlessness, an open country, and comparative accessibility.

The animals which appear in greatest numbers on the plains are zebras, hartebeests, and two kinds of gazelle, *Gazella Grantii* and *Thomsoni*. On a favourable day, it is hardly an exaggeration to say, that from the train one may see miles of zebras walking parallel to the railway in long lines. Like all the game, they are not at all shy as long as the train is in motion, though it is said that they will make off if it stops and the passengers descend. I myself have seen a zebra approach the line, halt about twenty yards off while the train passed, and then cross with the utmost calm. This fearlessness is due to the fact that the whole territory to the south of the railway between Nairobi and the Tsavo River is a game reserve where shooting is absolutely forbidden, and the limits of this reserve are extended for one mile on the other side of the railway. The result is that animals have come to know that they are always safe near the line. It would seem that the zebra, like most horses, has not much fear of man. When young it is very easily tamed, and will follow its owner about like a dog, enter his house, and jump on his bed, signs of affection which are somewhat embarrassing in a hoofed animal, and make one realise what horse-play means. The adult zebra is also tractable, but has not hitherto proved of great practical utility on account of a certain weakness in the shoulder compared with horses or mules. Experiments in training them have been fairly successful, but hitherto better results have been obtained in German than in British territory, as the herd of zebras kept at the Government farm near Naivasha were attacked by intestinal worms, which occasioned very serious mortality. In their wild state they would probably have found some herb, which when eaten destroys the parasite.

Next to the zebra, perhaps the most numerous and conspicuous animal is the hartebeest (*Bubalis Jacksoni* and *Cokei*), large, heavy antelopes of a somewhat bovine build, but with a suggestion of the giraffe in their appearance, as the back slopes downwards from the neck to the tail. The bases of the horns are close together, and set on a sort of pedestal rising from the forehead, which is characteristic of the genus. Near the hartebeest may sometimes be seen the less common wildebeest, or gnu, remarkable for the tufts of hair on its throat and face, which give it a strange appearance, and also for the extraordinary antics and capers in which it from time to time indulges.

Slighter and more graceful than these great beasts are the beautiful gazelles, which are found in thousands on the plains. I have seen the country near Elmenteita, in the Rift Valley, literally covered by them, so that it appeared of a sandy yellow. The *Gazella Thomsoni* is small, measuring only about 25 inches in height at the shoulder, and has a well-developed dark lateral band. The *G. Grantii* is larger, about 34 inches at the shoulder, but the lateral band is indistinct.

As a rule, too, the traveller will see ostriches from the train in small families composed of a cock bird and two or three hens.[1] If he has luck, he may also see giraffes, lions, or rhinoceros.

The mention of this last word reminds me of a problem which has tormented me all the time that I have been in East Africa, namely, what is the plural of rhinoceros? The conversational abbreviations "rhino," "rhinos," seem beneath the dignity of literature, and to use the sporting idiom by which the singular is always put for the plural, is merely to avoid the difficulty. Liddell and Scott seem to authorise "rhinocerotes," which is pedantic, but "rhinoceroses" is not euphonious.

But whatever the plural of rhinoceros may be, most people are quite satisfied with meeting one of them. The creature is an exception to what I believe to be the general rule of nature, namely, that animals are good-tempered unless they are defending themselves or pursuing their prey. But the rhinoceros has a really bad, cantankerous temper, and that without much excuse, for his food is vegetable; he is so extremely ugly and well-defended, that he need not worry much about his enemies, and he is attended by a bird which makes it its special task to relieve him of ticks. The only infirmity from which he is

---

[1] South African experts report that the east coast or Somaliland ostrich has poor plumes, but that the northern variety, which is found in the Rift Valley, has very fine feathers.

known to suffer is short sight, and possibly the annoying surprises which he meets as he stumbles through life are a sufficient cause for his conduct. Occasionally one sees a shrub or small tree which has been battered down and knocked into the ground, and one is told by the natives that this is due to a fit of temper in a rhinoceros, which has taken a sudden objection to the plant's existence. It is also said that he attacks and gores ostriches and other animals. To mankind he is particularly objectionable on account of his habit of charging through caravans, when his formidable horn may do the most serious damage if it comes in contact with the human person. I do not know whether it is a mere coincidence, or whether the unreasonable animal has any special prejudice against pots and pans, but in two cases of which I know he attacked the cook's portion of a camp, scattered the utensils right and left, and pierced several by tossing them on his horn.

The giraffe is perfectly harmless in all its ways, but of all living creatures I have seen is the most grotesque, and, did it not really exist, the most improbable. When you first see them jogging across a plain, their necks held in a line with their sloping backs (not upright as in pictures), you rub your eyes and ask if you are dreaming, so strange are the creatures' shape and movements, as if they were visitors from another world or relics of some distant age when the principles of mechanics were different. They look perhaps most like telescopes set on four legs. Except for its extraordinary appearance, the giraffe appears to be a perfectly commonplace creature, and does nothing remarkable. The Masai quaintly call it "the beast that wants a long bed"—Ol-o-ado-kiragata.

Neither the hippopotamus nor the elephant, being sagacious beasts, are much given to showing themselves, though their tracks are common. The former is abundant in most places where there is water—in the rivers on the coast, whence they sometimes make short excursions into the sea, in Lake Victoria, and, above all, in the higher reaches of the Nile where it issues from Lake Albert. Elephants are perhaps commoner in Uganda than in the accessible districts of the East Africa Protectorate. They are, however, found near the Kedong, on the Mau, and in Kavirondo, and appear to be abundant in the little-known northern territories. I have only once seen an elephant. It was in a forest near the Nile, and the impression left on me was that a huge brown table was being dragged through the trees. The Carthaginians used elephants in warfare, but since that time there are few records of the African as opposed to the Indian variety being domesticated, though Mtesa, the king of Uganda, is said to have given one to Sultan Barghash of Zanzibar, which was subsequently sent to India and proved quite tame. Various proposals for experimental domestication have been made lately, but have all fallen through on account of there being no sufficient local market for the animals when trained, such as is supplied in India by the many Rajas, who regard them as a necessary part of court ceremonies. There seems to be no reason to think the animals are less docile than their Asiatic kinsmen, but I confess that I see no opening for their use, though it is a pity to waste such intelligence. In native stories the elephant does not figure as a particularly clever animal, but he is generally credited with being a human, respectable sort of beast. There is a story at Taveta that a native woman once met a huge tusker, who appeared to be in a furious temper and was disposed to stop her. The poor woman was half dead with fear, but with feminine intuition she picked a bunch of grass and offered it to the elephant. The creature's demeanour at once changed; he accepted the present, picked another bunch himself, and, with a graceful wave of the trunk, handed it to the lady, for whom he now most courteously gave way.

Lions have perhaps contributed more largely to the beast epic of Africa than any other animal, and are the chief actors in stories, some of which are exaggerated, but more of which are true than the sceptical stay-at-home public are inclined to believe. Unfortunately true is the terrible narrative of how a lion took a passenger out of a first-class carriage on the

Uganda Railway. Gruesome as the story is, it has always seemed to me that there is a touch of humour in the emphasis laid on the fact that the tragedy took place in a *first-class* carriage, as if it were what third-class passengers might naturally expect. Three sportsmen went to a small station called Kima (now abolished), near Makindu, in order to shoot a well-known man-eating lion. There being no other accommodation they slept in the carriage, one on the upper berth, one on the lower, and one on the floor, taking it in turn to watch with a loaded rifle. Possibly the man on the lower berth dozed when he should have been watching. At any rate he paid dear for his error, for the lion which he and his companions had intended to stalk was in reality stalking them. He apparently opened the door of the carriage, stepped on the man who was lying on the floor, and, seizing the man on the lower berth, jumped with him through the window. The body of the victim partially devoured was found next day; and it is some gratification to add that an old lion with bits of broken glass in his back, who can hardly have been any other than the culprit, was subsequently shot.

Terrible too, though less tragic in its conclusion, is the story of a native boy who was pursued by a lion one night in a remote railway station, and took refuge in an iron water reservoir, which, though fairly roomy inside, had only a small aperture. The lion could not enter himself, but thrust in his paws. The boy, by crouching in a corner, was able to get into a position where he was just beyond the effective grip of the lion's claws, but was still exposed to the most alarming scratches. His only weapon was a box of matches, which he struck one by one, and thus burnt the lion each time he renewed the attack. The night passed in this way, and at daybreak the lion retired and the boy came out. Africans have good nerves, and it is not related that his hair turned grey or his skin white.

I cannot vouch for the accuracy of the most remarkable lion story that I know, and can only say that it was related very often by an excellent man who appeared to believe it himself, and resented incredulity in others. It was to the effect that he was marching up country with a caravan of donkeys, which generally went very slowly. One day they went at the most unusual speed, all except one which lagged behind. It was as much as the rest of the caravan could do to keep up with them. When they arrived in camp a very simple and natural explanation of this haste was discovered. A lion had got in among the donkeys the previous night, and had devoured one entirely, ears, hoofs, and all, with the result that he over-ate himself to such an extent that he could hardly move. In the grey, uncertain light of dawn he had been taken for the missing donkey and saddled with the rest. In his gorged and torpid condition he offered no resistance, and trudged along under his load, but the other donkeys, recognising his smell, were much alarmed and ran ahead as fast as they could.

It would appear that not only may lions be mistaken for donkeys, but that dogs may be mistaken for lion cubs. A traveller came out to East Africa with two very fine Airedales, and marched up country from the Coast. A high functionary of the Protectorate was at the same time marching down to the Coast, and shooting as he went. He fell in with the Airedales, which had run ahead of their master, and, being struck with their appearance, disposed of them with two well-placed bullets. As he was examining the corpses and discussing with his suite what they were, the owner came up. He explained what the animals were; he also said what he thought the functionary was.

The variety of antelopes which are fairly common, though not quite so numerous as the hartebeest and the gazelles, is very great, and it would require a treatise on natural history to merely enumerate them. Among them may be mentioned the eland, a stoutly-built creature of bluish colour, half ox and half antelope. The eland as well as the buffalo was nearly exterminated a few years ago by the rinderpest, which attacked

TAPPING A COCOANUT PALM FOR TODDY.

THE ZEBRA FARM NEAR NAIVASHA.

not only domestic cattle but also wild animals allied to them. Thanks, however, to the game regulations under which the slaughter of both buffalo and eland was for some time absolutely forbidden, their numbers have considerably increased, and both animals are now fairly abundant. Not uncommon, too, is the beautiful impala, a red antelope, remarkable for its bounding gait, which makes its bright colour vividly visible as it leaps every now and then out of the high green grass or scrub, which it frequents in preference to the plains. But perhaps the palm of beauty must be awarded to the greater kudu (*Strepsiceros Capensis*), a large striped antelope, of reddish or bluish colour, with spirally-twisted horns. It is not uncommon on the hills near Lake Baringo. Hardly inferior to the greater kudu is the sable antelope (*Hippotragus niger*), with a coat of rich glossy black and scimitar-shaped horns. It is not common in East Africa, but is found on the coast near Gasi.

A pretty antelope, somewhat different from what one expects under the name, is the diminutive paa (*Madoqua Kirkii*), which is common near the coast. This tiny creature is not much bigger than a fox terrier, and so slender and delicate that it seems too fragile to stand the rough ways of the animal world, and awakens a sense of pathos and pity which is wholly unreasonable and unmerited, since it is quite able to take care of itself and is a rather quarrelsome little creature. It frequents dry and arid places.

East Africa has not yet produced any sensational mammal which can be compared to the okapi, but there are stories of the existence of a gigantic pig-like animal, unknown to science, in the forests round Kenya and in the districts west of Nandi (Tiriki, Kakamega). It is called Mbiri in the latter locality, and the natives say it is about the size of a zebra. Fragments of the skin have been seen, but not sufficiently large to show the creature's size. There is, however, no particular reason to suspect the account given. Though European sportsmen are prone to romance and exaggeration in speaking about game, natives are observant and matter of fact. There is also a story that a small kind of chimpanzee inhabits the tops of trees in the Mau forests, but, as far as I know, it has not been killed or captured.

With some striking exceptions, the birds of East Africa are remarkable for their large size rather than for their numbers or their brilliant plumage. Besides ostriches, there may generally be seen from the Uganda Railway, between Makindu and Nairobi and in the Rift Valley, large storks and bustards, as well as an occasional secretary bird. On the borders of lakes and rivers, water-birds—cranes, pelicans, or flamingoes, according to the locality—are generally present in enormous crowds. Particularly beautiful are the crowned cranes and the snow-white egrets. A very conspicuous bird in the uplands at some times of the year is Jackson's weaver. The male, which has immensely long tail feathers that give him somewhat the appearance of a flying tadpole, is generally accompanied by a whole harem of females, before whom he is said to display his charms by dancing in a specially constructed bower or playground. A characteristic inhabitant of the lower forests is the hornbill, a large bird with a huge beak. It is of very friendly disposition, and will follow a caravan for many miles, chattering all the time. Among game-birds, whose flesh affords excellent eating, may be mentioned the kanga or guinea-fowl, the lesser bustard, wild pigeons, and various kinds of spur-fowl, belonging, I believe, to different genera from those found in other parts of the world.

Except in Lake Victoria, the fish are neither abundant nor good eating. In the lakes of the Rift Valley, though not entirely absent, as has been reported, they are very small, except in Baringo. In the rivers they rarely attain a fair size, and even then are bony and muddy in flavour. It has been proposed to introduce trout experimentally into the up-country streams, but hitherto nothing has been done. Fresh-water crabs are common, but crayfish are absent.

One of the most curious sights that I have ever seen

was the employment of a native fish-poison at Shimoni, a station on the coast near Vanga. The leaves of a tree, whose name I have unfortunately never been able to ascertain, were pounded up until they formed a green paste. This was then thrown into a large pool, about ten feet square, left by the tide, in which were a quantity of small fish. Consternation was visible in a moment, the whole pool was full of tremor and alarm. At the end of three or four minutes, all the fish were either lying gasping and swollen on the surface or had actually thrown themselves out of the water to escape the intolerable effect of the poisonous leaves. It is said that the use of this poison does not render the flesh of its victims unwholesome.

In respect to reptiles, the Protectorate deserves a good character among tropical countries. Venomous snakes are not numerous, nor are deaths from their bite often heard of. The best known and most dangerous is the puff-adder, a bloated, sluggish brute, which has a way of lying in the middle of paths and not moving till it is trodden on, when it at once retaliates with fatal effect. The most remarkable and dangerous reptile is of course the crocodile. It is not found in the Highlands except in Lake Baringo, where it is said to be harmless and to feed on fish only, so intending settlers need not be alarmed about it; but it is common in Lake Victoria and in the rivers Juba, Tana, and Sabaki. It appears to be established that in Jubaland crocodiles live for long periods out of the water. Lake Hardinge, or Deshek Wama, frequently dries up, and it is said that crocodiles may then be seen lying in piles, one on the other, under the bushes round the bed of the lake in a somewhat torpid condition, but quite alive and waiting for the return of the water.

Among minor fresh-water animals of interest may be mentioned the Medusæ of Lake Victoria, discovered in 1904 by Mr. Hobley. They are closely allied to the Limnocnida found in Lake Tanganyika, if not identical with it. It will be remembered that the presence of this form in Tanganyika was used as an argument for proving that lake to be an old sea, but it appears to me that a more commonplace explanation is possible, namely, that Medusæ are not exclusively marine animals. After all, they are not very far removed from the common fresh-water hydra. The mollusca and other forms found in Tanganyika, which are supposed to have marine characteristics, are not recorded from Lake Victoria.

Like reptiles, noxious insects are not very abundant. Mosquitoes are a serious nuisance only in some parts of the coast (especially Witu, the lower Tana, Vanga) and on the shores of Lake Victoria. In the Highlands they are practically absent, though it behoves the authorities to use vigilance in seeing that they do not spread, for the borrow pits from which soil was taken for the construction of railway earthworks become filled with rain water and afford most favourable breeding-places. Other dangerous diptera are the tsetse fly, which occurs in belts near the coast but not in the Highlands, and is well known as a danger to horses, and the nearly allied *Glossina palpalis*, which around Lake Victoria appears to be the means of disseminating sleeping sickness. Venomous spiders and scorpions are not heard of in houses, if they exist at all, but it is necessary to be careful of a burrowing flea, known as jigger, which penetrates into the skin, generally in the toes, and deposits eggs which may produce disagreeable ulcers if not extracted. This pest appears to have been brought from South America to the West Coast, and to have spread right across Africa. Some years ago, when the standard of accommodation and general comfort was lower than now, it was a serious danger, but at present seems less frequent and less virulent. Its wounds are dangerous only if neglected, and need occasion no apprehension if the insect is extracted at once, which most natives can do with a needle.

Speaking generally, neither gorgeous nor disagreeable insects are very conspicuous compared with those of other tropical countries. The finest butterflies are perhaps the large papilios, which may often be seen lazily fluttering across forest clearings in Kikuyu and on the Mau. Orthoptera are abundant on the plains, and a grass fire rarely fails to drive out of their haunts crowds of mantidæ and phasmidæ, strange long-legged creatures that look like living twigs and straw. Locusts are seen occasionally in considerable swarms, but, as far as I know, there is no record of their having done serious damage to cultivation. The beetles discovered by collectors are said to be numerous and interesting, but they do not show any undue forwardness in obtruding their presence on human beings.

Closely connected with the subject of game in East Africa are the Game Regulations. They have given rise to a good deal of criticism, and justly; but it must be admitted that they have attained their object, namely, the preservation of game at a moment when the extermination of many interesting animals seemed probable owing to the indiscriminate slaughter practised by many Europeans. Under these regulations preservation is accomplished in two ways, by creating game reserves in which shooting is absolutely prohibited; and by allowing animals to be shot elsewhere only under a licence, and then only in limited numbers. There are two game reserves, one to the north of Lake Baringo, comprising Lake Sugota and the adjacent districts, and the other constituted by the space between the river Tsavo and the Rift Valley,[1] and bounded on its remaining sides by the Uganda Railway zone and the frontier of German East Africa. The former reserve, though it may at any time become effective, is merely nominal at present. It is remote and visited by few Europeans, and perhaps those few have not always maps accurately marking the limits within which shooting is forbidden. But the second reserve between the railway and the German frontier has proved useful and efficient. It is a practically uninhabited country, full of huge herds of zebra, hartebeest, and other animals which range from the Athi plains to the Tsavo River,

[1] Strictly speaking, the limit is the old (prior to 1902) boundary of the Uganda Protectorate.

according to the season, and as long as game is preserved there, the principal varieties will be safe.. ....

Less satisfactory are the provisions of the game regulations which deal with licences and the amount of game which may be shot.   It is with extreme diffidence that I offer any criticisms on them, for not only am I not a sportsman, but I hold in all seriousness what seems to most Englishmen the fantastic opinion that it is wrong to kill any animal—whether an elephant or a partridge—for pleasure.   The temper which makes a man who sees a beautiful antelope walking in its pride across the plain long to bring his rifle up to his shoulder and convert it into a bleeding mass of lifeless flesh seems to me devilish, and I confess that I am a little sceptical as to the regulations for preserving game made by sportsmen. They are apt to assume that the object to be attained is that animals should be killed only in a sporting manner, and that legislation can attain this object.   I, on the other hand, think we should prevent the destruction of animals as much as possible, but still recognise that the impulse to kill is a part of human nature, and that people who cannot pay £50 for a licence will give way to it as surely as those who can produce that sum.

Further, one must admit that even among average law-abiding citizens there is a feeling that game regulations, like customs regulations, belong to that class of enactments which have no moral force, and may be violated without loss of moral character when they can be violated with impunity. An officer who was out shooting once saw some very plump antelopes, but hesitated to shoot them, as he had already killed the number allowed by his licence.   His native gun-bearer, who was longing for a meal, could not tolerate his hesitation, and said, "Don't think of the rules, master, think of the fat."   Most people do think of the fat.   It is therefore peculiarly desirable that legislation should be simple, easy to enforce, and put no strain on obedience.   But the existing game regulations are complicated, impossible to enforce, and with the best will in the world (which is usually wanting) not easy to obey. They assume that the sportsman can distinguish the species and sex of every animal at sight, whereas mistakes are constantly made even by the most experienced hands, and are inevitable in the case of new-comers.

The general principle is that under a licence a certain number of animals of certain kinds may be shot. There are two classes of licences, the sportsman's, costing £50, and the settler's, costing £10. The former entitles the holder to shoot ten antelopes of the common kinds and two specimens of most other animals, including the elephant, rhinoceros, and hippopotamus. The settler's licence allows the holder to shoot five antelopes of the common kind every month and in the whole year two hippopotami and ten individuals of various kinds of wild pig.

Of the two licences the sportsman's is the fairest. It is expensive, but as long as people will pay the price, it is justifiable to ask it, and if the sportsman shoots two elephants with moderately good tusks he easily covers his expenses. Also the provisions can be enforced, for most holders of the licence are travellers who wish to send their trophies out of the country, and the custom-house check the number exported and confiscate any in excess of the amount allowed, so that there is little inducement to exceed the prescribed number of victims. But in the case of the settler's licence for inhabitants of the Protectorate there is no such check. A man may hide the trophies he has obtained, or even shoot merely for meat and throw them away. There is no adequate machinery for bringing offenders to justice, and if there were it would only produce universal discontent. The fee of £10 is too high for practical purposes. It is useless to demonstrate that it is a fair equivalent for the amount of game it allows, for the fact remains that settlers will not pay it and that they still shoot, so that there is a universal conspiracy to defeat the regulations. If the licence were reduced to 45 rupees

(£3) it would probably be paid by most settlers, and both the revenue and the game would benefit by the change.[1]

The real difficulty of the position is not so simple as the mere cost of a licence: it touches the relations of game and private property. As long as all the land belonged to the Government the latter had, at least theoretically, the right to say what animals might or might not be killed. But now, when considerable areas are owned or leased by private persons, serious difficulties arise. Whatever the law may be, the sense of private property naturally increases the disinclination to be bound by strict and inquisitorial rules, and it becomes doubly necessary to have regulations which are easy to enforce. Further, there arises the difficult question of the damage done by game on an estate. However interesting the hippopotamus may be, he is capable of eating up a whole garden in a night, and frequently does so. One cannot expect landowners to tolerate this or be content with shooting two of the destructive animals in a year. Much the same may be said of elephants in the districts where they are abundant, and many apparently harmless animals may do unexpected damage. Monkeys will pull up young plants, and zebras break through and destroy fences. The existing game regulations were made by sportsmen and zoologists, who had no object before them but the preservation of wild animals. They should now be revised by a committee representing not only these objects, but also the interests of landowners and the general public.

What conclusions of detail such a committee may arrive at I will not attempt to predict; but it seems to me that in future we must rely for the preservation of animals rather on game reserves than on rules limiting the number to be shot. By a fortunate combination of circumstances, the districts in the Protectorate which are most abundant in game are also those which are least likely to be required for European settle-

---

[1] Since the above was written I believe a new regulation has been made, by which the owner of a farm can have for £3 a licence allowing him to shoot on his own land the animals which fall under a sportsman's licence.

ment, and are inhabited chiefly by the Masai, who do not kill game. There is at present no sign that the reserve between the Uganda Railway and the German frontier will be wanted for other purposes. Planters may perhaps utilise the country between Makindu, the Tsavo and the Kyülü Hills for growing fibre and cotton, which would necessitate the removal of this strip from the reserve; but compensation, if necessary, might easily be made by prolonging the reserve in the south of the Rift Valley or in the Serengeti plains between Voi and Taveta. Also there would probably not be much objection to making a reserve south of Lake Baringo. The country is hot and barren, but, though it does not support such extraordinarily numerous herds as other districts, the number and variety of species to be found is perhaps greater than in any other part of East Africa.

Apart from game reserves, it will always be possible to protect any animal or bird which threatens to become rare by forbidding its slaughter entirely; but, except for such restrictions, I am strongly inclined to think that Europeans ought to be allowed to shoot freely on their own land. I do not think it follows, as some people seem to suppose, that they would at once set about to exterminate game. Many are sportsmen, and would preserve it for its own sake; many others would preserve it as a speculation and let their shooting for money to the numerous sportsmen who visit the Protectorate, for the time is not far off when all the districts in which game is found will be either reserves or private estates.

CHAPTER XIX

A JOURNEY DOWN THE NILE

THE countries mentioned in this chapter are not in the East Africa Protectorate, but are closely connected with it. The Uganda Railway has rendered accessible the sources of the Nile, the southern Sudan, and the western parts of the Congo Free State. The large questions affecting general policy and internal communication in Central Africa which these regions present are a sufficient excuse for going beyond the frontiers of the Protectorate in this chapter; but I must ask the reader to remember that we are now dealing with an entirely new country—not the high temperate districts suited for white colonisation, but the great forests, jungles, and waters of Central Africa.

In making the journey which I am about to describe, I started from Mombasa by train at the end of June 1902, crossed Lake Victoria in the steamer *Winifred*, and then drove in a buckboard right across Uganda and Unyoro from Lake Victoria to Lake Albert. Here I took a sailing boat at Butiaba, and went by river to Nimule, where begin the highest rapids of the Nile. As no boat can pass through these, the traveller has to march about six days from Nimule to Gondokoro, where the rapids terminate, in the hope of meeting there a small steamer to take him through the swamps of the southern Sudan to Khartum. In all, the journey from Mombasa to Khartum occupied about six weeks. Excluding stoppages, the time actually spent in travelling amounted to about a month, and for any one who is willing to go quickly I think this ought to be sufficient, provided he is not kept waiting for the steamer at Gondokoro. I had an unusual advantage in being able to drive across Uganda and Unyoro with relays of mules prepared by the kindness of Colonel Sadler, H.M. Commissioner; but on the other hand, I had only sailing and rowing boats on the Nile as far as Nimule, whereas I believe that a steam launch is now available.

I would warn the reader that the word Uganda has a double geographical significance. First, there is the Uganda Protectorate, which comprises all our territories in East Africa which lie to the west of the East Africa Protectorate and to the north and west of Lake Victoria; and secondly, there is the much smaller Kingdom of Uganda, a protected native state, from which the whole Protectorate takes its name, and which lies on the north-west shore of Lake Victoria, and extends towards Lake Albert until it meets another native state called Unyoro. This kingdom of Uganda is a striking contrast to the other side of the Lake. In East Africa there are some European and Arab cities, but there is nothing built by African natives which can be called even a town, and no native roads which are anything more than tortuous paths. In Uganda, on the other hand, one finds a large city of nearly 80,000 souls, and the roads, though somewhat like a switchback owing to the uncompromising directness with which they go straight up and down hill, are wide and suitable for wheeled traffic. The capital, which is about seven miles from Manyonyo, the port on the Lake, labours under the disadvantage of having several names. All these designations really refer merely to quarters, and the question is which part shall be chosen to represent the whole. Like Rome, the city is built on many hills; on Kampala is the Government station, on Mengo the king's palace, on Nakusira the quarters of the troops, on Namirembe and Rubaga the Protestant and Roman Catholic cathedrals respectively. As a collective name for the city the alternatives are Kampala and Mengo. On the whole the former is most used at the present day, though missionaries often speak of Mengo.

The most conspicuous objects in Kampala are the cathedrals, forts, and other European edifices, which crown the various hills, but the native structures are less visible, being generally low and hidden by the groves of bananas planted round every house. The most characteristic feature in the architecture is the extensive use made of reed-work, formed by plaiting together in symmetrical patterns the stalks of the tall elephant grass. All the best streets are lined with fences of this material, which resembles the fabric of straw hats on a gigantic scale. Behind these plaited fences are houses which, in the case of rich people, are approached through several courts enclosed by walls of similar work. In the royal palace on Mengo one has to pass through about twenty of these courts before the king's apartments are reached, and important persons have sometimes six or eight. This reed-work architecture, though not imposing, is clean and neat, and leaves an agreeable impression.[1]

Like their towns, the people of Uganda stand alone in East Africa, and are distinguished from most other natives by at least two characteristics—a taste for clothes, and a passion for education. In striking contrast to most of the neighbouring tribes, both Bantu and Nilotic, the Baganda[2] have an almost Oriental care for decency and a horror of nudity, particularly in men, and every one who respects himself wears sweeping garments. The native material is bark cloth, made by beating out the bark of a species of fig-tree, but nowadays flowing robes of white linen are worn by every one who can afford it.

Equally unlike the ways of the surrounding tribes are

[1] Entebbe, the official centre of Uganda, is a modern and purely European town on Lake Victoria, about twenty miles from Kampala. It consists merely of Government offices and the residences of officials and merchants. The name means "a chair." The place is also called Port Alice, but this name is dying out.

[2] The inhabitants of Uganda are called Baganda, equivalent to the Swahili Waganda. Strictly speaking, the correct name of the country is Buganda. Europeans made the acquaintance of both the land and people through Swahili-speaking natives. Hence the forms Uganda and Waganda.

their ceremonious habits. One is generally struck by the entire absence of outward signs of respect among Africans, who seem to get on together like a herd of wild animals, and show their reverence for the strongest by material concessions as to food and comfort, but not by bowing and scraping. The Baganda, on the contrary, are among the politest people of the world, and not only use elaborate verbal salutations, but kneel when addressing their superiors. It is very curious to observe how, when a native of position walks in the streets, others will run up to him and fall on their knees as they make some request or deliver some message. This ceremoniousness may perhaps be due to the tyranny of native kings in the past, for, as Sir H. Johnston points out, there is nothing like centuries of whacking to teach good manners; but I think that the civilised habits and social development of the Baganda must indicate some connection by race or contact with Egypt or Abyssinia. At some period Uganda and the surrounding countries were invaded by a race from the north, whose blood still remains in the aristocracy, known as Bahima, and who probably belonged to the stock known as Hamitic, though all trace of their language has disappeared. They were probably connected with, or in touch with, some of the civilised peoples of the Nile. What may have been the date of their southward movement we have no means of telling; but it was sufficiently ancient to allow other tribes to close round Uganda on the north and obliterate all trace of the route by which they arrived or of their earlier halting-places. Before the arrival of Europeans, the people of Uganda, representing a mixture of this aristocracy with a Bantu population, possessed a social system culminating in a king, and comprising nobles, a middle class, and peasants, and a form of religion based on the worship of departed spirits, which was far in advance of the superstitions of the surrounding tribes.

Not less remarkable than this rudimentary indigenous civilisation is the eagerness with which the Baganda have welcomed European education and inventions. No such example of assimilative power can be found except perhaps among the Japanese. Though it is less than thirty years since the first missions were established in the kingdom of Uganda, all the inhabitants, except a few who profess Mohammedanism, are nominal Christians, and large numbers can read and write. The love of books and education is remarkable, and all classes are very quick, both at arithmetic and learning foreign languages. I have noticed that Baganda children appear to be able to read a book held in any position, and can make out the words when it is upside down or sideways as easily as when it is held in what we call the right way.

The early history of the missions in Uganda is not altogether edifying, owing to the unhappy mixture of religion and politics, and the quarrels between the Catholic and Protestant factions, which ended in civil war; but now that all this is at an end and peace has been established, it may be said that the introduction of Christianity has been an inestimable boon to the country. Among the most conspicuous and terrible features of the old régime were the constant executions and massacres ordered by the kings, which were a veritable scourge. Even now one not infrequently sees persons who have been horribly mutilated. One of the most frightful distortions of the human face imaginable, and worthy of being introduced into any representation of the Inferno, is produced by cutting away the lips and cheeks and leaving only the yawning cavern of the mouth. This was a favourite punishment of Mwanga's, and there are still some unfortunate creatures, grinning ghosts in human shapes, who have suffered it and not died. This Mwanga, the late king of Uganda, appears from all accounts to have been a monster of cruelty and vice, who was deservedly deposed by his subjects, and subsequently deported by the British authorities, first to Kismayu and then to the Seychelles Islands. He was, however, a man of some intelligence, and deserved literally the title suggested for the late Dean Stanley, "an honorary member of all religions." He was a catechumen of nearly all the missions, including the Swedish Church, but his vices were so flagrant that none would baptize him. He was succeeded by his son, a little boy of about seven, who now rules with the help of three regents, of whom the chief bears the name of Apolo. The missionaries are careful to explain that this name represents the Apollos of the New Testament and not the Greek god; and indeed it is easy to see that the regent, though a man of much dignity, does not recall the physique of the deity of Delos. He visited England at the time of the coronation, and wrote a very entertaining record of his impressions.

The kingdom is divided into twenty districts, each of which is managed by a chief responsible to the king, and there is an elective native parliament or council, the Lukiko. Taxation is limited by law, and steps are being taken to survey the country and register all private property in land. Judgment in cases where only natives are interested is delivered by native courts. Such institutions may seem nothing very wonderful to the casual European reader; but those who have had any experience of the blank, amorphous barbarism which marks the institutions of most East African tribes cannot fail to be impressed with the superiority and pre-eminence of the natives of Uganda among their neighbours in matters political.

The road from Kampala to Lake Albert must be described as monotonous. As I have several times pointed out, the Protectorates are not monotonous in the sense that they only offer one kind of scenery. On the contrary, they present most remarkable varieties and contrasts, but a particular class of landscape is distributed so to speak in large chunks; what you see one day you will probably see for the next week, unless you travel very quickly. But the real fact is that Europeans are too exacting in the matter of scenery: most parts of the world are somewhat uniform, certainly North

America and the northern and central parts of Europe and
Asia, to say nothing of Arabia and deserts generally.   The
exception is southern and south-central Europe (and perhaps
the same parts of Asia), where the natural variety of the
scenery, the alternation of mountains, rivers, lakes, and plains,
as well as the versatility of human taste as displayed in cities
and buildings, tend to present a new spectacle every hour of
the road.   *That* one never gets in Africa, and in many parts,
particularly in the forests of the centre, one is oppressed and
dwarfed by the interminable uniformity of nature.

It is not that nature is particularly grandiose in these
regions ; striking views,· high mountains, or even large trees
are comparatively rare, but the enormous masses of commonplace vegetation seem to have grown over and smothered the
human race.   In Uganda itself man is fairly conspicuous, but
as one advances further towards the centre of the continent,
one feels that he does not play the same part as in Europe or
Asia.   There, the work of this highly developed ape is everywhere visible ; whether he builds temples or factories, whether
he makes or mars the landscape, we are conscious that the
character and appearance of the country depend on him.
Here in Africa man has little more to do with the matter
than have his humbler relatives the gorilla and chimpanzee.
He is the cleverest of beasts, and kills by his cunning animals
much larger than himself, but he in no way dominates or
even sensibly influences nature.   His houses produce no more
scenic effect than large birds' nests ; he cannot lift himself
above the scrub and tall grass : if he cuts it down, it simply
grows up and surrounds him again.

It is this dense pall of vegetation, exciting no emotions,
offering no prospects of anything new, if one goes on further,
which has so held in bondage the spirit of African man,
and deprived him entirely of that inventiveness, energy, and
mobility to which other races have attained.   Even in animal
life these forests and glades of high grass—if one may call
them glades—seem strangely deficient.   Beasts, of course,

there are; but, in contrast to the eastern plains where they are so conspicuous, they are rarely to be seen. In my whole journey from Kampala to Lake Albert, the only wild mammals which I saw were a party of baboons in Unyoro. They were crossing the road, which was cut through the usual tall grass, a little way in front of me, and stopped for a moment, and turned with interest to see what the strange creature was. Prudence got the better of curiosity, and as I came near they retired into the grass, where they stood in shelter, holding apart the stalks with both hands and still peeping with lively interest.

Almost the only other four-limbed creature I saw was a chameleon. Most natives of East Africa dislike and kill this creature, probably on account of his forbidding appearance, but various curious stories are current as to the origin of their dislike. One which I once heard in Zanzibar imputes to the beast the introduction of natural death into the world. A long time ago, when things went better than they do now, people used to die for some sufficient reason—when they were killed by their enemies or eaten by their friends, for instance—but they did not grow old and decay in the deplorable modern fashion. The consequence was that there were too many people, and not enough rice and bananas for thém to eat. The kings and political economists of the period became alarmed, held a conference, and decided to send an embassy to the powers of the other world and ask for the introduction of natural death, at the end of a certain term of life. They selected the lizard as their messenger.

The populace, hearing of their deliberations, determined to anticipate this petition by one of their own, and to beg that the request of the kings might be refused. Their choice fell on the chameleon as messenger on account of his great family connections, for he is nearly related to the powers of the other world, as you will clearly see if you look at him. Observe the contemptuous deliberation of his movements because he knows no other animal dare touch him, and the cold, incurious stare in his diabolical eyes, which he turns superciliously round without moving his body. The chameleon admitted that he had influence with his relations, and undertook the task, but, instead of going straight and quickly, sauntered off in his usual listless way. On the road he saw a pleasant shrub, and, forgetting what he had promised, sat upon it for three days catching flies with his long, sticky tongue. At last he arrived at his destination, and found his near relatives, the powers of the other world, sitting in their dim, mysterious hut by a swampy river. They received him with great deference and cordiality, and he sat there twelve hours being entertained and exchanging greetings. Then at last he mentioned the object of his visit. His relations exclaimed at once that if they had only known that he took the faintest interest in such things they would have been most happy to meet his wishes, but the lizard, they said, had been there a few hours before he arrived and had taken natural death with him. The chameleon was annoyed, but said nothing for another twelve hours, when he suddenly observed, " I have an idea." " What is it, dear cousin ? " inquired his relatives with interest and anxiety. " We might send after the lizard and stop him." " To hear is to obey," they said. "We have a messenger who is as quick as thought; we will send him after the lizard." The messenger went, but returned almost immediately and reported that the lizard had just arrived and had handed the fatal invention to the kings. So natural death entered the world all through the laziness and apathy of the chameleon.

One form of animal life is, however, very abundant in these regions, butterflies. They are found in a somewhat unusual place, namely, the puddles on the road. The fact is that the butterfly has an entirely false reputation for refinement and delicacy of diet. Many of the tropical specimens at any rate scorn the gorgeous flowers where they might drink nectar so easily, and debauch themselves with low carouses in dirty water, particularly if there is a little filth or carrion in it. Indescribable quantities of these insects had settled on the road in many places, forming bright spots of white and yellow, and were so engrossed in their uncleanly banquet that they let the trap drive over them without stirring.

The route from Kampala to Lake Albert passes first through the kingdom of Uganda, and then through that of Unyoro; but though the road somewhat deteriorates as one goes further west, the scenery of the two countries is very much the same, being composed of hills with low-lying marshy country between them. The road scales the height and wallows in the marshes with the most inflexible determination, and no reason or obstacles can induce it to deviate from its straight direction. The ups and downs are terribly steep, and in some places white ants have erected solid fortresses in the centre of the highway. In Uganda the people were more demonstratively polite than further west. They accorded me most elaborate receptions at the various rest-houses, and, as far as our limited powers of communication permitted, were most anxious to obtain information about Europe and European ways. It cannot be doubted that, as far as the desire to buy goes, Uganda offers a most excellent market for European products of all kinds, from such simple substances as linen and jam to electric bells and steam-engines. Unfortunately, its inhabitants, like many other excellent people, suffer from a want of cash ; but the most recent reports say that currency is finding its way into the country. This is good news, for whatever harm money may do, it is pretty certain that as long as the purchasing power of the Baganda is so limited their really great capacity for progress and development will not have free scope.

For a few days on this journey I was without a lamp, and none could be found in the most civilised Baganda villages. This experience deeply impressed on me the meaning of the "Dark Continent" or "In Darkest Africa," and I think it is not fanciful to connect the backwardness of the negro with this want of illumination. In equatorial countries there are practically all the year round twelve hours of light and

T

twelve hours of darkness, and for ordinary natives this dark half of their lives is enlightened by nothing better than a fire. In more northern latitudes the tremendous nights of winter call for some remedy, and stimulate the illuminative faculties; but in the tropics this dull, heavy darkness produces sloth, not resistance, and for half the duration of his mortal life man is little more than a somnolent animal.

Unyoro is in most ways a repetition of Uganda, somewhat less Christian and progressive, but apparently possessing much the same aptitudes as its more advanced neighbour. Before the introduction of the British administration, it was ruled by a celebrated king called Kabarega, who, though unusually tyrannical and cruel, even according to African standards, appears to have been a personage of considerable ability and undoubted courage. By successful wars and a machiavelian policy of setting his chiefs to fight one another, he managed to found a considerable kingdom. For a long time he resisted European influence, and availed himself of the mutiny of the Sudanese in Uganda in 1897 to make a last effort of rebellion against our authority. He was, however, captured and ultimately deported with Mwanga to the Seychelles Islands.

After passing Hoima, the pretty capital of Unyoro, the ups and downs of the road increase in severity as one approaches Lake Albert, and terminate in a final precipitous descent. This lake, which is far more picturesque than the Victoria Nyanza, is surrounded by a low level plain, two or three miles wide near Butiaba where I approached it, from which rise cliffs about 1500 feet high. The soil of the plain is impregnated with salt, and supports but little vegetation. When I was at Butiaba the waters of the lake near the shore were of an opaque but vivid green. This colour, which I believe to be abnormal or occasional, appeared to be due to the presence of some organism in incalculable numbers. The water produced violent fever in all the natives who drank it.

Butiaba, though it possesses more claims to be a place than many names which figure on East African maps, inasmuch as it consists of three, if not four, sheds and a pier, must not be thought of as a town, for there are no inhabitants of any kind. It was therefore with great relief that I found a boat, wafted from I know not where, waiting at the pier, and ready to take me to Wadelai. The crew were most efficient, and certainly the most enduring oarsmen I have ever seen, for from sunrise to sunset they worked with the rhythmic, untiring regularity of a machine, without showing the smallest sign of fatigue.

A conspicuous contrast to their unceasing motion was afforded by the calm of a Sudanese soldier, brought with us as a hippopotamus shooter. His duties proved to be *nil*, but it was understood that our life was in his hands, and that he might at any moment be called upon to deliver us from the attacks of hippopotami, who are said to be ferocious in these regions. It may be true that old males will sometimes attack a boat, thinking, in their insensate jealousy, that it might appeal to the heart of a female hippopotamus, but, as far as my own experience goes, I must give them a good character. All the way from Lake Albert to the Rapids, particularly in the neighbourhood of Wadelai, we continually passed through schools of twenty or thirty of these huge creatures, who rose to the surface round the boat, which they treated with the most phlegmatic indifference. It would appear that they are more dangerous when they become a little civilised, and learn that grain is sometimes carried by natives in canoes. When once they have acquired this fatal knowledge, they will upset almost any kind of boat in the hope that it may contain the coveted food. In frequented parts of Africa the hippopotamus is extremely cautious, and lies under the water with only his nostrils and the tips of his ears emerging from the surface; but on the Upper Nile, where he has not been molested, he throws his whole head and neck out of the water as he opens his mouth to take a huge breath of air. In general effect, the head thus appearing is that of a gigantic cart-horse, and one sees why the Greeks called the creature a river horse.

When out of the water, his shape is like that of a monstrously overgrown pinkish pig (the colour being much lighter than is generally supposed), in comparison with which even a cart-horse would look fairy-like.

I have spoken of the still loneliness of African forests, but the waters and banks of the Upper Nile between Lake Albert and the Rapids are full of life, and offer a display of water-birds as remarkable in its way as the antelope and zebras of the Athi plains. Some run about on the flat leaves of the water-lilies; some chatter in the riverside trees, where they construct whole cities of bottle-shaped nests; and many stand on one leg contemplating the scene with that air of philosophy, not unmingled with grave disapproval, which characterises the family of cranes and storks. Hippopotami, as mentioned, are everywhere bobbing up and down in the quieter parts of the stream; but crocodiles, which might be expected to be numerous, are not conspicuous, probably because the river does not offer any of the sandy or muddy banks where they love to bask and doze. This part of the Nile has in fact no banks, and it is very hard to say where the water ends and the land begins, for a carpet of vegetation and flowers spreads from the land over the edge of the river, while the river overflows the land and creates a shallow marsh a few inches deep. All this renders landing and river-side existence very uncomfortable, but pictorially the effect is pleasant. The water is softly opalescent, particularly in evening lights, and the double line of mountains affords a good frame for the landscape, while the velvety carpet of vegetation, which borders the sides and backwaters, is redeemed from monotony by beautiful white and blue lilies, and occasional flowers of more gorgeous hues. The whole scene reminded me of some Far Eastern picture of Sukhavati, the Buddhist heaven of measure-less light, where the souls of the pious dwell among shining lakes and lotus flowers, in the eternal light which radiates from the face of Amitabha.

But with the evening the resemblance to the happy land

disappears. Mosquitoes come forth in clouds, and life is, as a rule, tolerable only in houses protected by wire gauze. The insects, however, appear to frequent only the low ground on the banks of the river. At Nimule, for instance, some new quarters built a few hundred feet above the level of the water are quite free from them. In the centre of the native villages is often seen a small platform, ten or twelve feet high, supported on poles. It is said that this slight elevation affords a satisfactory refuge from the mosquitoes when they are so bad that they trouble the inhabitants.

Man and his works are, as usual in Africa, inconspicuous, for which in this case there is the additional reason that the banks of the Nile, even as far south as this, were, until a few years ago, harried by the Dervishes, which caused the population to retire for about ten miles from the river. The Nilotic races are a great contrast to the inhabitants of Uganda and Unyoro, who call them "the naked people," in allusion to one of their most remarkable characteristics, namely, the absolute nudity of the male sex. They also appear to have acquired some of the characteristics of water-birds, for they have long thin limbs, and will stand for considerable periods on one leg, applying the other foot to its knee. In character they appear to be intelligent and independent, and less barbarous than their nudity suggests. The tribes on the east bank near Lake Albert are called Acholi, and are chiefly remarkable for wearing two skewers of white glass in a hole in the lower lip. A little more to the north come the Madi, then the Bari, and then, in the swamps of the southern Sudan, the Dinka. All these races build fairly comfortable conical huts; the lower part of the wall is made of stone, and the upper part of palm leaves.

From Lake Albert to Wadelai is a journey of about two days by boat, and another three days brings one to Nimule, where begin the Rapids, which impede navigation until Gondokoro, so that this part of the journey has to be done on foot. These Rapids are a most impressive spectacle—far more so than the Ripon Falls at Jinja, where the Nile leaves Lake Victoria. For a short space the whole volume of the Nile is forced through a channel cut in the rock, only fifteen metres wide, and of unknown depth, and then leaps out with mingled indignation and relief into a boiling caldron of foam, surrounded by black polished cliffs and dense, dark vegetation. Other, but less remarkable, rapids succeed, and the river is not free for navigation until within a few miles of Gondokoro, where the character of the stream changes, and the swampy vegetation of the southern Sudan begins to make its appearance.

In giving one's impressions of the country traversed in marching from Nimule to Gondokoro (about six days), it is not easy to be impartial, for the extreme badness of the road distorts the recollection of the beauty of the country. It cannot certainly be compared to the better parts of the East Africa Protectorate; but, on the other hand, it is not monotonous, and, if one can form an opinion on such a point in one brief journey, it is not unhealthy. Particularly pleasant are certain large, spreading trees, which afford a most grateful shade, and when, as sometimes happens, these are scattered over an open, grassy meadow, the view is restful and attractive. But the road is bad, even according to African standards; sometimes one has to scramble over rocks, and sometimes to wade through marshes or overflows; often one has to march through grass six or seven feet high. In going through this latter one is drenched with a cold, clammy moisture until about 10 A.M., for the heavy dew settles on the long stalks, and defies the sun for several hours.

Also, there are three rivers to be crossed, which illustrate the three methods used in Africa for overcoming these obstacles, the expedient of a bridge being practically unknown, except in semi-civilised parts, such as Uganda. You may either walk through, or be carried, or be ferried over on a raft. The first mode is generally adopted in deep, swift rivers, but has obvious disadvantages, considering the limited supply of clothes

A Swampy River.

and boots which a traveller can carry. The second is perhaps the best way of crossing wide, shallow streams. It begins well and comfortably, but is rather apt, particularly when the bearers are stalwart Nubian soldiers, to end by resembling the mediæval punishment, in which the victim was torn to pieces by being tied to four horses, who were driven in different directions. The use of a raft is rare; in fact, I have only seen it on the river Assua, a rapid and rather formidable stream, which flows into the Nile a few miles to the north of Nimule. The rafts are made of ambatch, a very light and buoyant kind of wood, and their management, which requires considerable skill, is the special trade of the natives, who live near the junction of the Assna and the Nile. The process is somewhat alarming, as numerous rocks can be seen, both above and below the surface of the rushing torrent, and the only guidance is supplied by a native who swims at the side of the raft. But he really understands his business, and the passage is accomplished without any mishap except the wetting, which is the inevitable tribute exacted by every African river, however you try to cross it. In this case the moisture is due to the fact that the raft is so light that the moment a heavy body is placed on it it sinks some inches below the surface.

In this part, the eastern bank of the Nile belongs to the Uganda Protectorate, but the western bank forms the so-called Lado Enclave which we have leased to the Congo Free State. There are Belgian stations at Mehagi, above Lake Albert, and at Dufile, Lado, and Kiro on the Nile. As far as can be seen from the river, the country consists of a wooded plain, from which occasional hills arise. As on our side, there are few inhabitants near the bank, on account of the old raids of the Dervishes; and here, as in other places, the Belgian administration has not the reputation of dealing kindly with the natives. It is generally said that our officers can always reduce natives to obedience by threatening to deport them to the Belgian side of the river. It is certain that there are no villages for many miles round the Belgian stations. These stations are constructed on a different and more sociable principle than ours. Every officer has a sleeping-room for himself, but there is a common hall in which they all meet for meals. I remember a similar arrangement was once advocated for a station in the East Africa Protectorate; but it was objected that the staff would probably consist of two men not on speaking terms, dining at separate tables at each end of the room, and clamouring for a partition to be erected.

The neighbourhood of the Nile, north of Gondokoro, and especially between Bor and Lake No, is one of the strangest and most desolate countries in the world. The Bahr-el-Gebel here ceases to have any banks at all, and spreads itself over huge marshes, whose extent is unknown, but amounts to many miles on each side. The course of the river is represented by a narrow and extremely tortuous channel, which sometimes widens out into lagoons, but is generally confined between two walls of dark-green papyrus, absolutely useless, since it is no longer wanted for making paper. Like the locust in the animal kingdom, the papyrus is an appalling example of the power of mere numbers. Weak though the reed is in itself, the strength of the host is irresistible; it invades, conquers, monopolises, and, unlike the locust, it does not go away. You may cut down a few million stalks: millions and millions more remain, like the spears of a countless army, and as soon as you have cut down, re-growth commences. It is for the water what scrub is for the land. Though each separate plumy shaft is a beautiful object, the mass of vegetation, when seen extending for hundreds of miles, has no grace of form or colour, but is merely a dull stretch of green, irresponsive to effects of light and shade. It seems uncongenial to animal life, at least to the more cheerful forms. Crocodiles and fishes abound, likewise mosquitoes in clouds; but birds are scarce, and even the hippopotamus, though not unknown, appears not to much like these dreary surroundings.

For about four hundred and fifty miles the steamer wanders

in this maze, sometimes actually going south, in order to follow the bends and twists of the stream, but never meeting any salient feature to break the monotony.   This is the region of the now famous sudd, the Arabic name (meaning barrier) given to the masses of vegetable growth which obstruct the river.   It would appear that this sudd is not here, as it is in some places, the result of the gradual collection of floating water-plants.   The prime cause is the papyrus, aided by other reeds, one of which is called Umm Suf (the mother of wool).   The roots of these plants grow together, and unite with the soil to form a compact mass.   When, as is frequently the case, violent storms sweep over the swamps, the vegetation shows a mixture of strength and weakness.   Large masses are torn off, but they carry their roots with them, and the roots carry earth and mud.   Sooner or later these islets collide, and become piled on the top of one another, leaving the water to force its way as best it can below them.   The river thus becomes covered with a layer of earth and vegetable matter, ten or even fifteen feet thick.   In 1900 this monstrous growth entirely obstructed navigation between Gondokoro and Khartum, and communication was only restored by cutting through it.

One rarely goes to a bad place without having the consolation of hearing that there is a worse.   Horrible as are the sudd districts of the Bahr-el-Gebel, it is said that the region watered or soaked by the Bahr-el-Ghazal surpasses them.   It is described as steaming marshes, where what appears to be solid ground generally proves to be nothing but fetid water overgrown with plants, and where the mosquitoes are so numerous and venomous that at evening, when they are most active, the whole native population adjourn to the lagoons, and remain for some time with only their heads above water.

The part of the Nile which I have described hitherto is known as Bahr-el-Gebel, or the mountain river, a name which suits well enough the beautiful reaches south of Nimule, but is not appropriate to the swamp just described.   At the end of that swamp is a lake called No, so overgrown with weeds that it is hard to say how large it may be. Here the Bahr-el-Gebel meets the Bahr-el-Ghazal coming from the west, and the united stream, known as the Bahr-el-Abyad or White Nile, turns sharply to the east, until, after receiving the Sobat, it resumes its northerly direction. Certainly the scenery of the White Nile cannot be said to reach a high standard of variety or interest, but it is an undescribable relief to feel that it is possible to escape from the papyrus; to see banks raised a little above the water, a few trees, and an occasional village.

The only locality of note before Khartum is Fashoda. When one looks at this celebrated place, which consisted when I saw it of a few native huts and one European house in the centre, all set in a swampy backwater of the river, the first thought is amazement that two great nations like England and France can have been nearly at war about so remote and unattractive a spot. It looks like a place which no one would want, and which every one would gladly hand over to his enemies as a residence. Yet that great issues were involved in its ownership is clear, and our position in Eastern Africa would have been very different if at this point French influence had stretched across the Nile. Also one must not forget the power of symbolism which can still invest simple objects with the sanctity of an idol. There was a question of removing the flag, and had we been unwise enough to meddle with that sacred strip of linen, what bloodshed might have ensued from the sacrilege! And every nation is the same. It has often seemed to me that the cultus of the flag—for it is literally nothing else—is one of the most remarkable manifestations of religion in our times.

I have taken the reader a long journey through monotonous districts where man seems nothing and nature as unamiable as omnipotent. It may be that I have produced the impression that we had better leave these countries to the papyrus and hippopotamus; but that is not the impression I should wish to leave, nor, as I believe, the right impression.

The whole civilised earth must have been reclaimed and transfigured by man, and in historical times much of central Europe, including Great Britain, must have consisted of forests and marshes as hopeless and forbidding in that day as those of Africa are now, if one considers how inferior were the means at man's disposal for overcoming natural obstacles.   I do not despair of seeing the eastern side of Africa take its place among the countries of the world as a theatre of great enterprises and a successful struggle with nature.   And the way in which this will begin is already indicated.   To my mind the most interesting book of this young century is Sir W. Garstin's "Report on the Basin of the Upper Nile and Proposals for the Improvement of that River," which has just been published (August 1904), and the enterprise therein foreshadowed one of the greatest and most useful which have ever fired the imagination of humanity.   That enterprise is to govern and regulate the waters of the Nile from the great Equatorial Lakes to the Mediterranean; to drain marshes and remove the danger of floods; and to secure a constant and sufficient system of irrigation to all districts which are capable of being fertilised.   The river is already under control below Aswan, in consequence of the construction of the dam there, but there remains the far more grandiose and stupendous task of bringing the upper reaches under a similar discipline.

I may briefly remind the reader of the course of the Nile, which from its source to its mouth is wholly under British control, with the exception of the part of the west bank leased to the administration of the Congo Free State.   It issues, under the name of Bahr-el-Gebel, from Lake Albert, which is connected with Lake Albert Edward by the river Semliki; but it has a double origin, inasmuch as the Victoria Nile enters Lake Albert just below the point where the Bahr-el-Gebel leaves it.   This Victoria Nile leaves Lake Victoria at Jinja, and passes through the Kioga Lake; in its course are the Ripon and Murchison Falls.   The Bahr-el-Gebel on leaving Lake Albert is at first fairly wide, but becomes much constricted after Nimule, in passing through the Rapids. After Gondokoro it spreads out in the papyrus marshes, where a great part of its water is wasted, so that the discharge at the end of the marshes is only about half what it was before the river entered them. On leaving the marshes it is called the White Nile, and is joined first by the Bahr-el-Ghazal on the west, which is mostly lost in swamps and adds little to the volume, then by the Bahr-ez-Zeraf, then by the Sobat, and at Khartum by the Blue Nile coming from Lake Tsana in Abyssinia, all these affluents being on the right bank. There has been considerable discussion as to whether the White or Blue Nile was the principal factor in the river below Khartum, but the conclusion arrived at by Sir William Garstin is that it will be best to reserve the waters of the Blue Nile for the improvement of the countries through which it passes, and use the White Nile for the supply of Egypt and the countries north of Khartum. For this purpose it is necessary first to regulate the great lakes which feed the Bahr-el-Gebel, and secondly, to prevent the waste of water which now occurs in the swamps of the southern Sudan. The work of controlling the lakes would be accomplished by the establishment of a regulator on the Ripon Falls, and by lowering their crest. The river would then have to be embanked for about fifty miles of its course through Lake Kioga, and another regulator would be established at the outlet from Lake Albert. Having thus regulated the supply from the lakes, it remains to see that it is not lost, for at present hardly half the water that leaves Lake Albert in summer reaches the White Nile, and in flood the proportion of loss is much greater.

Between Gondokoro and Bor, where the sudd begins, it would probably be possible to confine the river to a single channel by closing the spill channels with barriers of wattle and earth; but after this point it is proposed to cut a new channel direct from Bor to the mouth of the Sobat (rather more than 200 miles), so as to avoid the swamp region altogether, and pass on the water to the White Nile without any serious diminution of discharge. Another regulator would be built at Bor, so as to completely control the new branch. If further survey should show that the construction of this canal presents unexpected difficulties, it would be necessary to improve and embank either the Bahr-ez-Zeraf, or the part of the Bahr-el-Gebel which passes through the swamps; but these works, though apparently possible, would cost more than the canal, which is to be preferred if it proves practicable.

The magnificent boldness of this conception must strike and fascinate every one. That it is not foolhardy to thus freely correct and remodel nature's arrangements is shown by the success of the dam at Aswan, which also demonstrates that such works, though costly, are in the end financially profitable. But the aspect of the scheme which interests me here is the way in which the different spheres of British influence in East Africa, Uganda, and the Sudan co-operate with one another, and show that the toil and money expended on these regions has not been wasted. The Egyptian Nile can only be regulated by controlling the waters of Uganda. Uganda has only been made accessible for practical purposes by the construction of the Mombasa-Victoria Railway, and it is clear that the whole project presupposes a certain familiarity with Central Africa, which we have attained only by the establishment of our two Protectorates. But besides this, the future of Uganda will be assured, and the needful impetus to her development given, when it is found that she can help Europe in this great work.

In the greater part of this kingdom nature is not unfavourable, and the population, as I have pointed out, is exceptionally intelligent and progressive; but hitherto they have remained, even with the railway, somewhat isolated, and have had little dealings with the rest of the world, in commerce or otherwise. But the execution of these great waterworks, which would doubtless be accompanied by the construction of roads and possibly of railways, would give a stimulus which would react in many ways. Uganda would certainly supply the labour for the constructions in connection with Lakes Victoria and Albert, and probably also for those further north in the swamps of the southern Sudan, where the native population is scanty and unaccustomed to work. This would mean the introduction of a considerable sum of money among the natives as wages, which would be expended largely in the purchase of European articles, with a consequent increase in trade. Also, European engineers would probably settle in the country. Although the west of Lake Victoria does not offer the same attractions to European colonists as the eastern side, all that I have heard goes to prove that the hills near the Nile are at least relatively pleasant and salubrious. The Liria range behind Gondokoro has a good reputation both for climate and beauty.

Uganda appears to me to be a particularly promising and interesting corner of the world, inasmuch as its people are an unusually progressive and teachable race, though they will probably be long hampered by their inland and isolated position. They are also an important factor politically, because, as a Christian nation, they offer a barrier to any possible southward movement of the Sudanese and other northern Mohammedans. But as the people of Uganda grow and develop they will require careful handling. East Africa will probably become in a short time a white man's country, in which native questions will present but little interest; but a series of quite different and more difficult problems may arise in connection with an energetic and possibly domineer-'ing race.

CHAPTER XX

CONCLUSION AND RECAPITULATION

THE account given of our East African possessions in the previous chapters will, I hope, convince the reader that they merit the serious attention of statesmen and the public. It is curious that they have been hitherto treated with comparative neglect, for they affect in a striking manner so many great national interests. Politically, they give us excellent harbours and a commanding position in Central Africa, whence we can control the sources and whole course of the Nile, and, if we desire it, open up communications with the Congo and the Cape. The foundation of the two Protectorates was largely due to religious and humane motives. As far as the suppression of the slave trade is concerned, the task has been successfully accomplished, and it is a great and noble achievement; but for all who are interested in the evangelisation and improvement of the African races these territories must still rank among the fields which offer the greatest scope and promise to philanthropic work. Economically and commercially, they are of great importance, for they present in large districts the conditions necessary for a European colony. They yield a variety of valuable tropical products, such as rubber, ivory, and copra, but also afford first-class pasturage and a soil and climate which have been shown to be excellent for the cultivation of European vegetables, wheat, cotton, and coffee.

Financially their position cannot be said to be favourable, but it invites consideration and action, for the capital invested is large. We have spent about six millions on building a railway without, I think, quite knowing why we did it, though

the instinct was just.) It behoves us now not only to utilise
the wider political opportunities which that railway has created,
but so to develop the remarkable lands through which it
passes that they shall become self-supporting and offer some
return for the outlay made. I believe that this can be done
in a few years, but it cannot be done without care and energy.

Our possessions in these regions fall into two divisions—
the East Africa Protectorate to the east of Lake Victoria, and
Uganda to the north and west of it. Speaking roughly, the
former may be said to be a white man's country and the
latter a black man's. Uganda holds the head-waters of the
Nile, and, as a Christian state, constitutes a barrier against a
possible southward movement of Mohammedanism. In few
parts of the world inhabited by dark races will the missionary,
schoolmaster, and engineer find so good a reception, for it has
a large and unusually intelligent native population, who show
a striking readiness to adopt European ideas and inventions.
For the same reason it offers an extensive market for European
goods, and the prospects of creating a considerable trade are
encouraging. Though it is not as unhealthy as the west
coast of the continent, it contains few, if any, localities which
in their present condition are suited to the permanent
residence or long sojourn of Europeans, and it is likely to
become a native state placed under European supervision and
guidance.

I must confess that I am not sanguine as to the future
of the African race, nor do I see any ground for hoping that
it will attain to the same level as Europeans or Asiatics. In
so large a division of mankind there must be many variations
and exceptions, among which the people of Uganda stand out
prominently, but it still remains to be seen whether the later
phases of their development will maintain the vigour and
rapidity of its beginning. It is, no doubt, most unscientific
to lump all Africans together as negroes; but it does not seem
to me to be proved that the distinction drawn by some
authorities between Bantus and pure negroes is of much

practical value, or that the former have any considerable power of progress. According to all accounts, the natives of West Africa have reached a far higher standard in art, in religion, in political and social organisation than the Bantus of the eastern territories and of Uganda. Yet it was from the West Coast that negroes were exported to America, where their nominal equality and real inferiority to the white man, combined with their growing numbers, constitute one of the most formidable problems which this century has to face. There is no indication that for a measurable period it will be consistent with the welfare of the world to let the African races pass out of a state of tutelage. The best chance of improving them, at any rate in East Africa, is to encourage mixed breeds—not, of course, between Europeans and natives, but between the various tribes. The Masai and Somali are a superior, though somewhat unruly, strain which might be advantageously blended with the Wanyika and Wakamba.

The East Africa Protectorate differs from Uganda, and from most equatorial regions, in containing a considerable area suitable for European colonisation. This is due to the fact that volcanic action has raised a plateau from 5000 to 10,000 feet high at a distance of about 200 miles from the sea along the greater part of the East African coast. An experience of some fifteen years has shown that these regions are not only healthy for adult Europeans, but that European children can be reared and thrive in them. The fruits, cereals, and vegetables (particularly potatoes) common in temperate climates grow well, and can be exported. Among indigenous plants of commercial importance may be mentioned various species of india-rubber and fibre. The timber is good. The pasturage up country is exceptionally excellent, and the prospects for grazing and stock-raising remarkably favourable. A considerable export of hides has already sprung up.

The opening up of this country, though long delayed, has at last come with curious suddenness. A railway was built

U

through it before there was any general knowledge and appreciation of its character, or any adequate system of administration. A year ago it united the conditions found in the most backward and in relatively civilised countries. Hence the advent of the first European settlers was a very qualified success. The Government had assumed too much responsibility to let them squat where they liked, and fight it out between themselves and the natives, after the manner of pioneers in other colonies and in earlier times; but, on the other hand, legislation, administration, and survey were all deplorably backward and imperfect, and quite incapable of dealing effectively with the problems which they were called upon to solve.) Now that the Protectorates are passing under the control of the Colonial Office, the moment seems opportune to inquire what should or can be done to make better use of their great natural advantages and resources.

The measures necessary are not sensational, and the only real difficulty is money. It may seem unreasonable to urge further expenditure, seeing that so large an outlay has been made on the Uganda Railway; but I think that most persons who have a practical acquaintance with East Africa will agree that this outlay was unnecessarily lavish, and the expenditure on the rest of the two Protectorates disproportionately parsimonious. Up to 1901 about five millions had been spent on the railway, and only about £750,000 on all other branches of the administration since the foundation of the Protectorate in 1901. It would be thought hardly reasonable for a landowner to devote such a proportion of his money to making roads on his property and omit to adequately improve or keep up his estate in other respects. Yet this is practically the case in the East Africa Protectorate. It contains land of the best quality, and yields valuable commodities; but it has a very scanty population, and offers hardly any market. It is therefore not likely to prove progressive or remunerative unless it is helped by active intervention and European immigration, to which latter it fortunately offers many attractions.

It may be justly said that these attractions should produce their effect without interference from Government; a colony should draw colonists to it by its own excellence. This may be true as a general rule, but it is the construction out of public funds of an expensive railway, supposed to be worked as a commercial concern and at present worked with an annual deficit, which gives such a peculiar character to the financial and economical situation, and calls for active measures. If we neglect the territory as a whole, we are likely to lose or indefinitely delay the return for our outlay, and to continue paying a heavy yearly subsidy. The latest official report [1] endorses the opinion that there is no prospect of the Protectorate paying its way, or being anything but a financial burden to the home Treasury, until it is developed by white settlers.

As one specially interested in East Africa, I should certainly wish to see its finances directed in a far more liberal spirit, and as a matter of business I believe this would be the sounder policy; but I recognise the extreme practical difficulty of obtaining a larger grant, and therefore plead only for a better, not for a more costly, administration. Accepting the present contribution from imperial funds as the most that can be obtained, there should still be a sufficient margin to provide for the changes which I advocate. The revenue, which has grown steadily, should increase by at least £10,000; retrenchment in military matters is possible; and the charge for defraying the annual deficit on the working of the Uganda Railway (estimated at £45,000 in 1904–5) should disappear in two or three years if traffic increases, as it is undoubtedly doing at present.

The principal changes which appear to me needful are the following:—As a measure of defence, and to prevent a most awkward situation which may arise at any moment, it is desirable to effectively delimitate the northern boundary of the

[1] Report on the East Africa Protectorate, 1903–4 ("Africa," No. 15, 1904), published in January 1905, p. 29.

Protectorate with Abyssinia as soon as possible. It is also desirable to terminate the present arrangement by which the Coast is regarded for international purposes as the Sultan's dominions and subject to the treaties which bind Zanzibar. This arrangement is of no advantage to anybody, it seriously hampers our authority and our finances, and as long as it exists there must always be a fear of complicated and vexatious contentions with foreign powers.

On the whole, I think it would be better to unite the two Protectorates under one authority. It is true that they present considerable differences, though not greater than those between the Coast and the Highlands of the East Africa Protectorate; but for some time to come, at any rate, their interests in administration, finance, and military matters must be closely connected and best served by being considered together. Even if the European element in the East Africa Protectorate increases so rapidly as to require a large measure of self-government in the near future, it would still be advisable that the authorities in charge of the eastern territory should have an interest in the welfare of Uganda, which might otherwise suffer.

To facilitate European settlement, the chief requisites are a proper survey of the country and the formation of an adequate Land Department. Progress is probably being made in these matters; but as late as this month (January 1905) I have heard complaints that applicants who have applied for land many months ago cannot get it surveyed. A certain outlay will no doubt be necessary to provide survey, but it will be to a large extent immediately and directly remunerative in the way of fees and rent, and, as long as the land is not surveyed, trouble and loss must continue. It is important, not only that there should be a larger staff in the Land Office, but that all legislation and all questions affecting land should be considered by officials who have practical knowledge respecting such matters, and experience gained in other colonies. Early applicants were encouraged a short time ago by very large concessions, amounting to as much as 500 square miles, and it may still not be amiss to stimulate real pioneer enterprise in remote parts by grants, not on this scale, indeed, but of say 25,000 acres. But it is admittedly desirable not to let the land fall into the hands of a few capitalists and syndicates, and in the accessible parts of the Protectorate, where the soil is of good quality, 5000 acres for grazing and 1000 for agriculture will probably be found sufficient. In some parts the inferior quality of the soil, or the irregular distribution of water, may necessitate larger estates. It is now probably too late to legally modify the lease (with right to purchase) of 500 square miles given to the East Africa Syndicate; but no more concessions on such a scale should be allowed, and care should be taken to oblige landowners, and particularly the holders of extensive areas, to use and improve their land. It is not to the interest of the country to grant large concessions, which, like that of the East Africa Syndicate, are practically merely options, and leave the concessionaire free to lock up considerable tracts without being under any obligations to utilise them. Now that there is a steady influx of European English-speaking settlers, I deprecate the establishment on the Uasin Gishu plateau of a colony of foreign Jews, and also the grant of land to Indians in the Highlands.

It is also most desirable to make more roads and bridges, particularly in the Kenya province and on the southern part of the Mau range. The Government cannot be expected to undertake further railway construction; but if private companies are disposed to build feeders to the Uganda Railway, for instance, from Nairobi to Kenya, such enterprises should be encouraged.

Closely connected with European colonisation is the question of native rights. This difficulty is lessened in East Africa by the paucity of the native population, and I think that the obstacles which it has been supposed to present to European settlement exist in prejudiced imaginations rather than in reality. Natives must be protected from unjust

aggression, and be secured sufficient land for their wants; but
with this proviso, I think, we should recognise that European
interests are paramount.   Nomad tribes must not be allowed
to straggle over huge areas which they cannot utilise, nor
ought the semi-settled natives to continue the wasteful and
destructive practice of burning a clearing in the woods, using
it for a few years, and then moving on and doing the same
elsewhere.

As a general principle, I am opposed to the creation in
this Protectorate of native reserves, meaning by that name
not plots of land kept here and there to meet the needs of
natives, but territories in which natives are segregated and
left to themselves.   I do not see any necessity for such
reserves in East Africa, and by isolating natives they tend
to perpetuate bad customs and to retard civilisation and
missionary work.   There is, however, no objection to the
proposal to move the Masai to Laikipia, provided that when
they are moved there efforts are made to induce them to
adopt a settled life and to abandon their present predaceous
and pernicious habits.   The idea of the Foreign Office that
the best land in the Rift Valley lying along the line
should be made a native reserve seems to me politically
and economically a lamentable error, and I think it has
been finally abandoned.   The arrangement could not be
permanent, and would almost certainly cause a racial conflict
as well as retard the progress of the country.   In general, I
think that the right way to deal with the native question
is by education, to which our administration has hitherto
paid scant attention.   There is no real opposition between
European and native interests, or cause for hostility.   There
is land enough for both, and the East African tribes are
not sufficiently numerous to feel the pressure of European
immigration, and they are not united by any national or
religious idea which is likely to give them a sentimental
objection to our rule or combine them in a movement of
resistance.   The danger, no doubt, is that Europeans will

be irritated by thefts—particularly thefts of cattle, to which all tribes are prone—and take the law into their own hands.

For the general control of local matters the Commissioner or Governor should be assisted by a council containing non-official as well as official members. A government consisting exclusively of officials on the spot, controlled only by officials in London, is not a satisfactory form of administration in any country where there is a considerable white element in the population. The example of German East Africa shows that the establishment of such a council would not be premature. It should be consulted on all matters of purely local importance, and in such matters its opinions should not be rejected without special reason. It is most desirable that there should be greater elasticity and greater power locally in the allocation of expenditure. The exigencies of the Protectorate as well as the just requirements of the auditing offices would probably be satisfied by more frequently assigning a lump sum to certain objects instead of requiring the details of expenditure to be fixed many months (it may at present be as many as seventeen) beforehand.

Military expenditure might, in my opinion, be reduced. I have explained in greater detail elsewhere my reasons for thinking that no extensive military operations are likely to be necessary, as far as we can foresee the future. There should be little real military work, but we want a great deal of quasi-military work in the way of preserving order. With a volunteer corps of Europeans, and an increased force of police (who are cheaper than soldiers), a battalion of troops ought to be sufficient. It is also advisable to have a small body of white police. Natives should be used as irregulars as little as possible: they are most efficient auxiliaries from a purely military point of view, but the practice of employing them strengthens their natural proclivity towards pillage and fighting, which we should endeavour to eradicate.

We should extend our effective administration over the

Kenya province and the Lumbwa-Kossova country. It is probable that this can be done without provoking any quarrels with the natives; whereas, if we let European stragglers penetrate into these districts before we have effectually asserted our influence, collisions and murders are only too probable.

Jubaland and the Somalis should be left alone for the present, unless the delimitation of our frontier with Abyssinia, or some clear commercial advantage, makes it advisable to establish a more direct control over this turbulent and inaccessible region.

It is not necessary to perform any great feats of organisation in East Africa. Some of my suggestions will probably strike those who are not acquainted with the country as being so obvious that it is hardly worth while to make them. But all who have lived in the Protectorate know that what has been wanting hitherto has been the most elementary essentials of administration, and the ability to organise anything in a coherent system. As I have repeatedly indicated in this book, I believe—and most residents share my belief—that if the East Africa Protectorate only receives reasonable care and attention, it will prove one of the most valuable and interesting of British possessions, and, in large parts, a thriving European colony.

APPENDIX A

LATEST INFORMATION RESPECTING THE PROTECTORATE

MANY readers will probably think that in this book I have taken an unduly sanguine view of the financial and commercial prospects of East Africa, of the chances that the Uganda Railway will pay its way, and that any considerable number of settlers will be willing to occupy land. The latest available information will therefore perhaps be of interest as enabling us to judge what deductions may be drawn from the data furnished by the year 1904.

According to statistics just (January 1905) received from Mombasa, the calendar year 1904 (not the financial year ending March 31, which is the term generally selected for statistics), when compared with 1903, shows an increase of over fifty per cent. in exports and about thirty-three per cent. in imports. The value of exports from Mombasa was £159,809 as against £104,424 in the previous year, and the value of imports £484,294 as against £359,646. These figures refer to Mombasa only,[1] which is the principal, but not the only, port of the Protectorate, and the value of the whole trade for 1904 must be about £175,000 for exports and £575,000 for imports.

Taking the exports, the largest increase is in hides, which have risen £29,000 (£66,660 against £37,659), rubber about £4500, fibres about £2500, and copra about £2000. All the staple products show a more or less considerable increase, and there are some interesting additions to the lists of previous years. Ostrich feathers appear for the first time, with a value of £1312. This industry must be quite in its infancy, for it was not in existence in July last, but it is probably capable of great expansion; and the same may be said of beeswax, which is an important export from German East Africa, though in 1903 only £83 worth of it was exported from our part of the coast. In 1904 the value rose to £3467. Interesting, too, is the item

---

[1] Also they refer to trade goods only, and do not include imports on behalf of the Government and Uganda Railway or specie.

zebras and wild animals, £3467, which is no doubt chiefly made up by zebras exported to Germany.... The only item which can be regarded as disappointing is cotton—£652 as against £128 in 1903. It may be hoped that far greater quantities of this product are in course of exportation.

In the imports the most remarkable increases are £30,000 in cotton piece goods and £14,000 in glass and' hardware, doubtless representing the demand for these articles among the natives of the interior. Most articles used by Europeans show a small increase, but the tendency to replace imported articles by local products is also seen in such items as £528 for imported fruits and vegetables against £1829 for 1903. Though European imported provisions show a rise of £15,000, and spirits of £12,500, it is remarkable that tobacco has fallen £1700, which must mean that Europeans find the local varieties smokable.

This rise of 50 per cent. in exports and 33 per cent. in imports can only mean that, under the guidance of Sir Donald Stewart, which is highly spoken of, the Protectorate has not only continued its steady economic progress, but also shows signs of making that advance by leaps and bounds which I have foreshadowed in these pages. It must also mean that the Uganda Railway has materially decreased the deficit on its annual working, and is in a fair way to cover its annual expenditure by its annual earnings in a few years. I may remind the reader that the abolition of this deficit is a matter of great importance, not only because it is disadvantageous to run a Government railway at a loss, but because the money now expended in meeting the deficit ought, when no longer required for that purpose, to be available for improving the administration of the Protectorate. As the figures respecting trade, quoted above, refer only to the port of Mombasa, which has no production to speak of, it is probable that the down-traffic of the railway must have increased nearly 50 per cent. An increase of 33 per cent. in the Mombasa imports is probably equivalent to an increase of about 25 per cent. in the up-traffic.

I am also told that Europeans from South Africa continue to arrive in large numbers, and to bring money with them. The fact that East Africa is to be colonised from the south of the continent (if it proves to be a fact) is not without importance for the future of the country. It should tend to establish and develop a trade in grain and vegetables between the east and the south, and it might have a powerful influence on the communication between Lakes Tanganyika and Victoria. The weak point of the proposal to build the Cape to Cairo Railway is that so few people want to go from the Cape to Cairo, and in any case the difficulties of constructing a railway through the swamps of the southern Sudan would be extreme. But the prospects of building the southern portion of the line will be greatly increased if the European colony in East Africa have commercial and other connections with the British possessions in the south. British territory touches the southern end of Lake Tanganyika, and the distance from its northern end to Uganda is not long, though the territory through which the future road or railway would pass is not British.

If the tide of European immigration continues to flow freely into East Africa from the south, it is to be hoped that the Government will reconsider the propriety of establishing a colony of foreign Jews on the Uasin Gishu plateau. If this project had any clear and real philanthropic value, I should raise no objection to it, but I cannot see that the sufferings of the indigent and persecuted Jews in eastern Europe would be appreciably alleviated by settling a few hundreds of them in the interior of Africa; for even if the experiment succeeded beyond all expectation, there is not room in the limits assigned to the colony for the reception of any number which would sensibly reduce the Jewish population of other countries. The application for land on behalf of this settlement was made, like many others, at a time when the resources of the Protectorate were little known and its future doubtful. Steps were not taken at once to profit by the permission granted to settle, and meanwhile all the circumstances of the case have changed so markedly that I think the offer should not be kept open longer than is necessary under our express obligations. In establishing this Zionist Colony we shall be devoting a fine piece of country, of which the ordinary British agriculturist could make good use, to an experiment whose success is more than doubtful, and which if successful is not likely to prove of any utility to those in whose interest it is made, but rather to provoke racial conflicts. I may add that as long as Mombasa remains part of the Sultan's dominions, in which foreign subjects are not justiciable by the British Courts, it is very unwise to encourage a large number of foreigners to enter the Protectorate; for though Mombasa is not supposed to be their destination, it is probable that many will stay there.

In the *Geographical Journal* for February 1905, Lieutenant-Colonel G. E. Smith says of the country on the German frontier 80 miles from Lake Victoria: "By that time we had risen some 6000 feet above sea-level, and had reached an excellent climate with fine open grass country—some brush, but not much. Population was sparse." He adds that the Dabash is a fine river, 70 yards broad in the dry season, and that the whole country is well watered and affords excellent grazing.

·APPENDIX B

THE TEMPORARY BRITISH PROTECTORATE OVER
MOMBASA IN 1824

THERE is some discrepancy in details as to this Protectorate. Local information, as represented by the "Handbook to East Africa," published in Mombasa, and by Burton ("Zanzibar," vol. i. p. 296), ascribes its proclamation to Captain Vidal, of H.M.S. *Barracouta*, whereas those who have written elsewhere, and with access to official sources, such as Badger ("Imâms and Seyyids of Oman") and Lucas ("Geography of South and East Africa"), ascribe it to Captain Owen, of H.M.S. *Leven*. The facts seem to be that in December 1823 Captain Vidal was asked to hoist the British flag at Mombasa, but refused. Nevertheless the Mazrui hoisted it on their own authority; Captain Owen found it flying on February 1824, and established a provisional Protectorate. Hence, though the Protectorate was really Owen's work, it is very natural that it should be attributed to Vidal, since the flag was hoisted after his visit, and not taken down till the British Government declined to recognise the Protectorate.

The "Narrative of Voyages to Explore the Shores of Africa, Arabia, and Madagascar, performed in H.M. ships *Leven* and *Barracouta*, under the direction of Captain W. F. N. Owen" (London, 1833), consists of various journals edited and partly cast into narrative form by H. B. Robinson. The arrangement of this work is not always chronological, as the doings of the *Barracouta* and *Leven* are recorded separately, and as a rule only the day of the month is given. Also it is often hard to make out whether the editor or one of the naval officers is speaking, the changes between the first and the third person being most perplexing. The last three chapters of vol. i. (xx.–xxii.) are extracts from, or founded on, the journal of Lieutenant Boteler of the *Barracouta*, and terminate with

January 1824, so that the events previously reported happened at the end of 1823.

"On the 3rd of December (1823) we arrived at the cele-brated port of Mombasa. . . . In the morning the nephew of the Sheikh or Sultan . . . begged Captain Vidal to authorise them to hoist the English flag, and place their town and territory in the hands of his Britannic Majesty."

Captain Vidal was ill, and next day sent Lieutenant Boteler with his answer. Lieutenant Boteler was much interested by the petition of the Mazrui chief, who had already made over-tures to Bombay, but, according to his instructions from Captain Vidal, refused to hoist the British flag. "But they used so many arguments," he says, "and were so earnest in their solicitations, that I began to think they intended to make me hoist the English flag either with or without my consent. . . . However . . . they begged that if the captain could possibly leave his bed he would pay them a visit. Accordingly Captain Vidal and myself again attended upon them the following day, but, as may be supposed, the result was the same." The *Barracouta* left on December 7, and the British flag must have been hoisted soon after.

Earlier in the book (vol. i. p. 367) we have an account of the chronologically later proceedings of Captain Owen of the *Leven*, Captain Vidal's commanding officer. He left Maskat on January 1, 1824, and "on the 7th (February) we saw the British colours flying on the fort of Mombas. A son of the Sheik's . . . recapitulated all the arguments before used to Captain Vidal, and concluded by requesting Captain Owen's permission to place themselves under the British Government. . . . The following morning (February 8) Captain Owen went on shore. . . . The members of the council . . . acknowledged having hoisted the English colours without any authority, but unanimously craved permission to place the whole country under the protection of the British nation. Captain Owen informed them that provided they would assent to the abolition of the slave trade he would transmit their proposal to his Government for their decision, and that he should have no objection to hold the place in the meantime. To these condi-tions they readily assented, and made a formal cession of their island, that of Pemba, and the country from Melinda to Panghany. Our third lieutenant, Mr. John James Reitz, was made commandant."

Reitz died on "the 29th," that is, May 29, 1824, as it would seem, though the chronology is hard to follow, and some phrases leave the impression that it was May 29, 1825. "In the September following this melancholy event, Commodore Nourse . . . appointed two midshipmen named Emery and Wilson . . . to act, the one in the place of Lieütenant Reitz at Mombas, and the other . . . in the *Leven*." (Vol. ii. pp. 147–8.)

It is certain that Owen's action was disallowed, and the Protectorate repudiated. It is generally said that it lasted about two years, but I have not been able to find any record of its formal termination. It would appear that Seyyid Said attacked Mombasa with the consent of the Indian Government in 1829. (Badger, "Imâms of Oman," p. 349.)

INDEX

ABA-KISII. *See* Kisii
Aberdare Mountains, 77
Abubakari, Seyyid, 58
Abyssinian frontier, 76; delimitation of, 121, 183–84, 306
Abyssinians—
  Gallas suject to, 118
  Slave-raiding by, 237
  Southward advance of, 183–84
  Turkana harried by, 144
Acacia, 59, 62
Accommodation for Europeans, 152–53
Acholi, 110, 129, 132, 293; language, 148
" Across Masailand " cited, 25
Administration—
  Amalgamation of Uganda and East Africa Protectorates proposed, 180–81, 308
  Centre for, proposed, 187
  Centres of, 186
  Civil, cost of (1903), 191
  Council to assist Commissioner, desirability of, 203–4, 311
  Currency, 206
  Finance—
    Elasticity of allocation of expenditure, need for, 175, 204–5, 311
    Expenditure (1903), 191–92
    Revenue, 190
    Table of (1902–5), 189 *and note*
    Taxation, 191 *and note*[1], 197
  Improvements in, suggested, 307–9
  Johnston, Sir H., proposals of, 181
  Land questions. *See* Land
  Method of, 186–87
  Parsimony of, 175, 188–89
  Penal Code, 197–98
  Police, increase in, proposed, 201, 311
  Under-staffing of, 175, 188; economic advantage of additional officers, 189
Afmadu, 36, 76
Aga Khan, 44
Agriculture—
  Implements for, 161
  Prospects for, 160–68, 178

Ainsworth, Mr., 73
Akamba. *See* Wakamba
Akikuyu. *See* Kikuyu
Albert, Lake—
  Discovery of, 24
  Green organisms in, 290
  Nile source at, 299, 300
Albert Edward, Lake, 299
Albusaidi (Bu Saidi), 10, 20 *and note*, 26
Ali, Sultan, of Zanzibar, 35, 234
America. *See* United States
Anderobo. *See* Wandorobo
Anderson, Mr., shambas leased by, 53
Angata-oo-l-Kak (Regata Elgek), 81 *and note*
Angata-pus (Engatabus), 78
Antelopes, 263, 270–71
Ants, white, 82, 289
Arabic, 114, 117
Arabic chronicles, 11
Arabs—
  Characteristics of, 41, 42, 235–36
  Cocoa-nut plantations of, 162
  Costume of, 44
  Inland route of, 24
  Mazrui. *See that title*
  Portuguese relations with, 9–10, 18–19
  Present position of, on the coast, 31
  Slave-trading by, 42, 57, 232, 239
  Swahilis descended from, 42, 107, 111, 112
  Towns of, south of Tanaland, 52
  Yorubi, 10, 18, 20, 26
  Zanzibar made the capital by, 20, 21
Arabuko forest, 52, 161, 162, 164
Arkell-Hardwick, —, cited, 75 *and note*[3]
Armenians, missions among, 240
Arms, importation of, to natives, 182
Assua, River, 295
Athi Plains, 67, 170, 173, 219
Athi River—
  Cable-way on, 70
  Course of, 70–71
  Natives on, 124
  otherwise mentioned, 53, 68, 69

BABOONS, 287
Badger, —, cited, 316

Bagamoyo, 24, 252
Baganda—
    Advancement and intelligence of, 99–100, 302, 304
    Ancestor-worship among, 97
    Characteristics and customs of, 282–83
    Clothing customs among, 93; at Court, 130
    European products desired by, 289
Bahima, 110, 283
Bahr-el-Gebel, 296–97
Bahr-el-Ghazal, 297, 298, 300
Bailie, John C., cited, 90 *note*
Bajun (Wagunya), 39
Baker, Sir S., 24; cited, 133
Bamboo, 75, 78, 164
Bantu element—
    Religious ideas of, 97–98
    Sphere of, 109, 110, 114, 129–30
Bantu language. *See under* Languages
Barghash, Seyyid, 27, 233, 268
Bari, 132, 139, 293
Baringo, Lake—
    Crocodiles in, 273
    Fish in, 272
    Game south of, 279
    Kudus near, 271
    Natives near, 134
    Region of, 83
    Soil round, 145
    otherwise mentioned, 67, 77
Bayazi sect, 18
Beans, 165
Beeswax, 227, 313
Belezoni canal, 47
Belgian administration, 295
Benadir coast, 38, 248–50
Birds—
    Song, absence of, 262
    Species of, found, 272
    Water, 292
Blood-drinking, 138, 144
Blue glass beads, 148
Bor, 300–301
Boran country, 76, 77
Boran natives, 107, 119
Boteler, Lieut., 316–17
Boundaries, uncertainty of, 183–84, 307
Bricks, 160
Bridges, 71, 187
British East Africa Co., slaves liberated by, 246
British India Steam Navigation Co., 26
Bruce, Col., 157
Bryce, James, cited, 102; quoted, 103
Bu Saidi (Albusaidi), 10, 20 *and note*, 26
Buffaloes, 271
Bura, 60; mission at, 242
Burton, —, journeys of, 24; cited, 316

Butiaba, 290–91
Butter, Mr., 184
Butterflies, 274, 288–89
Buxton, E. N., quoted, 105

CAMERON, —, 24
Camoens cited, 15
Canning, Lord, 23
Cape to Cairo Railway, 314, 315
Caravan porters, 113
Castor-oil berries, 164, 165
Cattle, native and imported, 171–72
Central Africa Protectorate, situation of, 2
Cereals, 165, 167–68
Chagga country, 245, 246
Chameleon, legend as to, 287–88
Chaptilel (Japtulel) tribe, 90
Charra, 47, 49
Chibcharagnan, Mt., 87
Chills, 153
Chinese, traces of, in East Africa, 11
Chol River, 133
Clays, 160
Climate, 2, 150–51, 153
Clothing. *See* Natives—Nudity
Cloves, 32, 34, 223
Coal, rumours as to, 227
Coast. (*See also* Seyidie *and* Tanaland.)
    Climate of, 151
    Native civil administration on, 197
    Products of, 161, 162, 164, 168
    Provinces of, 185
    Sub-Commissioner for, proposed, 181
    Tonnage, total, for ports on (1903–4), 230
    Trade of, slave captains for, 236
    Zanzibar Sultan's territories on, 181–82, 312, 315
Coffee, 165
Collectors, 186
Colonisation, schemes of, 177–78
Colour *plus* intelligence, British dislike of, 122
Comoro Islands., 248 *and note*
Congo Free State—
    Founding of, 24
    Lado Enclave, 295–96, 299
    Uganda Railway in relation to, 221
Copra industry, 162
Consulates, 203
Cotton cultivation—
    Experiments and results in, 166–67
    Jubaland, in, 37
    Makindu, at, 68
    Nyando district, in, 65
    Tanaland, in, 49, 51
Crocodiles, 292, 296
Currency, 206
Customs duties, 190, 202

DA GAMA, Vasco, at Mombasa, 12-13, 55; at Melindi, 13, 52; at Kilwa, 253
Dabida Hills, 60
Dagoreti, 73, 74
Dar-es-Salaam, 252-53
Darkness, 289-90
Deer, absence of, 263
Delamere, Lord, estate of, 85
Deshek Wama, 76
Devils, belief in, 97
Diaz, Bartholomew, 14
Digi, 123
Dinka, 132, 293
Donyo Girri-Girri, Mt., 75
Donyo Sabuk, Mt., 70
Dorobo. See Wandorobo
Duruma tribe, 15-16

EAST Africa Protectorate—
Climate of, 2, 150-51, 153
Physical configuration of, 7-8, 63
Situation of, 3
East African Syndicate—
Concessions obtained by, 176, 177, 309
Exploring party despatched by, 66
Prospecting for minerals by, 158-59, 195
Soda deposit investigated by, 160
Eburu, 81
Education. See under Natives
Egyptians, traces of, in East Africa, 12, 147
Elands, 270-71
Elbolosoto, Lake, 78
Elephants—
Domestication of, possibility of, 172, 268
Hunting of, 149
Pits for, 89
Elgeyo escarpment, 67, 87; view from, 89
Elgeyo tribe, 90, 145, 237
Elgon, Mt.—
Language of neighbourhood of, 109
Marble north of, 160
Native name for, 64
Riff-raff north of, 196
Tribes near, 107
otherwise mentioned, 25, 87, 129
Elmenteita, Lake, 65, 213; salt water in, 80; pasture north of, 170
El-Wak, Abyssinians near, 183
Embi, 129
Embo, 75, 128, 195
Endabibi plain, 80, 170
Enderit River, 80-81, 170
Engatabus (Angata-pus), 78
Engoleni, 69
Entebbe, 228, 282 note [1]
Equatorial lands, climates of, 150-51
Erero, Abyssinian post at, 183

Escarpment station, 212
Euphorbia, 65
Expenditure, 191-92
Exports. See under Trade.

FAMINE of 1882, 154; of 1897, 74, 125, 128, 154
Fashoda, 298
Fever, 151-52; from Lake Albert water, 290
Fibre, 68, 163
Findlay, F. R. N., cited, 90 note
Fischer, Dr., 25
Fish, 272; native fishing methods, 148
FitzGerald, W. W. A., cited, 53
Flag, cultus of, 298
Flamingoes, 82
Food supply, 155
Forests, need for maintaining, 176
Fort Hall—
Rainfall at, 154 note
Telegraph from Nairobi to, proposed, 196
otherwise mentioned, 73, 74
Fort Ternan, 64, 213
Frere, Sir B., 246
Freretown, 54, 242, 246
Fruit cultivation, 69, 155
Fudadoyo, 35

GALLAS—
Classification of, 107
Golbanti, at, 49
Krapf's enthusiasm for, 243
Numbers and distribution of, 118-19
Rendile a branch of, 76
Somalis, relations with, 111, 118
Villages of, 46
Game—
Birds, 272
Licenses—
Grievances as to, 191
Kinds of, 277
Masai not hunters of, 138, 144, 279
Plenty of, 82-84
Regulations, complexity and inadequacy of, 276-77
Reserve for, south of the railway, 265, 275 and note [1]; north of Lake Baringo, 275
Gasi—
Antelopes near, 271
Name, meaning of, 57 note [2]
Situation of, 57
otherwise mentioned, 22, 30, 52
Garstin, Sir W., 255, 299-300
Gazelles, 61, 266
German East Africa—
Acquisition of, 25
Administration of, 257
Administrative districts of, 252
Arab route through, 24

German East Africa—*continued*
  Beeswax exported from, 227, 313
  British missionaries in, 48, 228, 247
  Commercial enterprise in, 229
  Comparisons with, 260–61
  Council assisting Commissioner established in, 203–4
  Education in, 259
  Expenditure on, 256, 257
  Extent of, 31
  Extradition treaty with, desirability of, 185
  Frontier of, 27, 185
  Gold in, 67, 159, 255
  Natives, relations with, 136, 258
  Plague in, 156
  Purchase of rights from Sultan of Zanzibar, 181
  Railways in, 260
  Roads in, 206, 256–57
  Rubber, export of, 255
  Scientific experiments in, 257
  Slavery in, 258–59
  Tobacco cultivation in, 167
  Uganda Railway a trade route for, 221, 255,
  Zones in, 254
Germans—
  Commercial enterprise of, in British East Africa, 228, 261
  Missions of, in East African Protectorate, 242–43
  Shipping trade in hands of, 229–30
Germany—
  Treaty with (1890), 27
  Witu Protectorate established by, 27, 45
Gilgil River, 81
Giraffes, 267
Gnu (Wildebeest), 265, 266
Goanese, 20, 34, 178, 242
Golbanti, 49
Gold reef, 67, 159, 255
Gona tribe, 77
Gondokoro, 132, 133, 280; road to, from Nimule, 294
Goro escarpment, 76
Gosha, 35, 161, 166
Government. *See* Administration
Gracey, Col., cited, 218
Grain, 167–68
Grant, —, expedition of, 24
Grazing land. *See* Pasturage
Gregory, Prof., cited, 7, 108, 127 *note*[2]
Gubbra tribe, 77
Guillain, —, cited, 11
Gulea, Mt., 68
Gurre tribe, 77
Gwaso-Marra River, 76
Gwaso-Narok River, 76, 78
Gwaso-Nyiro River, 70, 76

HALDAIYAN Hills, 76
Hamitic invasion, 110
Hannington, Lake, 77, 82
Hardinge, Lake, 273
Hardinge, Sir A., 216
Hartebeest, 68, 265
Hasan Burjan, 120
Highlands—
  Birds, absence of, 262
  Climate of, 151
  River systems of, 70
  Vegetation and scenery of, 8
Hinde, Mr., map by, 90 *note*
Hinde, Mrs., cited, 127 *and notes*
Hinds, T. C., cited, 90 *note*
Hippopotami, 267, 278, 291–92
History, epitome of, 109–11
Hobley, Mr., 146, 195
Höhnel, Lieut. von, 25
Hoima, 290
Hollis, A. C., cited, 58 *note*, 86 *note*, 118 *and note*, 133 *note*, 140, 143 *note*
Horses, 77, 172
Hospitals, native, need for, 207
Hunting tribes. *See* Wandorobo
Hut tax, collection of, 197
Huxley, Th., cited, 264

IBADHI sect, 18
Ibea, 27
Ibn Batuta, quoted, 12
Ikutka, 70
Immigration of Europeans—
  Necessity of, for development of British East Africa, 188, 306–7
  South Africa, from, 314–15
Impala, 271
Impala Valley, 83
Imports. *See under* Trade
India, steamship service with, 229–30
India-rubber. *See* Rubber
Indian Penal Code, 197, 198
Indians—
  Babus, British attitude towards, 122
  Colonists, as, 178–79
  Cotton grown by, in Kavirondo, 167
  Irrigation methods of, copied by Ja-luo, 101, 148
  Land grants in Highlands to, deprecated, 309
  Machakos, at, 69–70
  Mombasa, in, 31, 55
  Nairobi, at, 72
  Natives—
    Intermingling with, 107, 125
    Trade relations with, 188
  Plague among (1902), 156
  Shiahs, 44; Bohra sect, 55
  Uganda Railway, employed on, 125, 178, 211, 215
  Vanga, opening at, for, 57
  Wakamba, unions with, 125

INDEX

Indians—*continued*
Zanzibar, in, 32, 34, 179
Indigo cultivation, 163
Industrial missions, 160, 241-42
Industries, three classes of, 158
Insects (*see also* Mosquitoes), 274-75
Intoxicants—
Drunkenness from, 124, 131, 183
Importation and manufacture of, 182-83
Iraiini, 75, 195
Iron, 159
Irrigation—
Indian methods of, 101, 148
Tana River, on, 50
Taru jungle, prospects for, 154
Islands, proximity of, to shore, 39
Ismail Pasha, 23
Ismailiyas, 44
Italian Somaliland, 248-50
Italy, negotiations with, as to Jubaland, 38
Iveti, 70
Ivory—
Trade in, 226
Trumpets of, 13 *and note* ²

JA-LUO (Nyifwa)—
Classification of, 107, 132
Description of, 147-48
District and language of, 129
Nudity of, 130
Japtulel (Chaptilel) tribe, 90
Jenner, Mr., murder of, 120
Jewish settlement, site proposed for, 87, 177-78, 309, 315
Jiggers, 274
Jilore, 242
Jimba, 56, 243
Jinja, 294, 299
Jipe, Lake, 61
Johnston, Sir H., cited, 82, 88, 109, 131, 133, 144, 178, 181, 283
Jombo Hill, 56, 159
Jomvu, 56, 160
Juba River—
Cotton prospects on, 166, 167
Italian side of, 250
otherwise mentioned, 76, 119
Jubaland—
Cotton cultivation in, 37
Crocodiles in, 273
Military administration of, 37, 186, 193
Physical features of, 35
Policy as to, suggested, 312
Somalis in, 121-22
Jumbo, 38

KABAREGA, King, 95, 290
Kabras, 86, 159
Kach River, 63

Kakamega, 94
Kamagambo, 159
Kamasia, 145, 147
Kamasia Hills, 67, 86; view of, from Elgeyo, 89
Kamasia natives, 96
Kamenarok Lake, 89
Kamililo, 88, 145, 147
Kampala (Mengo), 281-82
Karamojo, 86, 110
Karuna Hill, 87
Karuri, 128
Kau, 46-47, 118
Kavirondo—
Beans from, 165
Blue glass beads found in, 148
Climate of, 104
Cotton cultivation in, 167
Labour plentiful in, 173
Population thick in, 103
Sleeping sickness in, 156, 157
Kavirondo Bay, disadvantages of, as a railway terminus, 214, 215
Kavirondo natives—
Bantu—
Characteristics and customs of, 130-31
Origin of, 129
Classification of, 107, 122
Intelligence of, 101
Linguistic divisions of, 65
Nilotic. *See* Ja-luo.
Nudity of, 94
Religious observances of, 96
Kayas, 123
Kedong, River, 80, 153, 212
Kedong Valley—
Climate of, 153
Masai in, 135, 136
Pasture in, 170
View of, 79
Kenya, Mt.—
Description of, 74-75
Height of, 8
Krapf's discovery of, 24, 245
Lava cap over, 159
Naiteru-Kop located on, 141
Population round, 74, 128
Railway from Nairobi to, suggested, 218, 309
Situation of, 77
Kenya province—
Cattle from, 172
Natives of, 74, 107, 122, 128
Roads needed in, 309
Silkworms in, 168
Stations in district of, advisability of, 195, 311-12
Kericho, 66, 84
Kerio River, 67, 89
Kerio Valley, 145; view of, 89
Khalifa, Seyyid, 27

Khartum, journey to, from Mombasa, time occupied by, 280
Kibigori, 64
Kiboko River, 68, 71
Kibos River, 148
Kibwezi—
　Description of, 68
　Fibre cultivation near, 68, 163
　·Glossina palpalis in, 157
Kibwezi River, 71
Kijabe, 79, 213
Kikumbuliyu, 70, 124
Kikuyu—
　Agricultural prospects in, 174
　Beans from, 165
　Cotton in, 167
　Grain crops in, 168
　Labour in, cost of, 173
　Maize, demand for, in, 165
　Missions in, 242
　Population thick in, 103, 104
　Ramie fibre in, 168
　Situation of, 128
　Teleki's visit to, 25
　Temperature and rainfall of, 153
Kikuyu Hills—
　Description of, 72
　Origin of name, 72 note[1]
　Railway in, 211
　Timber on, 164
　otherwise mentioned, 7, 70
Kikuyu natives—
　Characteristics and customs of, 74, 94, 127-28
　Classification of, 107, 122
　Distribution of, 74, 104
　Language of, 127 and note[2], 129
　Masai influence among, 106, 127, 134
　Nomadic habits of, 74, 94
　Numbers of, 128
　Origin of, 106
　Usefulness of, 100
　Workmen, as, 211
Kilaluma River, 48
Kilibasi, Mt., 8, 56
Kilifi Creek, 52, 53
Kilima-Njaro, Mt.—
　Height of, 8
　Lava cap over, 159
　New's ascent of, 246
　Rebmann's expeditions to, 24, 245
　Rubber on, 161
　Snow on, 75
Kilima-Njaro district, 255
Kilindini—
　Arab occupation of, 18
　Harbour of, 54
　Wharves to be constructed at, 210
Kilwa—
　Arabic chronicles of, 11
　Deportations from (1509), 16
　History of, 253

Kinangop, Mt., 77 and note, 78, 162, 163
Kinanjui, 128
Kinyolla, 126 ····
Kinyume, 117
Kioga Lake, 299, 300
Kipini, 47, 193
Kipipieri, Mt. (Kinangop), 77 note, 78, 162, 163
Kirau, 123
Kirk, Sir J., 246
Kisigau Hills, 8, 56
Kisii (Kossova) Country—
　Administration in, need for extending, 195, 311-12
　Situation of, 65
Kisii (Kossova) Natives—
　Classification of, 122
　Language, &c., of, 131
　Reports of, 66, 196
　otherwise mentioned, 129, 237
Kismayu—
　Deportations to, 198, 284
　Natives at, 119
　Slavery abolished in, 233
　Sultan of Zanzibar's territory round, 181
　Trade of, 38
　otherwise mentioned, 23, 35, 36
Kisumu (Port Florence)—
　Fish at, 155
　Murder case in, 198-99
　Name of, 64
　Railway terminus at, 210, 214
　Sanitation of, 194
　Taking over of, 30
　Tax collection in, 197
Kitui—
　Kivoi the chief of, 245
　Natives of, 124, 127
　Situation and trade of, 69
Kiunga, 39, 193
Kivoi, 245
Kivu, Lake, 255
Kohiti desert, 76
Koro-koro—
　Climate and products of, 48
　Fibre at, 48, 163
　Neglect of, 194
Kossova. See Kisii
Krapf, Ludwig, Kenya discovered by, 24, 245 ; career of, 243-45 and note ; quoted, 59 ; cited, 97, 118
Kudu, 83, 271
Kuja River, 63
Kulesa, 49
Kumbi, 76
Kunono, 148
Kwai, 257
Kyamvu, 73
Kyülü Mountains, 68

LABOUR, native, 173, 211

Lado Enclave, 295
Laibons. *See* Natives—Medicine-men
Laikipia—
  Description of, 77-78
  Masai, suggested removal of, to, 105, 170, 310
  Pastures of, 169, 170
Lamps, lack of, 289-90
Lamu—
  Climate of, 151
  Cocoa-nut plantations near, 162
  Cotton cultivation experiment at, 166
  Dialect of, 118
  German firms in, 228
  Importance of, 40
  Mangrove bark exported from, 45, 165
  Official at, 186, 193
  Situation of, 40, 44
  Slave establishments near, 236
  Timber exported from, 164
  Women of, 44
Lamu Archipelago—
  Civilisations in, various, 39
  Cotton prospects in, 167
  Officer required for, 194
  Persian settlement of, 11
  Said's operations against, 22
  Sultan's ownership of, 181
Land—
  Concessions, terms of, desirable, 309
  Official dilatoriness as to, 175-76, 203
  Staff in Land Office, increase in, required, 308
  Sudden demand for, 205
  Surveying of, 176, 203, 205, 308
  Tax not levied on, 191
  Urgency of question as to, 175-76
Languages—
  Arabic, 114, 117
  Bantu—
    Characteristics of, 114-15, 139 *note*
    Distribution of, 109, 122
  Igizii, 131
  Kamba, 126-27 *and notes*
  Kikuyu, 129
  Kinyume, 117
  Masai, 139 *and note*
  Nilotic, 132-33, 144 *note*
  Swahili, 114-18
  Uganda, in, 114
Latuka, 132, 133, 139
Le-eyo, legends of, 141-42
Lenana, 74, 135
Likyá, 85
Limoru—
  Climate of, 153
  Height of station at, 211
  otherwise mentioned, 73, 79
Linton, Mt., cited, 174

Lions, 268-70
Liria Hills, 302
Livingstone, —, journeys of, 24
Londiani Station, 86
Longanot, Mt., 79, 81, 212
Lorian Swamp, 76
Lucas, —, cited, 316
Lugard, —, work of, in Uganda, 28
Lambwa—
  Administration in, need for extending, 194-95, 311-12
  Agricultural prospects in, 169, 174
Lambwa natives (Sikisi)—
  Classification of, 107
  Kisii at feud with, 131
  Laziness of, 145
  Masai, relations with, 85
  Medicine-men of, 146
  Name of, correct, 134, 146
  Origin of, 146
  Relations with, 194-95
  Segelli annihilated by, 142
  otherwise mentioned, 43, 66, 88, 108
Lumbwa (settled) Masai), 134
Lusinga I., 64

MacGregor, —, cited, 127 *note* [2]
Machakos—
  European residence at, period of, 155
  Name, origin of, 69
  Natives of, 122, 124
  Rainfall at, 153
  Vegetable cultivation at, 69, 165
  Women murdered as witches at, 126
  otherwise mentioned, 71, 218-19
M'Killop Pasha, 23
Mackinnon, Sir W., 27
Madagascar, fauna of, 264
Madi, 132, 293
Mafia Is., 253
Magadi, 160, 220
Magalia River, 81
Magarini shambas, 53
Maize, 165, 167-68
Majid, Sultan, 22
Makandini, 75
Makdishu (Mogdishu), 11, 12, 249
Makindu—
  Agricultural prospects at, 174
  Climate of, 68
  Cotton prospects at, 167
  Fibre near, 163
  Height of, 211
Makupa, 17, 218
Makupa Creek, 210
Mambrui, 53
Manda, 61
Manda I., 44
Mangrove bark, 45, 165 ; poles, 164
Maps—
  Camping-grounds marked on, 36

Maps—*continued*
  Errors in, 77
  German, 257
Marble, 160
Margweti tribe, 90
Marmonet River, 80
Masai—
  "Ages" of, 136
  Blending other tribes with, proposed, 305
  Classification of, 107
  Customs of, 134–38
  Diet of, 138
  Districts inhabited by, 73–76, 134, 135 ; pasture-grounds, 78, 85, 170
  Ear-ornaments of, 87, 137
  Early invasions by, 110
  Education among, 100, 140
  Elmoran (warriors), 93, 136–37
  Europeans, attitude towards, 143
  Feudal service of tribes to, 148, 238
  Free love among, 133, 136–37
  Future of, 143–44
  Game not hunted by, 138, 144, 279
  Herdsmen, as, 173
  Hollis, Mr., on, 133 *note*
  Kikuyu natives influenced by, 106, 127, 134
  Language of, 139 *and note*
  L'Oikop and nomads, 134
  Lumbwa, relations with, 85
  Medicine-men of, 74, 95, 135, 140
  Merker's division of, 135
  Military organisation of, 94–95, 106
  Nilotic origin of, 108
  Occupations of, 144
  Peace proclaimed by, at Sangaruna Ford (1883), 142
  Proverb of, 174
  Raids by, 49, 60, 73, 124, 134, 142, 239
  Religious ideas and legends of, 96–97, 140–42
  Removal of, to Laikipia, proposal as to, 105, 170, 310
  Settlers, as, at Nairobi, 106
  Smiths of (Kunono), 148
  Stokers, as, 100–1
  Suk and Nandi at feud with, 145
  Tales of, 139–40
  Uasin Gishu, exterminated from, 88, 135, 142
  Wakamba, displacement of, at Machakos, 124
  Weapons of, 137
  Women of, 138
  otherwise mentioned, 25, 43, 200
Massacres, 98, 239
Mathioya River, 74
Mau escarpment—
  Climate and rainfall of, 63, 153–54
  Descent from, on the coast, 84

Mau escarpment—*continued*
  Forests of, 163–64
  Lava cap over, 159
  otherwise mentioned, 8, 80
Mau Plateau—
  Pasture on, 169, 171
  Railway on, 213
  Roads needed on, 176
  Wheat prospects on, 168
Mau-nanyokye, 85
Mau-narok, 85
Maud, Captain, cited, 75 *and note*[2], 76 ; quoted, 83
Maungu, 59
Mazeras—
  Height of, 210
  Mission at, 56
  Name, origin of, 69
  Railway ascent to, 218
Mazrui, 10, 19, 21, 22, 316–17 ; rebellion of 1895, 29–30, 51, 54, 203, 235
Mbagathi River, 72 *note*[2], 73, 74
Mbale, 60
Mbaruk, 29, 30, 56, 57
Mbatian, 135, 143 *and note*
Mbe, 129
Mbiri, 74, 271
Medusæ, 273–74
Melindi—
  Da Gama at, 14–15 *and note*, 52 ; his description, 13
  Drawbacks to, as a port, 227
  Milton's mention of, 52
  Murder case at, 198
  Railway to, from Mombasa projected, 218
  Slave establishments near, 236
Menelik, King, 183
Menengai crater, 82, 90 *note*
Mengo (Kampala), 281–82
Merker, —, cited, 135, 140
Meru, 75, 122, 134
Mica, 62, 159–60
Military force, suggestions as to, 199–201, 311
Military stations, 186
Minerals, 158–60
Missions—
  Church Missionary Society establishments—
    Coast, on, 56, 246
    German East Africa, in, 243
    Teita, in, 60, 242
  Distribution of, 242–43, 246–47
  German—in Tanaland, 48 ; at Ngao, 49 ; at Ikutha, 70
  Industrial, 160, 241–42
  Lutheran, at Jimba, 56
  Roman Catholic, 60, 241, 242
  Sects among, 242
  Swahili dialect favoured by, 118

INDEX

327

Missions—*continued*
Uganda, in, 28, 240, 284
United Free Methodist establishments, 56
Universities', 243, 247
Missionaries—
Education in hands of, 206
Hut tax approved by, 191
Value and work of, 240
Misunderstandings, 15 *note*
Mkonumbi, 45
Mnyiso, 75, 129
Mogdishu (Makdishu), 11, 12, 249
Mohammedanism—
Buildings, simplicity of, 40–41
Ibadhis, 43–44
Political dangers of, 241
Position of, in East Africa, 42–43
Slight progress of, in East Africa, 96
Utenzi, 117
Mohoroni, 66, 186
Mokwan, 87
Molo, 213
Molo River, 85, 86, 90 *note*
Mombasa—
Administration, impossibility of concentrating, at, 187
Arab siege of (1696), 18; their rule, 19
Bricks made at, 160
British protectorate over (1824), 21, 54, 316–18
Cliffs of, 56
Climate of, 151
Copra of, 162
Cosmopolitan character of, 55, 179
Customs levied at, 202
Da Gama at, 12, 14–15
Description of (1328), 12
Fish at, 155
Foreigners in, 315
Fort at, 16 *note*, 17, 55
German firms in, 228
Importance of, 9
Indians in, 31, 55
International situation in, 182
Minerals near, 159
Mission stations at, and near, 56, 160, 241
Port, as, importance of, 227
Portuguese governorship of, 17
Railway to Melindi from, project of, 52, 218
Rainfall at, 154 *note*
Ras-Sarani, 55
Roman Catholics in, 242
Situation of, 54
Swahilis of, tribes of, 113
Trolley system in, 55, 172
Troubles of, in 16th century, 15
Turkish raid on (1585), 16

Mombasa—*continued*
Water-supply of, 227
Morendat River, 81
Mosques, 40–41
Mosquitoes, 45, 49, 151, 262, 274; at Nimule, 293; on the Nile, 297; remedial measures against, 63–64
Mrima Hill, 56
Mtanganyiko, 53
Mtesa, King, 24, 95, 98, 239, 268
Mtito Andei River, 71 *and note*
Mtwapa, 54
Mukaa, 247
Mumia, 131
Mumias, 69, 85, 86, 131
Mumoni, Mt., 70 *and note*, 124
Murder—
Native punishment for, 238–39
Sentences for, 198
Muteyo tribe, 90, 96, 145
Mwachi River, 210
Mwanga, King, massacres by, 98, 239; misrule of, 284–85; deportation of, 284, 290
Mwanza, 255
Mwele, 56, 161, 162, 164
Mzara, 75

NABAHANS, 39, 40
Nairobi—
Administration concentrated at, proposal of, 187
Climate, temperature, and rainfall of, 153–55, 162
Cotton at, 167
German firms in, 228
Horse races at, 172
Masai settlers near, 73–74, 106, 144
Plague outbreak at (1902), 155–56
Railway headquarters at, 187, 211; unhealthiness of, 72, 219
Railway line from, to Kenya, suggested, 170, 218, 309
Road-making in, 206
Roman Catholics in, 242
School at, 206
Site and appearance of, 72–73
Telegraph from, to Fort Hall, proposed, 196
Vegetable cultivation in, prospects for, 166
View of Kenya from, 74
Otherwise mentioned, 61, 69, 128, 135
Naiteru-kop, 141
Naivasha—
Climate of, 153
En-aiposha a name for, 65 *and note*
Masai of, story as to, 88
Taking over of (1902), 30
Vegetable cultivation at, 165
Zebra farm at, 265
otherwise mentioned, 25, 74

Naivasha, Lake—
  Fresh water in, 80
  Pasture round, 171
  otherwise mentioned, 79, 170, 213
Nakuru, 170, 210
Nakuru, Lake, 80, 171, 213
Names of places, difficulties arising from, 64, 65 and note
Nandarua Mt. (Kinangop), 77 note, 78
Nandi—
  Agricultural prospects in, 174
  Bricks made in, 160
  Description of, 88
  Oats at, 168
  Pasture at, 169
  Railway through, abandoned proposal of, 214
  Sanatorium at, proposed, 194
  Vegetable cultivation at, 165
  Western, additional station in, proposed, 196
Nandi escarpment, 85–87, 162
Nandi tribe—
  Classification of, 107, 110
  District and description of, 145
  Masai non-combatants massacred by, 88
  Medicine-men of, 95
  Religious observances of, 96
  Segelli annihilated by, 142
  Thefts by, 147, 195, 214
Natit, 84–85
Natives—
  Alliances with chiefs of, 128
  Ancestor-worship among, 97
  Arms imported to, 182
  Artistic sense, absence of, among, 101
  Caravan porters, 113
  Characteristics of, 92–94, 99, 101
  Circumcision among, 136
  Classification of, 107
  Dances of (Ngomas), 53
  Dead, disposal of, 92–93 and note, 97, 131
  Decency, lack of, 92–93
  Devils, belief in, 97
  Dress, absence of. See sub-heading Nudity
  Drunkenness of, 124, 131, 183
  Education of—
    Baganda enthusiastic for, 284
    German East Africa, in, 259
    Missionary enterprise in, 206
    Need for, 206, 310
  European goods little in demand with, 220, 224
  Europeans, attitude towards, 188, 195, 196
  Family system among, 125
  Future of, 304–5
  Germans, relations with, 136, 258

Natives—continued
  Hair-dressing among—
    Masai, 137⋯
    Suk, 145
  Hospitals for, need for, 207
  Hut tax paid by, 191 and note[1]; collection of, 197
  "Hyaenas," secret society of, 49
  Indians, relations with, 188
  Interbreeding, Kikuyu precautions against, 128
  Intermingling of, desirability of encouraging, 106–7
  Languages of. See Languages
  Medicine-men of (Laibons)—
    Lumbwa, of, 98, 146
    Masai, of, 95, 98, 135, 140
  Missions to. See Missions
  Nomadic habits among, 74, 94
  Nudity of, 65, 93–94, 130, 133, 293
  Numbers, systems of, among, 144 note
  Ornament of (wire), 138, 147, 214
  Polygamy among, 125, 138
  Punitive expeditions against, 147, 200–1
  Religious ideas of, 95–98, 140–42, 283
  Reserves for, disadvantages of, 105–6 170, 310
  Rights of, 309
  Secret societies among, 49, 97–98
  Slavery, attitude towards, 231, 238. See also Slavery
  Soldiers, as, dangers of, 200, 311
  Villages of—
    Moving of, in Kavirondo, 130–31
    Protection of, by wall or hedge, 123, 130, 148
  Weapons of—
    Embo, 128
    Masai, 137
  Witch-doctors among, 98, 126
  Women—
    Kavirondo, 130
    Lamu, of, 44
    Masai, 138
    Nudity of, 65, 94, 130
    Position of, 125, 231, 238
    Shaving heads of, 133, 138
    Swahili, 113
    Wakamba, 125, 126
    Wanika, 244
    Widows, 138
    Witch-doctor practices on, 126
  Workshops, in, 173, 211
Natron, Lake, 134
Ndara Hills, 60
Negroes of North America, 99, 101–3
Negroes of West Africa, 103
Nengia, 69–70. See also Kitui
Neopara, office of, 113 and note
New, —, 245–46
Ngao, 49

Ngomas (native dances), 53
Ngongo-Bagas, Mt., 72 *and note*², 74, 128
Nile, River—
  Aswan dam, 299, 301
  Bahr-el-Gebel, 296, 299–301
  Bahr-el-Ghazal, 297–98
  Bahr-ez-Zeraf, 300, 301
  Blue, 300
  Course of, 299–300
  Nimule Rapids, 293–94
  Regulation of waters of, proposals as to, 299–302; probable effects of, 225
  Ripon Falls, 294, 299–300
  Sudd in, 297
  Victoria, 299
  Water-birds on, 292
  White, 298, 300
" Nile Quest, The," cited, 24
Nilotic languages, 132–33, 144 *note*
Nilotic tribes, characteristics of, 132–33, 293 ; nudity of males, 65, 93–94, 130, 133, 293
Nimule, 280, 293–94
Njamúsi, 83, 134
Njámusi, Great and Little (Njemps), 25, 83
Njoro River, 85, 86 ; opals in, 159
No, Lake, 298
Nsao River (Ndeo), 70
Nyando River, 63, 89
Nyando Valley, 142, 145, 148
Nyeri, 74, 128, 195
Nyifwa. *See* Ja-luo
Nyika (jungle plain), 58–59 ; droughts of, 123 ; missions in, 246
Nzaui peak, 69, 122
Nzoia, natives of, 129
Nzoia River, 63

Ogwalal Hill, 87
Officialism, 204
Officials—
  Increase in, economic advantage of, 189
  Leave of, 194
  Responsibilities and capacity of, 186–87
  Sanatorium for, proposed, 194
  Scarcity of, 175, 188, 194
Olive, forests of, 164
Omo River, 84
Opals, 86, 159
Ormania, 243–44
Ossagati Hill, 87
Ostriches, 173, 266 *and note*
Owen, Capt., 316–17
Ozi River, 47

Paa, 271
Papyrus, 296
Pangani, 45 *and note*

Pangani River, 142
Parsis—
  Funeral rites of, 93
  Mombasa, in, 55
  Zanzibar, in, 34
Pasturage, 169–71
Pate—
  Arabic chronicles of, 11, 40
  Founders of, 39
  Zanzibar acknowledged by (1866), 22
Pelicans, 50
Pemba I.—
  British protectorate over, 10, 27, 31, 317
  Climate of, 34
Persians—
  Shirazi, at, 57
  Traces of, in East Africa, 11
  Wagunya descended from, 39
Peters, Herr, 28
Piers, need for, 53
Place-names, 64–65 *and note*
Plague outbreak (1902), 155–56
Pokomo country, 246
Port Durnford, 38, 193
Port Florence (Kisumu), 64, 214
Port Reitz, 54
Port Tudor, 54
Port Victoria, 214
Portal, Sir Gerald, 28
Portuguese—
  Arab relations with, 9–10, 18–19
  East African settlements of, 6
  Henry the Navigator, Prince, 13
  Lamu Archipelago, in, 39
  Mombasa, at, 55
  Oriental empire of, divisions of, 15
  Zanzibar conquered by, 21
Portuguese East Africa, 250–51
Pottery, 160
Poyisia, 146
Price, Rev. W. S., 246
Provinces, list of, 185–86
Ptolemy cited, 10
Punitive expeditions, 147, 200–1
Pygmies, 107–9

Quiloa (Kilwa Kisiwani), 253

Rabai—
  Church opened at, 246
  Krapf at, 244
  Missions at, 56, 242
  Natives of, 124
  Rainfall at, 154 *note*
Rafts, 295
Rainfall. 153–54 *and note*
Ramisi, River, 57, 167
Rashid bin Salim, 29
Raspberries, wild, 78

Ravine station—
　Climate of, 86, 153
　Description and situation of, 85, 86
　Vegetable cultivation at, 165
Rebmann, —, 24, 243–45
Records, historical, 108
Reed-work, 282
Reitz, Lieut. J. J., 21, 54, 317
Rendile, 76, 107, 119
Rengata Elgek (Angata-oo-l-Käk), 81
　and note
Reptiles, 273. See also Crocodiles.
Revenue, 189–90
Rhinoceros, 266–267
Ribe, 56, 245
Rice, 49, 224
Rift Valley—
　Animals of, 262
　Climate of, 153
　Conformation of, 67, 77
　Diamond conditions in, 159
　Divisions of, 79–80
　Grazing lands in, 169–71
　Inhabitants of—Masai, 134; Suk,
　　145
　Labour in, 173
　Lava cap over, 159
　Ostriches in, 173, 266 note
　Railway in, 212–13
　Richest portions of, 83–84
　Soil of, 171
　Surveys of, faulty, 77
Rivers—
　Bars of, 47
　Crossing, methods of, 294–95
Roads—
　German East Africa, in, 256–57
　Need for more, 176, 206, 309
Robinson, H. B., cited, 316
Rogers, Mr., 121
Rubber, 51, 52, 161, 162
Rudolf, Lake—
　Discovery of, 25
　Frontier at, 184
　Gold prospecting at, 159
　Shores of, 84
　otherwise mentioned, 82, 86, 134

Sabaki River—
　Cotton prospects on, 166, 167
　Crocodiles in, 273
　Mouth of, 53
　otherwise mentioned, 70, 122, 123
Sadler, Col., 281 ; cited, 161, 220, 225
Sagalla, 60, 246
Sagana River, 48, 71
Said, Seyyid, 10, 20–22, 24, 29, 40, 244,
　318
Sambur, 76
Samburu, 59, 123
Sangaruna Ford, Masai peace at, 142
Scenery, 285, 286

Scrub—
　Constituents of, 59
　Fibre in, 163 ....
　Fuel wood and ebony in, 164
　Maize in, 168
　Railway construction through, 210–
　　11
Seasons, 153
Segelli, 142
Sekoki forest, 52, 161, 162, 164
Semliki, River, 299
Sendeyo, 135–36, 258
Serengeti Plains, 61
Sese, Is., 220
Settima Hills—
　Climate of, 153
　Pastures of, 169, 170
　Situation of, 77
Settlers—
　Difficulties of, 175
　Prospects for, 173–74
　Remoter districts, scheme for, 177
Seyidie—
　European influence dominant in, 51–
　　52
　Native civil administration in, 197
　Officials in, distribution of, 194
Shakabobo, Lake, 50
Sheep, 171
Shella, 44
Shilluk, 132
Shimba, 56
Shimba Hills, 56, 57, 227
Shimoni, 154 note
Shipping, 229–30
Shirati, 255
Shirazi, 57
Shungwaya, 123
Simba, 68
Sikisi. See Lumbwa
Silkworms, 168
Sio River, 63, 159
Sirgoit Rock, 87
Sirikwa, 87
Siu, 40
Slave Trade—
　Abyssinian raids, 237
　Arab enterprise in, 42, 232, 239
　Depopulation due to, 57, 191
　Eunuchs, making of, 232
　Geographical knowledge due to, 23
　Suppression of, 26 ; difficulty of,
　　232–33
Slavery—
　African attitude towards, 231, 238
　Coast strip, in, 232–34
　German East Africa, in, 258, 259
　Toleration of, in East Africa Pro-
　　tectorate, 234–35
Slaves—
　British East Africa Company's
　　liberation of, 246

Slaves—*continued*
  Manumissions of, 234, 237 *and note*
  Position of, 234–37
Sleeping sickness, 156–57, 220, 274
Snakes, 262, 273
Soba, 147
Sobat River, 110, 132, 298, 300
Soda, 160, 220
Sogorti, Lake, 76
Soil, kinds of, 160–61
Somaliland Protectorate—
  Cattle from, 172
  Ostriches of, 266 *note*
  Situation of, 2
Somalis—
  Beauty of, 36
  Biskaya section of, 36, 120
  Blending other tribes with, proposed, 305
  British dealings with, 37
  Campaign against, chances of, 199
  Characteristics of, 36, 121
  Classification of, 107
  Dislike of, by officials, 122
  Districts of, different from other parts of Protectorate, 180
  Europeans, attitude towards, 122, 188
  Future of, 121–22
  Gallas checked by, 111, 118
  Hertis, 119
  Mohammedanism of, 42
  North and South, 119
  Ogadens, 76, 119 ; punitive expedition against, 120–21, 199
  Political capacity of, 95
  Raids by, 39, 45, 49
  Siu, in, 40
  Trade with, possibilities of, 224
  Tumalods and Ramis, 46
  Wassegeju descended from, 123
Sosian, 85
South Africa, migration of Europeans from, to British East Africa, 314–15
Sotik, 66, 194, 237
Speke, —, journeys of, 24
Sport, 276
Stanley, H. M., 24, 28
Steere, Rev. E., cited, 117
Steggall, Mr., 246
Stephanie, Lake, 25, 82
Steward, Sir D., 314
Stone—
  Building, for, 160
  Knobkerries, 128
  Kraals, 87
Strandes, —, cited, 11
Subbu tribe, 77
Sugar-cane, 165
Sugota, Lake, 82, 83, 275

Suk—
  Appearance and customs of, 84, 145
  Classification of, 107, 110
  Number system of, 144
Sultan Hamud station, 68
Sunstroke, 152
Surveys, 77, 176, 203, 205, 308
Suswa, Mt., 79
Swahilis—
  Characteristics of, 112–13
  Classification of, 107
  Clerks, as, 100
  Language of, 114, 118
  Origin of, 42, 107, 111–12
  Religion of, 42
  Riff-raff of, north of Mt. Elgon, 196
  Tax-collectors, as, 197

TABORA, 24, 254
Tabtu, 76
Takaungu—
  Mazrui at, 22, 29, 53
  Rubber at, 52, 161
  Slave of Wali of, 236
Tana River—
  Climate of, 151
  Course of, 38
  Crocodiles in, 273
  Falls of, at Hameye, 70
  Fertilising overflow of, 48
  Fibre cultivation on, 163
  Mouth of, 47
  Natives on, 101 ; German spoken by, 243
  Source of, 8
  Upper waters of, 48
  otherwise mentioned, 71, 179
Tanaland—
  Administration of, inadequacy of, 193–94; civil administration by natives, 193–94, 197
  Biskaya Somalis in, 120
  Cotton in, 166, 167
  Cultivation in, 49
  Divisions of, 38
  Gallas in, 119
  Masai raids in, 142
  Stagnation of, 51
  Waboni and Wasania in, 149
Tanganyika, Lake, 273–74, 314, 315
Taptangale, 147
Taru jungle—
  Coal reported under, 227
  Maize crops in, 165
  Wells in, possibility of, 154
  otherwise mentioned, 61, 67
Tate, Mr., cited, 75 *and note*[1], 76
Taveta—
  Description of, 61
  Masai settlers near, 144
  Missions in, 242

Taveta—*continued*
 Natives of, 122
 Road from Voi to, 61, 255
 Timber in, 61, 163
 otherwise mentioned, 25, 59, 110
Taxation, 191 *and note*[1], 197
Teita—
 Labour plentiful in, 173
 Missions in, 241, 242
 Natives of, 122
 Situation of, 59
Teita Hills—
 Climate of, 151
 Marble in, 160
 otherwise mentioned, 8, 61
Teleki, Count, 25
Theoka, Mt., 68
Thika-Thika, River, 48
Thomson, Joseph, 25
Thomson's gazelle, 81
Thorns, 59
Thunguri, 247
Tigrish, River, 86, 159
Timber, 48, 52, 61, 84, 86, 163–64
Tiriki, 94
Tiwi, 57, 162
Tobacco cultivation, 57, 167
Torobo. *See* Wandorobo
Trade—
 British merchants' apathy as to, 228–29
 Exports—
  Increase in (1903-4), 221
  Value of (1902), 223; for five years, 226; (1904), 313–14
 Immigration of Europeans the condition of increase in, 220, 224
 Imports, value of (1902), 223; (1904), 313–14
 Slave Trade. *See that title*
 Stations for, Said's idea of, 24
 Uganda, of, 220, 225–26
 Zanzibar, at, 223
Tree-spirits, belief in, 97
Trolleys, 55, 172
Tropical lands, climates of, 150–51
Tsavo River—
 Agricultural prospects on, 174
 Fibre near, 163
 Mica found near, 160
 Scenery of, 61–62
Tsetse fly, 68, 157, 172
Turkana—
 Abyssinian raids on, 237
 Classification of, 107, 110
 Rumours as to, 84, 144
Turkwel River, 183
Turks—
 Characteristics of, 41
 Mombasa plundered by (1585), 16
Tursoga, 85
Twaka, 45

UASIN Gishu—
 Description of, 86–88
 Masai of, exterminated, 88, 135, 142
 Name, form of, 86 *note*
 Nandi originally from, 146
 Pasture on, 169
 Railway to, suggested, 170
 Wheat prospects in, 168
 Zionist settlement on, proposed, 177–78, 309, 315
 otherwise mentioned, 8, 65, 85, 110
Uganda, Kingdom of—
 Civilisation in, 202, 281, 283
 Mtesa's rule in, 95
 Mutilations in, 284
 Political institutions in, 285
 Protectorate distinguished from, 281
 Scenery of, 286
Uganda Protectorate—
 Amalgamation of, with East Africa Protectorate, advantages of, 180–81, 308
 Aristocracy in, 107
 Bahima invasion of, 110
 Birds, absence of, in, 262
 Black man's country, 103
 British Protectorate over, proclaimed, 29
 Christianity in, 28, 240, 284
 Climate of, 1, 151
 Countries included in, 1, 180
 Finances of, 202
 Future of, 304
 Hut tax in, 191 *note*[1]
 Language of, 114
 Military requirements of, 201–2
 Mission work in, fruit of, 240, 284
 Mohammedanism in, 43
 Mutiny of 1897, 30, 199
 Naivasha and Kisumu transferred from, to East Africa Protectorate, 30
 Natives of. *See* Baganda.
 Nile regulation works, probable effect of, on, 301–2
 Old caravan route to, 85
 Rubber cultivation in, 161
 Sleeping sickness in, 156, 157
 Trade of, 220, 225–26
Uganda Railway—
 Beginning of, 29
 Committee, 215–16
 Criticisms on, 215–19
 Expenditure on—
  Accounts of, 190, 191
  Amount of, 217; on working, 191, 219
  Criticisms on, 216–18
 Firewood for, 164
 Important places on, 186
 Improvements in, suggested, 218
 Inclines on, 212, 217

Uganda Railway—*continued*
  Indians employed on, 125, 178, 211, 215
  Journey by, time required for, 222
  Length and direction of, 210
  Lion story of, 268–69
  Mombasa, at, 55
  Name of, misleading, 209
  Native work on, 100, 211, 215
  Rift Valley viewed from, 79
  Route of, 64, 65, 209–13
  School at Nairobi, 206
  Tanaland affected by, 51
  Temporary lines, &c., 217–18
  Thefts from, by Nandi, 147, 195, 214
  Traffic prospects for, 188, 219–22; increase in traffic (1904), 314
  Viaducts of, 213
Ugaya, 65
Ujiji, 254
Ukamba—
  Barley from, 168
  Desolate appearance of, 69
  Divisions of, 70
  Fibre in, 163
  German missions in, 243
  Krapf in, 245
  Labour in, cost of, 173
  Mica in, 160
  Natives of. *See* Wakamba
  Northern, additional station in, proposed, 196
  Rainfall at, 153
  Soda in, 160, 220
  Sub-Commissioner of, 73
  Tobacco in, 167
  Western, neglect of, 67
Ulu, 70, 124
Umba, River, 57
United States—
  Commercial enterprise of, in East Africa Protectorate, 224 *note*
  Negro problem in, 305
  Uganda Railway viaducts made by firm of, 213
Unyamwezi, 254
Unyoro, Kabarega's rule in, 95, 290
Usambara—
  Climate and advancement of, 255–56
  Government plantations in, 257
  Krapf's visit to, 245
  Railway returns in, 222
Uwani forest, 46, 161

Vaneza district, 165
Vanga—
  Climate of, 57, 151
  Indians at, prospects for, 178–79
  Masai sack of (1859), 143
  Mosquitoes at, 274
  Timber exported from, 164

Vanilla, 168
Vegetables, cultivation of, 155, 160, 165–66
Victoria, Lake—
  Administration of, special, required, 194
  Cattle from, 172
  Climate of, 151
  Cotton prospects at, 167, 178
  Crocodiles in, 273
  Cruise round, time occupied by, 222
  Discovery of, 24
  Fish in, 272
  German frontier at, 185
  Gold at, 159
  Hippopotami in, 267
  Inaccessibility of district of, 6
  Indian cultivators near, 167, 178
  Medusæ in, 273–74
  Mosquitoes and *glossina palpalis* at, 274
  Rainfall at, 154 *and note*
  Rivers entering, 63
  Sleeping sickness on shores of, 156, 274
  Steamers on, 210; cost of, 190; success of, 221
  Views of, 64
Vidal, Capt., 316–17
Views, 64, 79, 89
Villages. *See under* Natives
Voi—
  Cotton at, 166, 167
  Road from, to Teveta, 61, 255
Voi River, 60, 162, 163
Vumba, 57–58 *and note*

Waboni, 46, 107, 148, 149, 238
Wadigo, 59, 123
Wadelai, 132
Waduruma, 59; village of, 123–24
Waganda. *See* Baganda
Waganga, 98
Wagiriama, 59, 123
Wagogo, 142
Wagunya (Bajun), 39
Wahadimu, 32
Wahehe, 142
Wakamba—
  Blending other tribes with, proposed, 305
  Characteristics and customs of, 124–25
  Classification of, 107, 122
  Clothing of, 93
  Distribution of, 124
  Language of, 126–127 *and notes*
  Masai attacked by, 143
  Villages concealed by, 69
  Women of, 125, 126
  Workmen, as, 100, 211
Wakefield, —, 245–46

Wakikuyu. *See* Kikuyu
Walker, Mr., surveys by, 158; cited, 68, 70 *note*
Waller's gazelle, 61
Wandorobo (Dorobo)—
　Appearance and customs of, 107-8, 148
　Dependent position of, 107, 238
　Legend of, 141
　otherwise mentioned, 46, 85
Wanyika—
　Arabs attacked by, 20
　Blending other tribes with, proposed, 305
　Block-houses against, 17
　Classification of, 107, 122
　Krapf's anecdote of, 244
　Origin and distribution of, 108, 123
　Religious ideas of, 97
　Tribes of, principal, 59
　Village of, near Samburu, 123-24
Wapokomo—
　Classification of, 122, 123
　Missionary influence among, 48
　Secret societies among, 49, 97-98
Wasania, 107, 148, 149, 238
Wasegeju, 17, 59, 123
Wasin, 58
Waso Nyiro River, 8
Watering-places, 36
Watoro, 35
Watt, Stewart, garden of, 69
West Africa—
　Advancement of natives in, 305
　Slave trade in, 232
　Sleeping sickness and plague in, 156
Whitehouse, Sir G., 211
Whyte, Mr., cited, 162-163
Wildebeest (gnu), 265-66
Wimbi, 66
Witu—
　Administration of, 45
　British East Africa Company's retirement from, 29
　British protectorate over, 45
　Court etiquette in, 46
　German protectorate over, declared, 27
　Military station at, 186, 193
　Mosquitoes at, 274
　Origin of, 27, 45

Witu—*continued*
　Rubber at, 161
　Slave establishment near, 236
　Sultan of, 45
Wray, Mr., 246

YALA River, 63, 148
Yatta escarpment, 68
Yonte, 37
Yorubi, 10, 18, 20, 26
Yusuf bin Hasan, 17

ZAMBESI River, 251
Zang empire, 10
Zanzibar—
　Administration of, 35
　Arab capital transferred to, 20-21
　British protectorate over, 10, 27, 31, 34
　Chuaka, 32, 33
　Climate of, 32, 33, 151
　Comoro islanders in, 248
　Consulate duties in, 203
　Copra of, 162
　Dunga, 32
　German trade with, from Bagamoyo, 252
　Grave Island and Prison Island, 33-34
　Indians in, 34, 179
　Khalid's revolt (1896), 35
　Natives of, 32
　Oman, independent from (1856), 23
　Population of, foreign, 34
　Portuguese conquest of, 21
　Roman Catholic bishop in, 242
　Scenery of, 32
　Swahili dialect of, 118
　Swahili name for, 34
　Trade dealt with at, 223
　United States Consulate in, 224 *note*
　Universities' Mission bishop at, 247
Zanzibar, Sultan of—
　Mainland territories of, 26; difficulties occasioned by, 181-82
　Title of, 10 *note*
Zebras, 172, 264-65; export of, 314
Zimbas, 16-17, 108
Zionist colony, question of, 177-78, 309, 315
Zulus, 123

Printed by BALLANTYNE, HANSON & CO.
Edinburgh & London

TURKEY IN EUROPE

By "ODYSSEUS"

Demy 8vo. With Maps. 16s.

OPINIONS OF THE PRESS

"There is always an attractive mystery about an anonymous book, wide possibilities of authorship, and a lively stimulus to the idle imagination. But, in truth, 'Odysseus's' book is far too brilliant to need the peculiar charm of the disowned. No one, however distinguished, need be ashamed to put his name to a study of modern Turkey at once so accurate and so penetrating, and set forth with such exceptional literary talent, as the book before us. We cannot recall any recent book on the subject, and scarcely any of the older authorities, of equal or even approximate merit."—*Spectator.*

"Whoever 'Odysseus' may be, his knowledge of a most baffling and difficult subject is both wide and deep. The book is an illuminating contribution to the understanding of the history of Turkey in Europe and the character of the Turk."—*Daily Telegraph.*

"Never were 'bag and baggage' more gracefully and gently hinted than in this delightful volume, which we recommend to all manner of readers, not merely as a repertory of mature and trustworthy observation, but as a brilliant example of how such a book ought to be written. Its style is as fascinating as its humour."—*Literature.*

"'Turkey in Europe' bears the stamp of a mind not only thoroughly familiar with its subject, but conscientiously impartial in the treatment of it. We have seldom read a book on Turkey indicating so minute an acquaintance with the country and all phases of its life, private as well as political, accompanied by so wide a sympathy with all classes of its inhabitants. This is especially true of those parts of the work in which the author deals with the actual condition of Turkey. His keen observation and many-sided experience enable him to present a picture both striking and suggestive, and illumined by flashes of humour which, though often unexpected, are never felt to be forced."—*Edinburgh Review.*

LONDON: EDWARD ARNOLD, 41 & 43 MADDOX STREET, W.

Telegrams :
'Scholarly, London.'

41 and 43 Maddox Street,
Bond Street, London, W.

January, 1905.

Mr. Edward Arnold's
List of New Books.

THE EAST AFRICA PROTECTORATE

By SIR CHARLES ELIOT, K.C.M.G.,

LATE H.M. COMMISSIONER FOR THE PROTECTORATE.
AUTHOR OF 'TURKEY IN EUROPE' (BY 'ODYSSEUS').

Demy 8vo.   With Illustrations and Map.   **15s. net.**

Sir Charles Eliot, whose authorship of the important work on the Near East, 'Turkey in Europe,' is now an open secret, had been, until his recent resignation, for nearly four years His Majesty's Commissioner for the British East Africa Protectorate.   In this book he gives a very complete account of the country, its history and its peoples, and discusses with great fulness its prospects as a field for European colonization.   He describes the present system of administration in the Protectorate, and makes a number of interesting suggestions for the future.   There are chapters on the Uganda Railway, Trade, Slavery, Missions, a Journey down the Nile, and Animals, the whole forming a comprehensive and valuable account of one of the most remarkable and, to the ordinary Englishman, least familiar possessions of the British Empire.

LONDON : EDWARD ARNOLD, 41 & 43 MADDOX STREET, W.

ALESSANDRO SCARLATTI : HIS LIFE AND WORKS.

By EDWARD J. DENT,
FELLOW OF KING'S COLLEGE, CAMBRIDGE.

Royal 8vo. With Portrait. **12s. 6d. net.**

To most musical people Alessandro Scarlatti is little more than a name, and even musical historians have been singularly cautious in their references to him. He is, however, a very important figure in the history of music, on account of his influence on the formation of the classical style—*i.e.*, the style of Handel, Bach, Haydn, Mozart, and Beethoven. His numerous works have almost all remained in manuscript, although he was quite the most celebrated composer of his time (1659-1725), and the difficulty of obtaining access to them has no doubt prevented musicians from studying him in detail. For this biography special researches have been made in the principal libraries of Europe, and much new material has come to light. Besides the story of Scarlatti's life, derived in great part from hitherto unpublished diaries and letters, a careful analysis is given of his most important compositions, considered specially in their relation to the history of modern tonality and form. The book is copiously illustrated with musical examples, and includes a complete catalogue of Scarlatti's extant works, with the libraries where the manuscripts are to be found.

FINAL RECOLLECTIONS OF A DIPLOMATIST.

By the RIGHT HON. SIR HORACE RUMBOLD, BART., G.C.B., G.C.M.G.

Demy 8vo. **15s. net.**

Sir Horace Rumbold begins the third and concluding series of his ' Recollections' in the year 1885 at the point to which he brought his readers in the volumes already published. He describes his life as Envoy Extraordinary and Minister Plenipotentiary to Greece from 1885-1888, and to the Netherlands from 1888-1896. In the latter year he was appointed Ambassador to the Emperor of Austria—an exalted position which he retained until his retirement from the Diplomatic Service in 1900. *[In preparation.*

THE UNVEILING OF LHASA.

By EDMUND CANDLER.

Demy 8vo.   With Illustrations and Map.   15s. net.
Second Impression.

With the exception of a short period during which he was recovering from a dozen wounds, Mr. Candler was with the Tibet Mission from start to finish.   The greater part of the book was written on the spot, while the impressions of events and scenery were still fresh.   The result is a singularly graphic picture, not only of the physical and political difficulties overcome in the course of this unique expedition, but of the many dramatic incidents which attended its progress.   The Gyantse operations, which occurred during Mr. Candler's absence, are ably described by an eye-witness, so that the reader has a continuous account of the whole affair.

' Mr. Candler's account of his experiences in Tibet is as breezy and suggestive as is the excellent sketch which stands on the frontispiece.   There is no attempt at a learned disquisition on the mysteries of Buddhism, no laboured effort to explain the intricacies of Indian diplomacy, but just a clear and impartial narrative of the toils and difficulties of the Tibetan Mission.   "The unveiling of Lhasa" is precisely the kind of book which the ordinary reader wants.'—*The Times.*

' The everyday incidents and accidents make the real romance of the enterprise. They are set forth in Mr. Candler's account with a vividness and charm which make the whole volume delightful reading.'—*Westminster Gazette.*

THE BURDEN OF THE BALKANS.

By M. EDITH DURHAM,

AUTHOR OF 'THROUGH THE LANDS OF THE SERB.

Demy 8vo.   With Illustrations and Map.   14s. net.

In this story of her sixth visit to the Balkan Peninsula, Miss Durham, after an historical survey of the causes of the present state of affairs, gives a most interesting account of her work as relief agent for the Balkan Committee, and finally describes Albania and the Albanian, ' the root of all the Balkan difficulties.' She endeavours to look at the situation from the point of view of each nationality in turn, combining with a keen sense of humour and the picturesque a discerning eye for all kinds of imposture.   The book contains a number of striking illustrations from sketches by the author.

FACTS AND IDEAS.

By PHILIP GIBBS,
AUTHOR OF 'KNOWLEDGE IS POWER.'

Crown 8vo.   **3s. 6d.**

As in the case of the author's previous book, the intention of these short studies of life, literature, philosophy, religion, history, and art, is to suggest ideas, subjects for investigation, and the like, connected with some of the great intellectual problems and achievements of civilization.

ECONOMIC METHOD AND ECONOMIC FALLACIES.

By WILLIAM WARRAND CARLILE, M.A.,
AUTHOR OF 'THE EVOLUTION OF MODERN MONEY,' ETC.

Demy 8vo.   Cloth, **10s. 6d. net.**

In this work the keynote of the first two parts is the stress laid on the essential character of the distinction which exists between the methods of investigation that are appropriate in physics and those that are applicable in sciences, such as economics, which belong, in truth, to the mental sphere.   In the third part the author brings his general line of reasoning to bear on the Fiscal Problem.   While he is an uncompromising Free Trader, he would throw overboard those Free Trade arguments that ignore the national point of view in favour of the cosmopolitan.

'Mr. Carlile is a hard hitter and an acute thinker. The dominant economical doctrines have had no more trenchant assailant for a long time.'—*The Times.*

OUTLINES OF THE SYNOPTIC RECORD.

By the REV. BERNARD HUGH BOSANQUET,
VICAR OF THAMES DITTON;

And R. A. WENHAM.

Crown 8vo.   **6s.**

'There is at the present moment a place for some such work as this, which, at once scholarly and popular, reverent, yet pervaded with the modern spirit, will put young students of theology and the educated laity in possession of the results of recent " higher " or literary criticism of the Gospels.'—*Scotsman.*

THE RUSSO-JAPANESE WAR:

From the Outbreak of Hostilities to the Battle of Liaoyang.

By T. COWEN.

Demy 8vo. With numerous Illustrations, Plans, and Maps. **15s. net.**

' Mr. Cowen's analysis of the events which led to the war is excellent. He puts things which we have all understood rather vaguely in a telling and direct fashion. He has evidently taken the greatest care to collate his facts, and the consequence is that we have a most enthralling and connected narrative of the naval operations round Port Arthur, enriched with small but convincing details such as could only have been related by eye-witnesses. Mr. Cowen's description of the Yalu battle is spirited, and his accounts of Kin-chow and Nanshan are quite the best we have seen.'—*Morning Post.*

THE REMINISCENCES OF SIR HENRY HAWKINS

(Baron Brampton).

Edited by RICHARD HARRIS, K.C.,

AUTHOR OF 'ILLUSTRATIONS OF ADVOCACY,' 'AULD ACQUAINTANCE,' ETC.

Two Volumes. Demy 8vo. With Portraits. **30s. net.**

Second Impression.

' A delightful budget of miscellaneous reading. The Reminiscences are light reading of a very easy and attractive kind ; but underlying them is the revelation of a strong and genial character, forcing its way to recognition by sheer merit alone. They are delightful, not alone by their wealth of anecdote, but also by their unconscious revelation of a strong and yet lovable personality.'—*Standard.*

POLITICAL CARICATURES, 1904.

By F. CARRUTHERS GOULD.

Super royal 4to. **6s. net.**

Also an Edition de Luxe of 100 *large-paper copies, numbered and signed,*
£2 2s. net.

' One looks twice before he is quite sure that the price of "Political Carica-tures" is only 6s. Where else for 6s., in a book or out of it, can we find so much good humour and so much hearty laughter ? "F.C.G." is still our one cartoonist, and his is the only brush which pictures the real history of our time in caricature.'—*Daily Mail.*

EDWARD AND PAMELA FITZ-GERALD.

Being some Account of their Lives
Compiled from the Letters of Those who knew Them.

By GERALD CAMPBELL.

Demy 8vo. With numerous Portraits. **12s. 6d. net.**

' No one interested in the '98 rebellion, in the gay and chivalrous and hapless Lord Edward, or in eighteenth-century folk and manners, can afford to miss this delightful volume.'—*World.*

' The frankness of the correspondence of Lord Edward's aunts and sisters makes Mr. Campbell's volume more entertaining than most novels.'—*Speaker.*

JERUSALEM UNDER THE HIGH PRIESTS.

Five Lectures on the Period between Nehemiah and the New Testament.

By EDWYN BEVAN,

AUTHOR OF 'THE HOUSE OF SELEUCUS.'

Demy 8vo. **7s. 6d.**

' These lectures deserve careful study by everyone interested in the history of how Hellenism and Judaism first came into contact.'—*Cambridge Review.*

STUDIES IN VIRGIL.

By TERROT REAVELEY GLOVER,

FELLOW AND CLASSICAL LECTURER OF ST. JOHN'S COLLEGE, CAMBRIDGE, AUTHOR OF 'LIFE AND LETTERS IN THE FOURTH CENTURY.'

Demy 8vo. **10s. 6d. net.**

' Mr. Glover has achieved a real triumph; he sends his readers away longing to take up their Virgil again.'—*St. James's Gazette.*

THE WHITE MAN IN NIGERIA.
By GEORGE DOUGLAS HAZZLEDINE.

Demy 8vo. With numerous Illustrations and a Map. **10s. 6d. net.**

The author of this graphic account of life in Northern Nigeria was for some time Private Secretary to Sir Frederick Lugard, the High Commissioner, and was thus in a position to learn the truth about the country and its problems.

'The author supplies some admirable pictures of the incidents which have led to the British occupation of Northern Nigeria. His theories are sane and wholesome, his descriptions graphic and informing. One would like every responsible tax-paying British subject to read them '—*Athenæum.*

'A really fascinating book, which, while stirring and picturesque, vivid and human throughout, is as full of facts of the rarer and more valuable sort as the driest and most scientific treatise could be. The book is certain to be read in France and Germany. By every law of common-sense it should be read, well and carefully read, in England. We hope it may be.'—*Pall Mall Gazette.*

SUNSHINE AND SENTIMENT IN PORTUGAL.
By GILBERT WATSON,
AUTHOR OF 'THREE ROLLING STONES IN JAPAN.'

Demy 8vo. With numerous Illustrations. **12s. 6d. net.**

'Mr. Watson has written a book which may be fittingly placed on the bookshelf between Sterne's "Sentimental Journey" and Robert Louis Stevenson's "Travels with a Donkey in the Cevennes." '—*Scotsman.*

ENGLAND IN EGYPT.
By VISCOUNT MILNER,
HIGH COMMISSIONER FOR SOUTH AFRICA.

Eleventh Edition. With additions summarizing the course of events to the year 1904. Crown 8vo. **6s.**

The great and far-reaching change in England's position in Egypt effected by the signature of the Anglo-French agreement has rendered necessary a further addition to Lord Milner's work, tracing the course of events from 1898, when the book was brought up to date by a chapter by Sir Clinton Dawkins, to the present time. This important task has been carried out by Sir Eldon Gorst, K.C.B., late Financial Adviser to the Egyptian Government, who describes in a masterly chapter the recent results of British rule in Egypt and the Soudan, and the hopeful possibilities of the future.

ENGLISH ESTATE FORESTRY.

By A. C. FORBES.

Demy 8vo. With Illustrations. **12s. 6d. net.**

Forestry is a subject the importance of which is by no means adequately recognised in this country. It is, indeed, seldom that one finds an owner of woodlands who has a competent knowledge of the scientific theory and practical possibilities of timber-planting. Mr. Forbes's book will be found a valuable corrective of the prevailing happy-go-lucky methods.

Mr. Forbes has produced a most excellent work, which should be on the shelves of all estate agents and owners of woodland property.'—*Saturday Review.*

Perhaps the soundest and most useful book on forestry yet written by an Englishman for the ordinary reader.'—*Estate Magazine.*

GHOST STORIES OF AN ANTIQUARY.

By MONTAGUE RHODES JAMES, Litt.D.,
FELLOW AND LATE TUTOR OF KING'S COLLEGE, CAMBRIDGE.

Crown 8vo. With Illustrations by the late James McBryde. **6s.**
Second Impression.

'We do not hesitate to say that these are among the best ghost stories we have ever read; they rank with that greatest of all ghost stories, Lord Lytton's '' The Haunted and the Haunters.'' '—*Guardian.*

COMMONSENSE COOKERY.

Based on Modern English and Continental Principles worked out in Detail.

By COLONEL KENNEY-HERBERT.

Large Crown 8vo. **7s. 6d.**

MY SPORTING HOLIDAYS.

By Sir HENRY SETON-KARR, C.M.G., M.P.

Demy 8vo.   With numerous Illustrations.   **12s. 6d. net.**

'The book which, like "Scolopax's" delightful gossip, informs the reader's mind without ever taxing his patience grows yearly rarer. Sir Henry Seton-Karr's volume is a very pleasing specimen of this class, the notebook of one who has wandered far afield in search of sport, and can write of his doings without egotism or vain repetitions. His sketches of Western society are very vivid pictures, full of insight and good humour.'—*Spectator.*

'This lively volume, which will be read with a great deal of pleasure by every sportsman who can get hold of it, records the author's adventures in search of sport during the last two-and-thirty years.'—*Illustrated Sporting and Dramatic News.*

PAGES FROM A COUNTRY DIARY.

By PERCIVAL SOMERS.

Large Crown 8vo.   With Photogravure Illustrations.   **7s. 6d.**

'It is not often nowadays that a writer on indoor and outdoor life in the country appears with a knowledge so matured and a style so mellow as that of Mr. Percival Somers. In fact, we do not believe that there could be a book which would better reflect the attitude of a country gentleman towards men and animals and affairs. His inimitable, genial manner is so effective that the reader is continually delighted, whether he is reading of a local steeplechase or how the author basketed some fine trout with the help of a phantom minnow when he was out with a party of dry-fly fishermen.'—*World.*

HOUSE, GARDEN, AND FIELD.

A Collection of Short Nature Studies.

By L. C. MIALL, F.R.S.,

PROFESSOR OF BIOLOGY IN THE UNIVERSITY OF LEEDS, AND FULLERIAN PROFESSOR OF PHYSIOLOGY IN THE ROYAL INSTITUTION.

Crown 8vo.   With numerous Illustrations.   **6s.**

Second Impression.

'Quite the best things of the kind that have appeared since nature study became a subject in the schools.'—*Field.*

'This admirable little work appears to be by far the best aid to the proper teaching of nature study that has hitherto come under our notice.'—*Nature.*

NEW FICTION.

Crown 8vo.   6s. each.

THE SEETHING POT.

By GEORGE A. BIRMINGHAM.

[*Ready immediately.*

THE RAMBLING RECTOR.

By ELEANOR ALEXANDER,

AUTHOR OF 'LADY ANNE'S WALK.'

Second Impression.

' In " The Rambling Rector " one finds the same delicate humour, imagination, and sentiment which distinguished " Lady Anne's Walk." ' '—*Manchester Guardian*.

' Miss Alexander has the goodly heritage of an admirable literary style combined with a sympathetic comprehension of the Irish people and a keen sense of humour.'—*Athenæum*.

PETER'S PEDIGREE.

By DOROTHEA CONYERS,

AUTHOR OF 'THE BOY, SOME HORSES, AND A GIRL.'

With Illustrations by Nora K. Shelley.

Third Impression.

' The story is very clever and amusing, brimful of real Irish fun and humour, and adorned with illustrations quite up to its own mark.'—*World*.

' This is one of the funniest books we have had the pleasure of reading for a long time, and is full of genuine humour.'—*Illustrated Sporting and Dramatic News*.

SCENES OF JEWISH LIFE.

By Mrs. ALFRED SIDGWICK,

AUTHOR OF 'CYNTHIA'S WAY,' 'THE THOUSAND EUGENIAS, AND OTHER STORIES,' 'THE BERYL STONES,' ETC.

Second Impression.

' Mrs. Sidgwick's bright manner of telling her stories, her delicate humour, and quick realization of the subtle pathos that is threaded through all Jewish life, appear on every page, and make the book both interesting and enjoyable reading.' —*Westminster Gazette*.

' A volume from the pen of Mrs. Alfred Sidgwick is always welcome, so alert is her intelligence, so keen her observation, so crisp and clear-cut her style. Altogether, this is an extremely vivacious and instructive volume.'—*Spectator*.

NEW FICTION.—Continued.

THE CELESTIAL SURGEON.

By F. F. MONTRESOR,

AUTHOR OF 'WORTH WHILE,' 'INTO THE HIGHWAYS AND HEDGES,' ETC.

Third Impression.

' In " The Celestial Surgeon," Miss Montresor is at her best. The character drawing, as is usual with the writer, is excellent; the characters are all living human beings, neither too good nor too bad for everyday life. The book is not one for girls just out of the schoolroom, but their elders will be glad to have it.' —*Guardian*.

' An immensely clever study of a group of temperaments, with the added advantage of a capitally constructed plot.'—*St. James's Gazette.*

THE SHADOW ON THE WALL.

By MARY E. COLERIDGE,

AUTHOR OF 'THE KING WITH TWO FACES,' 'THE FIERY DAWN,' ETC

Second Impression.

' A new novel from the pen of Miss Coleridge is an event the pleasure of which is enhanced by the comparative rarity of its occurrence. All who are able to emancipate themselves sufficiently from the tyranny of circumstance can hardly fail to recognise the charm of this delicately fantastic melodrama.'—*Spectator.*

THE REAPER.

By EDITH RICKERT.

' A simple yet strange story of a mind at once simple and strange; and throughout it the author would seem to have been guided by a delicate-unerring instinct for the central, the captain thought or word or expression.'—*The Times.*

' A novel the scene of which lies beyond the beaten track, and which will repay you amply for the reading.'—*Review of Reviews.*

CHECKMATE.

By ETTA COURTNEY.

' Miss Courtney has written an able novel, and one that will interest the reader from the first page to the last.'—*Sheffield Daily Independent.*

' The story is very interesting, and is told throughout with great cleverness and skill.'—*Outlook.*

THE EVOLUTION THEORY.

By Dr. AUGUST WEISMANN,
PROFESSOR OF ZOOLOGY IN THE UNIVERSITY OF FREIBURG.

Translated by J. ARTHUR THOMSON,
REGIUS PROFESSOR OF NATURAL HISTORY IN THE UNIVERSITY OF ABERDEEN,

And MARGARET THOMSON.

Two volumes, Royal 8vo. With many Illustrations. **32s. net.**

The importance of this work is twofold. In the first place, it sums up the teaching of one of Darwin's greatest successors, who has been for many years a leader in biological progress. As Professor Weismann has from time to time during the last quarter of a century frankly altered some of his positions, this deliberate summing up of his mature conclusions is very valuable. In the second place, as the volumes discuss all the chief problems of organic evolution, they form a trustworthy guide to the whole subject, and may be regarded as furnishing—what is much needed—a Text-book of Evolution Theory. The book takes the form of lectures, which are so graduated that no one who follows their course can fail to understand the most abstruse chapters. The translation has been revised by the author.

LECTURES ON DISEASES OF CHILDREN.

By ROBERT HUTCHISON, M.D. EDIN., F.R.C.P.,
ASSISTANT PHYSICIAN TO THE LONDON HOSPITAL AND TO THE HOSPITAL FOR SICK CHILDREN, GREAT ORMOND STREET;
AUTHOR OF 'FOOD AND THE PRINCIPLES OF DIETETICS.'

Crown 8vo. **8s. 6d. net.**

' It is difficult to praise this little volume too highly. It deals with one of the most attractive and satisfactory subjects in medicine, the treatment of children's diseases ; the style is excellent, and the illustrations, which, with one or two exceptions, are taken from photographs of the author's cases, are unusually good.'—*Nature.*

' Dr. Hutchison says in his preface that he does not intend to compete with the many excellent text-books on Children's Diseases, but we feel sure no student should be without this book, as, unable to spare time for the larger treatises, he will here learn many things which otherwise practice alone in after-life will teach him.'—*Guy's Hospital Gazette.*

ASTRONOMICAL DISCOVERY.

By HERBERT HALL TURNER, D.Sc., F.R.S.,

SAVILIAN PROFESSOR OF ASTRONOMY IN THE UNIVERSITY OF OXFORD.

Demy 8vo. With Diagrams. **10s. 6d. net.**

In these lectures, written for delivery before the University of Chicago, Professor Turner traces the history of modern Astronomical Discovery, first showing by what an immense amount of labour and patience most discoveries have been made, and then describing in detail many of the more important ones. Among his topics are Uranus, Eros, and Neptune, Bradley's discoveries of the aberration of light and the nutation of the earth's axis, the photographic measurement of the heavens, Schwabe's work on the sunspot period, and Mr. Chandler's discoveries in connection with the Variation of Latitude.

'A volume of unusual interest. In its fascinating chapters the story of some half-dozen discoveries is developed in an exceedingly attractive manner.'—*Westminster Gazette.*

THE BECQUEREL RAYS AND THE PROPERTIES OF RADIUM.

By the HON. R. J. STRUTT,

FELLOW OF TRINITY COLLEGE, CAMBRIDGE.

Demy 8vo. With Diagrams. **8s. 6d. net.**

'The author possesses to a remarkable degree the faculty of stating difficult questions in a simple way, and of expressing the answers in a language which is easily understood.'—*Nature.*

'The book may be confidently recommended to the general reader as a comprehensible and attractive account of the latest developments of scientific thought on the structure of matter.'—*Cambridge Review.*

AN INTRODUCTION TO

THE THEORY OF OPTICS.

By ARTHUR SCHUSTER, Ph.D., Sc.D., F.R.S.,

PROFESSOR OF PHYSICS AT THE UNIVERSITY OF MANCHESTER.

Demy 8vo. With numerous Diagrams. **15s. net**

This volume is intended to serve as an introduction to the study of the higher branches of the Theory of Light. In the first part of the book those portions of the subject are treated which are independent of any particular form of the undulatory theory. The author has endeavoured, by means of elementary mathematical reasoning, to give an accurate account of the study of vibrations, and has laid special stress on the theory of optical instruments. In the second part mathematical analysis is more freely used. The study of luminous vibrations is introduced through the treatment of waves propagated in elastic media, and only after the student has become familiar with the older forms of the elastic solid theory are the equations of the electro-magnetic theory adopted. The advantage of these equations, more especially in the treatment of double refraction, is explained, and the theory of ionic charges is adopted in the discussion of dispersion and metallic reflexion.

THE ELECTRIC FURNACE.

By HENRI MOISSAN,

PROFESSOR OF CHEMISTRY AT THE SORBONNE; MEMBRE DE L'INSTITUT.

Authorized English Edition.

Translated by A. T. DE MOUILPIED, M.Sc., Ph.D.,

ASSISTANT LECTURER IN THE LIVERPOOL UNIVERSITY.

Demy 8vo. With numerous Illustrations. **10s. 6d. net.**

This work embodies the original French Edition, together with the new matter incorporated in the German Edition. Moreover, Professor Moissan has written, specially for this edition, a chapter dealing with the most recent work. The book, while dealing largely with Professor Moissan's own researches, gives a general survey of the experimental work accomplished by means of the electric furnace up to the present time. The bearings of this work on technical processes are frequently discussed.

THE CHEMICAL SYNTHESIS OF VITAL PRODUCTS

AND THE INTER-RELATIONS BETWEEN ORGANIC COMPOUNDS.

By PROFESSOR RAPHAEL MELDOLA, F.R.S.,
OF THE CITY AND GUILDS OF LONDON TECHNICAL COLLEGE, FINSBURY.

Super Royal 8vo. **21s. net.**

The great achievements of modern Organic Chemistry in the domain of the synthesis or artificial production of compounds which are known to be formed as the result of the vital activities of plants and animals have not of late years been systematically recorded.

The object of the present book, upon which the author has been engaged for some years, is to set forth a statement as complete as possible of the present state of knowledge in this most interesting and important branch of science. The book will consist of two volumes, of which the first will be ready very shortly. The treatment is calculated to make the volume a work of reference which will be found indispensable for teachers, students, and investigators, whether in the fields of pure Chemistry, of Chemical Physiology, or of Chemical Technology.

HUMAN EMBRYOLOGY AND MORPHOLOGY.

By ARTHUR KEITH, M.D. Aberd., F.R.C.S. Eng.,
LECTURER ON ANATOMY, LONDON HOSPITAL MEDICAL COLLEGE.

A New Edition. Greatly enlarged. Demy 8vo. **12s. 6d. net.**

The greater part of the work has been rewritten, many of the old illustrations have been replaced, and a large number of new figures introduced. The alterations have been rendered necessary owing to the advances which have been made in our knowledge of the early phases of development of the human embryo, of the implantation of the ovum and formation of the placenta, and of the development of the heart, lungs and nervous system.

THE WALLET SERIES OF HANDBOOKS.

MR. EDWARD ARNOLD has pleasure in announcing the publication of a series of handbooks, ranging over a wide field, which are intended to be practical guides to beginners in the subjects with which they deal. The first five volumes, of which descriptions are given below, may be regarded as typical of the scope and treatment of the whole series, which is published at 1s. net per volume, paper, and 2s. net cloth.

ON COLLECTING ENGRAVINGS, POTTERY, PORCELAIN, GLASS, AND SILVER.
By ROBERT ELWARD.

'Really very interesting and constitutes in brief an admirable historical and artistic sketch. It forms an excellent handbook for the guidance of amateurs.'—*Scotsman.*

DRESS OUTFITS FOR ABROAD.
By ARDERN HOLT,

'To take more clothes than wanted is almost worse than not to have enough. . . . A perusal of this little volume, which is sensibly written, should enable any traveller, man or woman, to journey abroad suitably equipped.'—*Sheffield Independent.*

ELECTRIC LIGHTING FOR THE INEXPERIENCED.
By HUBERT WALTER.

'We really are delighted to meet with it ; common-sense, practical knowledge, and no small share of humour are marked characteristics of the work. . . . As a guide to the plain man, who wants to know how to set about getting his house wired and fitted . . . this is the best work we have seen, and we have pleasure in recommending it as such.'—*Electrical Review.*

HOCKEY AS A GAME FOR WOMEN.
By EDITH THOMPSON.

'Miss Thompson's book may be recommended to beginners as the very best that has yet appeared of its kind. It has the great merit of being quite practical throughout.'—*Queen.*

WATER-COLOUR PAINTING.
By MARY L. BREAKELL ('PENUMBRA')

'Miss Breakell's work is the product of knowledge and sympathy. She shows a thorough acquaintance with her subject, and is always able to illustrate her teaching by reference to the practice of great masters—past and present. The arrangement of the work is excellent.'—*Manchester Courier.*

LONDON : EDWARD ARNOLD, 41 & 43 MADDOX STREET, W.

CPSIA information can be obtained
at www.ICGtesting.com
Printed in the USA
BVHW070846291218
536681BV00001B/73